Nineteenth
Century
Ports

Publisher's note: This book is one of a four-book series comprising Vol. 1 of the AAG Project.

The four books are:
1. Cities of the Nation's Historic Metropolitan Core
2. Nineteenth Century Ports
3. Nineteenth Century Inland Centers and Ports
4. Twentieth Century Cities

Association of American Geographers

Comparative Metropolitan Analysis Project

Vol. 1   Contemporary Metropolitan America: Twenty Geographical Vignettes. Cambridge: Ballinger Publishing Company, 1976.

Vol. 2.   Urban Policymaking and Metropolitan Dynamics: A Comparative Geographical Analysis. Cambridge: Ballinger Publishing Company, 1976.

Vol. 3.   A Comparative Atlas of America's Great Cities: Twenty Metropolitan Regions. Minneapolis: University of Minnesota Press, 1976.

Vignettes of the following metropolitan regions are also published by Ballinger Publishing Company as separate monographs:

- Boston
- New York-New Jersey
- Philadelphia
- Hartford-Central Connecticut
- Baltimore
- New Orleans
- Atlanta
- Chicago
- St. Paul-Minneapolis
- Seattle
- Miami
- Los Angeles
- Detroit

Research Director:
John S. Adams, University of Minnesota

Associate Director and Atlas Editor:
Ronald Abler, Pennsylvania State University

Chief Cartographer:
Ki–Suk Lee, University of Minnesota

Steering Committee and Editorial Board:
Brian J.L. Berry, Chairman, Harvard University
John R. Borchert, University of Minnesota
Frank E. Horton, Southern Illinois University
J. Warren Nystrom, Association of American Geographers
James E. Vance, Jr., University of California, Berkeley
David Ward, University of Wisconsin

Supported by a grant from the National Science Foundation.

CONTEMPORARY METROPOLITAN AMERICA

2

Nineteenth Century Ports

Association of American Geographers
Comparative Metropolitan Analysis Project

John S. Adams, Editor
University of Minnesota

Ballinger Publishing Company • Cambridge, Massachusetts
A Subsidiary of J.B. Lippincott Company

International Standard Book Number: 0-88410-425-7 (set)

Library of Congress Catalog Card Number: 76-56167

Printed in the United States of America

Library of Congress Cataloging in Publication Data
Main entry under title:

Contemporary metropolitan America.

Includes bibliographies and index.
CONTENTS: pt. 1. Cities of the Nation's historic metropolitan core.—pt. 2. Nineteenth century ports.—pt. 3. Nineteenth century inland centers and ports.—pt. 4. Twentieth century cities.

1. Cities and towns—United States. I. Adams, John S., 1938-   II. Association of American Geographers. Comparative Metropolitan Analysis Project.
HT123.C635   301.36'3'0973   76-56167
ISBN 0-88410-425-7 (set)
        0-88410-467-2 (pt. 1)
        0-88410-464-8 (pt. 2)
        0-88410-465-6 (pt. 3)
        0-88410-466-4 (pt. 4)

Contents

Chapter Three
The Cities by San Francisco Bay
Jean Vance, San Francisco State University

List of Figures

CHAPTER ONE–BALTIMORE

CHAPTER THREE-SAN FRANCISCO

List of Tables

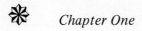 *Chapter One*

Baltimore

A Baltimore Rhythm

Two million people, three-quarters of a million dwellings, 2,000 factories, 1.4 million acres of land—this is the Baltimore region. We have to imagine it in motion—two million trips a day, 150,000 people moving into the city to work and out again, 3,000 arriving or taking off at the airport; the never-ending flow on the beltway, in and out to Washington, in and out to Philadelphia; giant food trailers to the warehouses, containers to the port, ships loading for Japan and South America; five TV and twenty-six radio stations all talking at once; and, underneath, the hidden circulation of gas mains, taps running 250 million gallons a day, current flowing, millions of switches and thermostats and valves connecting nature with the comfort of the two million.

The rhythms of every day define the parts of the city. They define the downtown, alive at noon with secretaries under bubble umbrellas, at 2:00 P.M. with men in wilted shirtsleeves, alive with teenagers in the afternoon, and Hare Krishna, pencils for the blind, the *Watchtower, Muhammed Speaks,* the balloon man. The rhythms of every day define the inner city—red brick and white stoops like a gigantic sundial, with people sitting or shifting to follow the patches of shade; roller skates racing buses; crowds proportional to the density of ambulances or fire trucks; children getting louder and later as the summer wears on. And in the suburbs, lawn sprinklers, kids on bicycles, damp green evenings, the sound of mowers, the action at the shopping center.

The system seems not much different from any other "two million city." But this everyday movement has its own rhythm, its own pace, and in the unique site and climate they give Baltimore its character. Spring overwhelms all the gardens with azaleas and roses and lasts for three days in April. Summer lasts forever. Blue flax two feet tall takes over the strips between the concrete dividers, and the humid haze varies from Blue Ridge beauty to a yellowish temperature inversion where you smother in a flapping breeze, and skidding newspapers and litter map out the microclimate at ground level. The weekend is defined by massive exodus and reflux from the Eastern Shore and 100,000 boats on the Chesapeake Bay. Fall is golden clumps of beeches in the coves of Druid Hill Park, tall straight tulip poplar on the plateaus, the purple of sweet gum and dark green scrub pine on the sandy coastal plain south and east of town. Winter can never make up its mind— the weather changes every eight hours, but night falls at 4:30, and all the houses in the row show a little bluish light in the front rooms and a warm yellow light in the backs.

And the rhythms of everyday define who's who—a social circulation in which the work trips, the shopping trips, the auto trips, the bus trips, the phone calls are assigned to different people in different parts of town. The azaleas, the air conditioners, the litter all have their geography. Rich and poor, young and old, black and white. Crab imperial, steamed crabs, crabcakes.

As the year turns, the system itself grows— 100,000 new cars, 25,000 building permits, 28,000 real estate transfers, a thousand buildings torn down; $100 million for an express- way, $20 million for a shopping center, $10 million for a high school. Baltimore has doubled in the past generation (thirty years) and its geographical features have changed radically. The leading edge of change is now defining a new and still different city, on a new scale.

Row House City

First impression and most persistent image of home is always the rows of brick, one room wide, two or three stories, with white marble steps (Figure 1). Only 40 percent of the households in the metropolitan area live in single family detached dwellings. Perhaps another 10 percent live in high-rise buildings. Half live in row houses. To the visitor from the Midwest or farther away, the brick rows produce a feeling of monotony, a threat of anonymity, and the anxiety of getting lost in the maze. A view from the railway embankment as you come from Philadelphia is grimmer—the black tarred roofs sloping back to the alleys by hundreds and thousands. The streets run straight and suddenly go off at an unexpected angle. But the longer you live in Baltimore, the more variety, the more solidity, the more character the brick rows seem to acquire, until you know just where you are and where you're going.

First, you know where you are in terms of the growth of the city. Like other cities, Baltimore grew ring by ring, a building boom every twenty years or so, annexing territory, filling it up, spilling out. The styles of the row houses of each great building cycle define their location in one of these rings. We are situated in time—new city, hand-me-down city, third generation city. . . . The brick landscape can be read like a drill core of coastal plain sediments or geologic history in a roadcut. The oldest houses were narrow, ten or twelve feet, four rooms or six, with peaked roofs and dormer windows. Some ran back a hundred feet or

were three stories high. This central ring of housing is disappearing rapidly as renewal spreads. Its very core, the Inner Harbor district, has been renewed not once but several times—a massive warehouse construction in the 1880s, a total fire and reconstruction in 1904, and total clearance over the ten years ending in 1972.

The next zone, which seems immense if you're on foot, is the inner city, extending to North Avenue (on the north) and beyond Monroe Street on the west. It "filled up" in the great building boom of the 1880s. It is characterized by the wavy fronts, yellow brick facades among the red, and a dozen variations on the bay window. The city's size was doubled by annexing part of Baltimore County in 1888, and the rows marched on. After World War I came another annexation, and most of the porch fronts, with more stone, more stucco, and more frame. These are today's "pop art" facades, where the porch gable and roof pinions are shared by pairs and each owner paints his half a color that pleases him—triangles of yellow and green and white and brown marching over the crest of the hill.

After a long drought in residential construction during the Depression, and the cramped rows of war worker and public housing built during World War II, row house construction took new forms—the garden apartments, two, three and four story blocs often placed gable end to the street. From the late 1960s developers varied these with attached "town-

Figure 1. Row house city. Source: Baltimore City, Department of Housing and Community Development.

houses," staggered to avoid the severely uniform facade and variously painted, shingled, and picture-windowed.

Not only do you recognize where you are in the urban stratigraphy, but from the row house landscape you can read a social landscape: Where do you fit in an income-stratified society? In each era row houses have been designed for rich and poor. We have today the elegant townhouses of Cross Keys, a Rouse Company development, which rent for up to $1,000 a month, and the good-looking Broadway-Orleans townhouses of a municipal project which rent for $100. Back in the 1840s and 1850s the very rich occupied townhouses on Mount Vernon Place, Baltimore's elegant and unique cross-shaped park centered on the Washington Monument. These houses are wide and splendid

and most have been turned into clubs or institutions. Certain working class streets of the same era near the B & O railroad shops at Mount Clare have become hidden alleys of white poverty, persisting from one generation to the next. The narrower "interior" streets have wood stoops painted white to look like marble.

The social landscape can be wonderfully complicated because a different society has occupied rows designed for an earlier one. Many blocks laid out in the 1850s or 1860s, for example, were first occupied by well-to-do families in the three story rows fronting on the wider streets, and working class households in the two story fronts on the narrower cross streets and interior streets or alleys. Frequently "Anglo" households lived in the large houses,

Irish and German households in the lesser streets or alleys. After the Civil War, such interior streets were occupied mainly by blacks —waiters, laborers, laundresses, and servants in the big homes of "Anglo" families on Bolton Street or Park Avenue and, later, Jewish families on Eutaw Place.

But the wealthy class repeatedly abandoned its homes for something modern, leaving the larger structures to be cut up into rental units, commonly one per floor. The conversions account for the remarkable concentration of dwelling unit sizes in Baltimore City rentals in the category of three room apartments. The perennial exodus of the successful, and social renewal by immigration (from abroad, then from rural Maryland, and from North Carolina and Virginia), turned some of these social landscapes inside out. Near Broadway, for example, a stable group of middle-aged black homeowners occupy the smaller houses on the interior street (Eden), while the larger houses on the outside of the block are subdivided and occupied by white tenant families from Appalachian communities of western Maryland and West Virginia, and by Lumbee Indians from North Carolina.

In other areas, particularly areas of black residence for more than a generation, considerable diversity exists and the houses one by one show signs of status achieved, of aspiration, or of despair—lace curtains, flowered plastic, or tattered shades; African violets, petunias, or plastic carnations; Victorian oak entry or broken screen; the pink porch, the black and olive trim, or a thousand fingermarks.

Some social boundaries are scarcely visible in the physical landscape, but as a general rule the physical patterns and variations designed in earlier generations are differentially occupied and maintained. The scale, grain, and texture built into the landscape continue to provide the set of sieves by which today's society sorts people in terms of income, race, occupation, and age.

Rowhouse building was at the same time street making. Street making can be considered the fundamental urbanizing process. Each extension of the urban street system into new territory represents a structure that may stand for hundreds of years, although its surface is renewed often and the public utilities beneath may be rebuilt. Buildings, fine or ugly, well- or ill-built, may last fifty or a hundred years.

This has been described as the bony skeleton of our social capital, which is fleshed out by all manner of faster circulating capital—new vehicles and new façades, shed and renewed continually, like the skin—and the yet faster metabolism of energy and materials—paint, fuel oil, water, newsprint.

One of the pleasures of a row house city is the large number of streets which have a human scale. The 19th century city authorized streets to be graded and paved in orderly sequence, a few blocks at a time. The habit of builders was to create a row at a time, or facing rows. One finds many combinations arising from a few standard street widths with two, three or three and a half story rows and with certain designs and patterns to the façade. Some streets feel like paths or canyons, some like plazas; some are homey, some elegant. The presence or absence of street trees adds another variant and people in some neighborhoods scream for trees while people in others object just as vigorously to their presence.

Each great building boom was characterized by a new street-making strategy. In general, there has been a progressive shift to lower overall densities, larger developments, more street area per house, and heavier investment in the street-associated underground utilities (Figure 2). The ways in which the rows are put together further help to define where we are in time and space. The patching together of rectangular street grids independently laid out on the old irregular manor properties of Maryland (Timber Neck, Ridgely's Delight) produces seams in the street system and angled rows, puzzling to a visitor from rectangular survey states. The working class districts of the 1890s have factory chimneys at the ends of their streets, while the middle class 1890s have their skyline punctuated by corner turrets.

Convenience shopping is by definition closely associated with residences and is therefore part of the row-and-street structure. The corner store and corner tavern trace out the pre-World War I city. Certain larger commercial nodes, circles, and strips reflect a streetcar pattern and zoning strategy of the 1920s. The gas station corners trace out a post-World War II city. Each of these commercial patterns allied with residence has produced problems of adaptation. The corner store and corner bar represent nuisance as well as convenience. The corner bars and commercial strips were the locus of the 1968 looting and burning and we now have

Figure 2. Town housing in East Baltimore. Source: Baltimore City Department of Housing and Community Development.

incredible architectural adaptations of "fortified" liquor caches. Gas stations have proved
exceptionally expensive to adapt to any other
use, to disguise, or even to demolish, and 250
derelicts remain in the city as relics of gas wars,
gas shortages, and the invasion of Baltimore by
multinational corporations.

With the annexation of 1888, as the city extended onto more rolling terrain and the upper
middle class bought into lower density "suburbs," the engineers came to grips with the
costs of paving, watering, and sewering it all.
They therefore abandoned the rigid grid street
plan and introduced a new sensitivity to terrain, building some fine viaducts, elm-lined
parkways, and winding rustic roads (for example Gwynns Falls Parkway and Windsor Mill
Road). The alley system was abandoned and
the old alleys were paved. The progress of the
automobile in the 1920s and again in the late
1940s fostered a preference for the dead-end
lane. The new scale of developers and cheapen-
ing of earth-moving favored immense grading
projects, and high and low priced postwar
developments can be differentiated by the
preservation of terrain, old trees, and vistas.
Each street-making strategy reflects a change
in the concept of an environment for living,
as well as changing notions of privacy.

DEPARTURES FROM THE ROW
HOUSE MODEL

What about the other half? We can treat the departures from the row house model as two
basic types—the detached dwelling and the
apartment house.

Detached dwellings are more numerous,
about 50 percent in Baltimore County and 75
percent in Anne Arundel County, the major
new postwar suburban area (Figure 3). The
detached dwellings belong to a "village" style.
They are not truly rural in origin since the
Maryland landscape was one of plantations,
isolated farms (in the piedmont), and wide
places in the road rather than villages. Bits and
pieces of "string towns" or roadside relays
are found as nuclei, as at Waverly and Reisterstown. The omnibus, the horse railway, and a
steam commuter rail line made possible gentlemen's villages like Mount Washington, Catonsville, Ruxton, and Lutherville. Marylanders who
could afford it adapted to the climate and its
health hazards by maintaining winter (town)

and summer (country) houses, as well as winter and summer rugs, drapes, and furniture.
By 1900 the existence of those villas and
villages, together with international trends
toward planned suburbs and the appearance of
the electric street railways, produced a new set
of villages designed for year round living of
upper middle class commuters—notably Roland
Park and Walbrook. In the 1920s the model was
extended to more modest classes, as at Dundalk
and Brooklyn, but a compromise was shaped
between the curving street and the row house.

Finally, after World War II, Baltimore participated in the national suburban development
boom. The vital elements, as elsewhere, were
the opening up of long term mortgages (FHA
guarantees) and the acquisition of automobiles.
We can map out the village model in terms of
the curves in street patterns. One of the more
comprehensively planned was Edmondson Village—around a "colonial" style shopping center, with a public library, school, etc. Single
family dwelling suburbs were seen as the modern way to live and symbolized the "anticity"
to which people leaving row house Baltimore
would flee. In the 1950s detached dwellings
were preferred by the affluent midwestern newcomers to central Baltimore County and the
somewhat less affluent newcomers from southern towns into Anne Arundel County. For
these outsiders, row housing was never identified with a middle class lifestyle. While hundreds of such "places" exist, distinctive as
Arbutus, Linthicum, and Pumphrey in one
small area, the suburban "villages" never possessed the sense of corporate solidarity of an
urban tradition. Social boundaries were maintained without legislative boundaries. The
counties do not contain incorporated towns
and cities such as hem in Cincinnati or Detroit.
Traditionally, the only important potential
boundary is the county line. The city has not
been part of Baltimore County since 1851.
They are independent jurisdictions and no annexation to the city has taken place since 1918.

APARTMENTS

Before World War I, when New York and
Chicago were building six story walk ups as
well as skyscrapers, Baltimore was building
six story warehouses, its skyscrapers could be
counted on one hand, and it took pride in having no tenements and an exceptionally large

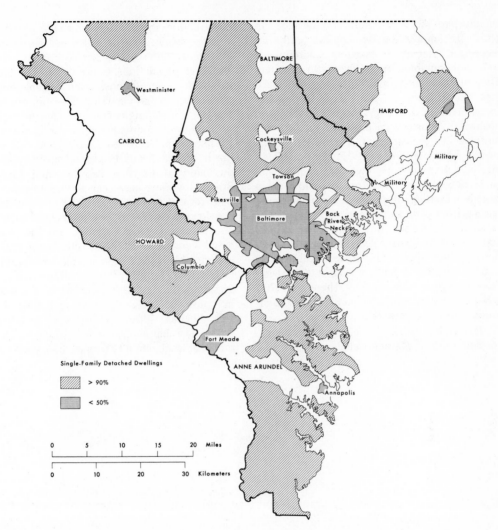

Figure 3. Row house city and suburban swellings. Only 40 percent of the region's housing units are single family detached dwellings, but they dominate a far greater portion of the region's land resource. The "row house" city is compact.

proportion of homeowners. Row housing, buttressed by a remarkable network of small mutual financial institutions and a British legal relic known as the ground rent (a family buys a home without buying the ground beneath), made homeownership cheap and popular and "stabilized" the working class.

In the 1920s new apartment houses and residential hotels of fifty to a hundred units were associated with grand views, pillars, and ballrooms. They were built on the new parkways or opposite city parks, as on Druid Park Lake Drive, Eutaw Street, Charles Street opposite Wyman Park, or the Mount Vernon area.

Many are now identified with shabby gentility, student ghettoes, or rip-offs of black tenant families who find themselves periodically without heat or hot water.

The next step in apartment construction was at the other end of the income spectrum. War time slum clearance projects were frustrated by the high densities per acre: planners could not rehouse the population and leave room to hang the laundry. About 1955 national prominence was given to ingenious designs for "high rise low cost" as at Pruitt-Igoe in St. Louis. Baltimore built in this style between 1955 and 1965 at central locations and the objections to this habitat have been felt here as elsewhere. In 1964 Baltimore's public housing authority recognized that these caged in environments were not suitable for families with children. They made a quick switch into high-rise apartment construction for the elderly in response to new federal housing subsidies. Public and nonprofit housing encountered much less resistance to the siting of apartments for the elderly—harmless and without automobiles—in contrast to all other low and moderate income populations. Therefore, we now see a curious sprouting of these high-rise buildings, ranging from plain to ugly, spotting the skyline of the city. These structures tend to house from 200 to 500 residents. Because federal regulations for their special funding are rigid in their income selectivity, they breed societies segregated by age and by income. There are 3,700 public units (low rent) and perhaps 2,000 nonprofit units (moderate rent).

Meanwhile, the same demographic trends, coupled with the rising value of land, new construction methods, income tax privileges, and the anxiety about violence, have favored the construction of high-rise communities for wealthier populations. Concentrated by zoning and parking regulations, several sizable apartment clusters have developed within the last ten years, including one at Towson (the capital of Baltimore County), one at the crossing of Reisterstown Road and Ford's Lane, and one north of the Johns Hopkins University campus along University Parkway and Charles Street. Investors have been extremely cautious with respect to luxury high-rise apartments in the downtown. There are clusters near Mt. Vernon Place and Charles Center, but "urban-oriented" professionals have also accomplished considerable reconversion and modernization of row houses. Favorite Sunday afternoon events in spring and at Christmas are "open houses" in renovation neighborhoods such as Bolton Hill, Charles Village, Federal Hill, and Fell's Point. The Baltimore rows continue to show remarkable adaptability for new lifestyles.

City of Neighborhoods

There are as many definitions of neighborhood as there are geographers, planners, and sociologists to debate them. Common notions include physical boundaries; a definite social network based on shared ethnic, cultural, or class identity; a sharing of certain facilities; and special emotional connotations. Neighborhoods combining all four elements, Suzanne Keller argues, are rare in modern cities.

But for some reason neighborhoods seem to be a real and universal phenomenon in the Baltimore region. I would attribute this to a remarkable correspondence of scale among physiography, the organization of the construction industry, pedestrian range, and the social units within which children play and grownups gossip and keep up with the Joneses. The elaborate and nearly indestructible differentiation of the physical landscape was the basis for gradual historical differentiation. Baltimore's topography also reinforces a strong distinction between walking spaces and riding or driving spaces, between neighborhood convenience stores and a regional shopping center or downtown, between neighborhood institutions and outside services, and between those who go outside to work and those who stay in the neighborhood in the daytime.

We are talking about a scale of ten to twenty blocks in the city, ranging up to 10,000 residents. In the counties the area probably ranges between half a square mile and a square mile. Is there any objective way to "find" such neighborhoods? Maps of street networks reveal several hundred small subsystems. In the outer ring of the city and in the suburban counties

highly connected nets appear, between which the only connection is a single link, a single through route, or a route with three or four entries. These are pedestrian nets joined by vehicular modes of travel. The rural-suburban edge can also be discerned. Within the city the grid is more completely connected, but one can nevertheless see unusual differentiation, with parks, watercourses and steep valleys tracing out barriers to everyday pedestrian movement. Industrial areas, highways, and railroads are perceived barriers, but historically their layout was also influenced by relief and drainage in the natural landscape.

Consequently, we can contrast the two major physiographic regions. In the coastal plain on the south and east, the *rivers* (tidewater inlets) dominate the shape of this isolation and differentiation of neighborhoods. The *necks* (peninsulas) govern the way roads and public utilities are laid out. Railroad yards and industrial proper-govern the way roads and public utilities are laid out. Railroad yards and industrial properties form barriers in this landscape and also contribute employment bases which give a certain cohesion to neighborhoods (see Figure 4). In the piedmont, the stream valleys are more often narrow, the land is rolling, and the controlling factor in construction and layout of roads is slope.

CONTROL BY DESIGN

On that complex natural foundation, cultural patterns were embroidered. In Baltimore the role of the large landowner, subdivider, or

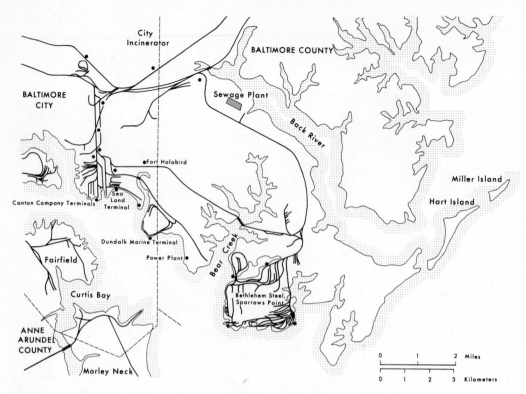

Figure 4. The industrial matrix of North Point Peninsula. Railroads ring the North Point Peninsula. Major industries form the rim on the North, West, and South. Along Back River are the city incinerator, land fills, the regional sewage treatment plant, and the islands scheduled for dumping of spoil from harbor dredging.

developer has always been important in the formation of neighborhoods. He transforms a marsh, a neck, or a hilltop into a neighborhood he believes will appeal to a certain market. His selection of price, location, and design creates a new social subsystem and a new bundle of property rights. The social system is vulnerable to change, as families grow up and regional housing market opportunities shift. But the people in the neighborhood generally want to maintain their social system—status, cultural group, and lifestyle. They develop institutions—formal or informal, legal or illegal—to protect the kind of neighborhood they have. Baltimore's scores of neighborhood improvement associations are a highly visible defense mechanism. So are local institutions such as school or parish, and shops which project a consistent market image. Less visible but important for perpetuating the social subsystem are the vested property rights and mechanisms for maintaining and transferring these rights. We

can get some idea of the variety of these mechanisms by looking at half a dozen communities, most of them along the Jones Falls valley between North Avenue and the city line.

One type of neighborhood social system based on property right is the company town. Over the nineteenth century, cotton mill owners developed strings of mill villages totaling 20,000 to 40,000 people along the mill streams or "falls". The easiest to visit are in the Jones Falls valley at Woodberry (below 40th Street), and downstream along Clipper Mill Road. These villages had a company store, Methodist chapel, and schoolhouse on company land and an occupationally structured arrangement of homes—stone duplexes for worker families, rooming house for single girls, detached dwellings with verandas farther up the hill for the supervisors' families, and, overlooking it all, the millowner's family mansion. For a hundred years they excluded sale of liquor and evicted residents who went on strike or took boarders not employed in the plant. The houses were sold off when cotton duck production declined in the 1920s. (In contrast, Bethlehem Steel has *consumed* its old company town at Sparrows Point for plant expansion.)

A variant is the "multicompany town" along the eastern city line. The Canton Company (incorporated 1830) progressively developed 3,000 acres by selling off waterfront lots for industry and inland residential building lots to housing developers. The plan assured a viable employment base for working class neighborhoods. The Canton Company retained the ground rents, and the various building and savings societies of the Polish, Bohemian, and German parishes enabled residents to buy up the rows of six room houses. Many homes have been inherited by a third generation. South of Patterson Park, for example, seventy and eighty year old brick houses with marble steps and stained glass lights shine like new all over, refitted with aluminum doors and windows and often with a patented imitation stone veneer.

New corporations in the 1890s adopted a strategy of developing purely residential neighborhoods. The Western Maryland railroad developed Sudbrook with F.L. Olmsted as architect. The Roland Park Company laid out a prestige community on the hills north and east of Woodberry. A commuter rail line, a private water company, large lots, a fine designer and architects, the rugged terrain, and an exclusive social group. The corporation structured the community through clauses in the contracts of sale and real estate deeds, to prevent commercial uses; the building of fences, walls, or additions; and occupancy by Negroes and Jews. They also required that property owners participate in a corporation of residents and levied a tax for certain services of street cleaning and maintenance. Over forty years they gradually extended their building strategy to other large tracts across the northern tier of Baltimore City (Guilford, Homeland, and Northwood). They adapted the devices to varying income levels.

The way in which the corporate developers of the elite neighborhoods planned and managed their communities reveals the pecking order of Baltimore society. The order of priorities, as worked out in practice, appears to have been the exclusion of blacks, the exclusion of Jews, and the exclusion of Catholic Europeans. The exclusion of people less affluent than the local norm overlapped with the other goals and the two conceptions were mutually reinforcing —social exclusion in order to protect homeowners' property values and economic barriers to insure social exclusiveness.

Naturally, as their economic conditions improved, excluded groups organized to create their own building and loan societies, build their own neighborhoods, and make them exclusive, too, further differentiating social areas and reinforcing a generalized pecking order. In this sense, Baltimore is a city of several hundred ghettos, each a little different.

Even where developers sold off all their property rights, a social subsystem could be maintained by mechanisms for limiting the homeowner transfer of property rights. In Hampden, on the plateau east of Woodberry and south of Roland Park, this applies to both homeowner and rental housing. Homeownership at workingmen's prices was coupled with a system for sifting and financing the entry of acceptable (white) replacement buyers through neighborhood realtors and savings and loan companies of local identity. Before World War II a large share of the still more modest rental homes were owned by several storekeepers on the "main street"; the Hampden bank was their principal lending institution. The relation of the neighborhood bank, a miniature downtown, the interlocking ownership of property and enterprise, and the manipulation of social structure are features of a model repeated in other neighborhoods, such as Highlandtown on the east, Little Italy near the center, or Glen Burnie in the suburbs.

Overall, this system produced certain painful contradictions. Because the choice of blacks in particular was so restricted, the black housing market became a pressure cooker. Blacks had to pay more for equivalent space, but whites would pay more for solid or "safe" property than for mixed or fringe blocks. These price differentials were incentives for realtors to organize the turnover of blocks or neighborhoods, one by one, at a rate that would just maintain the pressure. The process can be observed from 1900 down to the present moment. Only in the late 1960s did Maryland courts and the legislature begin to interfere in certain practices regarded as "private" property law—the restrictive covenant on the buyer's future resale, the owner's right to choose a buyer, the realtor's right to solicit business or steer potential buyers to acceptable areas, and the apartment owner's right to discriminate in renting and leasing.

New mechanisms, less racist and less explicit, are being developed to stabilize and protect a differentiated social structure and a neighborhood scale within large developments. In their village of Cross Keys, the Baltimore-based Rouse Company employed a high rent, long lease strategy. The village was built in the 1960s on the former golf course of the Baltimore Park Country Club, just north of Woodberry. Income exclusion remains solid, although great pains were taken to avoid racial exclusion. Partly on this prototype, Rouse planned the much larger "new town" of Columbia in Howard county. It is composed of residential villages, or neighborhoods, walkways and open space, industrial park, and town center. It already has 35,000 people, and is designed for 100,000.

The latest innovation is a joint plan of city government and private enterprise for Cold Spring, a "new town in town" for 12,000 people on a 500 acre quarry west of Jones Falls and just opposite Cross Keys. In the design Moshe Safdie (architect for Habitat in Montreal) uses a three dimensional concept of neighborhood, with clusters of high-rises and villages of townhouses (Figure 5). Lawrence Halprin, landscape architect, was involved, to protect the adjoining nature park (Cylburn) and develop the environmental assets—exceptional amounts of open land and vistas of the

Figure 5. Cold Spring model. Photo courtesy of Moshe Safdie, Architect.

Figure 6. The Constellation, moored in the Inner Harbor during the City Fair, 1973. Photo by Jim Kelmartin, *Baltimore News-American*.

rugged landscapes, natural and manmade. The developer is a Connecticut corporation, but some federal financial participation is assured to permit a wider, less exclusive range of rent levels. Rents must at the same time pay for a high quality physical environment and insure a sufficiently stable and protected social environment to attract people of that range of incomes.

Observers have suggested that there are signs of a renaissance of neighborhood, as there was in Baltimore in 1908–1910. Small neighborhood associations have become more numerous, won more legal and political victories, and formed large regional coalitions. As in other cities, neighborhood associations have—here and there—received support from the housing and urban renewal agency which assigns community organizers and the planning department which assigns district planners. Poverty and model cities programs seeded new neighborhood organizations in the inner city. A symbolic representation of this was the creation in 1970 of the September Baltimore City Fair. Modeled on the old-fashioned three day country fair, it has been enormously successful, attracting hundreds of thousands (Figure 6). Neighborhood associations annually take booths in which to sell their cookies or welcome mats, and with them their messages, political goals, and a neighborhood image. Nevertheless, the limited effectiveness of neighborhood defense strategies indicates the existence of powerful forces antagonistic to neighborhood. These forces determine the large scale segregations which are the subject of the next chapter.

Rings and Wedges

From the maps one can see a system of oppositions in the fabric of the metropolis. Among the most striking are maps of race, income, and private school attendance (Figures 7, 8, and 9). These are maps real and familiar to Baltimoreans. Many can draw these boundaries more consistently than the boundaries of their own "neighborhoods," and more accurately than they can map the major street pattern. Taken together, they map out deep-seated fears, envy, and mistrust. These tensions—open or concealed, conscious or unconscious—make the encounters of individuals in various parts of town comfortable or uncomfortable experiences that in turn generate a sense of security or anxiety about probable future encounters. On the basis of such expectations, people choose or avoid certain routes, locations, or trips in their everyday behavior, and so reinforce the boundaries and oppositions.

The three variables mentioned show extreme polarization. For example, most census tracts are nearly all black or nearly all white. Most individuals are socially defined as belonging to one of two "races," and two-thirds of all census tract populations are more than 90 percent of one race or the other. Likewise, the people of a census tract are either substantial users of private schools or they are not: only seventeen tracts out of 350 have more than 10 percent of their elementary children in private schools, but in half of these the figure is over 30 percent. Private schools, as classed in the U.S. Census, are distinguished from parish schools. Most of the parish schools are Catholic, but there are also Catholic private schools. Most tracts have figures under 1 percent. If we compare the frequency distribution of mean income by tracts with the overall income distribution of individuals in the total metropolitan area, they are much alike. This implies a high degree of spatial sorting by income. Most of the people in the "tails" of the distribution—the rich and the poor—must be living in different areas from everyone else.

The patterns of the maps make it clear that these polarities form large spatial discontinuities. They can be thought of in terms of the traditional urban patterns of ring and wedge—a black inner ring or core and a high income wedge in which many children go to private schools. A high income wedge is a feature Hoyt described in the 1930s for thirty American cities, and ring structures have proved basic in all urban multivariate analyses. It is likely that the unusually successful "tracting" of Baltimore and the strength of its neighborhood structure produce easier to read patterns than most cities. While Baltimore's pecking order may be more rigorous, it does not differ fundamentally from other U.S. cities. We will show here how the two sets of phenomena—rings and wedges—are related.

THE RINGS

The same variables which reveal neighborhood differentiation also reflect this larger scale op-

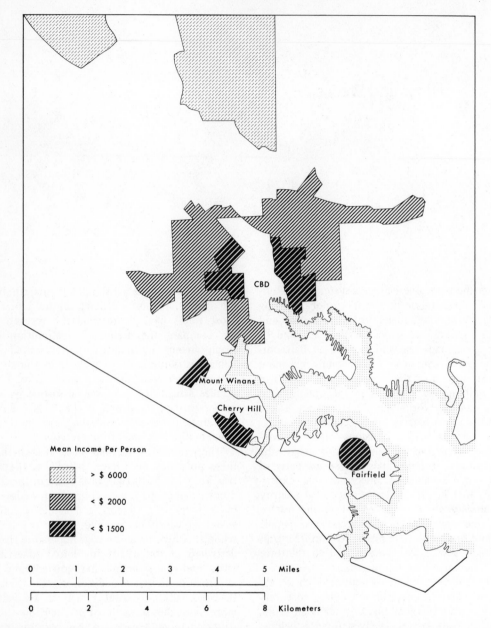

Figure 7. Extremes of mean income per person. Average income for each man, woman, and child in a tract shows the wedgelike distribution of the rich (over $6,000) and the inner ring of poverty (under $2,000). Public dependency is powerfully segregated: the lowest incomes (under $1,500) in the city are found in concentrations of public housing, and in the counties in institutional populations—state hospitals and prisons. Data for 1969.

position. For example, while there are dozens of distinctive black neighborhoods, most are grouped together into a black core or inner city. This core exists entirely within the city of Baltimore and is surrounded by a narrow, uneven, and fragile margin of change and an all-white periphery on the north, east, and south.

There has always been geographical expression of race discrimination in Baltimore. In the eighteenth century it was at the household scale—servants' dwellings over the backyard brick kitchens. In the nineteenth century it was at the row and alley scale of the city block. Three small black neighborhoods of the 1850s

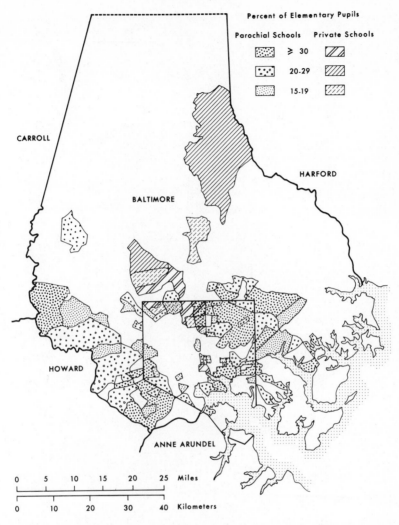

Figure 8. Use of private and parochial schools, 1970. A northern wedge of private school users overlaps on the east a wedge of Catholic parochial school users. A Jewish corridor (see Figure 10) overlaps the wedge of private school users on the west. Users of "parochial schools" in the north-west corner of the city are users of Jewish schools.

grew from narrow streets and alleys. They expanded before World War I (compare W.E.B. Dubois), and by 1935 there was a three-lobed "ghetto," defined by the city fathers as a "ring of blight" around the central business district (The South Baltimore black ghetto has been virtually demolished.) But it is only in the postwar period that immense opposition to racial segregation has emerged at the scale of the metropolis. It has crystallized into a formal political opposition—Baltimore City 45 percent black, Baltimore County 3 percent black. In the metropolitan area, 86 percent of the black population (five out of six persons) live in the city, of the white population 31 percent. A second major ring distribution is what sociologists or human ecologists sometimes call familism. It appears in factor analyses of nearly all North American census data as a multivariate dimension. It amounts to a concept of "standard family"—two parents and their children. Census data give us only a few clues to this structure, but it is an important contrast between city and suburb. We find that primary individuals (men or women living alone) are over 8 percent of the city population, but only 3.5 percent of the suburban population. To put it another way, one person

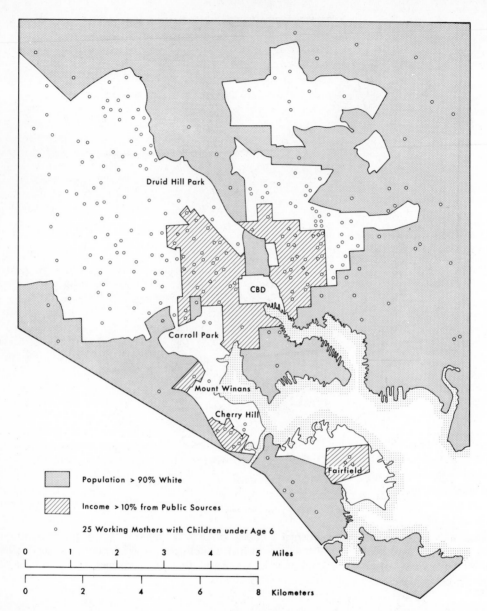

Figure 9. The core segregations—poverty, race, and structural dependency. Income from public sources includes social security, aid to dependent children. Because these incomes are low, in areas where they constitute over 10 percent of the total income the mean of the entire population must be low. The presence of working mothers with young children indicates a need for day care, but is correlated with inability to pay for it.

households are a quarter of all households in the city, but less than an eighth in the counties. Boarders and minors not living with either parent are twice as common in the city.

City-county differences in the percentage of women working outside the home are small, but this hides some important variations of work roles in relation to family life stages. Women with preschool children (under six) are only half as likely to work as women with school age children, grown-up children, or no children. In the two suburban counties, about one-quarter of the women with preschool children work; in the city 40 percent. The difference lies in the concentration in the city of black households in which the mother is much more likely to be in the labor force—half the mothers of preschool children (twice as many) and 62 percent of the other women. These figures apply regardless of whether the husband is present and reflect one of the ways in which the black family makes ends meet in spite of the lower average earnings per worker and more variable employment under "last hired, first fired" conditions. Labor force participation of white women is virtually the same in the city as in the suburbs.

ELEMENTS OF EXPLANATION

Row by row, neighborhood by neighborhood, the city pushed out from the core, influenced by great national booms of investment and tides of immigration. This kind of tree ring growth produced a ring structure of obsolescence at the center and, combined with the elaborate pecking order in Maryland society, organized a differentiation of the rings by race and income. Given also the high residential and job mobility of persons between eighteen and thirty-five, and their role in family formation, it might also produce the tendency toward rings in age distribution—young families in the new housing at the periphery, middle-aged settled families in intermediate rings, and the older generation in the center.

But that was a 200 year process. Other factors must be introduced to explain the new massive polarizations of the postwar years. The new phenomenon is the suburb. We have mentioned local suburban prototypes of the 1890s and 1920s, but massive suburban development was unleashed in Baltimore and Anne Arundel counties at the end of World War II. Rapid suburbanization resulted from a combination of technological change and social aspirations—an ideology of family life, the family automobile, the family-owned home, and the one family detached dwelling. These variables are geographically tied together in a suburban lifestyle. For example, outside a very small redeveloped center, there is an *old city* in which more than 80 percent of housing in every census tract dates from before World War II. The old city is belted by a narrow irregular zone in the annex of 1888, where the relief varies and radial routes pulled settlement into corridors. Around that is a broad and more continuous belt (the 1918 annex) in which less than 45 percent of dwellings are prewar. Most of these date from the boom of the 1920s. In the ring beyond that (two suburban counties) only 20 percent of dwellings are prewar.

The construction rings match closely the rings of present-day automobile ownership. Throughout the new annex three-quarters of all households have automobiles. And in the suburban counties, the basic design or strategy of development has made it almost impossible to function without a car, and households without cars rarely reach 10 or 15 percent. In Baltimore County 45 percent of the households have two or more cars.

In the 1920s, detached dwellings distinguished middle class from working class districts. The value system which preferred detached homes, private yards, the private family car, the nuclear family with two or three "planned" children and a "full time" mother existed full blown before the war. But after World War II it suddenly became possible for great numbers of people to realize this aspiration. As cars became cheaper, as factory workers' incomes rose, as more women took jobs, the suburban ideal became a realistic goal of more people. Wartime conditions had forced people to save money; then installment buying was invented. Also essential were federal strategies to insure massive private investment in long term home mortgages, homeowner income tax incentives, and massive public investments in road building.

Development of housing at a scale of scores and hundreds of dwelling units was not a new phenomenon in Baltimore as it was in many cities, but, because of the lower density, the new wave of construction required assemblage of large tracts of open land. It did not therefore fill in the old city, nor extend from block to block as row housing had done.

As the new low density developments spread, decentralization of shopping and jobs followed swiftly. The public transit system collapsed into a shell and none was extended into the new districts. The state legislature gave new charter powers to the suburban counties to provide urban amenities such as water and sewers, fire protection, and modern schools. Political development of the counties has followed in the wake of their economic development.

THE LOGIC OF DEPENDENCY

Suburbanization seemed to offer a new opportunity to all, but it nevertheless left some people behind—those unable to drive, those whose life expectancy or income expectancy would not appeal to the mortgage bank, and those who, not being part of a family, would not place a high priority on the standardized three bedroom house and yard. In other words, a development strategy aimed at the standard family market implied the neglect of another large and growing group of people peripheral to this family. Spatially, the development of the postwar suburban ring implied the simultaneous "undevelopment" of an inner city ring. The geographical reorganization followed a rigorous logic of dependency.

Dependency is the way in which a society defines the relation between its producers and its "nonproducers." In an individualistic society based on individual producers, all nonproducers are considered dependents and are divided into two groups. Insofar as possible, they are assigned to individual producers as "private dependents" and we have the family as the basic unit of consumption, redistribution, and reproduction of society. Those who cannot be assigned to families become "public dependents" and are regarded as a tax burden shared by all producers. As we shall see, this ideology is the basis underlying the new postwar ring segregations. Family type dependency is concentrated in the suburbs and public dependency in an inner ring of the old city.

Within the family relationships are considered noneconomic, although the producer role has much to do with the forms of domination which occur. In recent years the burden has shifted to a smaller number of dependents for each producer, but a heavier per capita investment in the rearing and education of each child for a longer period before he enters the labor force. The geographical concentration of families in the suburban zone is associated with heavy capitalization of the family, heavy investment in the new generation, and a new degree of isolation of the family on its individual piece of ground. As we have seen, its low density on the land is associated with the use of a family car (or two) and is unfavorable to mass transit. In other words, it offers a sense of mobility and choice within—and only within—that transport mode. This lifestyle also implies a heavy affec-tive load—or intensity of emotional relation-ships—within this small family structure. A sense of choice, mobility, and emancipation from one's parents is built into the mechanism of living in nuclear families. It provides the ties that hold the nuclear family together and the tensions that threaten it and at the same time reduces ties with the grandparent generation.

Meanwhile, in the core city, we see the segregation of public dependents, with high concentrations of "unrelated individuals" and nonproducers. Of the thirty-seven census tracts in which public transfer payments (social security, railroad retirement, aid to the aged, and aid to dependent children) exceed 10 percent of total income, thirty-four form a compact core. The other three are outlier neighborhoods of poverty, also in Baltimore City—Cherry Hill, Fairfield, and Mount Winans (evident in Figure 7). In the poverty core, we have 7 percent of the population of the metropolitan area, 7.5 percent of the housing units, but only 3.3 percent of the area's income. The income per person in this core is only $1,600, about half what it is in the remaining ring of the city and surrounding counties. The poverty arises from structural dependency. In this population, 9 percent are over sixty-five, 40 percent are under eighteen, and 12 percent (a quarter of the remaining producer-aged population) are at least partly disabled. In the region as a whole there is one dependent for each producer, but in this core there are two dependents for each producer. In fact most are nobody's dependents. As they do not have personal ties to individual producers, there is no personal sense of responsibility for their support and they receive smaller shares than private dependents in the overall social redistribution.

The stronger the family values and the pressures to invest in each child, the more families have tended to slough off their high cost dependents, particularly those who do not promise any return as future producers—for example, the physically or mentally disabled, the elderly, handicapped children, and those who are rebellious or ungrateful. The justification is that of a "normal" burden of dependency in relation to other producers in the society. For example, the retarded child is often institutionalized in order not to divert scarce resources from the child with greater potential. The number of public dependents therefore grows, and various classes of producers debate their shares of the burden of supporting them. This tends to reduce their maintenance. Regardless of where they are located, these dependents are more likely to be poor, as are half the "unrelated persons" over sixty-five. Of "poor" families, half have a woman as head of household (Figure 9).

But this squeeze makes it necessary to isolate the poor. Geographical separation makes the enormous differences of living standard less visible. The mean income of one census tract may be ten times that in another, but such tracts are separated by buffer zones, with continuous income gradients. The poor are not mobile and are not likely to be seen far from home; the 7 percent in the poverty core have a quarter of the carless households in the region. The wealthy have no reason to frequent the homes of the poor, as the homes of the poor have been gradually eliminated from the central business district itself, the suburban residents are doing more of their shopping in suburban shopping centers. In the five suburban counties, many of the poor are institutionalized. The only county tracts with per capita incomes as low as the core are the large state institutions for public dependents—those officially criminal, insane, retarded, or senile.

Geographical separation makes it easier for the majority in families to perceive the minority of public dependents as "other"—as a moral threat to the family as well as an economic burden, undeserving of any greater living standard. The core of Baltimore City is shared by greater than average proportions of abandoned wives, unwed mothers, the unemployed and the underemployed, the scarred and maimed, high school dropouts, alcoholics, old people, and communes. That is, geographical containment of various rejected populations produces a kind of moral contamination among the several groups as seen from the outside. A further guarantee of the sense of "otherness" is that the core population is 84 percent black. This makes it easier for the white suburban resident to resist any identification—"It's not *my* grandmother."

The poverty core is a human floodplain, where disaster strikes frequently and people are exceptionally vulnerable. Regardless of willingness, the capacity for mutual assistance is limited. Three-quarters of the households have no car (tracts range from 67 to 92 percent), and

two-fifths have no phone. Any breakdown of the postal service or public agency accounting machinery delays public transfer payments to 10 or 15 percent of the population and in some tracts withholds up to 25 percent of the total income of the area. Not only do bureaucratic catastrophes occur, but victimization is heavily concentrated here for fraud, violence, and theft. The demographic structures make this population even more vulnerable. The ratio of male to female runs as low as 75 to 100. Relatively low birth weights and high death rates of infants indicate the chains of secondary effects at the extremes of vulnerability.

The short-lived "War on Poverty" (1962-1972) and Model Cities programs (1967-1972) zeroed in on essentially the core area described here and attacked some of the problems. For example, a strategy of distributing free iron-enriched infant formula is credited with reducing infant mortality and anemia. Some day care and job training centers allowed women and ex-prisoners to get jobs and the banks were persuaded to cash public assistance checks. Social service jobs allowed some individuals and households to escape the poverty area and the programs reinforced citywide black political efforts to fight job and housing discrimination. But the situation in the core area itself is probably worse than before. The underlying problems of structural dependency remain, and inflation, increased property taxes, and interest rates have raised rent and food costs. Since 1950 the trend toward elimination of large chain food stores in the center city has virtually run to completion, while the small, higher cost "Ma and Pa" stores have been decimated. As consumers, core residents not only have too few dollars, but their dollars buy less than other dollars because they are a concentrated and captive market. This is also characteristic of the three outlier areas where there are also more women and children, fewer cars and stores.

THE GREEN WEDGE

If the core of poverty is a circle, wealth is a wedge. Where the circle is the shape of immobilization, the wedge or radial is the shape of mobility. In looking at the wedges in the Baltimore area, we find that they always indicate mobility and that geographical movement along these radials has been associated with

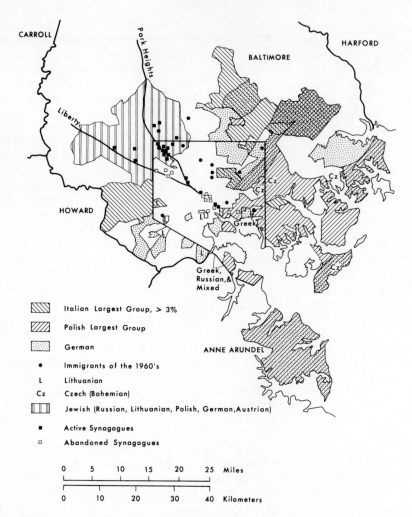

CARROLL

Park Heights

BALTIMORE

HARFORD

Liberty

HOWARD

Cz Cz

Cz

Cz

Greek

Greek,
Russian,&
Mixed

Cz

ANNE ARUNDEL

▨ Italian Largest Group, > 3%

▨ Polish Largest Group

▨ German

• Immigrants of the 1960's

L Lithuanian

Cz Czech (Bohemian)

▥ Jewish (Russian, Lithuanian, Polish, German, Austrian)

■ Active Synagogues

□ Abandoned Synagogues

| 0 | 5 | 10 | 15 | 20 | 25 | Miles |

| 0 | 10 | 20 | 30 | 40 | Kilometers |

Figure 10. Wedges by national origin. Locations of synagogues show the radial path of the Jewish community, complicated by religious differences and place of origin. For example, in the northwest corner of the city along Park Heights there are numerous Orthodox congregations of German origin, while the Liberty Road corridor includes more households of Reformed, as well as nonreligious and Gentile communities. A former Litvak congregation was located near the earliest settlement of Lithuanian Catholics. Concentrations of immigrants of the 1960s (one dot for 300 persons) occur near hospitals and universities and include a large share of Asians. Sources: Joseph Feld; Census of 1970.

upward social mobility from one generation to the next.

The high income wedge of classic type is a solid chunk as shown by the mean per capita income contour of $6,000 (Figure 7). It coincides with the private school users (Figure 8). The origin of the wedge lies, historically, in the present-day banking district of the downtown, where merchant families had their homes and counting houses, then "uptown" in the court

house vicinity or government district of the city, then in the Mount Vernon area around the Washington Monument and Bolton Hill (Figures 10 and 11). The wedge extends into Baltimore County. It is possible to say that the city is polarized into rich and poor, while the county is polarized into rich and middle income —a split which appears in the political life of the county. The creation of Roland Park (the point of the wedge on the income map of

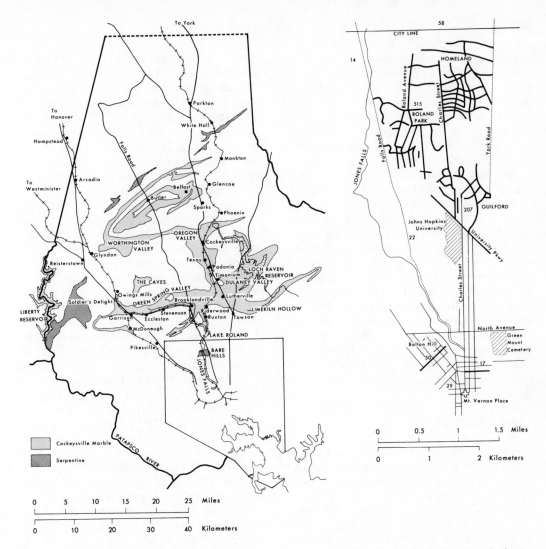

Figure 11. Blue blood and white marble. Radial mobility of families in the Social Register is shown by the difference of shading of street networks. Between 1912 and 1932, the streets in the older section (right figure, light lines) lost families, while the Roland Park Company suburbs (Roland Park, Guilford, and Homeland) gained. Figures in right hand map report by postal zone the number of Social Register families remaining in 1969. Of nearly 1,800 families in the register in 1969, all but a dozen lived in the towns and neighborhoods on these two maps, plus twenty-eight in Annapolis. Residential concentrations of Social Register families in Baltimore County show a linear pattern associated with two early commuter railroads which followed the valleys of the Jones Falls, Gunpowder Falls, and Gwynns Falls, and with the valleys developed on limestone. Marble is quarried near Cockeysville and Texas for the white stoops of Baltimore. It was used for the Washington Monument (Mount Vernon Place) and the marble trim on the surrounding homes. Source: Research by Mark Fleeharty.

1970) was the beginning of attention to "green" residential planning and respect for the admirable natural landscape. But with the exception of the century old city parks—Druid Hill, Clifton, Patterson, and Carroll—and its stream valleys, it has left the greening of Baltimore to the private market and the distribution of grass is the same as the distribution of greenbacks. Wealth is a wedge, poverty a circle. Likewise, green is a wedge and brick is a circle. Startlingly perverse is the distribution of air conditioners. If we consider the effects of natural terrain and microclimate, the effects of density and type of construction, there is no question that the heat dome of Baltimore centers over the poverty core. Here 9 percent of the households have air conditioners, while in the suburban ring over half do, and the percentage in tracts of the green wedge ranges between 65 and 99 percent.

The rent burden also has a perverse distribution. Average rents for dwelling units appear to be high in the central business district and low in the surrounding core, rising outwardly by rings. But if we consider variations in unit size and the frequency of homeownership, the wedge effect is evident, and if we look at rent in relation to income, the poverty core bears the heaviest burden. Perennial inequities in the property tax structure reinforce this burden. City tax rates are high, county tax rates lower, and within the city a 1974 study showed that properties in the green wedge were appraised for tax purposes below their market values, while inner city houses were overassessed.

ETHNIC WEDGES

We have already seen the striking central ring concentration of the black community, but one can also discern within it processes of radial mobility and a recent wedge or radial of extension toward the west, essentially the higher income movement along Druid Hill Avenue, then Ashburton and Forest Park, and out Liberty Heights Avenue and Liberty Road— the only sector in which we see a new concentration of black residents in Baltimore County (Figure 12 and 13). All the other enthnic groups show definite wedge structures. In fact, there exists a complete system of ethnic variations: everybody has a piece of the pie. This does not quite jibe with traditional descriptions of multiple nuclei of ethnic groups. Nevertheless, it is possible that a simple "Baltimore model" may apply to other cities. This dynamic model we might call a process of radial mobility.

The "ethnic wedges" are rather complicated to analyze because the census gives us not religion, but national origin, and national origin only in terms of first (foreign-born) and second generations. Each ethnic group has a different immigration history and a different balance of first, second, and third generations, etc. By examining in conjunction maps and

statistics of national origin, users of Catholic parochial schools, and the historical location of synagogues, we can trace out a process (see Figures 8-10). In the first generation we observe elaborate segregation by language and economic level, with a high concentration in the center city. In a second or third generation there is occupation of a larger area, farther from the center but still along an ethnic radial, with a greater mix of national origins but remaining within a higher order segregation by religion. This is consistent with sociologists' observations of "social distances" among such groups (Laumann) and it suggests that the notion of nuclei is illusory.

There exists a single broad wedge of Jewish settlement. Of the metropolitan region's 106,000 Jews, at least 90 percent live in this wedge. "Foreign stock" runs 20 to 40 percent (First and second generations), with a consistent national origin profile of Russian, Polish, Lithuanian, German, Austrian, and Rumanian in that order. The original heart of this corridor is eclipsed by recent black migrations, but can be seen in the presence of Jewish storekeepers and property owners and in the lovely restored building of one of the nation's oldest synagogues, on Lloyd Street near East Lombard. East Lombard Street is still the city's delicatessen row. The second foyer, in the Eutaw Place sector, is visible in the last remaining doctors' offices and a series of handsome synagogues, now Baptist and AME churches. The German Jewish immigrants who traced this path are also statistically erased because they are now in a third or fourth generation. In the early twentieth century a painful effort was made gradually to close the gap between highly educated and successful German Jews and the more recently immigrated East European Jews. The old differentiation of turfs between the groups is no longer apparent, but the Jewish wedge is extremely compact and extends into Baltimore County, where it is known as the Golden Ghetto. Jewish tenancy and ownership are still restricted from many other parts of the region. Two-thirds of the respondents in a study by Associated Jewish Charities described their neighborhood as all Jewish or mostly. Most expressed satisfaction with it "as is," not wishing it to be any "less Jewish."

The same study allows us to see how radial mobility produces both an ethnic wedge and a generational ring structure. It allows us to

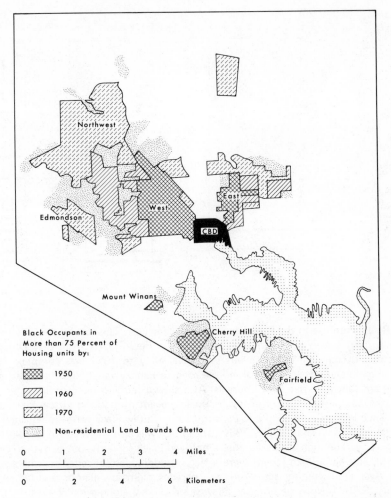

Figure 12. Expansion of the black ghetto, 1950 to 1970. The boundaries are defined arbitrarily as black occupancy of more than 75 percent of the dwelling units in census tracts. Stippling shows where the ghetto is bordered or contained by nonresidential land uses.

relate the process of intergenerational social mobility. In the twenty-five to forty-four age group, college graduates are 27 percent of the population, double the percentage in the generation forty-five to sixty-four (14 percent). Of the present college age generation (eighteen to twenty-one), 85 percent are actually in college. A full range of housing types can be found in the wedge, but home-ownership rises from 15 to 84 percent outward along the wedge, while length of residence declines. The sections outside the city contain two-thirds to three-fourths "standard families" with concentrations of young children, while the inner areas contain more of all other household types, more elderly, and more foreign born.

One can discover a very broad sector of Catholic occupancy, from due north clockwise around to the southeast, and a second wedge in the west and southwest. Within these sectors there are further discernible districts—several distinctively Italian wedges, a broad single wedge of Polish settlement, and extensive German Catholic neighborhoods, with considerable mixing along the fringes. Concentrations of a single national origin were strongest in old central locations or hearths, but some have disappeared. The importation of German-speaking priests to serve German Catholics (1840s) and the creation of "national" parishes, with parish schools and savings societies—five Polish, two Bohemian, one Lithuanian, several Italian—reinforced and

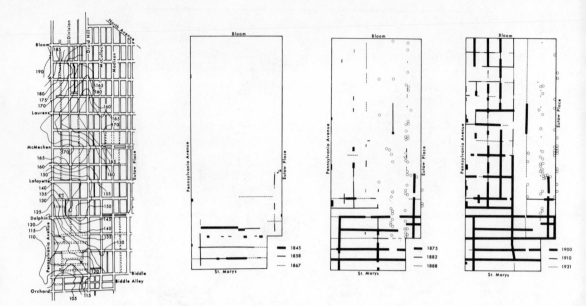

Figure 13. Racial mobility in the Pennsylvania-Eutaw corridor. The row-by-row extension of Negro occupancy has been traced by Raymond Snow and Andrew Frazier from City Directory listings. Movement outward from an 1833 nucleus in Biddle Alley to 1921 was complex, influenced by topography, commercial development along the road to Pennsylvania, and the width of the streets. Contour lines are shown at five foot intervals. Also shown (circles) are families listed in the Social Register in 1889 and again in 1921. They occupied elegant rows along Eutaw Place and Madison, the avenues which led to Druid Hill Park. Park squares in Eutaw Place were embellished in the 1870s and a fountain added in 1888. In the 1890s Eutaw Place was also the focus of the wealthiest Jewish families in the city. The high status families employed black servants, but twentieth century moves onto Druid Hill and McCulloch streets were a Negro middle class of school teachers and preachers. Pennsylvania Avenue became the scene of Easter parades, nighttime glamor, and famed Negro entertainers of the 1920s. Reconstruction has likewise proceeded along parallel axes. In the 1920s the Biddle Alley "lung block" (seven tuberculosis deaths a year) was demolished for school construction. By 1970 a pharmacy and another school, built over the avenue, replaced the heroin counter at Pennsylvania and Dolphin. New housing and a green network are planned further north, with Pennsylvania Avenue as the commercial and institutional backbone of "Upton." Along Eutaw Place, construction of the state office buildings was followed by consolidation of an institutional and commercial border for Bolton Hill and new garden apartments have been finished to the north. A steep social gradient still exists, from poverty on the west to upper middle class on the east.

stabilized Catholic immigrant neighborhoods almost as powerfully as sabbath restrictions produced compact neighborhoods of Orthodox Jews. The mixing of German, Polish, and Italian second generation is most evident in the suburban tracts. In these Catholic wedges one finds a wider range of variation in the proportions of immigrants of first and second generations. They add up to between 10 and 18 percent. Greek populations are often associated with Italian. There are also areas in which German stock populations are concentrated with-

out other Catholic groups present and some of these residents are German Lutherans.

Even very spotty ethnic "nuclei" such as the thousand or so Lumbee Indians from North Carolina appear to be developing an axis of outward hops and skips from the vicinity of Broadway and Fayette streets (East Baltimore) south to Brooklyn and thence to Glen Burnie in Anne Arundel County. The same path is followed by a sizable Appalachian population from western Maryland and West Virginia. People from South Baltimore along Light

Street tend to move to the same suburban areas.

Asians and "other Americans" (other than Canadian) are very recent immigrants, essentially the brain drain of the late 1960s favored by the change in immigration laws. They cluster around hospitals and universities. Asians are more strongly centralized than equally recent Caucasian immigrants and less centralized than black newcomers such as Jamaicans. Baltimore has a surprisingly small Spanish-speaking population. Cubans and Puerto Ricans have avoided Baltimore because in their search for jobs, education, and housing they are often treated as blacks. The Spanish-speaking people have not become established in distinct neighborhoods.

We have seen that people have been sorted by certain characteristics into wedge and ring distribution. This represents a certain amount of mobility within a context of apartheid. The ethnic variations are so elaborate that we cannot say who excludes whom: everybody excludes everybody else, except at the extremes —a wedge of white wealth and a core of black poverty. Income differentiation, while it is powerful in sorting at the neighborhood level, does not adequately explain the emergence of definite rings and wedges. A logic of producers and their dependents distinguishes the rings. In the next chapter, some classification of producer roles is proposed as a logic for ring and wedge.

The Tense Economy

At first glance the Baltimore economy looks very much like that of any metropolitan area in the nation, or a composite of them. It is not dominated by a single firm or line of production and has no pronounced image and no spectacular glamor sector. Overall growth rates are roughly in line with Baltimore's position as the nation's eleventh largest metropolitan area and fourth-ranking seaport and its location in Megalopolis. Its industrial and occupational structures, laid out in the census classes, are not unusual. They show little change, except for general trends in the national economy—more services are being produced and more clerical and professional workers are being employed. In its structural diversity the Baltimore economy is considered fairly well "buffered," and unlike Seattle or Detroit, it has not been especially hard hit by national ups and downs in the aircraft industry or oil prices.

But under the surface there is a great deal of turbulence. The Baltimore economy is an aggregate of highly specialized and differentiated activities, rather peculiarly knit together and undergoing complex changes. If we break down the production sectors to the right level of detail, we explode the apparent stability and discover the tensions, the vulnerabilities, and the sense of risk involved in its present growth strategies. Likewise, if we break down the occupational structure to the right level of detail by sex, age, and race, we discover a basis for the forms of social segregation and polarization described in the last chapter and get

some insights into current social changes and social tensions.

FIRST IMPRESSIONS

What does this factory town look like? A classic view from Federal Hill Park shows an immense foreground, the Inner Harbor, in various stages of total reconstruction. Looking east and north, through a forest of cranes in the ship repair yards, one sees a great gray-green sheet metal hulk steaming at water level —the chrome paint plant (Mutual Chemical), a visible example of the additions, accretions, and changes of 150 years' enterprise. Beyond, on the hill, sits the prestigious research and service enterprise, the Johns Hopkins Hospital, a clump of Victorian red brick turrets surrounded by assorted modern hunks of concrete, blind walls, air conditioning machinery, power house, and new parking tower. Farther east is Highlandtown, a hilltop covered with dingy glass and iron, the vast industrial cold frames of the 1920s. Off to the east a thin line of chimneys and a reddish haze mark the steel plant at Sparrows Point, its incredible scale, power, and din softened by seventeen miles distance. All of these industries show a tremendous resilience and vitality in their transformations. Each has reconstructed its techniques, its site, its markets, and its labor force, repeatedly building new values into its location.

To see the brand new industries, you have to travel out the expressway corridors or the beltway. Westinghouse and Western Electric plants built in the 1920s were the models for the modern low profile plant surrounded by vast parking lots and the sealed-off structures and brighter materials of the late sixties in the industrial parks at Timonium, Edison Highway, of the Baltimore-Washington corridor. The newer "dirty" operations such as the large chemical and fertilizer plants like Glidden or U.S. Gypsum, white with dust, have tended to concentrate in the outer reaches of the harbor, at Canton or Curtis Bay.

The basic geography of Baltimore industry is still the northeast-southwest axis, along the fall line or geologic contact of piedmont and coastal plain. Industry has spread out on the larger peninsulas and inlets of the coastal plain. This region has the advantages of tidewater shipping, ground water, relatively flat land, and a certain malleability. By filling and dredging, and by building piles, piers, and cribs, sites can be refitted and extended. The natural advantages have been reinforced by railroads and then highway construction, notably the Harbor Tunnel (1950s) and the North Point expressway (see Figure 4). The same geologic contact along the Atlantic coast is the basis for the commercial, industrial, and population growth of Megalopolis, which now reinforces the pull of this corridor for new distribution center and industrial sites.

THE LINKAGES OF GROWTH

We shall take three different angles for viewing the weblike growth of the economy and the ties between the private and public sectors. The first is the Baltimore-Washington corridor as a new industrial district. The second perspective is that of a large and specialized employer (Bethlehem Steel), linked into the regional economy. The third is an example of newly developed linkages within a diversified corporate structure (Easco). All have their geographical base in the coastal plain.

The Baltimore-Washington Corridor
New industrial sites in the corridor have grown by $5 and 10 million lumps on pockets of land. Piecemeal over fifteen years, public, private, and railroad initiatives have rebuilt the corridor and re-sorted the land values in a way that marries the old railroad access and the new highway access through spurs and feeders. Large amounts of land are devoted to railroad

car sorting and storage, truck terminals, and employee parking lots.

Corridor development is dominated by distribution operations and light or clean types of manufacture, oriented to product distribution rather than heavy raw materials or a large labor force. We find, for example, a GM parts depot for dealers in five states and distributors for foreign automotive enterprises—Volkswagen, Toyota, Mercedes, and Michelin. Marriott Hot Shoppes has a $9 million food-processing and distribution facility, while Macke employs 500 persons in a system for supplying food-vending machines. Carling's brewery (Canadian-owned) is one of six regional distribution centers in the U.S. After ten years of resistance, Baltimore's central produce markets have been relocated from the Inner Harbor to Jessup. Adjoining this site, Giant Foods has an automated warehouse with 4,800 gravity flow lanes and a central control console for picking off cartons of groceries.

Government services are a major growth sector in the corridor, as one might expect from the nearness of the federal capital and the state capital at Annapolis. The U.S. Department of Agriculture at Beltsville and the University of Maryland at College Park are a hundred years old and were jointly located, but they have expanded dramatically and independently in recent years. Both are large land users. So is the military base, Fort Meade. The new growth pole is the National Aeronautics and Space Administration. Its Goddard Space Flight Center cost $85 million to build over ten years and its Space Science Data Center near Greenbelt is newer and still more expensive. Of a thousand technical and professional personnel at Goddard, most have been recruited from out of state, and this has stimulated high value residential developments in Anne Arundel and Howard counties. Among NASA's important subcontractors in the region are the University of Maryland and the Johns Hopkins Applied Physics Laboratory in Howard County.

Another dramatic example of linkages between public and private enterprise in the corridor is in the vicinity of the Baltimore-Washington International Airport at Friendship. Three groups of developers acquired $1 million worth of land—about 180 acres—in three strategic strips, between 1966 and 1971. They have produced at least $50 million worth of development. The Sun Papers (April 5, 1972) traced the connections among numerous corporations, elected officials, and fund-raising politicians and thus documented a curious "complex," well known but rarely mentioned in textbooks of economic geography. In this complex we find a large motel and office buildings occupied by the National Security Agency and the state Board of Education and Department of Transportation. The Department of Transportation oversees the airport, interstate highways, motor vehicles, and port authority. Another large office group is the Greiner Company (Easco), private consulting engineers for airport expansion and state highway projects (see below). We also find among the owners and developers individuals tied to the airport limousine and taxi enterprise, state employees' and airport insurance contracts, the state liquor control board, the ownership of race tracks (state-regulated), and a pinball vending machine company.

Specialization

While a few resource industries are insignificant in Baltimore (leather, lumber, textile mill products), concentrations of most manufacturing sectors are in line with national averages. Proportionate to its labor force, Baltimore has its share of the nation's employment in food and apparel industries, printing and publishing, furniture making, paper, plastics, chemicals, fabricated metals, and electrical equipment. But if we break these sectors down into more detail there are decided differences. The location quotient for the subsector steel blast furnaces is five or six times the national average. Shipbuilding is three times the national average, while "other" transportation equipment is merely average. And shipbuilding is concentrated primarily in two firms—Maryland Drydock and Bethlehem—one of which is the major steel supplier as well. In electrical equipment, the bulk is produced by a few firms—Western Electric and Black & Decker, the region's largest locally owned firm, maker of home power tools. A large firm which appears diversified may be quite specialized, such as the Koppers Company (Pittsburgh) which has 3,350 jobs in the Baltimore region. Its five local plants produce an impressive variety of items—power transmission couplings, electrostatic precipitators, cooling fans, corrugated box machinery—but in fact half the operation is the production of piston rings and seals for diesel engines.

Bethlehem Steel, with a payroll of over $300 million, is a kingpin in the interlocking structure of the regional economy. Its linkages cut across private and public sectors. Its local sales include inputs to the other big export-base firms such as GM, Western Electric, and GE. Located near Bethlehem for convenient supply are Thompson Wire, Anchor Fence, and Ray-Met, a firm which supplies steel pile and does custom construction in an international market. A Venetian blind maker takes a million dollar's worth of steel each year. Bethlehem supplied the steel to a local bridge manufacturer for the state's new parallel Bay Bridge. Bethlehem interests are believed to have weighed heavily in the choice of technology for the regional mass transit system. The company's ship repair yards are essential to the local port and its shipbuilding division recently launched a new class of giant tankers. Their production thus directly and indirectly influences exports from the Baltimore region.

Bethlehem's investment program over the last ten years included $60 million for a new ore pier and channel to accommodate ore supercarriers and a still bigger investment in basic oxygen furnaces. They make steel in forty minutes, where the older open hearth furnaces took four to nine hours. These technological changes are closely related to another $28 million investment in special equipment for making light flat-rolled products such as chrome-coated can steel for the city's long-established can-making, food-processing, and brewing industries.

As part of an international complex with its main offices in Bethlehem, Pennsylvania, Bethlehem Steel is characteristic of a whole class of enterprises whose ownership and top management are outside the region. Of *Fortune's* 500, only two have their home offices in Baltimore (Easco and Black & Decker), while dozens have only branch plants. Baltimore businessmen complain of a "branch plant mentality." Baltimoreans tend to own shares in industries located elsewhere, while outsiders own the industries located in Baltimore. The ultimate threat is, of course, closing out of a branch plant and all its employment, as happened recently in the brass and copper industry (two century old firms) and the rayon mills (Mount Vernon-Woodberry). As Bethlehem's Sparrows Point plant is profitable and large new investments have been made, it sends no shivers down

local spines. But there are other side effects of
outside management. Some firms are resented
for their reluctance to invest in local cultural
and image-building activities. Baltimore's position in international banking is weakened because national corporations handle international
documents and foreign exchange through their
corporate headquarters and their New York
bankers.

Diversification

The new thrust of industry is corporate di-
versification. A large number of manufacturers
have adopted the strategy of diversifying into
service and real estate activities and then scat-
tering their risks in the metropolitan area or
still more broadly. For example, the McCor-
mick Company, a century old Baltimore spice
dealer and food processor, created Maryland
Properties, Inc., which developed Pulaski
Industrial Park on the east side, Security Industrial Park on the west side, and in the north,
at Shawan Road, Hunt Valley Inn, Golf Course,
and Industrial Park. The inn has become the
favorite executive club of the northern wedge,
and there are nearly 10,000 employees in the
industrial park.

The remarkable global expansion of multi-
product corporations like ITT have their modest counterparts in the Baltimore economy.
Easco is one of the two Baltimore-based corporations in *Fortune's* 500. Developed by acqui-
sitions and mergers, several of its operating
groups are headquartered in Baltimore. The
most important one locally is J.E. Greiner, an
engineering firm intimately connected with
Maryland state highway projects for seventy-
five years—in particular the Chesapeake Bay
Bridge, the new "parallel" bridge (next to it),
and the Interstate system in Baltimore City.
Its recent thrust is in engineering and environmental impact studies.

The Arundel Corporation also grew by successive mergers of firms in dredging, sand and
gravel, shipbuilding, ballast, and sanitary disposal. As their quarries were depleted and their
land fills finished (from dredging work), they
owned 8,500 acres, all in large parcels on prime
highway access in the industrial corridor. Their
ventures, evolving too fast to describe in full,
suggest the kinds of corporate linkages which
are emerging as the basis for a metropolitan-
scale economy of rising land values. Arundel
traded 722 acres in Howard County to the

Rouse Company for development of Appliance
Park, where GE will employ 10,000, adjacent
to Rouse's Columbia, designed as a "new
town." Arundel owns the 350 acre quarry site
for the Cold Spring "new town in town" project for 12,000 residents. Arundel is developing
a large industrial park at Linthieum and a 414
acre Arundel waterfront at Fairfield (opposite
Fort McHenry) is widely discussed as a site for
a large scale amusement and tourist center. Nationally Arundel has participated in huge joint
construction ventures on the Snake River and
water tunnels for Manhattan and Los Angeles.

When Henry Knott, one of the state's largest
builders, acquired an interest in both Easco and
Arundel, he effectively integrated these enterprises. Their growth is founded on the capture
of sites and environments privileged in the total
growth process of the metropolitan area. The
complex and ultramodern corporate structure
is built upon a remarkable continuity of family
strategies over two generations and on a tough
web of informal social (Irish and German Catholic) and political connections.

THE LABOR FORCE

Flux in the techniques of production, sites,
product lines, and corporate structures all imply adaptations for the labor force. Extreme
specialization and rapid technological change
mean that within the region there can exist
at the same time shortages of skills, skilled immigration (as of doctors from India and the
Philippines), unemployment among the highly
skilled (physicists and engineers), obsolescence
of older skilled workers, and unemployment or
underemployment of less skilled persons and
new high school graduates.

Not only are there changes in the job market—the supply and demand for various skills
—but there are important changes within the
region in the *locus* of job, residence, and journey to work. If we divide the entire urban work
force into five classes of jobs and look at where
they live, each class proves to be segregated
from the others to some degree and each has a
unique geographical pattern (see Figures 14
and 15). Even this crude division reveals the
relationships between people's residential situations and their roles in the economy.

The "primary" activities—mining and agriculture—are not discussed at length, as they
include only 1 percent of the work force, and

only 5 to 8 percent even along the northern "rural" border of the region in Carroll and Harford counties. More important (15 percent) are the "secondary" occupations—that is, manufacturing workers: skilled crafts, semi-skilled or factory operatives, and self-employed craftsmen. Most of them work in factories or workshops and handle materials, tools, and machines. The "tertiary" occupations include a great variety of service jobs—food service, cleaning service, security or "protective" personnel, nontechnical hospital workers, and personal services. They may work for an industry, an office, a government, or a retail establishment. The less familiar term "quarternary" workers applies to those (28 percent) who do routine information processing—such as clerks, typists, key punchers, programmers, and bank tellers. Most of them work in offices. "Quinary" workers also process information, but in nonroutine ways. They include professional and technical jobs, many management jobs, nurses, and teachers.

RESIDENTIAL PATTERNS OF THE LABOR FORCE

The most highly segregated category is the quinary. Although 21 percent of the work force is in this set of occupations, most tracts have a much larger or a much smaller percentage of their residents in such jobs. In a few tracts, quinary occupations are numerous and dominant; they account for 30 to 55 percent of the labor force. These tracts occupy a surprising share of the metropolitan area, as this class consumes a great deal of land. They occupy the green wedge north from Baltimore City into Baltimore County, a second southwest wedge (nearly all of Howard County), and three sizable areas south in Anne Arundel County. A map of quinary jobholders corresponds quite accurately to maps of high income, high homeownership, high home value, low density, and a high proportion of detached dwellings. The absence of quinary workers from certain districts is also striking. A large core area in Baltimore City has less than 10 percent in quinary occupations. In many tracts they are as rare as 2 percent.

Service jobs (tertiary) map out almost a mirror image of the quinary jobs. The city core, outside the central business district, has most service workers. Concentrations over

50 percent are chiefly the black ghetto neighborhoods. There are also sizable parts of Anne Arundel County over 40 percent and a narrow westward corridor through Carroll County.

These two groups of occupations are the most unlike in status and pay and in composition by race and sex (Figure 16). Their opposition suggests the way in which the polarization of residential space is built into the division of labor in the metropolitan economy. They represent the extremes—a highly specialized, highly educated and mobile elite work force, and a proletariat of service workers whose mobility—social and geographical—is relatively limited. Mobility of the quinary work force is evident, for example, in the concentration of brain drain immigrants of the 1960s from Europe, Asia, and Latin America into certain census tracts around research and educational institutions and hospitals and the concentration of highly technical and professional personnel from other parts of the United States around the NASA installations.

Quinary jobs can be regarded as decisionmaking occupations. These workers have a strong grip on decisionmaking within their highly specialized sectors of industry, technology, and government. They have a strong influence on the decision frameworks or range of choice of other sectors, through their role in the "quinary industries" such as banking and insurance, education, research and development. Moreover, when we relate this to the lifestyle of their residential districts, we see that they are decisionmakers in all domains of life. That is, they have a higher density of choice in their personal lives—the management of a house and real estate and a budget with credit options. Because they have automobiles, they have a farther range of decision, not only in choosing, trading, and financing the car, but in the daily choices of routes, shops, etc., and an extra degree of freedom in searching for another job or home. Accumulated experience in their education and career development has increased their mobility, their information network, and their flexibility in relating their personal decisions to opportunities and changes in the economy and the environment. People in this sector do not always see themselves as having an adequate range of choice or power of decision because they are limited to extremely specialized and narrow sectors in their work. Many

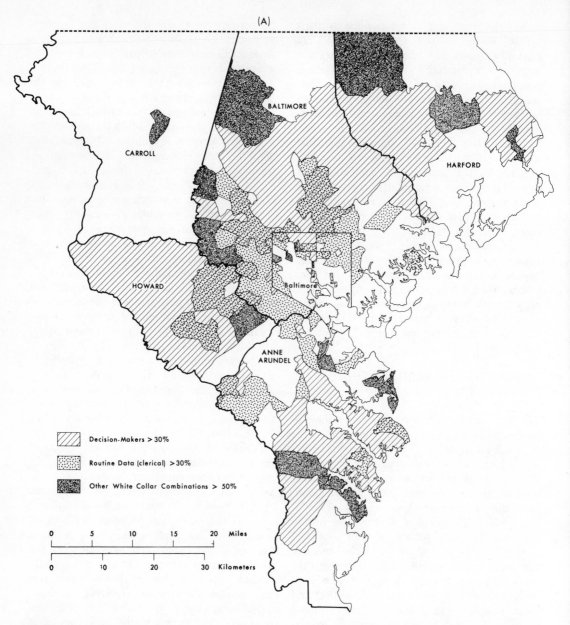

Figure 14. White collar (A) and blue collar workers (B) at home. (A) Residential patterns of decisionmakers (nonroutine handlers of data) and clerical workers (routine handlers of data) resemble the map of new, high value, resident-owned housing. (B) Manufacturing workers are concentrated in the industrial coastal plain corridor, while service workers are concentrated in the core region of public dependency.

work exceptionally long hours, but they have some ability to negotiate their work schedules, holidays, and vacation seasons. They appear to have characteristic maladies of tension, heart disease, use of alcohol, or tranquilizers. The

need for mobility and flexibility places great stress on the small family social unit.

In contrast, the core area where there are few quinary jobs is a nondecision zone. There is no room to maneuver. One rarely knows a

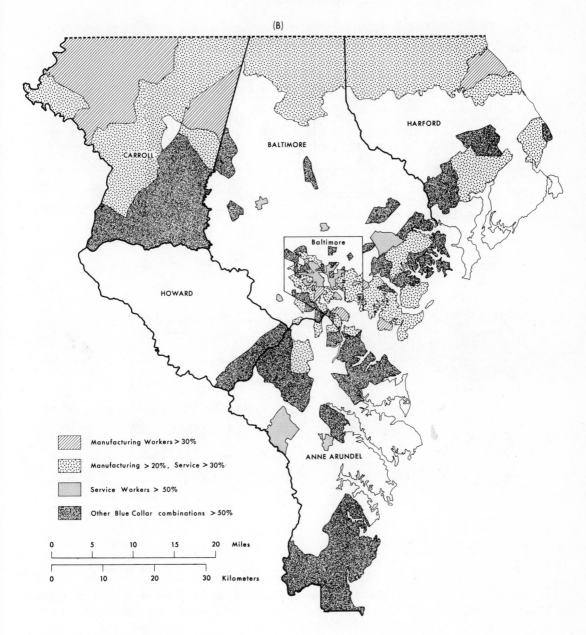

(B)

Manufacturing Workers > 30%

Manufacturing > 20%, Service > 30%

Service Workers > 50%

Other Blue Collar combinations > 50%

0   5   10   15   20 Miles

0   10   20   30 Kilometers

person whose job "changes" things. A large share of service workers have dirty jobs, night shifts, or variable schedules which they cannot manipulate. In daily life, residents are at the mercy of rigid bus routes and the weekly rent book. They have no financial flexibility and because income is smaller the range of shopping choices is more constrained. These workers have, on the average, much smaller household spaces to organize, maintain, or personalize

and much smaller public spaces to supplement them. Personal spaces are more frequently invaded—theft, fire, noise, odor—and there is a corresponding sense of lack of control of neighborhood—invasion by outside traffic and manipulation by absentee owners and businessmen. In addition to health problems directly associated with crowding and space (for example pedestrian accidents and respiratory diseases), some health problems appear to be

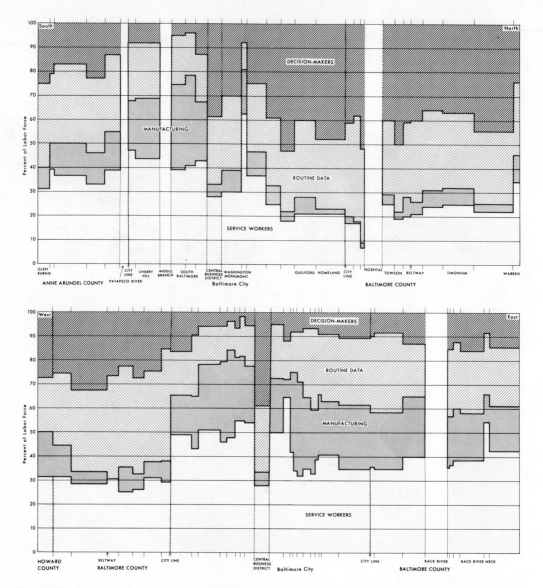

Figure 15. Labor force stratigraphy. The two cross sections, east-west and north-south through the center of town (Charles Center), show both a ring and a wedge effect. Blue collar workers (service and manufacturing) ring the central business district, but more so in the east and south.

associated with the constraints of "nondecision"—possibly the incidence of personal violence, use of hard drugs, and the common "ghetto headache."

Manufacturing workers have a degree of segregation comparable to the quinary workers, but they are not found in the same residential areas. There is more overlap between service workers and manufacturing workers than be-

tween manufacturing workers and either of the other groups. Together manufacturing and service can be regarded as "blue collar jobs," but manufacturing workers are generally unionized and better paid.

Quaternary workers (clerical) tend to share the geographical spaces of quinary workers. Both are "white collar" jobs, regarded as clean and "nonmanual." Quaternary and quinary

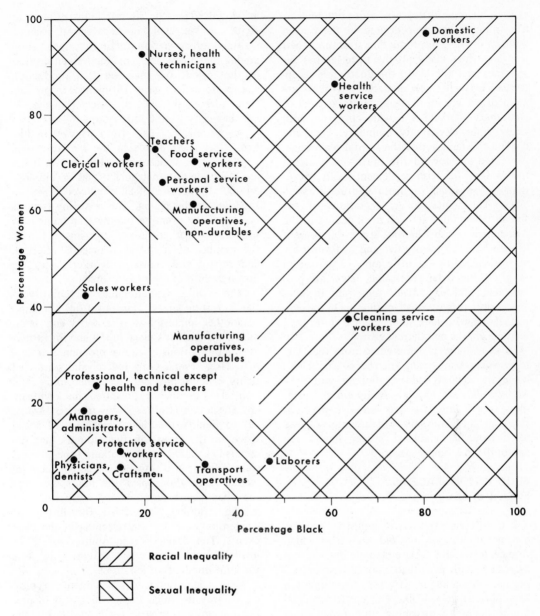

Figure 16. Metropolitan Labor Force by Race, Sex, and Occupation. Only one job category falls within the nondiscriminatory region around the "normal" percentages of blacks and women we might expect from their rates of participation in the region's total labor force. Occupations are ranked to approximate national norms of median wage and prestige. The ranking is crude because of race and sex differentials within each job category. The wide wage spread, from a median of $20,000 (1) to $1,700 (18), depends on maintaining race and sex wage gaps and a differentation of job types as shown. The three indicators of status thus tend to be mutually reinforcing. The wide spread of income provides mechanisms as well as "justifications" for segregations in housing, on the job, and in education.

workers share work space in office buildings. A large number are concentrated in the central business district. In production structures their jobs are often matched—the manager has his secretary and file clerk, the doctor his receptionist. In such cases, quaternary workers are more often women. The residential pattern of quaternary workers is a wide circle on both sides of the city-county boundary. The band does not extend across the coastal plain zone. An extension toward the northwest matches the wedge of Jewish settlement, with exceptionally low levels of manufacturing employment. The white collar aspirations of the Jewish community are well documented in the Associated Jewish Charities study—60 percent of men between twenty-five and forty-four are in professional or executive jobs, 12 percent in sales. Of the older generation, fewer are professionals and executives, more are in sales and proprietors of small business. Of the employed women half hold clerical jobs, and teachers are the next largest group.

A geographer is tempted to note that factory workers are living on the coastal plain, while the quinary and quaternary workers—white collar—are located chiefly on the piedmont (see Figure 15). It is not a simple matter of geology and soils, but a complex piece of history. Geographical spaces have been appropriated as social spaces.

PRODUCTION SPACE AS SOCIAL SPACE

The main concentrations of industrial workers are neighborhoods of old industry which formed distinctive local economic bases, often associated with a particular social base or ethnic mix. A simultaneous wave of immigration and industrial growth allowed a particular social group to develop or capture an economic base and a neighborhood. This process was repeated again and again. New production systems underlay new systems of social relations. Changes in the production system repeatedly disintegrated these local social systems and opened the way for reorganizations in the local social geography. Dozens of historical examples of these processes can be found—shipbuilding on Fell's Point, oyster packing in Canton, can making in Highlandtown, the cotton mills at Woodberry, the sweatshops of Old Town, dock work on Locust Point, railroad shops

at Mount Clare, the aircraft industry at Aero Acres. . . . We shall choose a set of complementary types of production systems from among the largest and most modern enterprises in the region. We shall see that production spaces are social spaces. Differences in production roles mesh with the social "distances" between classes and ethnic groups.

As we might expect from its size, Bethlehem Steel plays a role in the structure of a large series of social spaces (Figure 17). It has an elaborate internal society, as it employs 34,000—18 percent of all employed in manufacturing in the region. The company trend is typical of the overall economy: the number of production workers is not growing as fast as the number of technical, managerial, clerical, and service and transport workers, who are now one-third of their work force.

There were elaborate lines of seniority in the 217 shop units. Transfers from one shop to another implied loss of seniority and determined the worker's place in the line for further raises, promotions, training programs, or layoffs. Over several years federal and state civil rights commissions and the Office of Federal Contract Compliance pressured the company and the union (United Steelworkers of America) to modify the rigid framework of social space in the plant, on the grounds that the company's 8,000 black workers (one-quarter) were frozen into low-paying jobs. Environmentally, they occupied the hot spots, near the open hearth furnaces and away from the air conditioning, and filled the dirty and dangerous jobs like acid cleaning in the coke ovens. The limited compromises of 1971 involved unit mergers and reduction of tests for some hundreds of job classes.

Here again, Bethlehem was merely typical of the way in which the social spaces of production units were structured. In 1970 at the advanced materials works of Armco Steel in Baltimore, blacks were also more than a quarter of the production force, but no black had ever participated in the foreman training program, only one of ninety-nine plant supervisors was black, only one of 152 white collar management level employees, six of 216 clerical workers, and five of 198 professional, technical, and sales employees.

The Social Security Administration is a massive "white collar factory." Like the blue collar factories, it provides a local neighbor-

Figure 17. Sparrows Point steel plant. Bethlehem Steel Corporation's Sparrow's Point steel plant, one of the largest in the nation, occupies about 2,100 acres just southeast of Baltimore on the Patapsco River near Chesapeake Bay. The plant turns out a variety of steel products such as plates, pipe, reinforcing bars, wire rods, wire, nails and staples, wire strand, sheets, blackplate, and tinplate. Alongside the plant, at the left of the photo, is Bethlehem's Sparrows Point shipyard, one of the major builders of tankers and cargo vessels in the United States. Bethlehem Steel photo.

hood-building social and economic base. As the national records and data-processing center for the nation, Social Security employs more than 16,000 persons, 80 to 90 percent of them women. The majority are in the lowest four civil service grades, such as keypunch operators who are new high school graduates. This office alone would account for a third of the growth in the female clerical sector in the last decade, or 7 percent of all the quaternary jobs now in the region. The equal opportunity effort in federal jobs in the 1960s made this an economic base open to black women, as the post office had once been for men. The black community is now funneling large numbers of young women into the quaternary sector. The mechanism for a shift from the blue collar factory to the white

collar factory lies in the educational inputs and the black community like the Jewish community utilized the public schools and insisted on education for girls. The public schools have been most effective in fostering occupational success in the quaternary sector, as they teach routine processing of information and reward personal adaptation to the regimented, authoritarian, sedentary, and sanitary environment of the white collar factory.

Social Security has occupied various buildings in downtown Baltimore since it began in 1936, but its largest modern installation is at Route 40 West and Security Boulevard (Figure 18). Like Bethlehem on the east side, the white collar factory has generated a complex community space on the west side—row hous-

Figure 18. Social Security complex, 1973. Photo by Maps, Incorporated.

ing, apartments, and shopping centers. Its hiring practices have contributed to opening a thin wedge of black residential settlement in Baltimore County. Anxiety over that emerging wedge contributed to the decision that the further expansion of Social Security will take place at a center city renewal site.

Another white collar factory, the Chesapeak and Potomac Telephone Company (AT&T), appears to have a rigidity of social spaces complementary to those found at Bethlehem, Armco, and Social Security. C&P has some 14,000 employees in Maryland (not all in the Baltimore region). 1971 testimony to the FCC stated that only seventy of 2,000 managers were black. The segregation of shops and wage levels depended on a geographical structure for the various operating divisions. Most of the black women employees were operators

at inner city exchanges. There were no black personal secretaries, communications representatives, or engineering assistants at the downtown headquarters until recently, but blacks filled all the mailroom jobs. Blacks filled most jobs in the printing and typography operations in East Baltimore, but very few of the jobs in the central accounting office at Cockeysville, to the north.

SHIFTS IN THE DIVISION OF LABOR

It is apparent that the character of the four occupational groups is related to the elaborate segregation of production by race and sex (Table 1). By means of a more detailed classification of occupations, Figure 16 shows how strong these patterns of division of labor by race and sex are. Baltimore differs from other

Table 1. Occupational Groups by Race and Sex, Metropolitan Area, 1970

| | *Percent of People in Each Type of Job* | | | | | | |
Type of Job	Total Women	Total Blacks	WM	WF	BM	BF	All Workers
Decisionmaking jobs	27	10	68	22	5	5	100
Routine data handling	64	14	31	55	5	10	100*
Manufacturing workers	33	33	44	22	23	10	100*
Service workers	28	29	55	16	17	12	100
All workers	38	22	50	29	12	10	100*

*Figures do not add to 100 because of rounding.
Source: Census of 1970

metropolitan areas only in having a larger share of black workers.

Over the last ten years, changes in the composition of jobs and jobholders have shifted the percentages but have not changed the underlying structure of occupational roles assigned by race and sex. One hundred and seventy-five thousand new jobs were added to the labor force, largely in services and public sectors. As more women entered the labor force, they were absorbed into sectors traditionally reserved for women—nurses and teachers among professionals, clerical (about half), and health and food services. Many of the new jobs were at minimum wage. The only improvement in the wage structure was the disappearance of domestic household help. A slight shift from racist to sexist domination of jobs was not especially favorable to the black community in view of their high proportion of women wage earners.

The critical fact which reinforces this system is that we have not a mere *division* of labor, but a *hierarchy,* in which women are paid less than men, and blacks are paid less than whites. Limited alternatives in the job market create a different balance of supply and demand, which depresses wages in certain sectors. Interactions of "racism" and "sexism" produce an infinite number of options for playing off the interests of one group against another, with the result that Baltimore industrial interests in their economic development literature point to the unusually low family budget of Baltimore factory workers, low differential pay for shift work, and a lower rate of unionization.

Structural changes in the labor market are naturally reflected in labor organization. The growth of service and professional jobs and relative stagnation of factory labor have shifted labor-management conflict into the arena of public and service enterprise. But the job competition of various social groups has favored conflict *within* the unions. Effective unionization of new sectors has thus been limited by the social conflicts built into the division of labor. Three-quarters of manufacturing workers are unionized in the region, but a much smaller share of other workers. Baltimore has exceptionally large nonunion sectors in construction and trucking. Few women workers and black workers are unionized except in the clothing industry. A major breakthrough on all those fronts was organization of hospital service workers (Local 1199E). City teachers, policemen, and hospital workers became militant in 1974, but without significant gains. In the last few years most racially segregated locals have merged, but they maintained the seniority and preferential interests of the larger white membership (as at Bethlehem and in dock labor and construction). The city's black firemen formed the Vulcan Association to exercise a voice in the white-dominated firemen's union.

Over the next ten years, the sense of competition among groups for jobs can be expected to continue as a source of tensions, because of the changing proportions of various groups in the labor force. In this sense, conflict is structural in a competitive economy. The Regional Planning Council projects that the younger generation (twenty-five to forty-four) will increase from 40 percent (1970) to 50 percent of the labor force. Although the black work force will remain constant overall (one-quarter), in this age group it will nearly double. There are also more women among the younger workers. We may expect to see acute competition for low wage entry-level jobs, a struggle between younger and older generations for managerial and policy roles, and further pressures for early retirement and technological obsolescence of older workers. Because of the way demographic structure and labor force structure interact, all these forms of competition are likely to be expressed in the familiar rhetoric of race and sex.

THE REGION'S SOCIAL SPACE

The metropolitan region is a single area in terms of its economic structure. There are small differences among the counties in terms of the economic sectors for which people work. But in the actual occupational categories there are decided differences: city residents include half the factory workers of the metropolitan area, nearly half the service workers, but only 41 percent of the routine processors of information, and only 32 percent of the decisionmakers.

Geographically, the total growth of the metropolitan area requires a massive centrifugal movement of capital—capital formation, disinvestment or transfer from the central city, and investment on the new fringe. The development of residential spaces is only one aspect of this. In many ways movements of "human capital" resemble movements of fixed capital. The highly capitalized population—that is, quinary workers—has decentralized fastest and exerts immense pull on capital in the retail sector. We now find supermarkets and bank branches located in a suburban ring pattern. They have disappeared from a large inner city ring.

But this centrifugal movement does not imply a trend toward an equilibrium. The growth employment locations are cut off from public transport and the present dispersion of industrial operations is unfavorable to economical mass transit. Therefore, access to new jobs is reduced for the young, the less skilled, the lower paid, and married women in one car families. Even if no direct race discrimination were operating, the effects are discriminatory because blacks are overrepresented in all these categories and in their central residential location. In other words, the present setup in the language of development economists is a "low level trap." Occupational exclusion and residential exclusion reinforce each other and this

tendency is becoming more severe as industrial growth moves into Carroll and Howard counties.

Meanwhile, the technical growth of the economy produces at once demands for specialization, capitalization, and flexibility. The problem for the worker is much the same as the problem for the industry—he must invest more time and resources in his (or his children's) education, choose and concentrate on a narrower specialty. Yet he sees that these investments are subject to great risks of obsolescence and he has to preserve what flexibility he can.

At the level of neighborhood and social group, these processes continually produce disintegration and recoalescence. Neighborhoods appear to go through cycles of vitality and flight in which the movements of capital (mortgage money and public investments) run parallel with the movements of human capital —the young and educated households.

Because of the changing job mix and the changing labor force composition, old patterns of division of labor by sex, age, and ethnic group must break down. But traditions of racism, sexism, and paternalism provide a framework for venting frustration, hostility, and anxiety in the face of the personal threats of technical and economic change the individual cannot control. This context of structural conflict is the basis for the polarization of the region into spaces of control—home turf and places of threat.

At every scale in this local geopolitics— household, neighborhood, county—one discovers strategies of defense. In the suburban ring each household stakes a claim, creating a private hedge against inflation or a private speculation and defending it through local zoning restrictions. Older inner neighborhoods defend their investments, social identity, and status aspirations by struggling to keep the parochial school alive, retain the football stadium, or find enough young Italian couples to keep Little Italy alive as a restaurant district. In the very core, individuals buy guns or fierce dogs or they band together to fight off a new liquor license or to demand a community-controlled school. Many defense strategies have been cast at the scale of the metropolis—the city-suburban ring—because this is the basic political frontier between a zone of sunk capital and a zone of capital investment. Other struggles have been restructured into a geopolitical struggle at this scale, a level where public investments are made.

In other words, the Baltimore economy not only produces steel for the North Atlantic community and electric drills for the nation, distributes cars and groceries to six states, and fries chicken for Baltimoreans, but as a by-product it produces Baltimore society—the class structures of consumption and the geographical structures of distribution. It produces in some measure a "Baltimore person," with a sense of competition and vulnerability, and an awareness of the limits on his ability to control his own personal life.

Development and Redevelopment

The breakdown of old vital spaces and reconstruction of new vital spaces, as described for certain industrial districts, is an example of a more general process. Just as the vital space of the Susquehannock and Piscataway Indians was constrained, then broken up, destroyed, and reconstituted into an agricultural or planter economy, most of the agricultural space in the metropolitan area has in turn been constrained and broken up. It is now rapidly being reconstituted into suburban fabric. Some parts of the area have gone through further cycles of redevelopment which we recognize by the massive clearance of structures. Others are renewed by a more continuous and less obvious process, like the metabolism of the human body—the simultaneous breakdown and reconstitution of tissues.

We shall focus on the role of public enterprise in several different kinds of redevelopment—the port, the downtown, the inner city, and a series of speculative transformations of successive rings out to the fringe of conversion of agricultural land. These transformations, which seem like local phenomena and functionally distinct operations, are actually part of a single growth process. The metropolitan area is a whole and its physical transformation is only one facet of this process, a surface we can see. A second facet—the movements of people —can be traced with more difficulty. The third facet is an invisible movement of capital. We have to consider the total renewal process as this triple transformation.

THE PORT: PERENNIAL RENEWAL

Since 1730, the port of Baltimore has been recognized as the real urban potential, the growth frontier of the Maryland economy, and the squall line of competition with other cities. The port has grown, like the city, outward from its original all-purpose piers in the Inner Harbor (several times redeveloped), to a forty-two mile crocheted edging whose pattern can best be seen from a boat or plane (Figure 19).

But to maintain its competitive characteristics and accommodate the ever larger vessels in international trade requires ever greater investments in dredging—deepening and maintaining channels and anchorages. This trend was already evident 150 years ago, when Baltimore began asking for federal subsidy to maintain its sixteen-foot channel to Fell's Point. The current effort is to complete and widen the fifty-foot deep Chesapeake Bay channels and to improve the seventeen mile Chesapeake and Delaware sea level ship canal. The C & D Canal is a $100 million project; it is being deepened from twenty-five feet to thirty-five and widened for two way twenty-four hour operation.

In the economic geometry of ports, Baltimore's location has the characteristic trade-off of advantages and disadvantages of an inland type of port. It is relatively distant by sea from the major ports of northern Europe. Vessels must travel 150 miles (a twelve hour

Figure 19.   Baltimore Harbor, 1973. Photo by Maps, Incorporated.

run) up the Chesapeake Bay from Norfolk (Hampton Roads), or come through the C & D Canal. But the port of Baltimore is fifty to 150 miles closer than any other U.S. port to midwestern markets. In terms of cost structure, 150 miles ocean distance is short, while 150 miles overland is long, and rail freight structures tend to favor Baltimore. But to capitalize on the advantages of such a location requires also ever greater investment in overland transport systems.

The original Inner Harbor piers and warehousing were privately developed by merchants. In the next stage the entrepreneurs were charter corporations. The Canton Company built railroad belt and switching lines. It has extensive piers, warehousing, a new ore pier, and a new industrial park, and has expanded into industrial realty and freight traffic management beyond the region. Ironically, the Canton Com-

pany, owned by the International Mining Company of New York, is also port management consultant to the rival port of New Orleans. The B & O Railroad developed in succession the Locust Point coal piers, grain elevators, the European immigrant pier, and port facilities at Fairfield. In the early 1900s the city and the Western Maryland Railroad jointly developed the south side of the point. During World War II outlying specialized port installations were extended by heavy industries (See Figure 19).

But as the need for redevelopment emerged, the private corporations proved sluggish. In part this is an overall decline in the innovative capacity and financial health of railroads, but there are other reasons: they are interested in rather limited types of captive freight—the coal and grain traffic not subject to truck competition. B & O land is privileged: it is no longer locally owned, but by its early charter it does not pay the local property taxes which would force its redevelopment into income-producing property.

These conditions—the need for major capital, redevelopment, and effective total port management—led to creation of the Maryland Port Authority in 1956. The MPA's first ten year $67 million investment plan has turned into a twenty year $200 million plan, and the MPA is expected to unveil a still bigger program looking to the 1990s. The evolution of this plan gives insights into renewal strategies in the face of risk. The initial project was the creation of Dundalk Marine Terminal, with a new core-type pier, where ships tie up at marginal berths, in contrast to the older finger piers. This kind of mooring allows more flexible use of the total length of pier for ships of all sizes, and more flexible use of the back-up land area. Baltimore has become the most important port in the nation for importing foreign cars. Specialized rail yards and trucking facilities have been built to handle the inland hauls. A $20 million project for filling an entire cove at Hawkins Point is destined for automobile handling.

The dramatic change came in the container race. In 1955, at Bethlehem's repair shipyard, McLean Industries had the first ships converted for carrying trailer truck bodies. Their operating subsidiary, Sea-Land, created a container-handling port on a site leased from the Canton Company. Container shipping of general cargo reduces dock labor radically and makes loading and unloading faster, saving time in port for the ship. An hour's work for twenty men is turned into a ten-minute job for a small crane crew. It also means faster door-to-door delivery, less handling, significantly less damage and theft. The swift turnaround of capital is the basic strategy. By 1972 Sea-Land had ordered new fast ships built in Europe. Each will carry 1,100 containers and the Sea-Land fleet alone will have enough space to supply the projected North Atlantic commerce. They expect to go to a feeder or shuttle system, unloading at a few points and sending containers in smaller older ships to smaller ports. Baltimore has already been downgraded in this service by Sea-Land. The port of Greater New York is number one, but Baltimore is investing in new container-handling facilities in a race with Hampton Roads, Philadelphia, and New Orleans. The Dundalk Marine Terminal site has been expanded by 200 acres ($18 million) for six new container piers, and on Locust Point the MPA has exchanged land with the B & O, United Fruit, and the Western Maryland Railway for another massive container facility.

A related development is the "ro-ro" or roll-on roll-off ship. The whole truck—tractor and trailer—goes on the ship. The MPA is planning a $6 million ro-ro terminal on the south side of Locust Point. Martin Marietta's LASH system is a variant of this—lightering containers from large vessels onto barges and from barge to dockside supercargo plane. Their concept of intermodal access is calculated to recycle a thousand acres at Chesapeake Park into an industrial park. Originally an aviation enterprise, they have their own complete airport-seaport on Middle River, northeast of Baltimore.

It is evident that competition of the shipping corporations occurs at the national and international scale, in a climate of swift technological change. Large variations occur in bulk cargo movements, too. Grain exports, for example, were cut into by the Saint Lawrence Seaway opening to Chicago (1959) and by federally subsidized Mississippi River improvements favorable to New Orleans. The grain handlers union has declined since from 600 to sixty-five men. Baltimore interests complain that the grain elevators and handling facilities controlled by out-of-state interests are not being modernized to remain competitive.

The overall trend in the seaport, as in manufacturing, is toward heavier capitalization and specialization of facilities. It is essential to maintain flexibility in the use of land and facilities. The intense competition among East Coast ports and among interests within the port of Baltimore appears to stimulate overbuilding and high risk. Port management is therefore a tightrope act, in which state and federal governments are expected to perform, picking up the lumpiest and most risky investments. The same public initiative and risk-bearing are relied on for redevelopment of "over sixty-five" industrial spaces, such as the Camden station area and Highlandtown; the city recently agreed to redevelop half of Fort Holsbird (federal) as an industrial park.

DOWNTOWN RENEWAL

Baltimore's downtown experienced a forced renewal from a great fire in 1904 which leveled the financial district and the wholesaling and dock perimeter. It was immediately rebuilt, but very modest changes of plan were introduced—a few street widenings and a rearrangement of the docks. By 1960 the whole downtown was ready for retirement. It was physically obsolete, financially stagnant, and psychologically demoralized. Baltimore began to feel economic competition with other cities changing their skylines and fiscal competition with its own ring of suburbs. This produced a do-or-die sense of crisis among certain financial interests, including department store owners. They formed the Greater Baltimore Committee, which hired planners and in 1962 unveiled its

Charles Center plan to the mayor and the public.

This plan is a remarkable example of a strategy for change. (Atlanta is probably the other example of such a strategy.) A single large project—Charles Center—was calculated to generate a dynamic sequence (Figure 20). Like the port development plan, but more explicitly, it would lock in on ever larger investments and transformations. The strategy worked and most of the projected bigger efforts are now well underway. The criticism one can make is that it has proved hard to diverge from this strategy or from the interests and strategic control which this group

Figure 20. Strategy and tactics of downtown redevelopment. "As a nation we are deeply committed to an ethic of growth and development. . . . This growth mentality is a fundamental element of our economic system and a tremendous amount of money flow and rewards of the system are dependent on and involve physical growth. A city's physical growth is symbolic of the fight for life against death." (A) "The State Office Complex, Camden Industrial Park, and Charles Center acted as Phase I tactical moves. The Inner Harbor, University of Maryland, and Mt. Vernon plans (Phase 2) took advantage of the climate set by Phase 1 and began to exert counterpressures, as new places 'where the action is'. . . . The next set of moves will take advantage of previous tactics with new action thrusts, for example, the Community College, retail mall and the expected response of the private market as Phase 3. . . ." (B) Hard Structures: Shown response of the historical or visual importance, and new or bulky buildings and engineering structures. " 'Hard' means those buildings with stable, intensive uses. They are expected to remain indefinitely, and can generate new developments around them." Residential areas are also shown (R) but not defined as hard or soft. (C) Soft Structures: A matrix for action. " 'Soft' means those older buildings with high vacancy rates, and low assessments. . . . It is to the City's advantage to achieve the most aggregate total space and activity in Metro Center. It can do this by guiding new development into areas of generally smaller and older buildings." Source: Regional Planning Council and Baltimore City Planning Department, *Metro Center*, 1970.

represents. Large financial resources have been taken from federal urban renewal monies, but the strategy was conceived before these were available. With the reduction of federal funds, the city is still committed to very large investments.

Charles Center, an office building project, cleared thirty-three acres (Figure 21). It is elegant and modern and includes attractive and rather successful public outdoor spaces, yet the scale is very much a home place. A visitor alighting from the airport limousine finds himself in a human scale environment, a perfect introduction. The project was situated to promote future connections or extensions around the edges—west by the "Lexington Mall" toward Baltimore's wonderfully ugly retail shopping district on Howard Street, east down the hill toward the government offices and courthouse district, which is forever refurbishing its monumental character; southeast toward the finan-

cial district, originally the homes and counting houses of the shipping merchants.

The original Charles Center strategy would boost employment in the central business district, despite a small residential population. This implied more commuter movement, so the Charles Center included a maze of underground parking garages and created strong pressures for additional large public investments in expressways to serve commuters from the white collar districts on the north and west. A rail mass transit plan was redesigned as a star radiating from Charles Center, an expression of its overriding objectives as a downtown commuter and downtown shopper system.

Downtown renewal has to be considered incomplete. The retail position has continued to deteriorate, the convention role has not materialized, and Charles Center is ordinarily a dead space at night. Recognition of these faults has been built into larger projects and the re-

Figure 21. Charles Center, City Fair, 1973. Baltimore City Department of Housing and Community Development.

newal operation has been a learning process, as well as a pilot project for a much bigger venture on the south, the Inner Harbor, which is expected to increase its annual property tax yield tenfold. Successful features of the Charles Center as a planning operation were retained for the Inner Harbor project. The organizational structure—Charles Center–Inner Harbor Management, Inc.—is a nonprofit corporate subsidiary of the city's Department of Housing. A policy of strong architectural controls and design competitions has been continued. Mïes van der Rohe designed One Charles Center, Pietro Belluschi the IBM building, Louis Kahn the Constellation Place Hotel. The objectives were to restore a residential population and a night-life in the core. Staging has been calculated to prove its workability to the skeptics—first a nursing home and apartments for the elderly, then an entertainment complex, Science Center (Museum), a large hotel and restaurants, then high income apartments with waterfront views.

Meanwhile, a grand model and grand strategy known as Metro Center have evolved extending the downtown renewal to a much larger core and emphasizing the kinds of highly specialized activities which can be expected to grow as the metropolitan area grows. Into this strategic framework have been grafted a new campus for the Community College of Baltimore, a new federal courthouse and offices, and the state's World Trade Center. Still debated is a costly stadium and convention center. The original federal downtown renewal investments were intended as public pump-priming to stimulate private investments, such as the new buildings of U.S. Fidelity and Guarantee Company, IBM, and C & P Telephone Company. However, as in the port, one might infer that public and private investments have in fact primed the pump for much larger subsequent public investments.

The major gamble and the ultimate future for private investment appear to be high income downtown living. Shopping renewal hinges on this purchasing power. The attraction of private capital into these schemes requires the speculation incentive of the mass transit stations. But the residential strategy also requires a critical mass, endangered by competition among large projects and lifestyle alternatives in the Inner Harbor West, Cold Spring, and high-rise centers in suburban and exurban loca-

tions such as Towson, Columbia, and Lake Linganoke. All of these have been threatened with financial collapse in the "stagflation" of 1973-1975.

For redevelopment, the Metro Center plan conceives of the city as a mass of physical structures which are either hard or soft—that is, more or less susceptible to being remodeled (Figure 20). It illustrates the renewal process as an investment strategy, striking, as Churchill said (referring to a larger geopolitical stage), at the soft underbelly.

SLUM CLEARANCE

The first push for massive clearance of old residential areas occurred in the mid-1930s. Before federal low income housing programs or renewal subsidies took shape, Baltimore leadership staked out a belt of blight for clearance. During World War II the tactical program was housing for war workers, recast in 1947 as federally subsidized slum clearance and public housing, then as "urban renewal." We should also consider as slum clearance massive programs of expressway construction and inner-city school replacement.

There are three basic ideas behind all these forms of slum clearance. The first was a strategy of protecting a downtown. Clearing a ring of blight was a corollary of the downtown redevelopment strategy. This was already evident in the Emmart report of 1934. Concepts of a downtown labor force, downtown shopping, downtown image, and downtown security were connected to ideas of what land uses, populations, and purchasing power should be engineered in the surrounding belt. Expressway access tied in with this strategy.

The second goal always proposed is renewal of the city's tax basis. The return on public investments would come in the form of a future stream of annual property taxes. This is not a powerful argument for residential renewal itself, but when tied in with downtown renewal it pays off.

The third goal is a public health goal. Baltimore always attempted small slum clearance projects after great epidemics. In 1816 Ruxton Lane, the cholera lane, was demolished. A century later at the time of a polio epidemic, a strip along St. Paul Place was demolished for a monumental, beautifully landscaped park. In 1925 the "lung block" was torn down for a school. More recent demolitions include the flophouses on Pratt Street, the "Block" (a honky-tonk and vice district on east Baltimore Street), and the heroin corner on Pennsylvania Avenue. The conviction is irrepressible that deteriorated housing, deficient plumbing, and crowding into small dwelling spaces contributes to the spread of contagious diseases and perhaps to other threats such as crime, delinquency, drug addiction, illegitimacy, and mental illness. The presence of such pathologies always defined a soft underbelly for clearance and redevelopment, regardless of the new land uses proposed.

All these goals converged to make the black community the target. Relocation in postwar renewal projects has run 80 to 95 percent black. The prime obstacle to this overall program of physical and fiscal renewal has, from the first, been the massive displacement of people involved and the particular problem of people too poor to offer a profitable market for new private enterprise housing. In residential urban renewal, Baltimore has been a leader in the nation, and has exerted pressure for larger federal subsidies in public housing. The renewal program has been a politicized learning process over forty years. We can look at the process and ask what are the results.

Certain goals have been achieved. Baltimore has recycled more housing and more residential land than most cities of its size in the country and is continuing to demolish its pre–Civil War neighborhoods. There are now scarcely any dwelling units in the city without toilet and bath; central heating is swiftly becoming universal, overcrowding is radically reduced, and the population is generally better housed. Tuberculosis is declining and infant survival has improved. But the strategy and mechanisms by which this has been achieved have had dramatic side effects in the recycling of people. The number of households displaced by public actions (renewal, expressways, and school building) between 1951 and 1971 was at least 25,000 (75,000 people; see Figure 22). It is a small percentage of all the moves in the metropolitan area, but because of the concentration of actions in small spaces, short periods of time, and selected populations, the effects are intense. Between 80 and 90 percent of those relocated have been black, at least two-thirds renters, perhaps one-fifth single individuals. Most were relocated within the city. Government carried

out nearly all these operations. The rate of displacement accelerated over the period, from about 600 households a year in the 1950s, to 800 in the early sixties, to 2,600 in the late 1960s. In 1970 the city housing department had over 8,000 open cases for residential relocation.

THE CITY'S HOUSING STRATEGIES

The original public housing concept, modified to meet war worker housing needs in 1940, involved clearance of five to ten acre sites and construction of several hundred new low cost units, densely laid out, in two and three story rows. The wartime move ins were magnificently staged affairs, but it was impossible to replace the entire population on these sites. The scale of the relocation problems generated two kinds of experiments. The first was low cost housing on isolated fringe sites. This was reasonably adaptive during war time expansion of factory jobs, job training, and mass transit to work from these areas. But they have suffered since from the containment of manufacturing jobs, distance from the center, and the decline of public transit. All the projects were segregated by race. The white projects have proved viable as cooperatives or rental (Armisted Gardens, Aero Acres), but the black projects (Turner and Cherry Hill), located to insure maximum isolation, have suffered more from pollution problems and a lack of local shopping and institutional services.

The other experiment was rehabilitation of dwellings. Known as "the Baltimore Plan," the first effort (1952), in East Baltimore, became a code enforcement model for federal rehabilitation subsidy programs. It has since generated demand for more ambitious redevelopment in the same area. The second effort was Harlem Park (West Baltimore), where alley dwellings were demolished and inner block parks were designed with the participation of block clubs.

In the national architectural and financial context, the Baltimore Housing Authority moved in 1953 toward the construction of high-rises on cleared sites in two major clumps, east and west. They occupy whole tracts and fill whole elementary schools (Figure 22). Urban renewal projects were also extended over forty, fifty, or seventy acres, in order to coordinate design of schools, parks, fire stations,

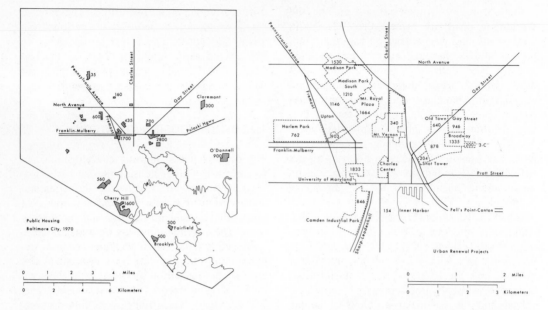

Figure 22. Units of public housing (left) and households displaced by urban renewal and public housing (right), Baltimore City, 1951–1971. Figures do not include displacement of the 1960s for highways, although the corridors are shown. The zones of massive displacement along Gay Street and Pennsylvania Avenue axes are now built up with large concentrations of public housing. Redevelopment lags generally ranged from three to thirteen years.

stores, and to get more flexibility in the rearrangement of the site. Nevertheless, difficulties of scheduling such large operations led to a housing gap in the mid-1960s. Massive relocations from the expressway coincided with renewal clearance. At the same time the city began to experience the environmental defects of high-rises, and the public housing waiting lists were filled with hard-to-relocate people. It became obvious to every one (it had always been obvious to the black community) that urban renewal meant black removal. The implications were laid bare and there was a crystallization of resistance—black resistance to removal, resistance of adjoining communities to a relocation spillover threat, and resistance of neighborhoods to construction of new projects.

The uproar resulted in a reorganization of municipal agencies, new stress on rehabilitation, fuller citizen participation, and smaller projects, including public reclamation and leasing of isolated vacant houses. The most popular new program is "homesteading": several hundred families are rebuilding abandoned "dollar homes"—in Stirling Street for example—with the help of municipal loans and technical assistance. By sharing contractors, designs, ma-

terials, and the crises of financial bureaucracy, their "barn raising" has restored social solidarity as well as physical environments at the scale of the block. Urban renewal has come to be seen as a therapeutic process rather than a grand scheme that would some day be complete. In this sense it began to look like the port or the downtown—redevelopment in ever-widening circles. The Community Renewal Program has the entire residential area of the city scheduled for differing degrees of remodeling, renovation, or conservation.

The city now has 15,000 public housing units. Yet its initiative and leverage in the metropolitan housing market is small and does not allow it to keep up with its ambitious rate of "slum clearance." There are another 2,000 "low rent" and 4,000 "moderate rent" dwellings, privately built and managed but federally subsidized. Social rigidity has been built into the various projects in terms of income and age segregations, which produces financial vulnerability for the public housing authority and for the households living in the projects. The projects are no longer officially segregated by race, but their location and use as a relocation resource favors de facto segregation. Of public housing occupants, 89 percent are black. Managers must tread a fine line. Because they must select people in greatest need, not served by federal home mortgage or private markets, two-thirds are dependent on public assistance. Only 9 percent are adult men, including some in their seventies. By federal policy, rents must cover management and maintenance costs, but the tenant's rent may not be more than a quarter of his income. This squeeze produces an intense concentration of households in a narrow income range. It also produces a narrow margin for management in responding to changes in fuel costs, or the need to replace refrigerators and roofs as whole projects reach a critical age. Baltimore's Housing Authority has been one of the most successful managements in the country, still solvent, and maintaining standards for maintenance, security, and tenant stability.

THE SUBURBAN FRONTIER

The energies of private enterprise, having largely abandoned the city, are being poured into the urbanization of the surrounding five county area. The fundamental geographic structure was already in place by 1960. The industrial advantages of large portions of the coastal plain were developed during World War II and affirmed by generous industrial zoning. The beltway and major radials of the interstate highway system were built or under construction. Suburban housing development had overflowed the beltway in the sixties on the southwest, north and northeast. But the rolling terrain and geologic variety of the vast semicircle of countryside north and west of U.S. 1, and a number of unspoiled necks and rivers (peninsulas and tidewater inlets) offered exceptionally attractive opportunities for further suburban development. Baltimore probably has more potential in this respect than any other metropolitan area in the country. The differentiated and fragmented character of the land is fundamental to the way in which development is taking place. As in nineteenth century Baltimore, the natural differentiation seems to lend itself to community building at a scale compatible with builders' economics—several hundred to a thousand dwellings—and with the buyers' conception of an exclusive neighborhood. The landscapes of central Maryland, more than most regions of the U.S., offer immense opportunities for the environmental and recreational lifestyles developers are now designing for high income people. At Lake Linganore, for example, west

of New Market, Brosius Homes built seven dams on a 4,200 acre site; one, a prize winner, has a water slide, lagoon, and fountain at the base. Its supernatural boulders were moved into place with machinery. (Its financial structure was less elegant, and the builder has since filed for bankruptcy.)

As Figure 23 shows, the basic ring of new single family developments is a zone in which half the households moved in within five years (1965 to 1970). It is beyond the beltway, and particularly strong just over the border of Harford County, deep into Howard County around Ellicott City and Columbia, and in Anne Arundel County along the Magothy and Severn rivers toward Annapolis. By 1971 Anne Arundel County was the leading area for single family dwellings. These new developments feature streams, private lakes or marinas, woods, and pasture for horses. The names hint at the premium combination of prestige and outdoorsiness, recalling the Maryland plantations, the hunts, and the English aristocracy—Fox Meadows, Camelot, Quiet Inheritance, Tanager Forest. Apartment developments, including garden and rental townhouses, are a more recent phenomenon and they are concentrated along the major radials at the beltway and beyond (Figure 26).

Beyond the construction zone, land is being held and transferred for speculation and future construction. In 1972 nearly 4,000 acres of land in Baltimore County (perhaps 6,000 acres in the region) were being taxed at a lower farmland assessment, although the land was already subdivided and zoned for business, industry, or multifamily. Anne Arundel County retains an unzoned category for areas not yet open to development. Harford and Howard counties retain lot requirements of three, five, ten, or even twenty acres for the same purpose, but Baltimore County recently removed its restriction. The object of the "nonzoning" tactic is to encourage orderly development instead of sprawl, but it also boosts land prices in the zones open for development and stimulates a race to capture and manipulate the future zoning of areas not yet open.

SUBURBAN DEVELOPMENT STRATEGIES

As the frontier moved out and population grew—26 percent in Baltimore County over the sixties, 44 percent in Anne Arundel, 50 in Har-

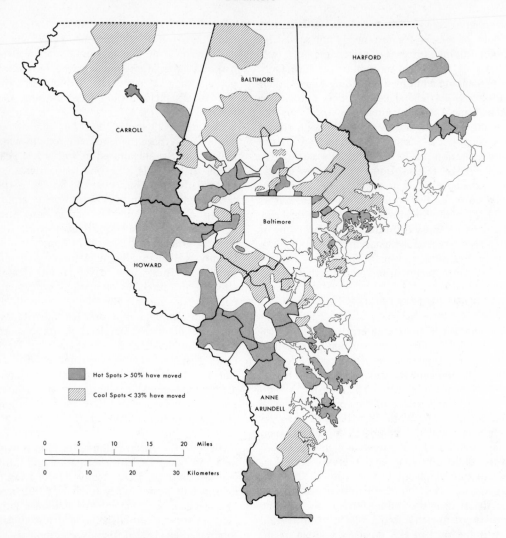

Hot Spots > 50% have moved

Cool Spots < 33% have moved

Figure 23. Residential turnover outside the city. This measure of turnover captures only one five year time frame in a moving picture. Suburban hot spots are zones of new construction. Many lie outside the sewered area. Beyond the line less than half the dwellings are connected to public sewers. The suburban cool ring is a zone of development of the ten years before 1965. The residents are staying put, paying the mortgage, and probably—if they are outside the line—having trouble with their septic tank system or their neighbor's.

ford, 77 in Howard—intense competition was focused on the large sites close to the junctions of beltway and radial expressways. These high access points were the obvious locations for industry, offices, shopping centers, and high-rise high density residence. There were immense rewards for the capture of these special locations at the right moment. But a sense of timing as well as spacing was essential to capture the right combination of buying price, interest

rates, and leasing opportunities. They were the object of geopolitical strategies—to achieve coordination in space and synchronization in time of public zoning actions.

The principal public forum for development issues has been zoning hearings. In 1968 Baltimore County reworked its entire zoning classification and maps and introduced a "cycle system" for considering rezoning petitions seasonally, to allow analysis and hearings focusing on one geographic sector at a time. In the 1970 cycle there were requests to rezone 2,000 acres in this county. The larger and more controversial sites have new value primarily because of government initiative. For example, a joint venture was proposed for the site adjoining a mass transit terminus planned near Owings Mills. County planners wanted to concentrate development into the beltway ring, into corridors already well served with water and sewers, and into high density *sector centers*. But this strategy added value to already appreciating nodal sites such as Towson, Reisterstown, Eastpoint, and Whitemarsh. For example, one developer requested rezoning for 500 acres in a proposed sector center at Kennedy Expressway and Whitemarsh Boulevard for a vast shopping district, motel, office park, and golf course. (He owns 900 acres more just across the expressway.) These conflicts produced a political crisis in Baltimore County. Thousands of citizens came to the hearings and expressed particular rage at the behind-the-scenes behavior of the county council men and a handful of well-connected zoning lawyers. All seven county councilmen are elected at large and the one most closely connected with developer interests apparently has never carried his own district.

SUBURBAN SOCIAL STRATEGY

Aside from the battle for "upzoning" of high value nodes, the other source of zoning controversy in Baltimore County involved protective "downzoning" of several of its twenty small black communities. It was probably a minor episode in their destiny, but reveals the underlying powerful agreement within the county on social strategy. The effort of several county planners to provide information to local communities and the public resulted in their being fired by the county executive. Evidence for the mechanisms by which a lily white Baltimore County was being created was brought out in hearings before the U.S. Commission on Civil Rights in August 1970. First, these small century old communities are isolated. In Edgemere, Turner, and Pines, the street networks do not connect with adjoining white communities except via the single main street. In other words, the positive factors that differentiate and reinforce neighborhoods also reinforce segregation by race; black neighborhoods are

isolated from white neighborhoods. Their small size insures a weak voice in local politics and makes possible the discrimination of public services. Small "colored schools" were operated at least until 1954. The county did not pave the streets and has not extended sewer and water lines to several of these communities, even where adjoining white communities are served. The residential pockets are kept at a rural level of services, while surrounding areas were brought to suburban standards.

Zoning was part of the strategy (Figure 24). Half the black communities in Baltimore County were zoned for industrial or commercial use. The environmental implications are obvious—the tankfarm, the sewage treatment plant, the quarry noise, the junkyard as neighbors. But more serious, the community cannot grow. It can be liquidated. Turner (near Dundalk Marine Terminal) offers this scenario: Several hundred apartments were built with federal money for war workers at Bethlehem Steel. In 1954 the management (the Baltimore City Housing Authority) tore down a third and sold off the rest to a private owner. In 1966 the owner tore these down, evicting 1,330 people who still lived in them, and redeveloped the land for industry. Fifty white-occupied homes on the same side of the tracks were not included in the industrial zone. In other cases, black communities were torn down to provide suburban amenities for others. More than fifty homes were demolished for Towson Junior High School, the county police and fire station, a new road, and a power substation. No relocation opportunities were made available. Many families had to move into Baltimore City, and the black population of Towson has declined by half. The remaining East Towson and Lutherville communities have been under threat for several years from a ring road. Expressways in the eastern part of the county are scheduled to wipe out Bengies and bisect Edgemere, and three freeways will reinforce the isolation of Turner.

The several discriminatory mechanisms are mutually reinforcing. Why perpetuate a residential community without sanitary facilities? But why extend sewers to an isolated community of a hundred homes when it is destined for industrial redevelopment? In the wake of the 1970 civil rights hearings, several communities (Chase-Bengies) obtained downzoning to residential status and East Towson resi-

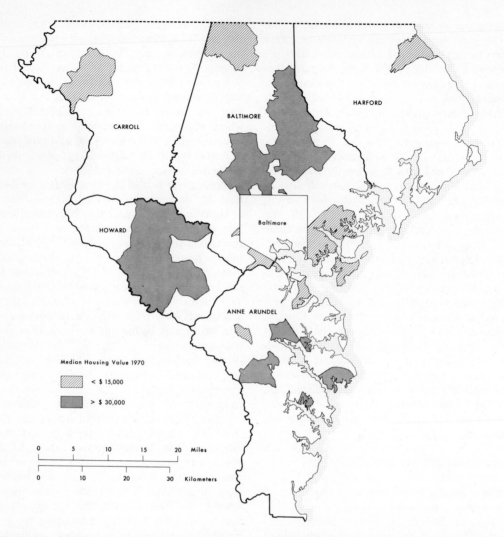

Figure 24. Median value of resident-owned homes, 1970. High value homes are found in the high income wedge to the north, a western wedge, and southern clusters of new white collar development. Lower value homes reveal an industrial belt of working class homeowners with a rather consistent mix of housing from the 1940s, 1950s, and early 1960s.

dents were promised some relocation in the county. But this is only the tip of an iceberg. These public debates over the survival of a few hundred homes reflected a broader policy, whose more important feature was keeping blacks out of new areas. The black population of Baltimore County increased by only 4,500 people in the 1960s, its white population by 124,000. The percentage black remained fixed at 3.5. Black families occupy less than 2 percent of owner-occupied homes in the county. Yet the black population of the city increased 30 percent. In the metro-

politan area they are nearly one-fourth of the population and the black middle class made income gains and could afford homes in the county. We can only infer some forces of resistance in Baltimore County.

How do these barriers work? As in other neighborhoods the front lines of defense are the real estate and financial institutions. Federal mortgage insurance was widely used by developers arranging homeowner financing, but it declined in the suburban area after 1962 when President Kennedy ordered the FHA to become colorblind. A Maryland fair housing law was passed about the same time as a federal fair housing law (1968), but enforcement is limited. The "steering" practices of at least one large realtor are now subject to continuous statistical evaluation, to insure his compliance with the law.

Baltimore County government is the third line of defense. The county council and voters have consistently refused to participate in federal programs of public housing, urban renewal, relocation assistance, or creation of a county "workable plan." Anxiety about these federal programs often comes to the surface.

The case is more complex in Anne Arundel County, with 12 percent black residents. Blacks are represented in school and city jobs, but not significantly in the police force. A quarter are concentrated in the ghetto fourth ward in Annapolis, but many others live in contained settlements. Isolation and limited services are common here, too, but they also occur in a number of white communities. Black families own 6 percent of the owner-occupied housing and 3 percent of the newly built homes of the 1960s.

The new town of Columbia in Howard county was the first serious and successful effort in the region to produce a new and stable integrated residential community of a large size. Population is believed to be 13 percent black and is not localized. This was possible thanks to the personal determination of the developer, James Rouse, the total community control in his hands, and the high income mix. Class selectivity reduced anxiety over racial integration. The location was ideal for federal civil servants and professionals already committed to and accustomed to integrated work environments. However, Columbia ran into financial trouble, and Rouse has not succeeded to the same degree in achieving a wider range of incomes and occupations.

As the Civil Rights Commission commented, "While protecting their own interests, suburban areas are legislating for the entire region." By 1970 there was no new single family housing being developed in the city and job development was also taking place primarily in the counties.

IN BETWEEN

As the fringe is built and the center is rebuilt all the in-between rings are being transformed

Some examples will show how the chain reaction occurs. Each link represents a shift of capital.

Clearance and relocation from central renewal operations produced strong impact on adjoining neighborhoods and certain corridors of "soft" urban tissue. Half to three-quarters of the people from a demolition area relocate within a mile. This effect observed in Baltimore resembles the diffusion models familiar to geographers or models of osmosis in body chemistry. The process is dramatic because of its swiftness. In the area south of Druid Hill Park, over two or three years, population increased 20 percent within the same set of three story houses. Elementary school population doubled, rent for a three room apartment increased, and rental income per house increased more. The same process was important along the Park Heights corridor (northwest), and along Greenmount Avenue, Patterson Park Avenue, and Washington Street. Windfall profits did not last long; they depended on permissive zoning and lagging code enforcement (Figure 25). The profitable phase was followed by progressive deterioration, high vacancy rates, depreciation of market values and assessments, and abandonment of the houses. An owner of 1,000 rental properties in this ring was tried in housing court for code violations on 200 properties. He was in federal prison at the time and claimed he could not make repairs because the federal government had frozen all his assets to recover $10 million in income taxes.

There seems to have been a rapid movement of capital into new construction and very little into maintenance and renovation. This is true in both the public sector (schools and city office space) and the private sector and has been favored by federal grant mechanisms and income tax rules. For example, the rule permitting deductions for depreciation of property over ten years favors nonmaintenance and resale or abandonment at the end of ten years. Abandonment of houses in Baltimore reached a thousand per year. This is not nearly as high as some cities, but is particularly serious in a row house city. Relocated households express intense frustration at seeing "slum" conditions of disinvestment and crowding follow them as they move.

Meanwhile, in the next ring out, racial turnover has occurred (see Figure 12). Conditions

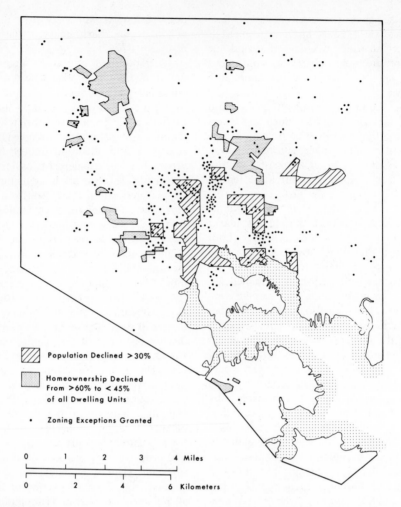

Population Declined >30%

Homeownership Declined
From >60% to <45%
of all Dwelling Units

•   Zoning Exceptions Granted

0   1   2   3   4 Miles

0   2   4   6 Kilometers

Figure 25. Rings of residential change in the city, 1960 to 1970. The ring of population decline over 30 percent (shaded) is associated with urban renewal clearance. Surrounding this is a spillover ring indicated by zoning exceptions granted (dots) for conversion of houses to multifamily dwellings, two to six in a house. Additional conversions occurred within zoning norms. Home ownership declined sharply in the outlined tracts, from at least 60 to below 45 percent of all dwelling units. The transformation of homeowner to renter in this third ring is associated with racial turnover and expressway impact, as in Rosemont. Sources: Harvey et al., 1972, and 1970 census.

"ripe" for block busting often include a sizable population of elderly homeowners and weak market demand by whites because young families are attracted to new suburban alternatives. The classic mechanism of the 1960s was documented by the Activists, Inc., from real estate records. In the Edmondson Village area (census tract 16–8) 94 percent of the 1970 households had moved in since 1960. Nine hundred houses changed hands, many of them twice, in 1962, 1963, and 1964. A single speculator, operating thirty real estate corporations, bought and resold a

third of the houses (half the transactions). The price to white sellers averaged $7,419, to black buyers $11,418. The speculator took the difference, as well as financing charges. The financial institutions were crucial to the operation. The three largest commercial banks in Baltimore provided him with working capital, $3.5 million in personal loans on three to six month terms. He arranged mortgages for his buyers from a savings and loan company. In most cases, he retained a second mortgage; later he had the transaction refinanced through the loan company. (Twenty-four other savings and loan associations in Maryland had also become captives of such speculators in the sixties.) When the FHA began offering loan guarantees in this area, 260 more sales were financed at an average price to buyer and seller of $9,357 and the speculator's operations were dramatically reduced. The FHA has, in the 1970s, replaced the speculator as the chief financial agent for neighborhood racial turnover, through its 221(d)(2) program in the city (See Chatterjee, Harvey, and Klugman).

In such turnover areas, the schools were quickly overcrowded, as younger families replaced older ones. A perceived decline in the quality of the school (crowding and low teacher morale) reinforced household decisions and hastened "white flight." The swiftness has to be ascribed to racism in the total housing market, availability of new housing for white families on the suburban frontier, and demolition of housing of less affluent and black households on the central renewal frontier. The squeeze hastened turnover in the middle ring, as blacks would pay higher rents than whites. Not only were black households squeezed financially, but they were frustrated by the feeling that, despite their financial sacrifice (higher labor force participation), the "ghetto" was following them. Some of these neighborhoods are very attractive, and feature beautiful gardens, as in Edmondson Village, Northwood, and Forest Park. They vary in income level, but in each case community effort to maintain racial integration has met tough obstacles. It became very difficult to obtain "respectable" mortgage money in the zone of turnover and maintenance investment on rental property was radically reduced, even while large sums were mobilized for investment and mortgage finance in the suburban fringe.

As documented by Harvey and Chatterjee, the partitioning of the housing market into submarkets, each with its own financial institutions and clienteles, has promoted over the entire market higher levels of indebtedness for housing, higher interest rates, and higher profits of developers and financial intermediaries.

Other curious opportunities have appeared in the metropolitan growth process. Each transformation requires a flow of capital and a scramble to capture the windfall of change, concentrated at particular locations. An example is the meteoric rise to wealth of wrecking contractors chosen to benefit from the city's demolition work. Another is the creation of a new chain of parking lots on vacant city-owned renewal lots, private lots "ripening" next door to them, and garages in the inner harbor renewal district. The expansion of the parking business has allowed a cluster of black entrepreneurs to enter urban capital formation. Somewhat on Ianni's model of Sicilian immigrant families who moved in a generation from illegitimate to respectable businesses, this group has developed from a springboard of "sportsmen's" activities (numbers) to politics, parking, real estate, construction, food processing, and supermarketing.

The growth strategy of city and county depends on capturing private capital. Despite state and federal revenue sharing, Baltimore City receives half its revenue from the local property tax. But to attract private investment, governments must invest heavily in organizing and equipping public spaces and income opportunities for private enterprise. The entire operation is a pyramid or chain letter in both the public budget and private real estate. Since the net movement of capital for urban construction is outward, Baltimore County or Howard County can be highly selective of industry, commercial projects, and homebuilders. The present political jurisdictions are structured for city-suburb opposition and they pursue different strategies of public investment. It is important to recognize that their different strategies are economically and politically rational. As in the labor market, conflict is structural. In this context, race discrimination and inequalities of income are played off against each other, reinforcing the very structure of inequality.

Mobility and Uncertainty

A civil rights commissioner asked a Baltimore County public works engineer in 1970:

> Might priorities for these projected roads be re-ordered if federal support for such roads weren't forthcoming?
> Yes, that is conceivable because, really, the top priorities for roads are to use up all the federal money we can. Certain roads qualify for federal aid where others will not, so it has been our aim to use up the federal funds wherever possible. (U.S. C.C.R., Transcript, p. 101)

Transportation investments are the biggest chunks of public urban capital. In transportation the most intensive, longest range, and most costly urban planning has been done. Current estimates for the construction of Baltimore's twenty-five mile expressway system and the first phase of a twenty-eight mile mass transit system are over $3 billion (1973). Even port development does not approach this. It is roughly the total real estate tax basis existing in Baltimore City. Each of these two schemes is described as a delicate and well-conceived system which cannot be tinkered with or modified. Nevertheless, the program has been changing for over thirty years and is still the focus of controversy and uncertainty. It is impossible to tell the full story of expressways in Baltimore in a few pages. I will simply try to sketch the dimensions of the two programs, emphasizing the ways in which they are connected and the way they bear on the problem of uncertainty.

Creating a beltway, like a lasso around the developed core, was not difficult, since it created new real estate values and opportunities at every exit and relocation problems were minimal. Likewise, it was not hard to build the Jones Falls valley expressway south toward town, although it took more leadership. State funds were voted in 1951, and once Congress created the Highway Trust Fund (1956) for federal subsidy, beltway construction moved fast (1961 and 1962). Its last link, the Outer Harbor crossing, is under construction. State Roads Commission projects for highways like spokes out from the beltway were also located without serious obstacle. But the program met resistance in the connections through the developed core.

The city had made plans as early as 1942 for an "east-west" highway to handle through traffic and the Franklin-Mulberry corridor was the first area in which the uncertainty was concentrated and over which it has hung ever since. This West Baltimore ghetto was the "soft underbelly." The corridor was bought up by a couple of land companies and gradually became derelict. The period of public acquisition and relocation—the tenants were mostly black and mostly poor—was in the mid-1960s—twenty to twenty-five years after the original plan was made.

Likewise, a firm plan was announced in 1956 for an expressway through Rosemont and Leakin Park. No further investments were made in the development of the park. The formal condemnation lines were fixed by ordinance in 1966, ten years after the threat. Rosemont was a community of middle-aged middle class black homeowners. The coincidence in 1966 of relocation of several thousand people from Franklin-Mulberry with the "taking" of homes in Rosemont provoked strong resistance. Neither group had reasonable relocation opportunities or adequate replacement values for their housing. Beyond the actual "take" strips, both communities were severed and homes were cut off from services and conveniences. There had already been many uproarious highway hearings, exposés, and confrontations, but the new resistance to black removal was a more serious threat because it resonated with nationwide vibrations. The mayor and the Interstate Highway Division responded with a new tactic. They contracted (1967) for a new, impressive planning instrument to match the magnitude and challenge of the problem. Known as the Urban Design Concept Team, it was a $5 million consultant team which incorporated engineering and architectural firms, landscape planners, and young specially hired "people-oriented" planners. Their task was

> to integrate the road by means of its form, scale and materials into both the man-made fabric and natural topography of the city . . . from the point of view of the driver, and from the point of view of the city dweller—objective was to bring these two views into harmony, to maximize the benefits to both.

The planning venture, applauded nationwide, was nevertheless under rigid constraints. The team was ordered not to deviate from the set of designated routes. Its paying client, the Interstate Highway Division, was an ambiguous structure composed of engineers and appointees of both city and state, committed to spending federal money (90 percent). Politicians and construction interests were eager to insure the local injection of federal funds.

The still simmering Rosemont resistance to acquisition was aired in three nights of hearings (August 1968) in front of professional flak catchers from the Interstate Division. The politicians did not attend and enraged citizens of twenty-four disparate organizations opposing the expressway formed a coalition known as MAD—the Movement Against Destruction.

The Design Concept Team, deeply split, recommended one deviation from the original route—to avoid Rosemont by going through a cemetery. The condemnation line was lifted early in 1971. Rosemont had been condemned for fifteen years in principle and for five years in law. During its "uncertainty" it had lost its solid homeowner character and become rundown. The city was holding 500 houses. Since then, $10 million has been earmarked for rehabilitation of the neighborhood to counteract the effects. It is a striking example of the fact that a city cannot live without a future and that parts of the city were sacrificed—deprived of their future and therefore of all investment—in the debate over the future of a "greater Baltimore."

ENVIRONMENT AND EXPRESSWAY

Baltimore's expressway struggle followed the major themes of American national life, and in 1971 the rhetoric of civil rights was replaced with the rhetoric of environmental concern. Resistance jumped from one neighborhood to another and different organizations in MAD took turns carrying the ball. Although the Concept Team has been dissolved, their environmental recommendations provide a guide to still unresolved conflicts. Their ingenuity of detail frequently indicates the severe contradictions of their mandate to bring conflicting views "into harmony" *without deviating from the route.*

In Leakin Park and Gwynns Falls valley, for example, to "integrate the road into rolling terrain and natural setting, minimize intrusion for park-users, and create a roadway experience in park for the driver," the team recommended the use of weathering steel for bridges "to give a natural weathered appearance". If their recommendations are followed, the great lawn of the Crimea estate of Victorian railroad engineer and entrepreneur Thomas Winans will be reconstructed after cut-and-cover construction of a 600 foot tunnel. Special irrigation will be installed and the grade in the tunnel will match the terrain so that "the driver is exposed to the shape of the park above". Barrier lighting will minimize "spill light" in the park. A new channel for Gwynn's Run will "simulate" the present natural channel in every respect.

Entrances to the city will be landscaped and lighting will "create areas of night-time interest" and "edge" residential and industrial areas. High pole lighting will be used where spill light is not considered a problem and "peach color" sodium vapor lights will delineate and differentiate certain types of intersections. Plans were recommended for stockpiling topsoil. The swampy landscape of Moore's Run (on the east side) will be improved by planting "weeping specimens."

The Concept Team recognized explicitly the problem of scale. The road is a new large scale phenomenon, like the newest downtown buildings (USF&G, World Trade Center, or state office complex), the newest port installations, and town developments like Columbia and Cold Spring. All these phenomena reflect the transformation of the entire urban fabric into a new metro-scale structure. This scale may be called heroic or inhuman to suit one's bias, but in either case it does not match the existing neighborhoods, buildings, and service systems. The problem exists in all cities developed over several generations. In both downtown renewal and expressways, Baltimoreans of the 1960s and 1970s—business leader, professional, and the man in the street—have in different ways expressed the values of the human-scale city and resisted the inhuman more effectively than the "high brow" cities of Boston, Chicago, and San Francisco.

The problem of integrating the road into the "complex human scale of the neighborhood" is most acute in the Fell's Point-Canton corridor, the Franklin-Mulberry corridor, and the inner boulevard. In Fell's Point, a high structure of concrete precast box girder or voided concrete was proposed, with a "bright underside" because it will have foot traffic and a playground underneath the expressway. Twenty-five to thirty historic structures of the 1790s will be moved "to a better neighborhood." "How do you move a row house?" one stubborn citizen kept asking. Acoustical barriers are "for the first time being systematically applied" where a residential area would suffer an increase greater than six dBA. In Fell's Point they are to be transparent, although at other locations "acoustical fence" includes six foot sheet metal siding.

In the Franklin-Mulberry corridor a depressed roadway was recommended, with plat-

form buildings—school, health center, and pedestrian overpasses—"to restore severed movement patterns." Its inbound traffic will pour onto a distributor bypass or boulevard, "something less than a freeway, but more than a street." It is designed for 30,000 vehicles per day, fifty mph design speed, and thirty mph average speed. The Concept Team recommended a system of parking corridors and large parking structures along the boulevard and at its junction with Franklin-Mulberry. The boulevard is also described as "a development tool," and its route is studded with joint development projects—the gems of federal subsidy held out to compensate impacted neighborhoods. Among the impacted areas are over 2,000 units of public housing. Here, at the junction of corridor and boulevard, many of the persons displaced from the corridor have been relocated. This appears to be the most alarming zone for air pollution.

SYSTEM THINKING

The theory of the Concept Team was system and careful attention was paid to consistent systemwide signs, safety design, and traffic monitoring, as well as lighting, planting, and aesthetic detail. It now appears, however, that the chief defects of the 3-A modified system and of the Concept Team's work lie in weaknesses of system thinking.

First, in the area of environmental impact, air pollution and noise problems were grossly understated because of segmented consideration. The federal Environmental Protection Agency protested in 1973 that they considered the environmental impact statements wholly inadequate because there was not enough attention to the overall system. Baltimore was supposed to reduce its carbon monoxide pollution level by 50 percent by 1975, but the expressway plans project an increase of automobiles coming into the central district. The concentration of pollution in the central district will be intensified, and it is necessary to consider *jointly* the effects of the several problem segments which compose an inner-loop—the Franklin-Mulberry, the boulevard, and the segment of I-83 which runs down the Fallsway toward Fell's Point. There are also difficult problems of air pollution involved in the Fort McHenry crossing, associated with the combination of industrial pollution and bridge approach. Expensive design detail could not compensate for the failure to consider environmental impact in the original location of the highways.

Air pollution and noise problems are associated with the operation of the system at its most intense levels. Yet official public reports are still reluctant to discuss the peak hour parameters. There have been well-argued accusations that the "delicately balanced" system may break down altogether under rush hour operations. The crucial points appear to be the major central interchanges and the boulevards by which traffic is to be dispersed into the old downtown street network. Innumerable schemes have been proposed for inner harbor crossings. One called for "two mammoth spaghetti-filled interchanges" less than a mile apart. Another required a fourteen lane bridge shaped like a cube. Still another proposed an expressway tunnel which would have collided with a planned mass transit tunnel. An inner habor crossing was finally abandoned and the Fort McHenry crossing adopted.

Doubts also remain as to whether the total system is needed. Superhighway planning is largely self-justifying—the traffic will go wherever you build the road. Because all hearings were rigidly focused upon a particular segment, just as the environmental impact statements were, the overall traffic handling of the system could not be fully debated. Assumptions shifted continuously as to whether a particular segment would serve through traffic or Baltimore traffic. No segment was designed to serve local or neighborhood traffic and it is clear that the basic problem is one of redistribution: the benefits and costs are not spread over the same people. The redistribution problem is therefore the fundamental geopolitical issue, and the effort to manipulate, soften, or conceal the costs has led to mistrust and fiscal distortion. City and state juggled traffic, street repair, and policing funds in order to conceal road costs. The state issued $23 million in bonds for the city's 12 percent share, because state bonds do not require voter approval, whereas city bonds do. City voters repeatedly rejected bonds for a relocation of police headquarters to express their opposition to the road, but the city administration built it anyway.

In November 1971 several councilmen were elected as expressway opponents and when they took office (January) a public hearing was staged in a small room of the public library. By this time, as the housing commissioner expressed it, "We [had] suffered most of the negative effects of the expressway and none of the benefits." The city had spent $50 million on the Jones Falls Expressway, $100 million on the 3-A system, had relocated at least 4,000 households, and demolished or depreciated three major corridors. The new system price tag exceeded $1 billion. At the hearing it was clear that "system" was a political idea—selling the package. The technical personnel, the municipal administration, and the Greater Baltimore Committee lobbyist argued that the system was so well integrated that removing any part would destroy its functioning—i.e., take it or leave it. The MAD coalition opposed the system: "We don't want NO road." This position was inevitable, in view of their experience of divide-and-conquer tactics, the politics of coalition, and the profound mistrust of the "highwaymen." The chairman of the city Planning Commission was not allowed to speak at the twelve hour hearing and the next day he resigned, regretting among other features this polarization:

> Nowhere was there to be found the rational middle ground—the case for *some* expressways. This case is solid. The one for a complete system is not. . . . The hearings were, in effect, one more charade in the history of the expressway saga. (*Baltimore Sun*, February 19, 1972)

Construction continues as a large pincers movement, boring in relentlessly on the controversial segments.

AUTOMOBILE-ORIENTED SETTLEMENT

Meanwhile, in spite of "systemwide" planning, a somewhat different system has gradually emerged. We have seen how massive relocation generated strong resistance (negative feedback), delaying numerous sections of the expressway program and diverting location. More important were positive feedbacks associated with the larger growth of the city, creating patterns of automobile-oriented settlement. The changes in settlement and mobility which occurred in the Baltimore region in the 1960s and which appear likely in the 1970s are classic examples of

Myrdal's circular cumulative causation. There are now 700,000 cars in the region. Virtually the entire labor force in the suburban counties drives to work. Only in the city do a substantial number of people go to work by bus. Only two-thirds of city residents now work in the city. The populations of Anne Arundel and Howard counties increased faster than the number of jobs there and they generate sub-

stantial flows toward the Washington metropolitan area as well as to Baltimore.

The automobile made possible the settlement of the suburban counties and the settlement of the suburban counties generates the demand for shorter travel time, more parking spaces, and more road for peak hour commuting. Figures 26 and 27 give some idea of the magnitude of the reciprocal movement—resi-

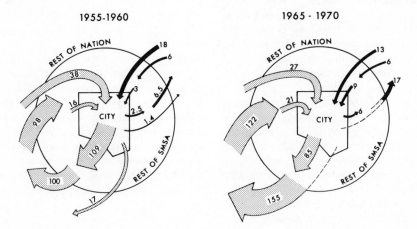

Figure 26. Migration streams by race, in thousands of moves during the five year interval. Residential movement between the suburban counties and the rest of the nation have intensified, but there was little change in the pattern. Blacks are underrepresented in all moves between counties, especially moves into the suburban ring. Moves out of the region are not reported in detail for 1970, but the majority of white outmigrants are from the counties, while the majority of black outmigrants are from the city. Source: U.S. Census.

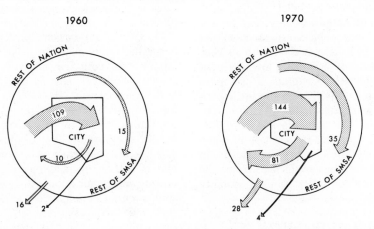

Figure 27. The journey to work, 1960 and 1970. Changes in the pattern of daily journeys to work result from the combined effects of residential moves (Figure 26) and the creation of new jobs. Commuting into the city has increased despite small growth of jobs in the city. Commuting from the city to the suburban counties and between adjoining suburban counties has increased markedly. Source: U.S. Census.

dential moves to the suburbs and daily commuter trips to the center. The kind of feedback involved here was pinpointed in a Regional Planning Council study of the situation at Social Security in 1970. Two-thirds drove their own cars, half alone; 28 percent were car pool passengers, and only 6 percent rode buses. Back in 1966, only a quarter of the employees drove to work alone. The changes resulted from the federal government having developed free and unrestricted employee parking, about 8,000 spaces, at $4,500 per space. Downtown likewise the city's off street parking commission has subsidized 8,000 garage spaces (since 1948) through low interest municipal revenue bonds and a property tax subsidy for the duration of the loans.

In spite of gasoline prices, there is every reason to believe that the process will continue. The Regional Planning Council forecasts rapid residential settlement of the outlying areas over the next ten to fifteen years in Howard and Harford counties and accelerated growth of jobs in Anne Arundel and Howard counties. This may limit the movements in and out of the city, but it will favor more beltway traffic and other movements within and between the suburban counties. Road development in the counties reinforces our expectation. Expressway type development extends much beyond the interstate highway system. A crisscross of limited access roads is consuming much land and fragmenting still larger areas, particularly in the coastal plain corridor of Baltimore County and Anne Arundel County.

Meanwhile, the problem will become yet more acute for the city dwellers without cars. The whole inner city becomes a low level trap —you cannot move out without a car and a steady job. You cannot get a job without a car. Yet the inner residential core without cars is the zone which has borne the impact of relocation and will now bear the greatest air pollution, noise, interruption to foot traffic—in short the greatest inconvenience from the secondary effects of other people's mobility (Figure 28).

WHAT ABOUT MASS TRANSIT?

The critical decision seems to have been made that Baltimore will have a mass transit high speed rail system. The price tag discussed in 1973 was $1.5 billion and rising. A first leg will connect downtown Baltimore with Reisterstown to the northwest and Glen Burnie and Friendship Airport to the south. But so far the public has not shown much interest (relocation is small) and does not believe that the system will materialize. Even the gasoline crisis of 1973 did not build up a head of steam.

The mass transit system is not designed as a substitute, but as a supplement to a highway sytem. Suburban commuters are expected to continue to own automobiles and are likely to use them to commute to the mass transit stations. The projected network of feeder buses is designed only for service intervals of thirty minutes in "high density" residential areas and an hour in other parts of the region. One segment will run in a median of the Northwest Expressway, apparently to help justify the construction of the highway (state-funded). Traffic expectations for 1990 (as of 1962) were that the expressway will be overloaded, with a capacity of 45,000 cars a day, while the transit line will be underutilized, with 13,000 passengers a day, a capacity of 60,000 per hour.

The overall system is conceived as a planning tool which will concentrate high-rise and commercial development around the stations, reinforcing the concepts of a Metro Center (downtown Baltimore), town centers and sector centers in the counties, and a corridor development pattern in higher density population ridges. It is expected to reinforce certain high value nodal locations and speculative opportunities (near the beltway and the inner boulevard).

In spite of the advantages, it is difficult to juggle the transit plans to make them equally attractive to both the city and the counties, anxious about cost sharing. An Anne Arundel county councilman said (1971), "A rapid-rail transit system designed primarily to serve downtown Baltimore must rank very low on our list of priorities." Yet to obtain support of city interests, convenience for downtown commuters and shoppers is billed as essential to downtown revitalization. All lines will radiate from a central station under Charles Center.

The overall mass transit strategy resembles the highway strategy. Its first objective is to capture the federal dollar. Two-thirds of the cost was expected to be paid by federal funds and intense pressures were built up "to maintain the rhythm of planning." In 1974 new interest in commuter adaptations of the rail-

Figure 28. The sump and the alabaster city. The Inner Harbor is the sink for untreated surface drainage from highways, and residues of oil, gasoline, zinc, and lead. More oil goes into the harbor from accidents and negligence on land than from vessels. This sump of water pollution is an old vexation. A century ago, before sanitary sewers were built, the issue was the summer stink. It is small, artificially deepened, and has a "three-layered" tidal circulation. Beck estimates that now the coliform bacteria level (indicating sewage) is attributable to the feces of the city's 100,000 dogs. The Inner Harbor renewal program has provided momentum for research and for a serious effort at enforcing water pollution laws.

roads was suddenly sparked by hopes of federal subsidy. *Both* road and rail transport programs have suffered from distorted priorities because of three-layered financing, three-layered technocracy, and county-city rivalries. They also suffer from more fundamental problems. We have seen how closely the settlement pattern and the transportation pattern are related. But housing is handled as a private sector for production and consumption, while transportation is treated as a massively subsidized or public sector. The essential question is, How are the costs and benefits from public subsidy distributed? The intensity of the expressway controversy suggests that either we do not all have the same expectations or else we do not all agree the redistribution is just.

City on the Falls

Baltimore's "fall line" location is the key to understanding its environmental assets—for industrial, residential, and recreational development. It is also the key to its environmental problems and politics. Baltimore is typical of the East Coast metropolitan areas strung along the fall line geological contact between the old uplands and the Atlantic coastal plain.

The physiographic term *fall line* refers to the fall of the streams, here usually fifty to one hundred feet over a stretch ten or fifteen miles, which allowed the development of water powered mills for grinding wheat into flour, later converted for making cotton duck sailcloth. The several "runs" or "falls"—the Patapsco, the Gwynn's Falls, Jones' Falls, Herring Run, and the Great and the Little Gunpowder falls—cross the geologic zone of contact, roughly from northwest to southeast, to flow into the Chesapeake Bay. As elsewhere, the millstreams were gradually abandoned as a major source of industrial energy. They became sewers for carrying off slaughterhouse wastes or were dammed for water supply reservoirs. As sources of energy, they were replaced by massive new industrial fuels introduced from outside the region and from the underground "stores": Appalachian coal and oil, then Venezuelan oil, natural gas, and nuclear power. The boost in total energy applied is a major factor in environmental crises. The dissipation of most of this energy is still handled by the basic gravity flow systems—underground and surface drainage, the circulation of warm and cool water in the bay, and warm and cool air in the atmosphere. Each of the two natural landscapes—piedmont and coastal plain—provides distinctive raw materials for human use and each forms a distinctive warp and woof into which man weaves his routes and pipes and wires. Just as the old row house grids still form a matrix for social sorting and social movement, the basic physiographic structure is still the matrix for the sorting and movement of material and energy.

The beautiful rolling piedmont provided a variety of building stones—marble for the steps, granite for the basilica, greenstone for Mount Vernon Place Methodist Church, sandstone for Franklin Street Presbyterian. It offered a wealth of local plant environments—white oak on the plateaus of Wissahickon schist, post oak and scrub pine barrens on the serpentine, pure stands of beech in the coves, sycamores on the valley floors. Each knoll or hilltop grove was first appreciated as a gentleman's estate or summer place and in later generations turned into subdivision, park or cemetery—Beech Hill, Chestnut Ridge, Marble Hill, Druid Hill, Green Mount. The valleys of that piedmont landscape have for seventy-five years been seen as a regional system of linear parks and parkways. The Olmsted brothers' plan of 1903, commissioned by the Municipal Art Society, was wonderfully sensitive to the rocks, trees, and landscapes unique to each piedmont valley. Thanks to reservoir development and the Civilian Conservation Corps in the 1930s, park development was most fully carried out in the Patapsco and Gunpowder Falls valleys. Each now has 10,000 acres in park and twenty miles of nature trails.

The old mill roads such as Falls Road and Franklintown Road and parkways of the 1920s such as Ellicott Driveway, Wyman Park Drive, and Chinquapin Parkway harmonized with the stream valley park concept, but expressways have been harder to blend in. The earliest successful linear park, along Gwynn's Falls, will be dismembered by an expressway. In the Jones Falls valley an expressway was completed, but the imaginative park plan (by David Wallace) miscarried. The Jones Falls mill dams, wild strawberries, and butterflies remain secret places of people who explore railroad yards.

The coastal plain, trending northeast-southwest, is Baltimore's great transport corridor to the rest of Megalopolis and the bay is its corridor to the rest of the world. The region's industries use the quaternary sediments of the coastal plain as ground water reservoirs and mine the sands and gravels for concrete, the clays for making brick and fire-brick. In former times they also recovered iron nodules. Where the streams enter the unconsolidated coastal plain materials they become broad and sluggish and are called rivers or creeks instead of runs or falls. Herring Run, for example, becomes the Back River. The rivers and margins of the Chesapeake contain the wetlands or tidal marshes important to the life cycles of blue crab, oyster, clam, menhaden, striped bass, and shad and to the weekend and seasonal recreation flux of the human population.

THE VULNERABLE FRINGE

Knowing that much biological and chemical exchange takes place in the interfaces—the earth's "thin skin" of soil between air and rock, and the coastal margins between continent and ocean—we can expect to find in the Baltimore region a critical biological zone along the tidal margins of the rivers and the bay—its piers and channels, its mudflats and wetlands. There is amazing variation from place to place, from hour to hour, and from season to season in temperature, salinity, and sediment content. The bay is vast and shallow, "paper thin" if we reduce it to a small model. Its variations provide a richness of niches for water life. This wealth of the necks and rivers landscape was as easily recognized by explorers and settlers as

the potential value of the falls. Muskrat trapping, duck hunting, and crabbing, already familiar to the Nanticoke, the Suquehannock, and the Piscataway Indians, promptly became the basis for economic and recreational values of both rich and poor.

But each local environment, each species' life cycle, each food chain is vulnerable to sudden change. Immense investments have taken place in the coastal plain. Industrial development implies concentrated application of energy and harbor development implies massive changes in the dimensions of the bay—filling whole coves and dredging to new depths. Each lump of capital has had important impacts on the ecosystem and has fired political controversy, scientific research, and popular environmental concern.

Channel and port development programs posed an urgent problem of disposal of spoil—dredged harbor mud (Figure 29). The dredging of the fifty foot channel and the container facilities was stymied for over two years because a site could not be agreed upon for dumping 2.3 million cubic yards of mud. (Another two million yards will be dredged annually as maintenance.) Older sites—deep places in the bay at Kent Island and Poole's Island—had been filled. The material is fine silt with 60 percent water. It is not easily compacted and drained and is not usable as fill for construction sites. Because the upper layer, perhaps a third, is contaminated by oil, lead, cadmium, molybdenum, nickel, manganese, and cobalt (but little mercury, in contrast to dredge fill elsewhere), the U.S. Environmental Protection Agency was opposed to dumping it in the bay without dikes to contain it. Over vigorous protest, the port authority finally chose the Hart and Miller Island area for a diked spoil disposal which will cost $13 million and take three or four years to build.

Except for the contaminants, the dredging spoils resemble deposits from the natural processes of hydrology, erosion, and sedimentation in the bay. The Susquehanna River, mighty tributary at the head of the bay, normally brings down one-half to one million cubic yards of sediment a year, but runoff and sediment occasionally increase dramatically. For example, in June 1972, the Susquehanna, swollen from hurricane Agnes, created new mud flats and chains of islands. The bay is the "drowned valley of the ancestral Susquehanna," and its

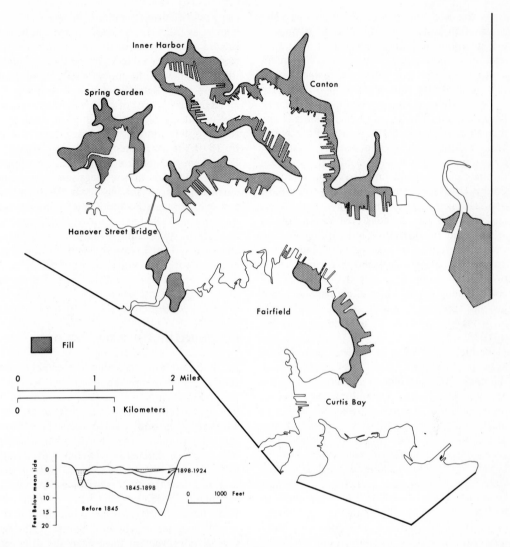

Figure 29. Sedimentation in Baltimore Harbor. Original shore line and sedimentation since time of colonial settlement were mapped by the Maryland Geological Survey. The cross section at Hanover Street bridge is from L. C. Gottschalk, *Geographical Review*, 1945.

complex ecosystem depends on gradual tidal mixing to produce the full range of salinity, from fresh water to sea water. The unusual outflow of fresh water caused by Hurricane Agnes killed oysters and clams (they require about five parts salt per thousand) and apparently contributed to fish kills from oxygen depletion in the brackish layer underneath. The Conowingo power dam on the Susquehanna is regulated with attention to that problem of oxygen distribution. There is concern that flows in the bay may be seriously affected by

deepening of the C & D Canal and diversion to Baltimore of more water from the Susquehanna River.

Nearly $1 billion was invested in power plants for the Baltimore area in the early 1970s and the environment effects are concentrated in the tidewater fringe. Baltimore Gas and Electric Company has developed a nuclear plant at Calvert Cliffs, in Calvert County to the south. Another is planned for near the mouth of the C & D Canal to the north. PEPCO (Potomac Edison) will build two others on the bay to serve the Washington metropolitan area. The constuction costs included millions "to protect the environment." Risks of accident and problems of disposal of plutonium wastes remain controversial issues, as elsewhere in the nation. But the everyday impact on the bay is merely an aggravation of that of other power plants. Because the efficiency of nuclear plants is less than that of fossil-fueled plants, more waste heat is disposed of to the water. A liquefied natural gas plant was built in the city and a gas turbine power plant at Perryman (Harford County). A large plant was built at the mouth of the Conemaugh coal mine in western Maryland, but the several older coal-burning plants around the Inner Harbor and Spring Garden were converted to oil because in the late sixties oil was the cheaper fuel and cheaper in terms of emission control. Ironically, some of the coal-handling equipment was actually scrapped just in time for the oil shortage and price increases precipitated by the Arab oil embargo of 1973.

Bethlehem Steel at Sparrows Point offers, as we might expect from it size, an example of the many effects of industrial energy use on the environment. It uses ten million tons of iron ore in a year, five million tons of coal, and much larger tonnages of water and air. It uses seven million gallons a day of filtered city water, larger amounts of well water, and circulates 700 million gallons of brackish harbor water for cooling and quenching. It releases great quantities of heat to the atmosphere as well as to the bay. But Bethlehem is also an example of the pressures and efforts involved in controlling such emissions and recycling materials. Bethlehem is part of a complex urban ecosystem. New electrostatic precipitators collect 167 tons of usable iron oxide dust daily from the open hearth furnaces. The city delivers 300 to 400 abandoned cars a day to a monster car shredder which in turn supplies scrap to Bethlehem. The steel company generates electricity from surplus blast furnace gas, coke breeze, and fuel oil and participates in the regional electric power pool with BG&E. Bethlehem delivers its slag to a specially built plant of the Arundel Corporation for making road materials. Most remarkable is Bethlehem's purchase of the entire treated effluent of the city's principal sewage treatment plant—130 million gallons a day. The use of the effluent as an industrial water supply was devised to overcome ground water problems which be-

came severe during the industrial spurt of World War II, as the entire industrial area can be considered one great well. Intensive pumping caused the water table to drop radically, brackish water began to move into ground water aquifers, and Bethlehem was forced to seek an alternative source of fresh water.

Current problems at the giant steel plant relate to deterioration of surface water quality. In 1970 the state stepped up its pressure on Bethlehem to control effluents contributing to fish kills. Among the illegal discharges were cyanide, phenols and oils from the coke oven and benzol plants, and zinc and cadmium from the wire mill. Bethlehem attributes a tenth of its recent investment program to pollution abatement. The Baltimore County Council has arranged for the company to use the county's federal tax-exempt status to issue $28 million in low interest bonds to finance air and water pollution control devices.

CLEANING UP THE BACK YARD

In Baltimore's more affluent nineteenth century neighborhoods, the front and back of a row house symbolized a lifestyle. The fronts had bay windows, marble stoops, wide streets with sidewalks and street trees. In back, lining the ten foot alley, were the privies and stables, old "summer kitchens," dwellings of servants and laborers, the board fences, garbage cans and flies, and the gutters draining from kitchen and laundry. Many of the horrors of alley environments have been eliminated, notably typhus and infant cholera. Some of the factors of improvement have been the disappearance of the urban horse, the change from soft coal to fuel oil, underground sewering, and machinery built into houses—the toilet, washing machine, drier, and garbage disposal unit. The alleys were paved with cement and gradually the dwellings were removed from them. Postwar neighborhoods of garden apartments have layouts such that one can hardly tell which is the front or back of the row.

But modernized evacuation of wastes from neighborhoods requires sites for processing and disposal—sewage treatment for 200 million gallons a day, dumping grounds for 2,500 tons of solid waste a day, reprocessing for waste oil, a rendering plant for disposal of 30,000 dead dogs and cats a year. These activities were concentrated in certain tidal margins which we might call Baltimore's back yards or the alleys of twentieth century affluence. In East Balti-more, along Back River, are the region's largest sewage treatment plant and its largest inciner-ator. Off Back River are the old sludge disposal sites and the new sites for diked spoil. In the southwest, where Gwynn's Falls flows into Spring Garden, once the site of a white lead works, we find bus junk yards, the Westport powerplant, and the new liquefied natural gas plant. In the south, on the Patapsco River mud flats, are the often offensive Reedbird incinerator and landfill.

Baltimore has accelerated its efforts in the 1970s to reclaim and relandscape its back yards. What has been accomplished? The sew-age treatment plant at Back River is being re-built to increase its capacity and the flexibility of its processes. It is one of the largest trickling filter plants in the world. These photogenic rotating sprinklers are displayed in a wooded park open to the public (drive out Eastern Ave-nue). Low-sudsing detergents have eliminated the great suds which for years blew or flowed over Back River. Nearby, an ancient private dump "of last resort," long a site for the sport of nighttime rat shooting, was plowed up in 1973. A stratum of cockroaches was treated with chemicals. The terrain was totally re-constructed and aggregate was added to sup-port a landscaped expressway interchange.

In the lower Gwynn's Falls valley, the city has just built a spectacular new pyrolysis plant —an incinerator of high temperatures, more complete combustion, elaborate sorting, and reclamation. Metals will feed Bethlehem; the glass will be used for road-paving material. (A sample of the glinting surface, glasphalt, can be seen on downtown Charles Street.) The process will produce enough methane to operate the plant and sell surplus steam to the BG&E steam plant, which supplies heat to downtown build-ings. The pyrolysis plant, the first of its type and scale in the nation, was sited to eliminate auto junkyards and private dumps at the city's Washington Parkway entrance. The pyrolysis plant will also allow the city to phase out the Reedbird incinerator in South Baltimore. The adjoining Patapsco mudflats are gradually being developed as parkland.

THE CORE ENVIRONMENT

The city's original site astride the geologic contact zone and astride the millstreams makes it the hub of the transport system of the state, and places it in a critical position in the gravity flow systems of drainage, sanitation, and sedi-mentation. As in other fall line cities, its old and central location—that is, the "core" proper-ties of Baltimore—adds to its specific environ-mental problems and aggravates and conflicts with less built-up and more peripheral parts of the region. The very nature of a city is to concentrate people, goods, and information, to facilitate their exchange. At the core of the region, and in the core of the city itself, land values tend to be high, intensities of movement are great, and buildings are tall. Because this core has developed over a long period of time, some elements of its structure are obsolete or deteriorated and there are complex vested interests.

The core is, for example, the center of the metropolitan "heat dome," a basic urban modi-fication of the circulation of air and air pollu-tants. This is a factor increasing heat stress for people close to the core during extreme mete-orological conditions—the summertime heat wave. Columbia, the "new town" in Howard County, appears to be a small scale develop-mental model of the full blown urban heat dome and air pollution system of Baltimore itself. In 1967 only 200 people lived on the 28 square kilometers of the town. By 1970 there were 10,000, by 1974 35,000. (The population target is 100,000.) Helmut Landsberg has docu-mented the development and expansion of the urban heat island, with nighttime summer temperature differentials of 4.5°C between "downtown" Columbia and the countryside, a 4 percent decrease in relative humidity (day-time), a decrease of vapor pressure, and a greater recirculation of city air. He attributes the changes primarily to the replacement of vegetation with paved and shingled surfaces and the resulting changes in the rates at which heat flows into and out of the soil. Buildings also block wind and renewal of air. Baltimore City, by virtue of its greater size, taller build-ings at the center, and much more complete coverage with asphalt paving and roofs, has stronger differentials. The metropolitan area is so varied in configuration and land use that the climatologist John Lewis (of McGill Uni-versity, formerly of the University of Maryland) has been able to relate the profile of heat radiation to land use features. On infrared photographs Bethlehem Steel stands out as a distinct "heat island," while Druid Hill Park appears as an "oasis."

The major distinctions of form which we observed in Baltimore's social geography—coastal plain and piedmont, green wedge and suburban circle—appear to match patterns of variation in the basic environmental resources, and in particular the distribution of extreme environmental stresses. In Baltimore, mortality has always been highest in the hot months of July and August, although the recognized "causes of death" have changed from generation to generation. In spite of anxiety over "hot summers," there is still limited public information about the significance of urban microclimates to murder and mass violence. The murder rate radically increased in Baltimore in 1972 and has stayed up. Homicide accounts for 3 percent of deaths in the city. We do know that these phenomena are concentrated in the inner city asphalt core, as are air pollution, lead, rats, noise, and lung diseases. There phenomena have provoked highly emotional responses and curiously erratic control efforts. For example, year after year the city health department issued congratulatory reports on the steady decline of lead poisoning cases among children—down to seven or eight in 1973. But a strong research program of national importance had just begun in Baltimore in 1972 and the new evidence reveals thousands of cases of lead poisoning. Thirty percent of inner city children (both black and white) have higher blood levels of lead than is considered safe.

Another example of uncertain and emotional priorities is animal control. Baltimore, with federal assistance and in response to the intense emotional response of inner city residents, spent several millions on rat control and related sanitation problems in the 1970s. But there are fifty or sixty rat bites in the city each year and 7,000 dog bites. Dog bites have increased 50 percent since 1960. Baltimore was the research area for Alan Beck's ecological study of the urban "free-ranging" dog. He estimates the population of strays at 40,000 and pet dogs at perhaps 60,000. They present serious health threats, notably the transmission of tuberculosis and a worm which can cause blindness. The number of large dogs and potential biters (according to breed, sex, and degree of confinement) has increased in response to anxiety about crime. "Nearly every back yard bordering the alleys of Baltimore contains a captive dog," Beck reports. Stray dogs live in vacant houses, turn over garbage cans, and chase the cats who kill the rats. Dog feces are food for rats, breeding places of flies, and carriers of parasitic diseases. Dogs and children compete for space.

Children and elderly persons are most vulnerable to carbon monoxide, sulphur dioxide, heat stress, noise (interrupted sleep), and infections. They are also the prime pedestrian targets for automobiles. Pedestrian environments have deteriorated generally, in spite of unusual research effort by the city planning department on the social uses of the streets, and special planning in renewal areas. More garage and service entrances interrupt sidewalks than before. Automobile exhaust and traffic noise are most intense at pedestrian levels. Grades and approaches are controlled more rigorously for motor vehicles than for pedestrians and users of wheelchairs. Many suburban areas do not require sidewalks. Their shopping centers have protected pedestrian malls inside the treacherous zone of unpoliced vehicle traffic.

One response to the various environmental hazards has been the escape into sealed-off environments with air conditioning and wholly artificial lighting. However, the effects of such environments on behavior, health, and mental health are uncertain. Public schools and infant day care centers have been built without windows. Apartment houses, residences for the elderly, and nursing homes all feature maximum uniformity or control in the environment and total cutoff from weather, natural stimuli, and people outside.

All of those neglected or newly discovered environmental deficiencies affect above all the people who live in the core. The inner city concentration of the poor, the elderly, the black, public housing tenants, and children dependent on public assistance for food and medical care is associated with the strong concentration of heat, noise, lead, dog feces, broken glass, carbon monoxide, sulfur dioxide, and exceptional deficiencies of grass, shade, and privacy. Just as in the nineteenth century alleys, the tendency remains for certain populations—physically vulnerable, economically marginal, politically weak—to bear the hard to measure or hard to predict environmental costs.

PROBLEMS ARISING IN THE PERIPHERY

Environmental problems also occur in the periphery where there have been radical jumps in population, energy inputs, mobility, and intensity of land use. This is true of the residential, industrial, and recreational land uses in the periphery. The problems are associated with investment leads and lags. The total growth of the region produces system overloads, most apparent in "downstream" environments.

Most of the recent residential growth has occurred on the piedmont, upstream from the city which was founded on the harbor. Regional sanitary sewers generally run downhill to the big treatment plant at Back River and the new Patapsco plant. Likewise, the storm drainage of Baltimore and Anne Arundel counties courses through the city. This means that any defects in the disposal of these effluents has repercussions in the city. From time to time the state health department has declared moratoria on issuing building permits in parts of Baltimore County, in order to limit the severe overloading of sanitary sewers and "overflow" sewage pollution of the Gwynn's Falls and the Jones Falls in the city.

Half the dwellings of Anne Arundel, Howard, and Harford counties depend on septic tanks for sewage disposal (see Figure 23). They are the same areas which rely on ground water for domestic supply.

We are spending millions of dollars in the eastern part of the county providing water and sewers. At the same time, we are letting subdivisions go into the rural areas where they are beyond the reasonable water and sewers and certainly sometime in the future a problem is going to develop there because the septic tank sooner or later will fail. With good maintenance and good soil conditions it can last for many years without troubles, but sooner or later the soil becomes fully saturated.

(U.S. Civil Rights Commission Hearing)

Suburban development has produced sizable changes in storm drainage parameters. Storm drainage is handled mainly by the "natural" stream channels. The same manmade radiating surfaces which create a change of heat flux and circulation of the air also produce changes in the flux of water into the ground and in the surface runoff. The runoff from urbanized watersheds with mostly paved or roofed surfaces is much swifter than from wooded or grassed surfaces or even from plowed land. Therefore, in the Maryland pattern of heavy summer rainstorms, the runoff peaks are swifter and more intense, producing more frequent flash floods and aggravating the rare events such as Hurricane Agnes (June 1972) when twelve inches of rain fell in one day. The flood damage also occurred downstream.

The hazards of work environments have not yet become a major public issue in Baltimore, although the metropolitan area presumably has a cross-section of the problems of other regions, such as excessive noise levels, unlabeled chemicals, acid spills, and noxious dusts and fumes. Many of those subjected to maximum hazards are workers in the outer harbor—construction workers and those in heavy metal manufacturing, oil and chemical plants, and paints. Blue collar census tracts in the city and in eastern Baltimore County have the highest rates in the region for disability among persons of working age. Many disabilities and chronic illnesses are never traced to their work environment sources.

The first indication of work environment hazards more severe in the Baltimore region than elsewhere comes from recent epidemiological studies of cancer. Mason and McKay's statistics of cancer deaths by counties of the U.S., 1950 to 1969, reveal decided excesses for Baltimore City in certain cancers which have elsewhere been linked to handling of specific industrial chemicals (carcinogens such as vinyl chloride). Men's city rates for cancers of the bladder and kidney and the more common cancer of the lung run 50 percent higher than state and national averages. (These contrast with rather low local rates for cancers of stomach and brain, and women's averages for cancer of the breast and cervix.) Radford's more specific study of 1973–1974 deaths among employees and pensioners of the Bethlehem Steel Sparrows Point plant shows still higher death rates in precisely the same categories. The rates for the population of steelworkers over age thirty-five ran 50 percent higher than what would be expected from city averages, already 50 percent higher than national averages.

Those initial results are especially interesting because they also indicate the life and death significance of the social structure of the job market and the social space in the factory. The distinctive distribution of jobs by race at the steel plant discussed earlier was matched by sharply different incidence of cancer deaths —kidney and liver cancers among blacks, bladder cancers among whites. "Excess deaths" were greater among whites, more of whom had served at least twenty years in a particular sector of the plant. Among the shipyard workers there were more deaths from lung cancer (and other respiratory diseases), consistent with their known exposure to asbestos. The new trend toward hiring blacks and women in a wider range of jobs ironically exposes them to new hazards. New industrial techniques have also introduced new risks—such as exposure to powered chromium salts in chrome plating—whose consequences have not yet shown up in death statistics. Once again, Bethlehem is merely an example, better documented because of its size and union concern, but indicative of conditions in other firms. Baltimore's very old copper and chrome smelting plants which shut down in the early seventies have left contaminated areas on the north rim of the harbor (Fell's Point, Canton, Highlandtown). On the south rim (Fairfield and Curtis Bay), dusts and fumes are frequent signs hinting at the invisible hazards within the plants. Hazards increased in the boom of the late sixties and early seventies when oil and chemical industries were working to capacity and overloading their systems. 1973-1975 layoffs undermined the bargaining position of employees.

We have seen how residential construction and industrial growth generate environmental changes on the periphery that have powerful impacts downstream and at the urban core—floods, deaths, disability payments, medicare costs. Likewise, if we look at the recreational zone still farther out on the periphery, we shall see a chain of impact which reaches again all the way to the core. What appear to be distinguishing traits of the periphery and the core are two sides of the same coin. Environmental problems on the periphery and environmental deficiencies in the core boil down to the same basic problem of access. Maryland's extraordinary variety of scenery, wildlife, and water life had survived in its piedmont stream valleys and tidewater wetlands because of their remoteness or high costs of draining and building. Less wetland, for example, has been lost than in other states, even though nearly all of it is privately owned. But carownership, roadbuilding, and a shorter work week have suddenly made these distant resources beyond the metropolitan region more accessible to more people and converted the elite styles of recreation such as duck hunting and sailing into mass activities. The new accessibility has posed new problems. The intensity of recreation

activities reduces some of the recreational values. Hunting has become so popular that the sport is risky for the hunters. Fishing has become a collective rather than a solitary pastime at Loch Raven, Broening Park, and Curtis Bay. Holidays and summer weekends are traffic jams at the Bay Bridge and campgrounds have become quasiurban installations. Recent projects for Worcester County wetlands include a "campominium" on a thousand acres, with six campsites per acre, a trailer park for a thousand trailers, and a resort camp of 3,300 acres. Machine access to recreation sites threatens even the survival of recreation environments. The newly acquired National Seashore on Assateague Island must rigidly restrict camper vehicles, cars, and dune buggies because of the danger of having its fragile dunes erode. Coastal erosion would follow. At Ocean City, land costs have shot up, private hold on the entire beach is reinforced, and high-rise construction now aims at luxury condominiums and year round convention business, while family vacation use is diminished.

But the more distant recreation opportunities have not been equally accessible to everyone. New problems of distribution have emerged, revealing the connection between development problems at the core and the periphery. Because the new mobility is *auto* mobility, the recreation gap has widened between people with and without cars. Streetcar lines and electrics no longer offer access to commercial swimming pools and amusement parks. Growth of harbor and industrial activity has fenced off or polluted more of the causal crabbing, boating, bathing, and fishing places. Community associations in the city's green wedge and in the suburbs have sponsored membership pools, but there are only the four sizable outdoor municipal swimming pools of 1920. Fifty small "portable" pools purchased after the 1968 riot were designed for regimented use by children and were spotted on blacktop playgrounds, but as the "hot summer" threat receded they have been left in mothballs. None was installed in 1974.

WHOSE ENVIRONMENT?

The problems described arise from the growth of the total Baltimore region—in population, wealth, energy use, and mobility. As the region develops, some resources become more abundant or accessible, others become more scarce or more costly. What makes these problems controversial is their distributional aspect. Who will share in the new abundance? Who will bear the added costs? We have seen how threats to the magnificent environmental resources of the bay arise from the scramble for site values and access. Each household, each neighborhood or identity group, each corporation enters a competition for environmental resources. Each struggles to capture benefits and evade costs. Consequently, environmental conflict is channeled by the legal and political framework. Property lines set up jurisdictions between householders. Political boundaries set up jurisdictions between groups of taxpayers. Environmental issues arise whenever resources or costs must be shared across these boundaries.

For example, developer proposals for extension of sewers into the areas around Loch Raven reservoir, Soldier's Delight, and the Worthington Valley raised the question of environmental planning. The debate hinged on the issue of distribution. The beautiful limestone valleys called Green Spring, Worthington, and Caves, some 45,000 acres, are part of the horsey country of gentleman farming north of Baltimore. A community council of 5,000 families invited Ian McHarg and David Wallace to develop a plan in 1962. Their plan would protect the more fragile environments. The steep valley walls would remain forested. The floodplain and open valleys on Cockeysville marble would be reserved for agriculture, pasture, and low intensity institutional open space. Residential development would be allowed on the wooded plateaus, with high-rise towers on the promontories. The planners showed that total land values would be greater than with "uncontrolled growth." While the proposal helped delay random subdivision, and has so far prevented the sewer extension, there has not yet been agreement on a program of implementation or redistribution of rising land values. In spite of their appreciation of use values of the habitat, the resident owners are committed to the game of individual private risk and private manipulation of market values.

The problem is similar in the tidewater zone. Virtually the entire tidewater margin of Maryland is private property, parceled into thousands of jurisdictions. In the city it is all zoned for industrial use; in Anne Arundel County most is zoned for low density residential use, accessed by private roads. Vacant sites remain with potential for recreation and other uses,

but all are "encumbered." In order to protect wetlands, state legislation was passed in 1970 establishing strong state powers and a permit system for all dredge and fill and some state enforcement has begun. One developer was obliged to restore a wetland site. This controversy was characteristic of the race between owners to capture new market values and other citizens to assert rights to user values.

How and where to provide water mains and sewers are issues which involve redistribution across county lines as well as among households. The developed city has excellent, well-integrated water and sewage treatment plants adequate for the next generation. These plants serve to some extent the suburban populations, which share in operating costs. But the fast-growing peripheral counties need to build systems of comparable size over the next twenty years. They are therefore eager to spread capital costs over a metropolitan district, which, according to Abel Wolman, "of course, means that the City of Baltimore would be disproportionately paying for something it doesn't need." After years of study and negotiation, a regional water and sewer authority acceptable to the several technical administrations has been designed, but its political fate is uncertain.

The same kind of structural conflict of interest occurs with respect to public parks. Because recreation is generally a low intensity land use, it seems rational to purchase lower priced peripheral land. But residents of the peripheral counties, owners of cars and private yards and private mortgages, do not yet feel an urgent need for public parks. Fiscal rivalries aggravate public tightfistedness: no community wants to subsidize a recreational resource for its neighbors. Marina owners do not want to provide sewage dumps for boaters, as Anne Arundel County has not provided public sewers and pumping stations on the low lying recreational peninsulas. Baltimore County has resisted developing parks for regional use and concentrated on insuring developer participation in tucked away neighborhood parks. Howard County adopted a comprehensive park plan and appropriated a large sum, but has fallen far short of target rates of acquisition. These are instances of Kevin Cox's argument that collective (environmental) goods will be underproduced and negative externalities (pollution) will be overproduced. In the opinion of experienced observers, metropolitan government does not appear to be politically feasible in the

Baltimore region, but there is a growing tendency to demand new forms of redistribution or "equalization" through state government. The Regional Planning Council (a state agency) has, for example, called for state acquisition of 200,000 acres of open space. In terms of funding and purchase, the state government has served the appetizer—the purchase of the unique Soldiers Delight serpentine barrens for a state park.

In spite of its capricious legislature and councils, Maryland has a long and distinguished tradition in environmental science and engineering. Seventy-five years ago, when the Olmsteds prepared the stream valley park plan and the city built its sewer system and rebuilt its burnt downtown, there was a flowering of many new forms of environmental planning, with the collaboration of public agencies, private citizens, neighborhoods groups, and professionals, notably the geologists, water chemists, oyster biologists, and civil engineers at the young Johns Hopkins University. A Hopkins economist at that time argued that the key to environmental problems was distribution, and the first thing to consider in distribution was the socioeconomic order based on the legal institutions of property. The renewal of public interest in environmental problems since 1970 is important because it is the only area in which Marylanders appear to be challenging the institutions surrounding property and the transfer of property. Environmental problems are essentially "common" problems, not individual ones, and our environmental concerns reflect the idea Richard T. Ely expressed: "Society lives in a condition of solidarity."

The Institutional Neighborhood

There are three-dozen-odd neighborhoods in the Baltimore region. One neighborhood of a thousand has seven men to each woman, only two dozen children, nobody over sixty-four, and no disabled or unemployed. In another neighborhood of 4,000, half are over fifty-six. There are only two men for each three women. A third live alone. In a neighborhood of 2,400, with a comparable portion of elderly, nobody lives alone, and 5 percent have moved in the last five years. In another neighborhood of more than 3,000 people, half are under nineteen, three-quarters are white, three-fifths are male, but only 6 percent are in the labor force. In yet another, of 1,400 residents, nearly all are men, two-thirds black. Three-quarters have moved in recently and a quarter are separated from their wives.

What these five neighborhoods have in common is their institutional character. The first is an army installation, the second adjoins a university, the third is a state mental hospital, the fourth is a training school for the retarded, and the fifth a prison. Each institution is unique, yet they represent a large class of neighborhoods. There are in the region five such military bases (15,000 residents in barracks) including Fort Meade and the U.S. Naval Academy. There are five such large mental hospitals and several smaller ones—9,000 beds. The general hospitals of the region have another 9,000 beds, but turnover is swifter and their occupants are not considered residents. There is a prison population of roughly 6,000, and a comparable number in the dormitories

of universities and colleges. Half the 60,000 people classed as living in group quarters are concentrated in these neighborhoods. The rest are in smaller institutions of several hundred, such as the 10,000 in nursing homes and homes for the aged—two-thirds run for profit, one-third nonprofit.

The nonprofit institutions, whether public or private, are an important force in the local economy. The military bases and college campuses are large users of land. The Johns Hopkins medical institutions are one of the largest employers in Baltimore City. As purchasers, they affect specialized sectors such as water use, laundry, laboratories, vending machines, and hotels. They affect neighborhoods in terms of housing markets, parking demand, vehicle traffic, pedestrian movement, and evening or nighttime activity. They also have a privileged position in the tax structure. In the city, 28 percent of land is tax-exempt—or nearly a billion dollars value. About one-third is accounted for by universities, hospitals, schools, and churches, another 40 percent by the city's own enterprises, including the public schools.

Is it reasonable to lump together these institutions with their diverse objectives? Is it reasonable to regard them as residential neighborhoods? Certainly their designers, architects, and managers regard them as specialized residential neighborhoods. They are the ultimate in planned communities. While they reflect to some extent the ideas of specialized professionals in the nation at large, they also reflect political and financial priorities of the local community over many years. They add up to an intricate system which sorts people or differentiates among them and isolates them for longer or shorter periods of time, to greater or lesser degree, from others in the community. In the largest and most isolated institutions— the mental and penal institutions—contrasts of race and sex dramatize the extent to which the assignment of caretakers *in loco parentis* reflects the same pecking order apparent in the labor force and the housing market.

Institutional peculiarities and new thrusts must reflect the peculiar dimensions and dynamics of Baltimore's social life. Changes are taking place in institutional structures, particularly medical, educational, and caretaking services. These are apparent in the geographical arrangement. By looking at the location and relocation patterns, we can discover some aspects of an institutional crisis and, woven into it, a crisis of values. The basic problem is the effectiveness of institutions with respect to their goals in a continually changing society. Like the physical plant itself, the institutional organizational structure tends to become obsolete. In the context of urban geography, the city is changing and moving and institutions must change or move also.

Many hospitals and schools were originally located and designed for a definite type of service and a definite clientele. Baltimore had, for example, a Jewish hospital (Sinai), a German Protestant orphans' home, a farm school for colored boys, a Lithuanian parochial school, a grade school for Irish children (without regard to religion), public "English-German" schools, and so forth. All were created and endowed to respond to certain needs. But what happens when there are no longer many German orphans or no ready markets for black farm labor? What happens when the Jewish population moves to another part of town and the hospital is surrounded by black Protestants? The Baltimore Urban Parish Study is an account of the cumulation of such problems for the parochial elementary schools of the archdiocese.

It is also necessary to appreciate the fiscal context. As a nonprofit service enterprise in a profit-structured society, each organization had built into it some conception of social responsibility, personal responsibility, and common values which could be mobilized to support and pay for the services. These were not easy to organize. At the turn of the century, the creation of a Jewish hospital, recre-

ation center, family and youth services, and charities involved tense alliances between rich and poor, newcomer and establishment, German and Russian, Orthodox and Reformed. (Some of the nuances are described by Isaac M. Fein.) In the 1960s raising $1 million in the Negro community to build a modern building for Provident Hospital has also involved complex tensions and strategic considerations. After the institutions are established, they remain vulnerable. The three-cornered relationship between financial backers, professional managers, and users is continually subject to change. One cannot make the "equilibrium" assumptions of a private enterprise in which interests are automatically reconciled in the balance sheet. All these institutions are initially defined as money losers. The problem lies in the "glue" which holds such machinery together.

PROBLEMS OF SITE AND ENVIRONMENT

Certain large institutions traditionally preferred large, isolated, suburban or rural tracts. Such sites had the advantages of fresh air and sunshine, and land which could be farmed or pastured to provide work therapy, fresh milk, or economies of growing food. Moreover they provided security, either to protect a vulnerable population of children, youth, retarded, or senile against a threatening society, or to protect society from a threatening population, criminal or contagious.

This pattern of location has produced two types of obsolescence. We shall look at some examples of each, with the several kinds of institutional response or reorganization which followed. The first is the set of remote sites which are no longer suitable for a changed role of the institution in modern society. The state mental hospitals are all in isolated locations which have become handicaps as their philosophy has changed. Visiting is difficult, outpatient treatment and follow-up care are impractical, and employment outside the institution is impossible. In other words, the institutions were located for indefinite or permanent alienation from society and these locations are not easy to adapt to the strategy of reintegrating the individual into normal patterns of work and interaction. Something similar has happened with the tuberculosis hospitals, now that tuberculosis is also largely treated with drugs on an outpatient basis. Juvenile "villages" and houses of correction are also locations of this type.

The new philosophies of treatment have therefore required the creation of a new set of institutions on a smaller scale in the community or close to population centers. The logic is convincing and since 1970 funding has begun in earnest. For example, the state Department of Corrections has plans to decentralize half the prison population into community correction centers of 198 residents each. For delinquent or disturbed youth, several new "group homes" have been organized in the past three years and the intent is to abandon the larger institutions. The state Department of Mental Health has created several specialized outpatient services for psychiatric treatment of alcoholics, drug addicts, and persons prone to violence or suicide, and also several new small scale residential facilities for retarded persons and "halfway" houses for people able to leave the state hospitals.

But the effort to locate all such new facilities has repeatedly come into conflict with the defensive strategies of residential neighborhoods. Their chief resort is the zoning laws. The public continues to regard the people returning from institutions as alien and threatening populations. The facilities so far located are clustered in areas of old mansions and large daytime populations, on the outer fringes of the central business district.

The second type of obsolescence appears where the city has overgrown a remote countrified location, destroyed its rural assets, and hemmed it in with urban traffic, high value land uses, and urban environmental threats. One institutional option was simply to exit (see Albert Hirschman's work), particularly where the traditional clientele had exited or where the users had no clear ties with the neighborhood. For example, most of the colleges, boarding schools, seminaries, and convents moved to larger and greener sites in the suburbs. This process was continuous over 200 years, but there was a notable spurt in the 1950s, leaving an immense amount of underutilized and ill-maintained social capital behind.

Leaving the truly critical gap, doctors and several hospitals moved out, in response to a mix of more and less rewarded services. Three hundred doctors have private practices in the city, as compared with 950 thirty years ago and 500 now in Baltimore County. A dramatic restructuring of health facilities was inevitable

to compensate for the exits. The large hospitals experienced dramatic expansion of demand in their outpatient clinics and emergency rooms. The phenomenon has been even more severe in Baltimore than other cities. Federal financing contributed to this important shift in the delivery of medical services—Medicare, Medicaid, and HEW construction funds. The rising capital-intensity and specialization of new medical technology also favored the creation of comprehensive pediatric clinics and "primary care" facilities now under construction. These developments help to fill the vacuum in the inner city, but they cluster around established hospital sites precisely the same set of growth poles as for mental health services, halfway houses and services to the aged.

The same type of institutional concentration has appeared in the suburban ring, at Towson (Sheppard-Pratt, Greater Baltimore Medical Center, and Saint Joseph's hospitals adjoin), on the east (Essex Community College and Franklin Square Hospital), and at Catonsville. But the beltway ring sites are relatively favorable to readaptation, on site expansion, and improved access, whereas the most centrally located hospitals, among the oldest and most diversified, have acute problems of site expansion. The University of Maryland (1820), Johns Hopkins Medical Institutions (opened 1891), and, near Mount Vernon, Mercy Hospital (1805) and Maryland General, were once country locations. They are now the favored locations for new services for the core area of public dependency, as well as the highly specialized Metro Center activities in medicine, education, and research. (A trauma center with heliport, for example, has been located at Maryland General.) Urban renewal has been a prime means of delivering land with federal subsidy, notable for the expansion of Johns Hopkins and University of Maryland hospitals. The city's off-street parking commission, formerly concerned with boosting downtown shopping, is now devoting its effort to providing garages for the hospitals.

A CASE OF INSTITUTIONAL RENEWAL

The exit of institutions required painful adjustment in abandoned communities. But adjustments have also been painful where institutions chose to stay. The case of the Johns Hopkins Hospital is an example of exceptional scale and

drama. Successive projects on the perimeter of
the Johns Hopkins Medical Institutions in the
1950s produced a medical residence with a
small outdoor swimming pool; a fenced-in
"compound" for families of medical personnel,
with barred windows and playground; a hotel
for out-of-town relatives of private patients;
and a huge parking garage—all on the site of
several thousand dwellings. The evicted residents live in the surrounding area. Most are
black, poor, and use the hospital. But the
medical personnel were white. This is the
premium medical educational institution of
the South. Negro doctors and their private
patients were not accommodated until the
last few years. Since 1965 there has been a
rising percentage of Asian immigrant personnel.

Seething resentment came to a boil in the
late 1960s over the issue of a black top "football field" which the renewal projects had
created for Paul Laurence Dunbar High School
(Figure 30). This conflict generated a political
movement, a promise of an entirely new school

and multipurpose center, and, to plan it, the
extraordinary "Dunbar charette." This was a
continuous fourteen day brainstorming effort
by a hundred people, including parents, teachers and students from the high school, other
representatives from the neighborhood, and
personnel from the hospital. From the larger
community came others—from the institutions
of black leadership—Provident Hospital and
Morgan State College—from the archdiocese,
city school administration, and federal education consultants, plus the architects and "organizers." As J.H. Harrison reported,

> In the view of the Dunbar community resi-
> dents, there exists no meaningful commu-
> nity in the Dunbar area. The area is essen-
> tially underdeveloped. . . . There is no land
> available that does not involve someone's
> dislocation.

The fourteen days were stormy and harried.
More important than the innovative character

Figure 30.   Dunbar High School. Photo by Julian Olson.

of the building is the vision around which they designed it, of a community that would emerge —not a community within the school, but the Dunbar facility as the focal point of a real neighborhood.

The educational program recommended by the charette involved contract learning, student choices of learning methods, and councils and review boards of the faculty, students, and community. They demanded a strong liberal arts curriculum open to all and a vocational curriculum oriented to growth occupations in which black workers are underrepresented— management, entrepreneurship, sales work, and a unique range of health careers, but not blue collar manufacturing. The hospital is to contribute to the facilities, teaching, motivation, and job opportunities for graduates in the health sector.

The buildings are arranged so that the swimming pool, cafeteria, and movie theatre can be used at different hours by students and others from the community or the public at large. Residents of the entire neighborhood will be served by the information center for job placement, career planning, and occupational counseling. A "neighborhood city hall" was envisioned, with offices for the area's councilmen and voter registration outreach, "to develop in the people of the second ward a feeling of their own political potency".

The Dunbar episode shows how institutional renewal must occur simultaneously on many fronts—in the hospital, in the overall system for delivering medical care, in public education, in political redistricting, in the job market, and in personal soul searching. The painful process of reorganizing and reforming so many institutions took place in the specific geographical context of a neighborhood. The institutional bureaucracies themselves could not have accomplished their renewal individually or jointly. It was their unwilling neighbors who got it together, because the changes required for "neighborhood development" spilled out of the neighborhood. The "glue" which held the charette together through moments of hostility and hours of stalemate was Baltimore's experience of the burning in April 1968, less than a year earlier.

Will the Dunbar effort succeed? The school is operating. The tension still remains between a struggle for "meaningful community" at a neighborhood scale and the pressures on Hopkins Hospital to grow and extend on a scale which does not relate to this neighborhood— its citywide children's trauma center, its research of national importance, its surgical pioneering, and its international programs in public health. Hopkins is undertaking a building program which dwarfs the sorely felt renewal of the 1950s. The Hopkins picture is just one example illustrating the neighborhood-battering force of institutional growth. The institutions have burst out of the topographic cadre, out of the pedestrian scale, out of the ethnic scale.

The Dunbar community, in spite of its new physical center and the community experience by which it was obtained, is also caught in a larger structure which severely limits educational opportunities—the whole structure of residential segregation at the scale of the metropolis. In the Park Heights corridor (northwest corner of the city) also, community aspirations and political power have mobilized imagination and talent to rethink and remodel their educational institutions, and there, too, the community is hemmed in by the metropolitan ring and wedge structures which limit the range of variation of pupil experience and family resources. Even at the scale of the whole city, that basic structure remains the stumbling block to all schemes for "desegregation" by race and "equalization" among income groups. The "low level trap" which restricts the job mobility of the work force also constrains the educational development of tomorrow's work force, perpetuating the inequality.

INSTITUTIONAL DECISIONMAKING

Institutional growth must also be seen in the context of metropolitan-scale finance. In the nonprofit institutions, costs are visible and measurable, but the benefits are usually hard to measure. Cost shifts are therefore attentively examined, while shifts in benefits are ignored. Because there is always the risk that the donor will exit, those generous givers often influence decisions. In Baltimore there is a definite control of the boards of nonprofit institutions (whether public or private) by the directors and managers of the financial sector—the banks and utilities. U.S. Congressional Banking Committee hearings (1967) showed a tighter interlocking of directorships among Baltimore banks than for other cities. Manufacturing industries may be underrepresented because so few are home owned and the archdiocese may be closer to the core than in other cities, but the pattern is the usual one of a close knit core of white, male, moneyed respectability, aloof from "politics" and unknown to most people. They live in the green wedge and their close knit web contrasts with the extreme fragmentation of the clienteles or users of the institutions—unevenly assigned by race, religion, means, and residence.

Vigorous and sometimes violent confrontations have dented that power structure in the past ten years. Tenants' councils have been organized in public housing. New appointments were made to the city school board in order to allow parents of public school children to outnumber those who sent their children to private or parochial schools. The city's Civil Service Board was induced to add bonus points for city residence (as for veteran status), because more than a third of the city's policemen, firemen, and hospital employees lived outside the city (coincidental with an underrepresentation of blacks in these jobs). Hospital and university boards have hastened to add token blacks and women, while the financial sector promoted at least one Jewish member into the inner circle of 150. Nevertheless, change does not seem to have touched the core of this structure. Likewise, in the political structure, even the election of a Republican governor in Maryland, his accession to the vice-presidency, and a heavy Republican vote for president in 1972 produced no hint of a viable Republican party in Maryland. Maryland democracy remains a solid one party system of Byzantine intrigue. Many political, professional, and financial roles are, like family businesses, inherited. The extraordinary stability of the financial elite and the political order affects the quality of leadership and the rate of change which can be expected in institutional and social process and, therefore, in the form or pattern of the urban space.

The Image: Does It Matter?

A PLACE TO VISIT

The mayor and business leaders are concerned about the city's image among port users, in international trade, and in national tourism (Figure 31). Baltimore was known for the Preakness and for its sports teams—the Colts, the Orioles, the Bullets, and the Clippers. Does it matter whether the teams are sold to some other town? Which of dozens of promotional schemes—aquarium, floating restaurant, scale model of the harbor, hotel school—will put across a Baltimore image? Will a $100 million stadium make Baltimore more visible? Or will it make it look more like Dallas? Does it matter that the B & O Railroad now calls itself the Chessie, that the excursion boats have no place to go, that a New Orleans decor was proposed for an amusement park in Howard County? Is a police headquarters with golden windows more of an enhancement for the Baltimore image than the famous but seedy "Block" of nightclubs?

Baltimore was simply not built for tourists. To visit Baltimore, you have to look for it. You have to keep moving. Go in search of something—azaleas in May and roses in June, the fringed gentian in November. If you want flag-draped neighborhoods on the Fourth, try Hampden, Locust Point, and Highlandtown. For Christmas decorations, drive through Windsor Hills and Forest Park. If you came in by the Jones Falls Expressway, take the old Falls Road out. Or drive out Wilkins Avenue, and come back in by Washington Boulevard. Every-

thing you visit—Fort McHenry, the B & O railroad museum, the Basilica, the Lexington Market, Mencken's home or Poe's, or Babe Ruth's or Mother Seton's, the pagoda in Patterson Park—grab the chance to explore the neighborhood around it. Stop in for a soda or a coffee or a beer on the corner and let yourself get drawn into the banter and the warmth. Because Baltimore is a place to live. As one citizen at an expressway hearing put it,

> I say first the city is a place to live in. They say first the city is a place to make money in. Whether I am right or they are right makes the big difference.

A PLACE TO LIVE

What kind of image do we have of ourselves? Does it matter that we have no hometown firms, that we work for Bethlehem, but Bethlehem's identity isn't Baltimore? Must our productive power be a massive secret all around us? Must every factory be surrounded by parking lots and cyclone fences? Must our port remain invisible?

And why shouldn't we be proud of taking in each other's washing? The quickest way to get a grasp of our dependence on each other is to spend Saturday night in the emergency room. Does it matter that our hospitals look like penitentiaries and that operating room lighting has been extended to the streets around them?

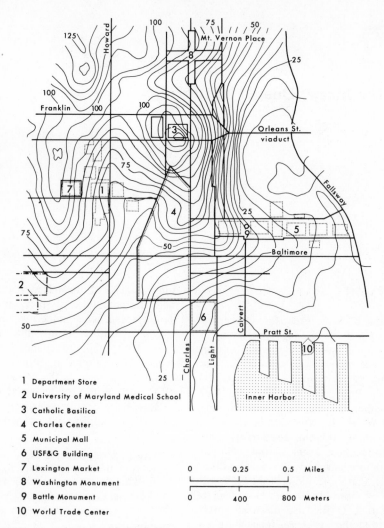

1 Department Store
2 University of Maryland Medical School
3 Catholic Basilica
4 Charles Center
5 Municipal Mall
6 USF&G Building
7 Lexington Market
8 Washington Monument
9 Battle Monument
10 World Trade Center

Figure 31. Downtown in 3-D. The generation of the War in 1812 saw the rugged topography of Baltimore as a stage for architectural monuments—the Catholic Basilica, the Washington Monument, the Battle Monument, the University of Maryland medical school, and the Lexington Market. A "progressive" and efficiency-minded generation 100 years later took advantage of terrain for a municipal mall, a sewer system, the Fallsway (over Jones Falls), and the Orleans Street viaduct. The generation of the 1960s used the terrain of Charles Center for walkways above traffic, underground parking, and vistas of the older monuments. They have designed a waterfront skyline with two new monuments to finance and trade: The USF&G building has forty stories, the World Trade Center will have thirty-two. The department store gully is still unreclaimed.

Baltimore still has a potential for integrity in its fine scale or grain. Baltimore is not part of the Roman Empire, in spite of the grandoise office schemes of the federal and state governments. In the neighborhoods, street life depends on the scale of the streets and houses. Even the downtown has a neighborhood quality. Charles Center, compared with such projects in other downtowns, is intimate and fits into a pieced-together fabric of buildings of eight generations—the rectory of Saint Paul's, the steeple of Saint Alphonsus, the Shot Tower, the Basilica. In order to be itself, Baltimore must, like New England, accept its own provincialism and revel in its patchwork.

H.L. Mencken, one of Baltimore's orneriest citizens, appealed to that sense of identity and integrity of Baltimore's self-image. In the 1910s he argued for beer and Sunday concerts. In the 1920s he ranted against filling stations and suburban houses (no privacy) and the so-called skyscrapers: "There was never any need of them here." In the thirties he vented his spleen on the east-west viaduct.

Wasting millions on such follies is simply not Baltimorish. Every enterprise of the sort is a kind of confession that Baltimore is inferior to New York, and should hump itself to catch up. No true Baltimorean believes that. He accepts the difference between a provincial capital and a national metropolis as natural and inevitable, and he sees no reason why any effort should be made to conceal it. He lives in Baltimore because he prefers Baltimore. One of its

Figure 32. Kids running, the dome of city hall, a patchwork of downtown land uses.

greatest charms, in his eyes, is that it is not New York.

Studding the inner city are symbols of its ethnic patchwork. Baltimore's social mix differs from Boston or New York or Cleveland or Los Angeles, just as their mix of industry differs and their house types differ. Two blocks from the Baltimore Symphony is the Left Bank Jazz Society. By a hair's breadth, the Jewish community saved the Lloyd Street Synagogue and the Sulpicians restored St. Mary's Chapel before they moved out of the seminary. Each of those buildings has the power to communicate the sense of prayer by which a whole community survived and each is a doorway to one of Baltimore's hidden worlds. Does it matter that one is only open one afternoon a month, the other never? "Beautiful Baltimore" and "Black is Beautiful" are slogans of the moment. The third term—"Baltimore is Black" —is rarely posted. Blacks made the bricks and blacks keep downtown alive, but their aspirations, generation after generation, need stronger symbols at the center (Figure 32).

A PLACE TO GROW

Baltimore neighborhoods are a wonderful radius of action for a child. Hopscotches are drawn like nowhere else. We eat sauerkraut with our Thanksgiving turkey and black-eyed peas for New Year's. We all go out on new roller skates on Christmas even if it snows, and visit the "Christmas garden"—model railroad displays at the firehouse. We take in the state fair in August, the City fair in September, the Fell's Point Fair in October, and all the lesser street fairs.

But what happens when you outgrow the neighborhood? There is the new "undistricted" high school complex of 4,000 students. What kind of neighborhood is that? In Locust Point and Canton some of the boys still slip out of childhood right into a warm spot next to dad at the tavern and the hiring hall. Some of the girls still move from courting on mom's front steps to scrubbing their own white stoop three doors down or around the corner. But not so many. The adolescent and the newcomer share a need for an arena, a smithy in which to forge identity and solidarity. Although the region has 40,000 full time college students, it lacks a student quarter and consequently has no bookstore, no home for political life, mature artistic life, or ideological debate. Mount Vernon Place has some potential, but escapes its old gentility only by perennial outrage. The Maryland Institute of Art had a vision when they bought Mount Royal Station (B & O), but the state has now, by design or default, acquired most of the surrounding land and shows no sign of grasping that vision. Fell's Point may yet survive the highway project, now scheduled to be "sunk" in the mud off the point, but designs for the Inner Harbor East campus of the Community College of Baltimore appear to be as sterile as the University of Maryland complex.

Meanwhile, the place to discover Baltimore and discover yourself is at public meetings. Nineteenth century Baltimoreans loved public hangings, town meetings, and the hustings. Officially, jousting is the state sport, but in fact the courtroom is from colonial days to this moment the real Maryland jousting place and our favorite source of gossip. One can also rely on daytime attractions at the School Board, the Liquor Board, and the Board of Zoning Appeals. Baltimore's public life is an emotional rollercoaster. Urban renewal community meetings offer nightly guerrilla theatre. Expressway hearings and cycle zoning hearings in the counties are less frequent but clearly polarized: you won't need a score card to tell the players. The observer should be warned, however, of the risk of involvement. The candor and the vehemence are contagious. People rarely succeed in remaining neutral.

Bibliography

Amourgis, Spyros. "Baltimore—A Design Concept for the Inner Core of the City." Occasional paper of the Johns Hopkins University Center for Metropolitan Planning and Research, 1975.

Archdiocese of Baltimore. *Baltimore Urban Parish Study.* Baltimore, 1967.

Associated Jewish Charities of Baltimore. *The Jewish Community of Greater Baltimore, a Population Study.* December 26, 1968.

Bachrach, Peter, and Baratz, Morton S. *Power and Poverty, Theory and Practice.* Oxford University Press, 1970.

Baltimore Citizens Planning and Housing Association. *Bawlamer, an Informal Guide to a Livelier Baltimore.* 1971.

Baltimore City. *Municipal Handbook.* 1969.

Baltimore City. Department of Housing and Community Development. *Annual Reports.*

——. *Oldtown Development Guide and Upton Development Guide.* August 1970.

Baltimore City. Department of Planning, and Johns Hopkins University Center for Urban Affairs. *Census Notes.* Irregular issues, 1971.

Batimore City. Urban Renewal and Housing Agency. *Displacement and Relocation, Past and Future, Baltimore, Maryland.* Stage one staff monograph 5.4, March 1965.

——. *Harlem Park, a Demonstration of Rehabilitation.* June 1965.

Baltimore Sun, 1961–1973.

Baltimore Evening Sun.

Baltimore New American.

Barker, Constance L. *Relocation and the Housing Market in Metropolitan Baltimore, 1968–1975.* Regional Planning Council, 1968.

Beck, Alan M. *The Ecology of Stray Dogs, A Study of Free-Ranging Urban Animals.* Baltimore: York Press, 1973.

Bedini, Silvio A. *The Life of Benjamin Banneker.* Scribner's, 1972.

Bennett, Robert R., and Meyer, Rex R. *Geology and Ground Water Resources of the Baltimore Area.* Maryland Geologic Survey bulletin no. 4. 1952.

Chatterjee, Lata; Harvey, David; and Klugman, Lawrence. *FHA Policies and the Baltimore City Housing Market.* Baltimore: The Urban Observatory, April 1974.

Council of Churches and Christian Education of Maryland and Delaware. *The Negro Church in Baltimore.* 1934.

Crenson, Matthew. *Survey of Organized Citizen Participation in Baltimore, Final Report.* Baltimore Urban Observatory, Inc.

Crooks, James B. *Politics and Progress, the Rise of Urban Progressivism in Baltimore, 1895 to 1911.* Louisiana State University Press, 1968.

Educational Facilities Laboratory. *Experiment in Planning an Urban High School: The Baltimore Charette.* Case Studies no. 13. 1969.

Ely, Richard T. *Property and Contract in their Relation to the Distribution of Wealth.* Boston: Thomas Crowell, 1914.

Emmart, William W. "Report on Housing and Commercial Conditions in Baltimore." Studies prepared for Mayor Howard W. Jackson, October 1934 (Municipal Reference Library).

Fein, Isaac M. *The Making of an American Jewish Community, the History of Baltimore*

Jewry from 1773 to 1920. Philadelphia: Jewish Publication Society of America, 1971.

Feld, Joseph A. "The Changing Geography of Baltimore Jewry." Paper, Johns Jopkins University, August 1968.

Geyer, John C. *Ground Water in the Baltimore Industrial Area.* Maryland State Planning Commission, publication no. 44, May 1945.

Gottschalk, L.C. "Effects of Soil Erosion on Navigation in Upper Chesapeake Bay." *Geographical Review* (1945), pp. 219–38.

——. Sedimentation in a Great Harbor. *Soil Conservation* 10, 1 (July 1944): 3–5, 11–12.

Haeuber, Douglas H. "The Baltimore Expressway Controversy: A Study of the Political Decision-Making Process." Occasional Paper, The Johns Hopkins University Center for Metropolitan Planning and Research, 1974.

Harrison, James Haywood, ed. *People, Planning, and Community and the Creation of a New Paul Laurence Dunbar High School in Baltimore, Maryland.* March 1969.

Harvey, David. *Class-Monopoly Rent, Finance Capital and the Urban Revolution.* University of Toronto, Department of Urban and Regional Planning, Papers on Planning and Design, no. 4. March 1974.

——. *Social Justice and the City.* London: Edwin Arnold, 1973.

Harvey, David, and Chatterjee, Lata. "Absolute Rent and the Structuring of Space by Governmental and Financial Institutions." *Antipode* 6, 1 (April 1974): 22–36.

Harvey, David, et al. *The Housing Market and Code Enforcement in Baltimore.* The Baltimore Urban Observatory, Inc., City Planning Department, July 1972.

Hirschfeld, Charles. *Baltimore, 1870-1900: Studies in Social History.* Baltimore: Johns Hopkins Press, 1941.

Hirschman, Albert O. *Exit, Voice and Loyalty.* Cambridge, Mass.: Harvard University Press, 1970.

Keller, Suzanne. *The Urban Neighborhood: A Sociological Perspective.* Randon House, 1968.

Laumann, Edward O. *Bonds of Pluralism: the Form and Substance of Urban Social Networks.* John Wiley, 1973.

Marx, Karl. *Grundrisse.* Translation of Martin Nicolaus. Pelican 1973.

Maryland, Department of State Planning. *Maryland Chesapeake Bay Study, Report.* Wallace McHarg Roberts and Todd, Inc., March 1972.

Maryland Geologic Survey. Topographic Maps of Baltimore County and Anne Arundel County.

Maryland Historical Magazine.

Maryland, Regional Planning Council. *General Development Plan for the Baltimore Region.* September 1972.

Maryland, Regional Planning Council, and the Baltimore City Department of Planning. *MetroCenter/Baltimore, technical study.* Wallace, McHarg, Roberts and Todd, 1970.

Maryland, State Planning Commission, Baltimore Regional Planning Council. *Water Supply and Sewerage.* Technical Report no. 4. May 1959.

Mason, T.J., and McKay, F.W. *U.S. Cancer Mortality by County, 1950-1969.* Bethesda, Md.: Department of Health, Education and Welfare, Pub. no. (NIH) 74-514, 1975.

National Education Association. *Baltimore, Maryland, Change and Contrast—the Children and the Public Schools.* Washington, D.C., May 1967.

Olmsted Brothers. *Development of Public Grounds for Greater Baltimore.* 1904.

Porter, John. *The Vertical Mosaic, an Analysis of Social Class and Power in Canada.* Toronto: University of Toronto Press, 1965.

Radford, Edward P. "Cancer Mortality in the Steel Industry." Paper presented at Conference on Occupational Carcinogenesis, New York Academy of Sciences, March 27, 1975. mimeographed.

Reutter, Mark. "The Endless Road: Baltimore's Expressway Controversy." Paper, April 16, 1973.

Rothman, David J. *The Discovery of the Asylum.* Boston: Little, Brown, 1971.

Sennett, Richard. *The Uses of Disorder: Personal Identity and City Life.* Vintage, 1970.

Snow, Raymond W., and Frazier, Andrew S. "Racial Development of the Pennsylvania-Eutaw Corridor." Paper, Johns Hopkins University, December 1969.

Sober, Marc. "The Baptist Churches of Baltimore." Paper, Johns Hopkins University, December 1969.

Stanton, Phoebe B. *The Gothic Revival*

and American Church Architecture. Baltimore: Johns Hopkins Press, 1968.

Thomas, Brinley. *Migration and Urban Development*. Methuen, 1972.

University of Maryland. Cooperative Extension Service. *Maryland Soils*. Bulletin 212, May 1967.

Urban Design Concept Associates. *Segment Area Reports,* November 1, 1968; *Point III Reports,* July 1970; and *Roadway Corridor Design, Baltimore Highway System 3-A,* December 1970. prepared for Maryland State Roads Commission and Interstate Division for Baltimore City.

U.S. Commission on Civil Rights, Maryland State Advisory Committee. *Transcript of Hearings, Baltimore, Maryland, January 1971.*

U.S., Congress, House. Committee on Banking and Currency. Control of Commercial Banks and Interlocks among Financial Institutions. 90th Cong., 1st sess. Staff Report, July 31, 1967.

Waesche, James F. *Baltimore Today . . . A Guide to its Pleasures, Treasures, and Past.* Bodine and Associates, Inc., 1969.

Wallace, David A., and McDonnell, William C. "Diary of a Plan." *Journal of the American Institute of Planners* 37, 1 (January 1971): 11-25.

Wallace-McHarg Associates. *A Plan for the Valleys.* 1964.

Whitman, Ira L. *Physical Condition of Streams in Baltimore and Their Relation to Park Areas.* Report to Departments of Recreation and Parks, and Public Works, Baltimore, December 1966.

Wolman, Abel, and Hoffman, Janet. Interviews in *Metro News* (Johns Hopkins University Center for Metropolitan Planning and Research) 3, 1 (September 15, 1974.)

Wolman, M. Gordon. "A Cycle of Sedimentation and Erosion in Urban River Channels." *Geografiska Annaler,* 49 Series A, 2, 4 (1967): 385-95.

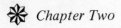 *Chapter Two*

New Orleans—The Making of an Urban Landscape

Frontispiece A. Aerial photograph of metropolitan New Orleans, looking northwestward across the Mississippi toward Lake Pontchartrain. See Frontispiece B for key to locations. Also see Figure 3, map of New Orleans and vicinity. (Photograph by Sam R. Sutton, courtesy Board of Commissioners for the Port of New Orleans)

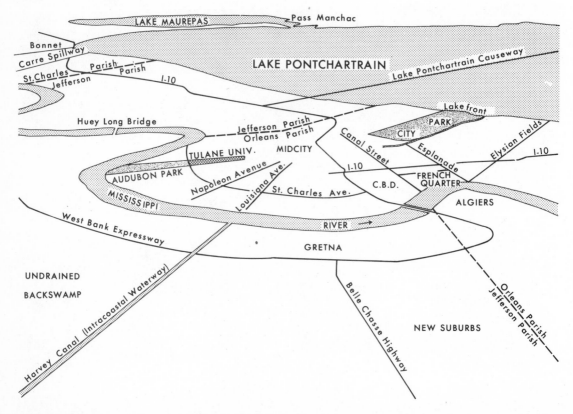

Frontispiece B. Key to locations, Frontispiece A. Only main landmarks are identified.

Foreword

A town is saved, not more by the righteous men in it than by the woods and swamps that surround it.

—Henry David Thoreau, 1854

It is not entirely a disadvantage to be born a member of a small isolated metropolis instead of a great central one. If the seed of its population be good and strong, if the geographical situation be a fortunate one, if the detachment from, and the connection with, the civilized world be nicely adjusted, the former being definite and the latter difficult (and surely these conditions were met with a century and a half ago on the banks of the Mississippi), there follows for the smaller metropolis a freedom of development with a resultant cleanness of character, which is as great a gain for a city as for an individual. In such a smaller mother-city, individual acts assume an importance, individual lives an intrinsic value, which it would be absurd to attribute to inhabitants of a great centre; our gods seem closer to us, our fates more personal. . . .

—Grace King, 1904

Because we [Southerners] started later, and because we were poorer than our fellow city dwellers in the North, we have had neither the time nor the money to immortalize—in concrete—quite as many of our mistakes as they did.

—Joel L. Fleishman, 1972

. . . and while neither Atlanta nor New Orleans yet vies seriously with New York, Chicago, Los Angeles as irreclaimable disaster sites, they are trying hard and cheerfully, and, given time, may well succeed.

—Reynold Price, 1972

The future of our city . . . cannot be foretold by looking to other places. It is to be found by looking at what we've been and what we are. . . . I know politicians are not supposed to wonder about these things. I'm a politician, but I'm also a New Orleanian, and that means I'm different.

—Moon Landrieu, 1972

Apologia and Acknowledgments

I accepted John Adams' and Ron Abler's invitation to write this "vignette" about New Orleans in large part to satisfy personal curiosity—I wanted to know more about New Orleans and about myself. I saw a chance to educate myself about a legendary part of America—a place which was terra incognita to me and, judging from the dearth of scholarly writing about New Orleans, not very well known to most other American geographers either. I was also curious to know whether one could "learn" a big city in a short time—not perfectly, of course, for even old-timers cannot do that, but well enough to explain how a city's gross patterns of internal geography get to be the way they are, and to explain how they relate to their neighboring areas. Above all, I wanted to see if one could draw a holistic picture of a place like New Orleans, where romance and reality are so cheerfully inter-changed—on the one hand recognizing the romance without wallowing in it, on the other hand recognizing the hard economic realities of urban life without treating the city as an economic machine. I had been telling students for a long time that all these things were possible; it was time to put up or shut up.

The reader must decide whether I have succeeded, for I am too close to this venture to judge, and I have grown too fond of New Orleans to be very dispassion-ate. (I have learned, if nothing else, that it is possible to fall in love with a city on short notice, even if one may not understand her perfectly.) To the degree that I have succeeded, however, it is less my success than the success of the throng of people who helped me, supported me, and educated me during my encounter with New Orleans. I owe the most to Sam and Joyce Hilliard, of the Louisiana State University Department of Geography, who nourished me in mind and body, and whose kindness I shall never be able to repay; to James Lewin of the New Orleans City Planning Commission, who showed me his adopted city and why he had fallen in love with it; to Dr. Milton B. Newton, Jr. of LSU, who argued me through the redneck country beyond New Orleans; and to John Chase, that extraordinary and literate gentleman (can one say more?), who helped me more than he may know.

I also owe a great debt to Captain Paul Vogt, and his fellow bar pilots at Pilot-town, who showed me the amazing business of getting ships in and out of the Mississippi River and showed me once again that Southern hospitality to strangers still thrives; to John and Ann Fluitt of the University of New Orleans; to Dr. Ronald Lockmann of the University of New Orleans geography department; to Ada Newton and Joyce Nelson for access to the excellent archives of the geography department's map room at LSU in Baton Rouge; Mrs. Connie Griffith and Mr. William Cullison, III, of the Special Collections Division of the Tulane University Library; Mr. Colin B. Hamer, Jr., of the Louisiana Division of the New Orleans Public Library. All gave me free access to invaluable archival material. Captain Albro Michell, Jr., of the bar pilots, essentially loaned me his entire library on the port of New Orleans.

I am also indebted to the officials of the remarkably hospitable public bodies of the New Orleans area: Dr. Gordon A. Saussy, assistant director of the Division of Business and Economic Research, UNO; Mr. Alfred C. Nichols, public relations and advertising manager of the Greater New Orleans Tourist and Convention Commission; Mr. William Smollen of STAR/NASA at Michoud; Mr. Robert Smith, manager for news and publications for the Board of Commissioners of the Port of New Orleans; Dr. David Slusher, state soil scientist for Louisiana; the geologists of the New Orleans District of the U.S. Army Corps of Engineers; Mr. Hugh N. Ford, director of the Jefferson Parish Planning Department; Mr. Peter J. Nogueira, research analyst for the Chamber of Commerce of the New Orleans Area; and Mr. Thomas W. Schnadelbach, Jr., senior planner of the New Orleans Regional Planning Commission. Special thanks go to Mr. Hugh G. Lewis for cartographic help, and to Mrs. Colleen Kristula for long hours of typing and retyping of manuscripts. Richard Ormrod, Helen Chelius, and Fred Kniffen all called my attention to things I would not otherwise have noticed. None of these kind people, of course, are responsible for my errors.

I owe a particular debt to those who read the entire essay in manuscript, and whose careful criticisms helped me find and hopefully eliminate some of my more egregious blunders: John Chase and Maurice Ries of New Orleans, Donald Deskins of the University of Michigan, James E. Vance, Jr., of the University of California at Berkeley, Donald Meinig of Syracuse University, and John S. Adams of the University of Minnesota at Minneapolis.

Finally, I am grateful beyond measure to my wife, Felicia, and to Miss Malvina Evans, who endured my day to day crotchets and eccentricities without reproach. The same goes for the people of New Orleans—a fine folk.

—Peirce F. Lewis
University Park, Pennsylvania
November 1973

The Eccentric City

Americans have rarely been very fond of their own cities. Poets, statesmen, and armies of crackerbarrel philosophers have repeatedly told us that virtue resides in rural places, while cities are dens of vice and iniquity. Thus, when headlines cry scandal in city governments; when city streets are fouled with garbage and air corrupted by smog; when we learn that people are fleeing the crime-ridden city for the green lawns of suburbia—we shake our heads in disapproval, but we are not surprised. Although the United States is one of the most urbanized countries on earth, our cities are not very successful creations. Most Americans know it, and many accept it as inevitable.

But there are exceptions—a select company of big American cities beloved by their residents and praised by visitors. This essay is about one of them—New Orleans, a city that has been admired perhaps more enthusiastically and persistently than any other American city. Nor has New Orleans gained its reputation by boosterism, either. (Unlike Los Angeles, Houston, New York, and other boastful places, New Orleans has rarely thought it necessary or seemly to broadcast its virtues to the world.) The ordinary Orleanian *assumes* that everyone else shares his admiration for his native city—*assumes* that outsiders envy his own happy condition and would instantly move to New Orleans if they only had the chance. From time to time, other Americans—especially those in upstate Louisiana who live outside the magic circle—have found this Orleanian attitude smug and have said so loudly. But it no more dis-tresses an old-time Orleanian to be called smug than it does a native of Boston or San Francisco —two other American cities that resemble New Orleans in civic self-assurance. Orleanians know very well that their native city occupies a special niche in America's small chamber of urban delights. It has been so for two and a half centuries.

Obviously, any city with a million people in its metropolitan ambit will possess defects, and New Orleans has more than a few.* Furthermore, the flaws are not merely cosmetic blemishes. Nobody who knows New Orleans, for example, would urge other cities to imitate her dreary record of chronic political rascality, her ominous racial affairs, the egregious quality of her public school system, or even the homicidal way her expressways are designed. But one can admire Paris without endorsing living standards in Parisian garrets. It is the same with New Orleans: we need not approve every particular to know that in its elusive *genre de vie* (what we inelegantly render in English as "lifestyle"), New Orleans is almost in a class by herself.

It is tempting, then, in this era of urban decay, to hold up New Orleans as a model—a place for other American cities to admire and

*More precisely, the 1970 census counted 1,046,000 people in the New Orleans SMSA (Standard Metropolitan Statistical Area) of Orleans, Jefferson, St. Bernard, and St. Tammany parishes. (A "parish" is the Louisiana equivalent of a county elsewhere in the United States.) The SMSA boundaries are highly artificial, however, and it would be more accurate to say that the population lay somewhere between 1.0 and 1.1 million in the city and its contiguous suburbs.

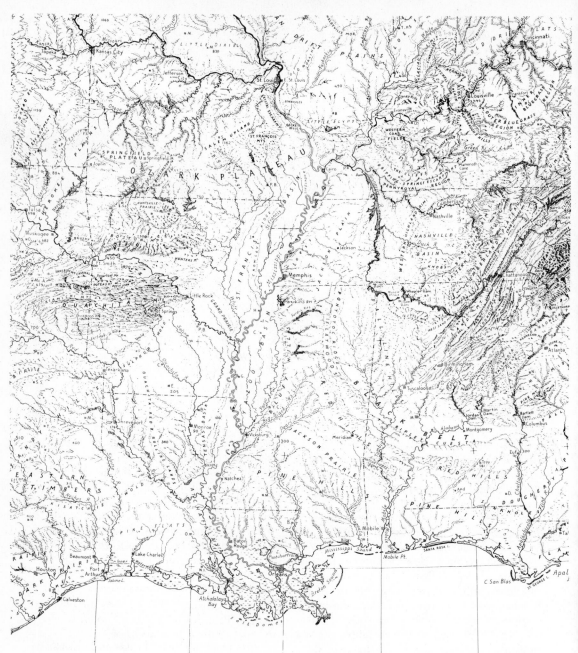

Figure 1. Landforms of the lower Mississippi valley. Many of the river's important peculiarities are shown on this superb *Map of the Landforms of the United States* by Erwin Raisz (1957). Note that the river's alluvial plain extends north of Cairo, Illinois, wherein access to the river is difficult; Memphis, Vicksburg, Baton Rouge, are all located where well-drained land briefly abuts the river. Even tributaries have trouble crossing the Mississippi's natural levees and flow parallel to it for hundreds of miles. Note also abandoned channels and deltas of lower Mississippi, creating alternation of swamps and lakes with levee ridges, and making East-West transportation difficult. Note absence of deltas on other rivers. Access to New Orleans is obviously easiest by river, or Lake Pontchartrain; overland routes from the upland South are difficult and costly. (Copyright Erwin Raisz, used by permission)

perhaps to imitate. New Orleans serves that function imperfectly, however. In the first place, it is by no means certain that New Orleans can long retain her most delectable qualities. As we shall presently see, sins of the past are catching up with her, as they have with other American cities, while increasingly she is pressed by economics and by fashion to re-model herself in a more conventional image. Second, many of the things that make New Or-leans special and admirable cannot be duplicat-ed by other urban places in the United States: many of her most important attributes spring from a history and a geography that are ec-centric to the mainstream of American urban experience. (Indeed, the cities that might profit most from a study of New Orleans are not American ones, perhaps, but those old cities in preindustrial countries that seek to retain traditional virtues but find it hard to make a living in the modern world at the same time.) And finally, New Orleans is not even an easy place to study. For a city of its size, age, and prominence, there is an uncommon scarcity of serious scholarly work on the city. To be sure, there are studies of certain aspects of New Orleans, and some—notably in local architecture and history—are distinguished and entrancing. But serious comprehensive studies of the contemporary city are hard to come by; published works about New Orleans too often tend to be narrow in scope, esoteric in topic, or dripping in saccharine—sometimes all three. This special quality of New Orleans scholar-ship is no accident, however, for it stems from the special qualities of the city itself.

A ROMANTIC SORT OF PLACE

From the outset, New Orleans was a foreign city, and it has never completely lost its foreign flavor. If Americans have never been very good at understanding cities, they have been even worse at understanding foreigners. Further-more, when Americans bought the city in 1803, it was no mere frontier village, but a robust place with a mature personality. By standards of the time, it was a good-sized city: the 1810 census counted New Orleans as the fifth largest city in the country—a position it maintained off and on until shortly before the Civil War (see Figure 5). Clearly it was big enough to resist assimilation into the American mainstream for a long time, and to keep its foreign ambience.

(French was spoken by a good many Orleanians until well into the twentieth century. When Louisiana seceded from the Union in 1861, the articles of secession were published in both French and English—as were all of Louisiana's laws.)

These Orleanians, furthermore, were a dif-ferent breed of foreigners than Americans were accustomed to dealing with. The American East Coast gentry, of course, had plenty of experi-ence in dealing with foreigners, but all obvious-ly of a rather inferior kind—half-naked "foreign" Indians, wretched Africans in chains, and a good many Europeans who came as indentured servants and the like—supplicants who no more merited esteem than Indians and Negroes. But the New Orleans Creole* was another sort, prouder even than a Bostonian. He considered his Franco-Spanish civilization obviously su-perior to that of England, and planets apart from the unwashed Kentuckians who landed, spitting tobacco, on the Mississippi levee. As H.W. Gilmore put it much later on, it was "the only case of its kind in American history . . . [when the] spreading American frontier ran into a culture which, on the basis of manners and fine appearance at least, was superior to its own".

While the Creoles were revolted by the Americans, the Americans were stunned by the finery of this transplanted Mediterranean city, and it seems doubtful if they, or generations of successors, really expected to understand the place. From the Creole's standpoint, the more misunderstanding the better, since social inter-course with barbarian Anglo-Americans was a loathsome prospect. Both parties invented their own mythology, sometimes by accident or

---

*The word "Creole" is widely used in two quite different senses. It derives from the Spanish word *crillo* "a child born in the colonies"—according to John Chase (*Frenchmen, Desire, Good Children. . . .*). In this context, it came to designate native-born white Orleanians of Spanish (and French) ancestry. Over the years, however, the word took on broader meaning, to include anybody or anything that is native to New Orleans or is associated with traditional New Orleans. Thus, in spite of stiff-necked whites, many New Or-leans' Negroes call themselves Creoles, and with pride. In the same sense, a much-loved variety of southern Louisiana tomato is a "Creole tomato" and the assemblage of traditional New Orleans cooking practices combine to form the famous "Creole cui-sine." A Creole skyscraper, on the other hand, is unthinkable; although a Creole might own one or even build it, modern things just can't be Creole.

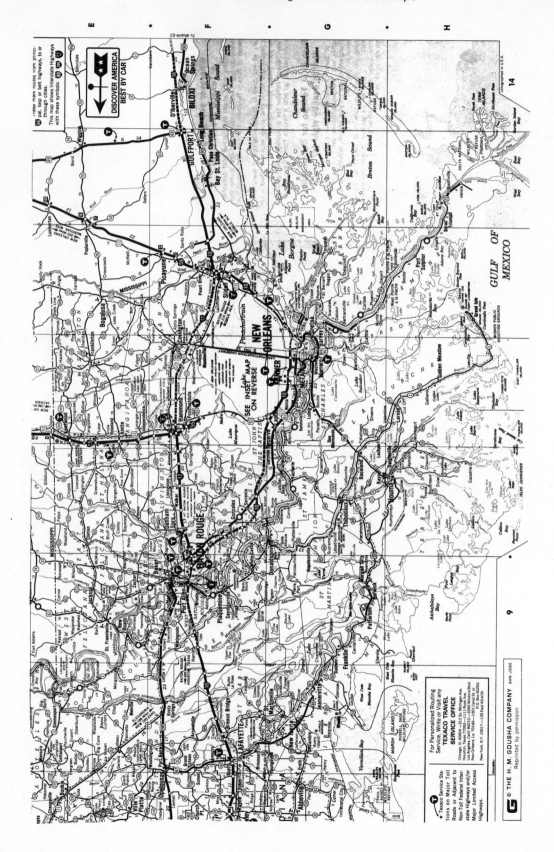

whimsy, sometimes through malice, but a city which was different enough to begin with became shrouded in an almost impenetrable fog of romance and fable. (Scholars evidently found the atmosphere excessively gassy, and fled.) The Civil War, which speeded the process of cultural convergence in many other parts of the country, only made understanding New Orleans more difficult. After all, New Orleans was by far the largest city of the South, and it was easy to believe that the wrongs inflicted at the hands of those same barbarian Northerners were more cruel and more numerous than the wrongs suffered by lesser places. So went the mythology, and so it grew. Whether the tales are true or not is quite beside the point; at the end of Reconstruction, New Orleans lay far outside the mainstream of American urban society and was quite content to remain there—in image if not in fact.

THE CITY LOOKED DIFFERENT

For a visitor, already prepared to believe that New Orleans is different, seeing the city is likely to confirm his convictions, for a good share of the city looks like nothing else in North America. It was so from early times. The urban historians Glaab and Brown remark that "by the 1840's travelers found a monotonous similarity in the appearance of American cities, particularly those that had been newly built in the West." Having made that statement, they immediately hasten to note that New Orleans was different—a foreign-looking city which most visitors found entrancing.

Part of the difference in appearance—and in the city's image—is simply the result of climate. New Orleans is a tropical city or nearly so; indeed, until fairly recently, the only tropical city of any consequence in the United States.* This

*By strict standards, most climatologists would call New Orleans *sub*tropical, not tropical. In January, the coldest month, the average day ranges between a low temperature of 45° F, and a high of 64° F, and

very fact enlarged New Orleans' image, for all Americans know that the tropics are both romantic and faintly corrupt. Visitors who came looking for an atmosphere of mildew and lassitude were quick to find it, especially in the summertime before air conditioning, when Orleanians quite sensibly paused for a lengthy midday siesta in the shade. Outsiders even blamed the long hot summer for the fetid condition of New Orleans politics, which had presumably rotted in the steaming heat. But visitors seldom failed to mention and admire the luxuriant vegetation, especially in the fashionable districts of the city, and even the slums looked somehow less slummy in a setting of banana plants and crepe myrtle. Many visiting authors seemed almost inspired. Even the misanthropic Mrs. Trollope, who entered the United States by way of New Orleans in 1827 and found nothing much to her liking, was "cheered ... by the bright tints of southern vegetation". When somebody took her for a walk in the nearby woods, "the eternal forests of the western world," they made her feel "rather sublime and poetical". (From what she wrote later on, one guesses she contracted spleen and vapors in the swamp.) Mrs. Trollope was not the last of the literati to be inspired by the combination of foreignness and tropical setting. According to C. Vann Woodward,

the weather bureau on one terrible February day a few years ago recorded a temperature of 7° F,—the lowest in thirty years and one which produced real suffering. But winter is short, and "cool" would be a more accurate description than "cold." Summer, by contrast, is sweaty and seemingly endless; temperatures in the 90s are recorded from March through early November, with drenchingly high humidity much of the time. The vegetation reflects the climate more tellingly than statistics—bougainvilla, bananas, sugar cane, and citrus all grow in and around the city. And, as in much of the humid tropics, there is no dry season at all. (For a fuller description of New Orleans' climate, see the U.S. Department of Commerce, Environmental Data Service's *Climatic Atlas of the United States*, [Washington, D.C.: U.S. Government Printing Office, June 1968].)

Figure 2. The environs of New Orleans. This splendid Gousha highway map of southeastern Louisiana illustrates the insular location of New Orleans, its isolation from the well-drained uplands of the "mainland" by the lakes and marshes of the backswamps. Only the natural levees are sufficiently well drained to support towns and farms. Where roads depart from the natural levees, they must be thrust causewaylike across uninhabited lakes and swamps. Note the importance of abandoned Mississippi courses and their natural levees as loci of Cajun population—Bayou Teche (Lafayette to Morgan City), Bayou Lafourche (Donaldsonville, Thibodaux, etc.), and dead-end roads in the old St. Bernard Delta east of New Orleans. (Copyright by H.M. Gousha Company, 1973; reproduced with permission)

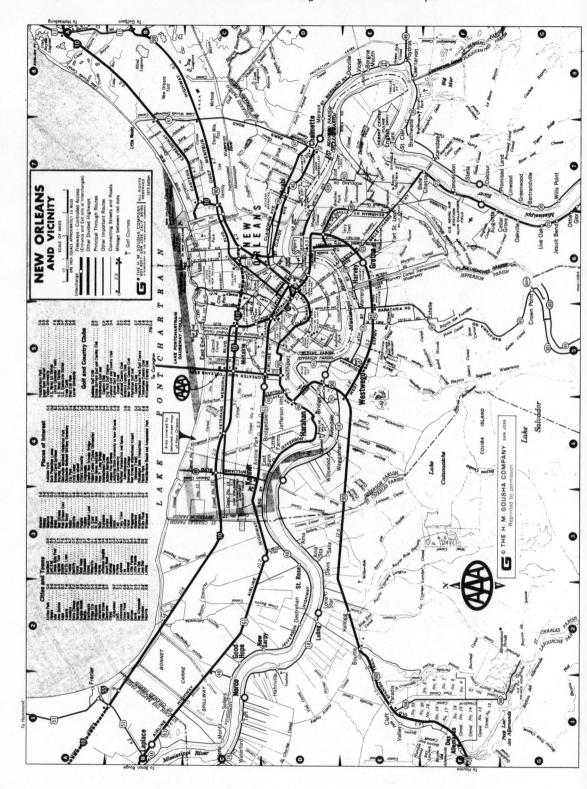

Lafcadio Hearn, who later won fame by celebrating the spooky romance of feudal Japan, found New Orleans enchanting, meantime pledging himself "to the worship of the Odd, the Queer, the Strange, the Exotic, the Monstrous." His books about New Orleans added considerably to the city's eccentric reputation, but did little to provide a dispassionate portrait of the city. With each additional author, the miasma grew thicker.

New Orleans buildings were foreign and eccentric too. It was not just the pastel stucco and cast iron of the French Quarter, nor just the flamboyant mansions of the Garden District, so celebrated in architectural literature. Even the modest houses of ordinary citizens (both white and black) were unusual. Part of the architectural flavor had descended through the Creoles from French and Spanish ancestry. Much more was imported from the Caribbean, where an early marriage of Indian and European ideas had given birth to picturesque houses that afforded maximum ventilation and shade. And more than a few stylistic quirks consciously aped changing European fancies, especially the more florid varieties which adorned the times of Victoria and Napoleon III. In a few instances, models for meaner domestic houses apparently filtered into the city from rural sections of the lower Mississippi valley, but standard American models were not much favored by the New Orleans elite, who generally set styles for the whole city. In architecture, New Orleans was foreign, not just in small areas, but for miles. If the mixture did not resemble any particular foreign city very much, it resembled the ordinary North American city not at all.

THE FLAVOR OF SALT

New Orleans' romantic differences are compounded by the fact that she is a seaport. All ports, of course, enjoy a certain worldly quality that comes from the constant mingling of products and people from far-off places, but again,

New Orleans is not even ordinary as a port. First of all, the port of New Orleans is big—ranking second only to New York in volume and value of cargo handled. Unlike New York, however, which does a good many things beside handling cargo, New Orleans embraces marine commerce with the same single-minded enthusiasm as Detroit makes automobiles. Manufacturing, by contrast, plays a relatively insignificant role in the city's economic life, and even that limited industry is mostly associated with the port—shipbuilding and the like.

This heavy dependence on the port has occasionally proved dangerous, for if the port is unhealthy, the city is in serious economic trouble. But shipping is a business that pays reasonably well, especially if that business is located at the entrance to the richest river valley on earth. Most of the time, New Orleans has stayed economically healthy, meantime thoroughly relishing her bigamous marriage to the river and the ocean. Obviously, going down to the sea in ships was a good deal more enjoyable than pouring pig iron or slaughtering hogs. There are still more poems written about Old Man River and the briny deep than about making machine tools or assembling transistor radios.

AN OLD IMPORTANT PLACE

Even if New Orleans had not been a romantic place, Americans would have found her difficult to ignore, especially in the early days of the Republic when so many of our national attitudes were forged and hardened. New Orleans occupied an extraordinarily important geographic location (never mind the romance), the possession of which was viewed as indispensable for our national well-being. Her command of the entrance to the Mississippi was like Québec's command of the St. Lawrence, and both cities were seen as gatekeepers to the continental interior. The possession of both cities by foreigners was threatening to merchants and frontier farmers—maddening to all red-blooded

Figure 3. New Orleans and vicinity. Note relation of well-drained natural levees and ill-drained backswamps away from the river; fine lines are drainage canals, carrying rainwater from levees into backswamp and generally follow old French property lines, perpendicular to river. Rectangular patterns in southwest are polders for agriculture. Compare heavily populated "East Bank" (north of river) Jefferson Parish with adjacent unpopulated St. Charles Parish, which lacks protection levees. Bonnet Carre Spillway lets Mississippi River floods pass directly into Lake Pontchartrain. (Copyright by H.M. Gousha Company, 1973; reproduced by permission)

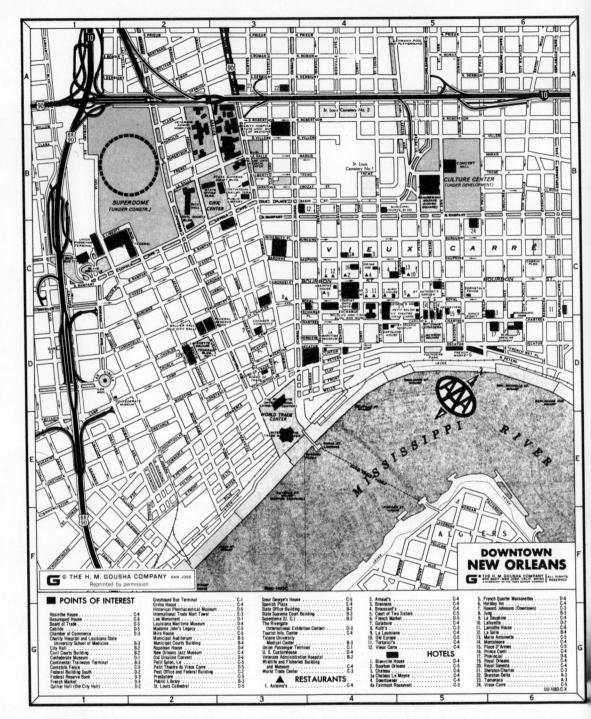

Figure 4. Downtown New Orleans. (Copyright by H.M. Gousha Company, 1973; reproduced by permission)

METROPOLITAN POPULATION, 1790–1970

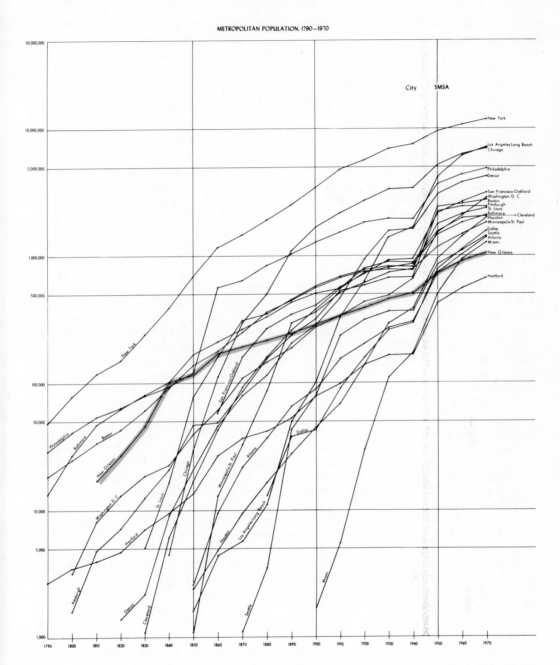

Figure 5. Population growth of America's twenty largest cities, earliest census to present. New Orleans joined the Union as the nation's fifth largest city and was on the verge of becoming the second city in the 1850s. Growth slackened abruptly after 1860, the result of railroad competition for the upper Mississippi hinterland. Thereafter, with slower growth, the city was in turn overtaken by two groups of cities—the railroad-industrial center of the North and East between 1850-1900; subsequently by the sun-and-space cities of the West and South, mainly between 1940 and 1960. (Abrupt jump in all cities between 1940-1950 is statistical aberration, resulting from census re-definition of cities as Standard Metropolitan Statistical Areas.)

patriots. American rage grew more furious after the Revolution, when permanent settlers began flooding into the upper reaches of those two great rivers. Despite several formal and informal raids on Québec, it presently emerged that America could not have her, and the national dudgeon subsided after the Erie Canal proved a better entry to the Great Lakes anyhow.

But New Orleans—as usual—was different. No imaginable canal could substitute for the Mississippi, which with its tributaries constituted a magnificent system of natural highways in the roadless territory that the newly independent Americans were about to occupy. While Québec was dangerous in imagery—a stone fortress brooding over an isolated river— New Orleans was a menace in fact, for in foreign hands it could throttle the commercial life of half the national territory. Ironically, the most succinct description of the city's importance came from that classic enemy of cities in general, Thomas Jefferson: "There is on the globe one spot, the possessor of which is our natural and habitual enemy. It is New Orleans. . . ."

Thus, New Orleans was important in myth and important in fact—indeed, in the company of American cities, uniquely so. Moreover, Orleanians have always known it and hastened to capitalize on the combination by deliberately surrounding the city with as much additional mythology as they could conjure. H. Brandt Ayers, the noted Alabama newspaper editor, has remarked that "you can't eat magnolias." Orleanians might disagree, for magnolias have paid the city handsomely. In early times, the image of Paris-in-the-Wilderness helped promote Creole separatism and was frequently used as a basis for claiming special treatment for New Orleans at the hands of state and national government. More recently, New Orleans has found that romance is a salable commodity and has built a tourist industry which ranks second only to the port in the city's economy. To read the brochures, New Orleans offers the tourist a variety of the less deadly sins, crusted with an antique patina, and smelling strongly of gardenias. If the metaphor is mixed, it causes little concern. It is the nature of romance to be inconsistent.

It is hardly surprising that this extraordinary city has spewed a prodigious outpouring of writing, by native Orleanians and visitors alike. As might be expected, some of it is very good: Lafcadio Hearn's gothic prose proved as much,

as did the novels and essays of George Washington Cable. Even today, the works of such native authors as John Chase, the gifted cartoonist and historian, can be sensitive and engaging. Equally, the majority of writing about New Orleans is very bad. A typical species is the semiliterate Victorian pseudopoetry that Mark Twain so loved to lampoon, and which was lamentably slow to expire in the swamps of the lower Mississippi. But good or bad, New Orleans writers have paid more attention to gumbo and hoopskirts, to scarlet women and duels at dawn, than to the harder realities of economics, geography, political science, or demography.

If Orleanians thought about this imbalance— and most of them surely did not—it must have seemed only reasonable. After all, New Orleans *is* a different sort of place, and what is more natural than to pay attention to eccentricities— especially when they are colorful and entertaining? After all, what other American city possesses a genuine indigenous cuisine—and, as Richard Collin vividly demonstrates, one of such variety and excellence? What other city, especially a Southern city, exhibited such tolerance to sin, or such an easy-going attitude toward race relations? What other American city is so strongly flavored with Mediterranean Catholicism, with carnivals that bridge the chasm between sacred and profane with such élan? Whose society was so brilliant, so exclusive, and so elusively foreign? What other city had such an illogical and dangerous site, but insouciantly went about its mixed business of commerce and fun in defiance of threats from pestilence, flood, and hurricane? Above all, what other city was so extravagantly charming?

Even scholars could convince themselves that New Orleans was different from other American cities in fundamental and important ways. What other Southern city had a demographic history like New Orleans—in fullest bloom while most of America was still rural, only to fall on evil days at the very moment that the country was being transformed into an urban nation? How had New Orleans managed to escape the racial tragedies of the 1960s, this despite her hateful history as the place to which slaves were sold down the river and despite the fact that the New Orleans metropolitan area contained a higher percentage of Negroes than any other city in the nation? Indeed, until the rise of Atlanta, what other big city did the South possess at all?

It is a useful and healthy thing for a city to

be proud of its heritage, to possess a sense of peculiar identity to cherish and preserve. But it is easy for Orleanians—too easy, in fact—to leap to the conclusion that their splended ghost-haunted city is so aberrant that the ordinary laws of nature do not apply to it. It may be worthwhile to study conventional cities, the Chicagoes, the Pittsburghs—even the eccentric Los Angeles, that wave of the urban future. But, the argument continues: there is scarcely any point for a scholar to study New Orleans, particularly if the scholar is predisposed to study cities in search of general urban theories. After all, if ordinary norms do not apply, then the city is not going to make any sense a priori. Equally unrewarding to the aspiring scholar, whatever he discovers about New Orleans remains particular to New Orleans and cannot be used as a reliable basis for the study of other places. It is enough to turn any scholar into other, more productive undertakings, and apparently it did.

The argument is much too pat, of course. Romance and curiosity are fine things, but a million people cannot survive by eating magnolias. New Orleans is an unusual city, but it is still a city: people live and work there, and, as in less exotic places, cause traffic jams when they travel to and from work. White and black people live in different parts of the city, and the geographic distribution of the races is not random. Many of the problems which afflict the "inner" parts of northern cities also afflict New Orleans, and just as Northerners are fleeing to the suburbs of Detroit and Omaha, so are Southerners doing it in New Orleans, albeit in somewhat different patterns. And so it goes. In many important ways, New Orleans is not unique, and it does not serve the city well to perpetuate the myth that she is.

On the other hand, New Orleans is not the average American city by any stretch of the imagination, and one may be grateful that she is not. Simultaneously unique and not unique, New Orleans has much to learn from the rest of the country's cities, even if it is nothing more than learning what *not* to do. Correspondingly, she may have a good deal to teach the rest of the nation as well, especially in the creation of gentle and humane urban environments.

THE ISLAND CITY

We shall have no "hyphenated Americans," Theodore Roosevelt used to say. Roosevelt, of course, was expressing both official policy and a deeply rooted national xenophobia. Foreigners are simply intolerable as permanent residents of the United States, and this country over the years has invented various ways to persuade or force foreigners to assimilate. One of the few ways that a foreign group can avoid being swept into the maintstream of American life is to find some island, some isolated nook where it can continue to grow as some exotic plant might grow undisturbed on some far-off Pacific atoll. (Thus the Mormons survived and flourished as an exotic culture in their Utah oasis.) It is true for cities as it is for national groups, and New Orleans has preserved its exotic individuality because it is a cultural island. And, as we shall presently see, the city is a cultural island largely because it was first a physical island.

New Orleans' cultural insularity persists at several different scales, much as a physical island might be located in several bodies of water at the same time—in a small estuary, which is the arm of a bay, which opens off a gulf, which in turn is an extension of the ocean. From least to greatest, New Orleans is an island in Cajun southern Louisiana, an island in the state of Louisiana, an island in the South, and an island in the nation. Each kind of insularity has affected her character and colored her urban personality.

Island Among Cajuns

Just as New Orleans began as a French city, much of southern Louisiana is French in ancestry. The city, however, is not just an extension of the countryside, as one might consider Wichita a creature of the Kansas prairies or Charlotte a creature of the Carolina Piedmont.

The rural southern Louisianian traces his ancestry mainly to French-Canadians, expelled by the British from New Brunswick and Nova Scotia in the mideighteenth century. These are the people from Acadia, and their descendents in Louisiana are called "Cajuns," a corruption of the word Acadian. Like their French-Canadian ancestors, the Cajuns are still a profoundly rural people, which the urbane Creole Orleanians emphatically were not, and are not now.

Outsiders often confuse Creoles with Cajuns, since French names dominate both groups, both are overwhelmingly Roman Catholic, and both have peculiarities of architecture and diet which set them apart from northern Louisiana and the rest of the South. But similar peculiarities also set them apart from one another. To take but one example, Cajun and Creole cuisine resemble each other as the bourgeois cooking of the French provinces resembles the haute cuisine of Paris; both are splendid, but they are not the same thing. So also the people —although both have French forebears, Creoles and Cajuns are entirely different species.

To the Orleanian, the Cajun is a hick from the swamps, a kind of hillbilly without hills. This country bumpkin is tolerated for his wildly accented jokes and tall tales, which are widely circulated by radio and on phonograph records. Otherwise, his influence on the cosmopolitan city is negligible. Nor has the city had much impact on the ordinary swamp Cajun; the main Cajun city in Louisiana, judging from names in the telephone directory and food on the restaurant tables, is not New Orleans at all, but rather Lafayette, 150 miles west.

Indeed, the Cajuns themselves are isolated; they could not have survived otherwise as a discrete ethnic group. The Mississippi Delta, where many of them live, is an area where transportation is extremely difficult by land, and not so easy by water either (see Figure 2). For example, it is forty-eight airline miles from the small town of Grand Isle into New Orleans; it is 109 miles by road, and until fairly recently there was no road. Even closer places like Lafitte and Delacroix sit amid swampland at the end of devious dead-end roads. They are not en route anywhere, and unless one is inextricably lost, he is unlikely to pass through either town by accident. Thus, as the Cajuns began their career in Louisiana as a profoundly nonurban people, two centuries of isolation did little to urbanize them. To the degree that they have joined the national mainstream, it is national television that has done it and not the influence of New Orleans. Meantime, New Orleans sits grandly aloof, occasionally patronizing the Cajuns, but usually ignoring them.

Island In Louisiana

If New Orleans is an urban island in rural Cajun Louisiana, she is an armed fortress in the context of Louisiana as a whole. In many American states, of course, there is considerable hostility between the rural and small town folk, as opposed to the people of the state's largest city. This, of course, is traditional "upstate-downstate" split which has set Chicago against the rest of Illinois, Detroit against Michigan, and New York City against upstate New York. In Louisiana the split is exaggerated to yawning proportions, for the difference is not merely between city and country, but between two disparate cultures (Figure 6).

Upstate Louisiana is the extension of what Professor Kniffen of Louisiana State University has called "the Upland South," the traditional South to most Americans, the South of Faulkner and Truman Capote. Its white ancestry is Anglo-Saxon, and heavily Scots-Irish, with almost no traces of ethnic groups outside the British Isles. Its religion is Protestant with a strong fundamentalist strain, and its home has been the complex of small dirt farms, hamlets, and small towns that dot the eroded piney hills where cotton once was king. The area is poor-dirt poor—and if it has lost some of its poverty in recent years, it is because many of the poorest farmers have given up and left their wretched little plots.

Politics in northern Louisiana have a strong Populist bias, stridently and colorfully represented by such men as Huey Long, a shrewd and sophisticated man who advertised himself to the public as an uncouth redneck and the mortal enemy of city slickers and big money capitalists. For Long, and the northern Louisiana constituency that reared him, New Orleans was wickedness incarnate, bad enough for its wealth and arrogance, but doubly detested for its Popery and foreign ways. When Long made occasional liason with the New Orleans political machine, he loudly announced how he disliked the job but had no other choice. (Long's private views were something else again. Once he had been safely elected governor, he set up permanent residence in New Orleans, where his sybaritic enjoyment of the city became something of a public scandal.)

The political antagonism is further complicated by the Cajuns, who are allied to New Orleans by religion and ethnicity, but linked to northern Louisiana in poverty and rurality. Even when Cajuns voted with their fellow-Catholics in New Orleans, southern Louisiana has only recently had the population to win statewide elections. As a result, New Orleans was often a political underdog and the subject of malevolent attentions from northern Louisi-

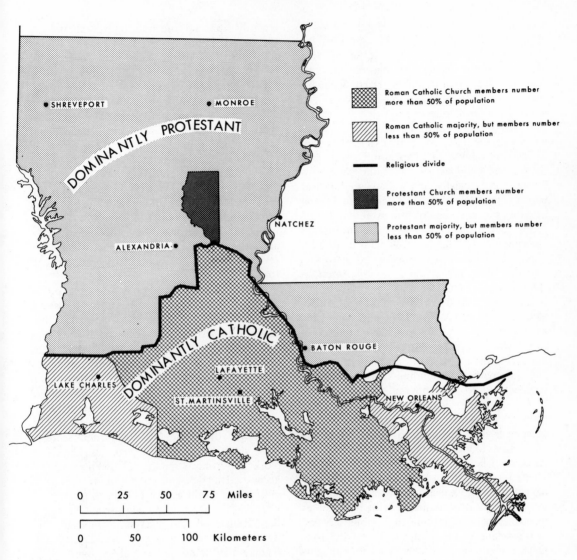

Figure 6. Religion in Louisiana. The sharp line between Protestant North and Catholic South is the most important social-cultural cleavage in Louisiana. Its earliest recognized boundary was the Amite River (cf. Figure 2), the ancient northern boundary of the Isle of Orleans. Note that metropolitan New Orleans is heavily Catholic, but not as overwhelmingly so as the more rural and isolated Cajun areas to the west. Source: National Council of Churches Division of Home Mission. "Churches and Church Membership in the United States," series C., no. 45, figure 64 (New York, 1957). Data are mapped by parish.

ana legislatures and governors. For a long time, however, the city possessed a formidable political machine known as the "Old Regulars," which held a balance of power in the state whenever factions of northern Louisianians went to war among themselves. Since such warfare was chronic in northern Louisiana, the North more often sought some kind of accommodation with the city, ordinarily with no particular regard for legal niceties. Thus, while Southern politics have a reputation for picturesque chicanery, Louisiana is in a class by itself, in large part because it was the only Southern state that had to contend with a big exotic city.

The results have been lurid in the extreme.

V.O. Key, Jr., perhaps the closest observer of the Southern political scene, subtitled his study of Louisiana politics "The Seamy Side of Democracy." The most vigorous description, perhaps, comes from T. Harry Williams, Huey Long's biographer, who quotes "an impressed twentieth-century critic" as writing: "Louisiana politics is of an intensity and complexity that is matched, in my experience, only in the Republic of Lebanon." According to Williams, "he decided that the state as a whole, but especially its southern section, was part of the Hellenistic Mediterranean littoral ... the western-most of the Arab states. Its people had a tolerance of corruption not found elsewhere in America. . . ." Williams continues: "Some [observers] have gone so far as to suggest that Louisiana is not really an American state, but a 'banana republic,' a Latin enclave of immorality set down in a country of Anglo-Saxon righteousness. . . . It is understandable that Louisianians have always had a non-American attitude toward corruption. They have accepted it as a necessary part of political life, and they have even admired it when it is executed with style, and, above all, with a jest."

A good many Orleanians, however, are not amused. The "toleration of corruption," they suggest, is not unrelated to the fact that the Mafia first found American roots in New Orleans, even before it had landed in New York. Then, too corruption is grossly wasteful, perhaps helping to explain Louisiana's chronically low ranking when compared with other states in quality of schools and other public services. Nor can one overlook the fact that the New Orleans public is justifiably suspicious of government *qua* government, with the result that a good many civic ills go unattended because the public is unwilling to support governmental attempts to correct them. It is true that most Americans distrust politicians, but in New Orleans that distrust reaches pathological levels.

Island in the South

The very fact she is a city, of course, makes New Orleans a foreigner in the South—a region which has been unurban in fact and antiurban in sentiment. (Populism has been endemic in the South in large part because the South has been traditionally the least urbanized area in the country.) Indeed, one can argue with some justice that the South had no real cities until

recently—that the true metropolises—Baltimore, Cincinnati, Louisville, St. Louis, Dallas, Houston, and even Miami, that exotic outpost of New York City—were located in the *rim* of the South, like a row of spectators standing on the brink but not daring to come in. The Nashvilles, the Chattanoogas, the Montgomerys, the Little Rocks have been small, sleepy, and largely lacking in the kinds of urban atmosphere that one associates with big cities. Even the densities of population within Southern cities have been low, with houses sitting on plots of ground that often look more like small farms than urban lots. That situation is changing now, and that is why metropolitan Atlanta and "the Atlanta spirit" are correctly viewed as revolutionary in the context of Southern culture.

If lack of urbanization has been an essential Southern trait, then one suspects that it may be wrong to call New Orleans Southern at all, that the city at best belongs to the outer rim. That may be true. In the fundamental things that set people apart from one another culturally—how they speak, eat, drink, dress, shelter themselves, and even how they view sex—Orleanians do not seem like Southerners. The New Orleans accent, for example, often sounds more like Brooklyn than like Vicksburg, and scholars have noted that New Orleans is like New York in having a number of distinct regional accents. The rich and cosmopolitan Orleanian cuisine is a world apart from the "hogmeat and hoecake" of the Upland South that Professor Sam Hilliard of Louisiana State University has described so artfully. As for drinking, the Orleanian may be no more bibulous than the Upland Southerner, but he drinks different things and under different circumstances. In her sexual mores, New Orleans has a reputation for permissiveness that may be undeserved, but is of long standing, as an 1853 gazeteer makes clear when it compares the "insalubrity of the climate" with "the morals of the city." The gazeteer goes on in a tone of indignation and surprise: "From certain flagrant features of open abandonment ... among a population so little American in its composition, it is not strange that an impression extremely unfavorable to the morals of the city should be produced." Today, the reputation of "open abandonment" is carefully nourished by bartenders, innkeepers, and other interested parties. That reputation is responsible for drawing libidinous conventioneers into town from great distances, and may help explain the disproportionate number of emancipated youths who wander the streets of the French Quarter at night, seeking adventure.

The Island as World City

But New Orleans' insularity emerges most obviously when the city is compared with other big American cities and, indeed, most other big cities in the world. The ordinary big city in the United States—especially one that relies on commerce for a livelihood—serves (and is served by) a hinterland which surrounds it and largely determines its character. Most of the midcontinental cities are obviously colored by their rural hinterlands, even those that are heavily industrial. Chicago, for example, as Carl Sandburg and Louis Sullivan have both said in their own ways, is a midwestern prairie city, just as Denver is a compound product of mountains and plains, and Seattle an offspring of the Pacific Northwest. The key to the economic and social character of each of these cities—as to a host of lesser places like Tulsa or Des Moines or Indianapolis—is the social and economic character of the territory which lies immediately adjacent to the city.

This is not true of New Orleans. To be sure, New Orleans serves as market town for the Cajun Mississippi Delta, and even for parts of Anglo-Saxon Louisiana and Mississippi that lie north of the city across Lake Pontchartrain—but that market is quite incidental and unimportant. New Orleans has a larger role—to link the distant and unimaginably rich interior of North American with the ocean.

Such phraseology may seem merely a pompous way of saying that New Orleans is a big seaport, but it is more than that. The richest part of New Orleans' hinterland is the *upper* Mississippi valley, not the lower valley, and that was true even before the boll weevil effectively wiped out the cotton belt of the old South—even while the bales still stood high on the levees at the foot of Canal Street. A large part of the agricultural and industrial products of the Midwest find their way to market by way of the port of New Orleans, and the port is the city's most important source of income. That wealth, because it comes from very far away, has allowed the city to ignore adjacent areas and even to ignore other ports which might potentially compete with her.

Phrase it in different terms. The hinterland of the ordinary inland city is shaped like an amoeba, spreading off into the surrounding countryside with fuzzy boundaries and uncertain impetus, but with a roughly circular shape. New Orlean's hinterland, by contrast, is shaped like a lollipop, with the city at the tip of the stem. Economically, the valley of the Mississippi is like a funnel, and New Orleans controls the outlet. Orleanians know it very well and see little reason for the city to concern itself with areas nearby, since they are irrelevant to her economic well-being. Indeed, their very poverty and lack of sophistication merely reminds New Orleans that the city is an especially favored place. If nearby people gnash their teeth in rage at the Orleanian's smug belief in his own superiority, it does them no good. New Orleans *is* rich, it *is* superior, and its nearest competitors are half a continent away.

Despite New Orleans' rather parochial pride, of course, she is not unique, for there are other cities like her, both in the United States and elsewhere in the world. But to list those cities merely reaffirms the eccentric brilliance of New Orleans, for the list includes some of the greatest and most glittering cities on earth. New York is like her, connected to the wealth of the Great Lakes by the umbilical cord of the Hudson and Mohawk valleys, its harbor open to Europe and the world, but scorning nearby New Jerseyites and other lesser breeds without the law. San Francisco is like her, commanding the Golden Gate, through which the Babylonian treasures of the interior West pour out to the Pacific and the world beyond—but culturally closer to Hong Kong and Singapore than to Fresno. The great colonial capitals—Calcutta, Alexandria, Shanghai—were like her, each secure in its marshy wilderness, each extending its tentacles into an unbelievably rich hinterland, while scorning the groundling masses who huddled nearby. So too the great imperial seaports—St. Petersburg in the Neva marshes; Venice on its islands at the foot of the Alpine passes; Byzantium commanding from its Golden Horn the Mediterranean to one side, the vast plain from the Vistula to the Caucasus on the other. Carthage was like her, on the edge of the desert, but demanding tribute from the trade between the eastern and western basins of the Mediterranean.

All of these cities are ports, to be sure, but that obscures the point. In a larger sense they

were oases like Samarkand and fabled Karakor-
um, which never depended on the area around
them, but instead defied and scorned them. The
wealth of these cities rests on distant, foreign,
and romantic places.

Such environments may breed great and rich
cities, but they do not breed humility among a
city's inhabitants. Nor do they breed a tendency toward introspection. If the Orleanian thinks
of his city in comparative terms, he usually
makes comparisons with other cities he believes
to be competitors—Mobile, perhaps, or the upstart Houston. The comparisons, quite naturally, are invidious. He rarely thinks of comparing
New Orleans with Byzantium or Samarkand,
and perhaps it is just as well. He has enough to
nourish his self-confidence already.

A Place on the River

THE IMPOSSIBLE BUT INEVITABLE CITY

When one glances at a small scale map of the United States, it is obvious that there had to be a city at the mouth of the Mississippi River. Common sense demanded one, and so did experience. Common sense also tells us that the location determined the kind of place New Orleans was to become.

Although the location of New Orleans is obvious on a small scale map, it is far from obvious when one examines a detailed map of the swamp where the Mississippi debouches into the Gulf of Mexico (see Figure 2) and even less obvious when one visits the area. The Mississippi Delta is a fearsome place, difficult enough for building houses, lunacy for wharves and skyscrapers. Nor have environmental problems disappeared under the onslaught of modern technology. Yellow fever was eradicated around 1900, but flooding remains a constant threat. Foundation materials are the consistency of glue in many parts of the city and there are few old buildings or sidewalks that have not settled or broken since they were built. Most dreaded are the hurricanes that boil out of the gulf with random ferocity, pushing flood waters ahead of them.

Yet the city is still there. The apparent paradox between excellent location and miserable location merely illuminates the distinction between two terms—"site" and "situation"—which urban geographers use to describe the location of cities. *Site* is the actual real estate which the city occupies, and New Orleans' site is wretched. *Situation* is what we commonly mean when we speak of a place with respect to neighboring places. New Orleans' situation is her location near the mouth of the Mississippi, and the fact that a million people work and make a living on this evil site only emphasizes the excellence of the situation. There is no contradiction. If a city's situation is good enough, its site will be altered to make do.

That is precisely what happened in New Orleans. The situation guaranteed New Orleans prosperity, but the site guaranteed that the city would be plagued by incessant trouble—yellow fever, floods, and unbearable summer heat. And because it was so difficult, the site also guaranteed that the form of the city's physical growth would be shaped by local environment to a far greater degree than in most other American cities.

In a word, New Orleans was shoehorned into a very constricted site. It is scarcely surprising that the shoe has pinched from time to time. Nor is it surprising that the city has taken some very strange shapes as a result. Further, some of New Orleans' most important internal patterns—the distribution of Negro population to name but one of many—can be explained directly or indirectly by the difficulties and curiosities of local environment.

RIVER, DELTA, AND CITY

To understand how these shapes have evolved, to understand the extraordinary difficulties of building and maintaining a city here, one must understand what the immediate physical site of New Orleans is like. That site, like the personality of the city itself, is an offspring of the Mississippi River, a direct result of the river's behavior in its lower courses over the last several thousand years. Like the city it nourishes, however, the Mississippi is unusual—quite different, indeed, from any other large North American river. And the difference is not just a matter of size.

To begin with, the Mississippi is unusual because it has a delta. Not only do most North American rivers lack deltas of any kind, their mouths are *embayed*—that is, the sea has entered the river mouth and flooded it (see Figures 1 and 2). Nearly every river in the world is that way, and the reason is the same. During glacial times—most recently about 25,000 years ago—sea level dropped because considerable ocean water was locked up in huge sheets of continental ice. At the glacial maxima, when sea level was lowest, rivers cut down to meet the new low sea level, and then, when the ice melted and sea level rose again, their valley mouths were flooded to form the estuaries that line the coast of North America today.

Finding a site for a city at the mouth of an embayed river poses no special difficulty. A host of big port cities—like London, Hamburg, and Old Québec—grew up quite naturally at the narrow inland neck of the estuary—the first place where ships were forced to use the same channel and the first place where land traffic could conveniently cross the river. But there is no embayment on the Mississippi, which is uniformly wide for hundreds of miles upstream (Figure 1). Correspondingly, south of Cairo, Illinois, where the Mississippi valley opens out into its great deltaic plain, no place on the river is much easier or harder to cross than any other, and bridges were out of the question until fairly recently. Nor is there any well-defined head of navigation until one reaches Minneapolis; indeed, the shallowest and most treacherous water in the lower Mississippi is across bars at the mouth of the river in the Gulf of Mexico. (To locate a city there, where the highest point is a tussock of salty grass, would be insanity.) In fact, there is no high ground on the lower Mississippi below Baton Rouge, more than 200 miles upstream from the Gulf (Figure 1). In sum, the Mississippi River demands a city at

its mouth, but fails to provide any place for one.

To make matters worse, the Mississippi's delta projects into the Gulf of Mexico and causes trouble both for seagoing ships and coastal vessels. Because the several mouths of the river are flanked by extremely low land— little more than grassy sandbars on mudflats— the river mouths are extremely hard to find, and equally easy to confuse with a myriad of bayous that lead into the coastal marshes and then fade away. Second, there is no way to get into the river by water except through the mouths, and no way for coastal ships to cross the upstream river. As a result, coastal vessels from a place like Pensacola, heading for Lake Charles or Galveston, or even for New Orleans itself, would necessarily leave the sheltered coastal waters and head out into the uncertain gulf, either to round the delta, or, optimistically, to find the mouth of the river. For shallow-draft coastal vessels to embark into the stormy gulf, the detour was at best risky, at worst suicidal.

Thus, from the very beginning, mariners had three basic questions, each bearing on where ships and boats could go, and in turn where a city could logically be expected to prosper.

1. Can the river be reached by deep-water vessels in any way other than by entering the mouths of the river far out in the Gulf of Mexico? (Masters of north-south ships were interested in the answer to this question.)
2. Can longshore shipping find its way through the delta by some sheltered inland route, and thus avoid crossing the open water of the gulf? (This question applied to ships traveling east-west.)
3. Is there any place in this featureless, slimy plain where goods can be off-loaded and stored for a time without risk of flooding?

The answer to all these questions was "yes," but a qualified "yes." And, in a faltering sort of way, they pointed to the place where New Orleans was ultimately to grow and flourish. To understand how that happened, and simultaneously what sort of site the city was to occupy, it is useful to turn the clock back and see what the river has been doing over the past few thousand years, and what sort of delta it has been building.

EVOLUTION OF THE SITE OF NEW ORLEANS

Foundations of the Delta: What lies beneath.

From Cairo southward, the Mississippi River generally follows a broad downwarp in the earth's crust. That downwarp, called the Mississippi Embayment, has allowed the ocean periodically to invade the continent as far north as southern Illinois (Figure 1). The southern end of the embayment in the New Orleans area is still sinking at a perceptible rate; an average figure, often cited, is about three inches per century. In some places, however, subsidence is considerably faster, and there are places in the delta where sugar cane fields, cultivated by eighteenth century farmers, are now completely under water.

All other things being equal, this crustal subsidence should have put all of southeastern Louisiana under water with an arm of the Gulf reaching north at least as far as Baton Rouge and perhaps much farther. If that had happened, of course, there would be no delta as we know it, and no New Orleans. What made the difference was continental glaciation.

Although the ice spread over much of the continent at least four successive times, it never came within 500 miles of the site of New Orleans. It did two things to the Mississippi River system, however, which ultimately made New Orleans possible and was to shape her development as a sculptor shapes his clay. First, the ice wiped out a number of preglacial drainage systems in the Midwest and rerouted drainage toward the Mississippi. As a result, the Mississippi River system was much enlarged. Second, the ice carried an enormous volume of miscellaneous debris, while simultaneously generating windstorms which deposited blankets of silt all across the upper and lower Mississippi basin. As the glaciers melted, both ice-borne debris and windblown silt eventually found their way into the river. The combination—an increased flow of water and an increased burden of material—caused the Mississippi to begin extending its delta at a rapid rate, filling the southern end of the embayment even as it was sinking.*

*The Mississippi, like all rivers, sorted material at the same time it was depositing that material. The coarsest material deposited by the melting ice— boulders, cobblestones, and gravel—were mainly left

Thus, if one imagines a cross-section cut through the delta from east to west, it would resemble a saucer made of preglacial bedrock filled with layer upon layer of deltaic material —silt, clay, lenses of sand, and a large bulk of soupy organic matter which results from the decomposition of swamp and marsh vegetation. The underlying bedrock which forms the floor of the saucer dates back to the Pleistocene geologic epoch, a million or so years ago, but is not really rock in the conventional sense. Rather, it varies between semicompacted clay, silt, and silty sand. Altogether, the cross-section rather resembles a shallow clay saucer filled with layer upon layer of warm jello.

North of Lake Pontchartrain, the Pleistocene "rocks" crop out at the surface to form a low bluff which parallels the lakeshore; north of the bluff the material has been eroded into low hills, now covered with spindly pines—a region so totally different from the flat delta around New Orleans that it seems another world. Although it is thirty miles and more from downtown, this rolling Pleistocene country is much beloved of New Orleans real estate dealers, who are luring exurbanites into the hilly woods with the enticement of inexpensive "quarter acre estates," with no foundation problems and freedom from danger of flood. With an interstate highway now completed from downtown New Orleans, the southern edge of the Pleistocene in St. Tammany Parish and in Hancock County, Mississippi, is beginning to look like Suburbia-in-the-Woods, and the sleepy country villages of Slidell, Louisiana, and Picayune, Mississippi, are turning into hives of land speculation (Figure 2).

The bluff on the northern edge of Lake Pontchartrain is caused by a group of faults, and the Pleistocene material has been dropped below the surface of the shallow lake, where it continues to dip gently southward below New Orleans. Under the city, it lies seventy to a hundred feet below the surface of the delta. This fact is of great importance to builders of skyscrapers and other heavy structures, for the deltaic material is usually too weak to support

in the upper river, far to the north. Thus, by the time the Mississippi neared the Gulf of Mexico, only fine materials were left—sand, silt, clay, and even smaller particles. Gravel and stone are so scarce in the vicinity of New Orleans that building contractors and cement manufacturers must have the materials shipped in by barge. Many children in New Orleans have never seen a rock.

much weight. If a builder has large scale ambitions, he must be prepared to sink pilings a
minimum of seventy feet to gain solid footing
on the Pleistocene, unless he is lucky enough to
find an old buried sandbar of the Mississippi
on which to rest his foundations. Either way, it
is a chancy and expensive business, and one
important reason why skyscrapers and big
bridges were late in coming to New Orleans.

The Surface of the Delta

Although the detailed geologic history of the
Mississippi delta is very complicated, the general mechanics of delta formation are well
known, and have been lucidly described by
Professors Fisk, Russell, and other geologists
from the Coastal Studies Institute at Louisiana
State University, as well as geologists Kolb,
van Lopik, and Saucier of the Waterways Experiment Station of the U.S. Army Crops of
Engineers in Vicksburg. At a general level, however, these mechanical principles are fairly
straightforward, and it is helpful to understand
them, since they help explain minute but sys-
tematic differences in elevation within the city,
as well as differences in subsurface material.

These may sound like trivial matters, but
in New Orleans they are not. Except for levees
and artificial hills, no part of New Orleans is
more than fifteen feet above sea level, a good
part lies within five feet of sea level, and much
of it is below sea level. Under such conditions,
even a few inches of elevation can determine
whether a particular area is habitable or not.
Differences in material are equally important.
Silt, for example, drains well and makes a
reasonable foundation. Organic material, by
contrast, drains badly and generally makes
wretched foundations. In sum, the river's
geologic history helps explain the city's human history, and its contemporary patterns of
growth and internal development.

Old Distributaries and New Land

A river like the Mississippi builds delta land
in two quite different ways, and the New Orleans metropolitan area contains both kinds.
The first is by depositing material where the
river empties into the sea. Often, such deposits
take the form of sandbars or mudbanks which
occur just off the river's mouth and often im-
pede the channel. If these deposits accumulate
substantially, an island will form and the river
will be split into two or more distributary chan-

nels. The contemporary Mississippi is doing that
today about twenty miles below Venice,
Louisiana, where it divides into three major distributaries called respectively Pass à l'Outre,
South Pass, and Southwest Pass (Figure 2).
(The latter two are the main deep-water ship
channels into the Mississippi, with the Southwest Pass carrying by far the larger volume of
traffic because it is deepest (see Figures 1 and
2).

Obviously, where the river separates into
several courses, no pass contains the scouring
power of the main river upstream. Although
the Mississippi is a very deep river in its main
channel—with one pool opposite the French
Quarter in the neighborhood of 200 feet deep
—the passes are much shallower and have the
disconcerting habit of silting up. In time the
river may abandon them completely. Such
silting in the distributaries occurs constantly
and unpredictably, both in the channels and
over the bars; indeed, the difference in behavior
between the distributaries and the sinuous main
river has a certain official sanction. The pilots,
who guide ships from the Gulf up to New Orleans, are divided into two independent organizations—the "bar pilots," responsible only for
piloting over the passes and Gulf bars; and the
"river pilots," who take over at Pilottown and
guide vessels upriver to the city (Figure 2).
The division point is where the river changes
character.

Keeping the river open, furthermore, is a
serious full time concern of Orleanians, for the
health of the port depends on maintaining a
deep channel. Significantly, one of New Orleans' folk heroes is Colonel James Eads, who is
nationally known for building the Eads Bridge
at St. Louis in the 1870s—the first big trans-
Mississippi bridge ever to be built. His fame
in New Orleans, however, rests with the "Eads
Jetties," which he built at the opening of South
Pass to force the river to scour a reliable, deep-
water channel for ocean-going ships. (By 1879
the jetties were in place, and the old sandbars
were gone forever). In contemporary times, the
job of keeping a clear channel of forty foot
draft belongs to the U.S. Army Corps of Engineers, which is also responsible for building flood
control and navigation works in the metropolitan area, as elsewhere along the Mississippi. The
corps has come in for acerbic criticism in many
parts of the country for alleged sins against nature, but the corps enjoys considerable popu-

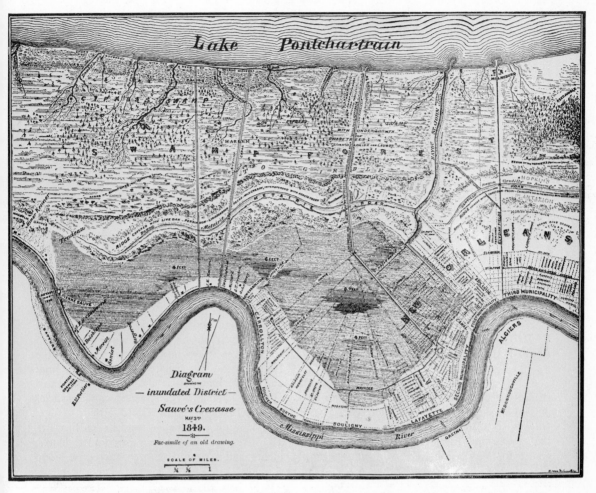

Figure 7. New Orleans after the breaching of Sauve's Crevasse, May 3, 1849. Natural levees of the Mississippi and Bayou Metairie remain unflooded (cf. Figure 8). Present-day "Mid-City"—at the convergence of plantation property lines—is under nine feet of water. Note also: Bayou St. John connecting with Carondolet Canal into back side of French City (First Municipality)—which newly built "New Orleans Canal" (New Basin Canal) links Lake Ponchartrain to American City (Second Municipality). Third Municipality was low income area. Village of Carrollton was separate suburb, created by horse railway along Nayades (St. Charles) Avenue. (Report on the Social Statistics of Cities, U.S. Census Office, 1887)

larity in New Orleans and—not surprisingly—wields considerable political influence.

Just as the river is making and abandoning distributaries today, so it made them in the past. Two abandoned distributaries meander through the New Orleans area, and both have left important marks on the city. One of them wandered away from the Mississippi at Kenner Bend, about twenty miles above the French Quarter, and strayed eastward toward the Gulf in a sinuous path roughly parallel to the river

and north of it (Figure 7). When the river abandoned the distributary, it was left as a discontinuous sluggish bayou west of town called Bayou Metairie, its eastern section variously called Bayou Sauvage or Bayou Gentilly. (In Louisiana patois a *bayou* is any stream or small river.) Although the Metairie-Gentilly Bayou was never important to Europeans as a route of water transportation, it is paralleled by a belt of fairly well-drained ground which provided a flood-free *land* route into the city—

from the west via Metairie Road, from the east via Chef Menteur Highway and Gentilly Boulevard (Cf. Figures 7 and 3). Metairie Road for most of its history was a rather bucolic path (*métairie* = farm), since there is another route into the city from the west, leading along the riverbank from Baton Rouge—the so-called River Road. Gentilly "Ridge," however, has always been the main road into New Orleans from the east, carrying both national highways (U.S. 90) and the main line of the Louisville and Nashville Railroad (Figure 2).

The other distributary—Bayou Barataria—is less important, if more colorful, since it heads south into the swamps where nobody except a few Cajuns and the pirate Lafitte ever lusted to go. More recently, however, real estate developers have been pushing their suburbs into the swamps by way of Bayou Barataria's banks, for reasons which we must now examine (cf. Figures 2 and 3).

NATURAL LEVEES, CREVASSES, AND AN UNDEPENDABLE RIVER

The river's other method of making delta land is more spectacular and considerably more important to the evolution of contemporary New Orleans. It involves nothing less radical than the Mississippi River abandoning its lower course for tens or hundreds of miles at a time and lunging out to sea by an altogether new route. When the river does this—as it does regularly every several hundred years—it leaves great gashes across the delta and, in combination with the sea, redistributes geography in a wholesale way. Consider how it happens and what it has done to New Orleans.

Begin with the river meandering across its floodplain to the sea (Figure 8). Most of the time, the river does little work; that is done at flood time, when fast-moving water picks up additional material that is normally untouched. Where the muddy river rises and spills over its low banks, its velocity is abruptly reduced, partly because the spillover is shallow and turbulent, partly because the current is checked by the friction of riverbank and dense thickets of vegetation. Consequently, the coarsest material is abruptly dropped to collect in a belt along the riverbank. (In the lower Mississippi, "coarse" material is mainly silt, since the coarser sand and gravel have mostly been left behind upstream or are moving down the bed of the river by traction.) Farther back from the river, as the overbank flow is slowed, finer and finer material is dropped, until almost nothing is left but nearly microscopic particles that may take days or weeks to settle.

The result is immediate and straightforward. The river systematically raises up its banks, higher and higher with each successive flood

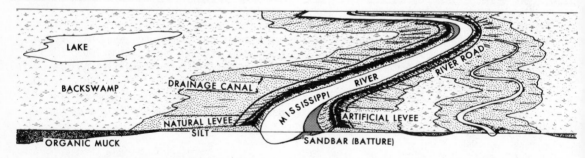

Figure 8. Idealized section of the Mississippi River, showing relationship of river to natural levees, backswamps, and human settlement. In flood, river deposits silt along its banks, creating very low broad ridges called "natural levees." Behind the natural levees, standing water creates habitat for swamp-loving vegetation; organic material accumulates in these low wet places, producing mucky "backswamps." Farms, roads, and towns are built along the natural levee and shun backswamps. Natural levees are made more habitable by digging drainage canals perpendicular to the river, which carries rainwater off into backswamp, and by building artificial levees atop the natural levees. Where river meanders, water is deepest in swift current on outside of bends; on insides of meanders, water is slack and sand accumulates in bars. In low water, these bars are exposed. Note that distributary channel also has natural levees, connecting with main river levees to form enclosed swampy basins; Mid-City New Orleans is such a basin.

(Figure 8). The French word is *levée*—meaning "raised up"—which is exactly what a levee is. One should not confuse the *natural levee* with the artificial levees later built atop them. An artificial levee may be thirty feet high and faced with concrete or rip-rap; it is one of the most prominent features in the landforms of New Orleans. The natural levee, by contrast, is so subtle that many Orleanians are unaware of its existence. At New Orleans, the crest of the natural levee is ten to fifteen feet above sea level and a mile or two wide. Obviously with such dimensions its slope away from the river is extremely gentle (a bicycle rider is scarcely aware of the slope), and its inner boundary where it merges with the *backswamp* can be defined only arbitrarily. From the ground, one must strain to see it, but from the air, it is the most striking feature of the landscape aside from the river itself. It is a simple fact that *the natural levees of the Mississippi and lesser streams provide the only well-drained areas in the whole of southeast Louisiana* (cf. Figures 2, 3, 7, and 8). Nearly all settlement, both urban and rural, is located on natural levees—partly because for a long time the river provided the only reliable transportation in this watery wilderness, but mainly because the natural levees provided the only place that was reasonably safe from flood and the only easy place to build roads and buildings.

For the first 200 years of New Orleans' history, the city was chiefly confined to the natural levee of the contemporary Mississippi, or, as we have seen, along Bayous Metairie, Sauvage, and Barataria—natural levees of abandoned distributaries of the river (see Figure 9). The hideous alternative was to build in the backswamp, the low perenially flooded area back from the river a mile or two—during most of New Orleans' history a pestilential morass whose most polite description was "back of town." Less politely, these swampy fringes of the city were called variously Crawdad-town or the "Quarter of the Damned." With most of the silt and much of the clay already left behind, the floodwaters had only submicroscopic material left to deposit—ooze, to put it charitably. There was plenty of vegetation, however, and, as centuries passed, rotting organic material would accumulate to great depths. In time, the material would become peat and eventually soil, but as David Slusher, Louisiana State Soil

Scientist, points out, one cannot dignify most it by calling it soil—not yet at any rate. It is simply a black, slimy material that varies in consistency between thin soup and dense glue. In sum, the backswamps are not very attractive places to build cities, and for most of New Orleans' past not even the most poverty-stricken inhabitants would venture to live there. The city simply came to a stop at the edge of the backswamp.

Although backswamps are generally odious places, New Orleans' are particularly so, especially in the Uptown end of town. ("Uptown" generally means "upriver"; see Appendix A.) The reasons are simple and deadly. The Mississippi rounds the Uptown area in a great semicircular meander, with the result that the Mississippi's natural levees bound the area on three sides (Figure 9). The side to the north, however, is also blocked by the lower but continuous natural levees of the abandoned Metairie distributary. In all, the middle of the Uptown area, later to be dubbed "Mid-City," is surrounded completely by natural levees which have turned it into a shallow bowl whose center lies below sea level. At best it was wet, but after heavy rains or a flood it filled up with water, most of which stayed to form a noisome swamp (Figure 7). Within this century the city has found ways to pump the water out and make Mid-City habitable, but in prehistoric times, when water rose high enough in the bowl, it spilled northward over the lowest place in the Metairie levees. That low place eventually turned into a channel—a small, sluggish, but profoundly important stream called Bayou St. John (Figure 7). This miserable stream, flowing into Lake Pontchartrain, was one of the main access routes into early New Orleans. We shall return to it presently.

As the river builds its natural levees however, it is also extending those levees into the Gulf. The combination sounds innocent enough, until one recalls that the river *requires* a certain gradient, no matter how slight, in order to maintain a current. If the current slackens too much, material is deposited in the riverbed, which literally lifts itself by its own bootstraps. Thus, as a matter of simple geometry, as the river's mouth extends farther and farther, any particular upstream stretch imperceptibly rises higher and higher with each new flood and each new increment to the natural levees. In time, the river will stand some considerable eleva-

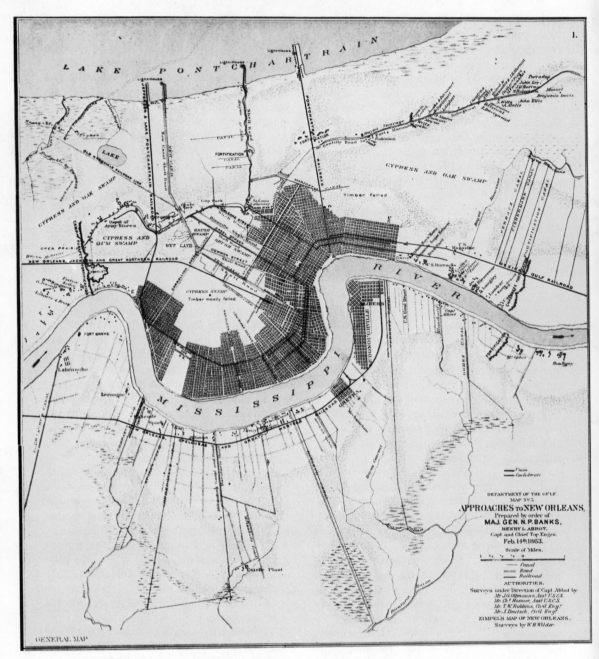

Figure 9. The superb "Banks Map" of 1863 was prepared by the Union Army for military purposes. It is one of the best nineteenth century maps of New Orleans. Note how closely the city is confined to the natural levees of the Mississippi (cf. Figure 8). "West Bank" (south of the river) is still rural, but farms, roads, and villages are also confined to the natural levees. The only other permanent settlements are located along Bayou Metairie-Gentilly, an old distributary channel of the Mississippi with its own small natural levees. Note that military defenses are necessary in only a few places, because there are only a few places whereby the city can be approached—via the natural levees, via the river, or via the canals from Lake Pontchartrain. (Courtesy of the Louisiana Collection, Special Collections Division, Tulane University Library)

tion above the adjacent floodplain (cf. Figure 8).

That is the reason why small streams in southern Louisiana do not flow into the Mississippi as tributaries, but instead flow away from it, or parallel to it, always avoiding the natural levees of the larger stream. (See Figure 2; but the same is true of the whole lower Mississippi valley; cf. Figure 1). For the same reason, intracoastal shipping could not be taken through the Mississippi Delta in a simple sea level canal, but had to wait for the building of locks—not completed until 1909. At New Orleans the river is about ten to fifteen feet above sea level and above the city, and that is exactly why the city that is nourished by the river also lives in dread of it. To puncture the natural levee, whether by natural or artificial means, would invite a flood of Noachic proportions.

Now it is obvious that a river perched on a ridge is in an unnatural and unstable condition. With a river the size of the Mississippi, flowing between ridges over ten feet high at New Orleans, about double that height at Baton Rouge, the instability is very great. Any large flood can cause the river to break through its natural levee and vomit out into the backswamp. Such a rupture in the levee—locally known as a "crevasse"—was dreaded above all things by the early settlers. The natural levee, after all, was the only farmland worth owning, and a crevasse in one's farm could literally erase one's holdings and dump them into the backswamp as a sheet of mud.* The river roads which always followed the crest of the levee would instantly be cut, and since the river roads were the sole dependable means of land transportation in the delta, a crevasse could paralyze the whole tenuous road network.

But to the Orleanian, a major crevasse posed two other overriding threats. First, of course, was the danger of a break in the levee near the city. The last time the Mississippi burst into the

city out of control was in 1849 via Sauvé's Crevasse, and it was a serious inconvenience (Figure 7). (Since then, the city has seen no general uncontrolled floods, which demonstrates that artificial flood control has worked fairly well.) But above all, and most to be feared, was the very real prospect that once the river got out of its banks into the backswamp, there would be no getting it back. The river would have changed its course for good.

The map of Louisiana shows multiple evidence that the river has done just that many times. The last 5,000 years have left geologic evidence of numerous old channels, each with its own delta (Figure 10). Three of them can be seen on a good road map (cf. Figure 2), and their location determines the patterns of roads and rural settlement in the whole of southeast Louisiana.

The westernmost and oldest course that is still plainly visible is now occupied by Bayou Teche, now an insignificant stream which traces a path from Opelousas southward to the Gulf of Mexico. (Just as the city of Lafayette is the urban heart of Cajun Louisiana, the natural levees of Bayou Teche form its main artery, and such Techeside towns as St. Martinsville, Breaux Bridge, and New Iberia are still overwhelmingly Cajun in population and general flavor, remarkably "foreign" places in the context of contemporary America.*) About halfway between the Teche and New Orleans is a more recent ancestor of the Mississippi, Bayou Lafourche, whose natural levees apparently mark the Mississippi's course in its penultimate stage, just before it jumped its banks to adopt its present course near the town of Donaldsonville. Perhaps the best marked of the three deltas—although not the best marked channel— is the so-called St. Bernard Delta east of New Orleans. Drowning and alongshore currents

---

*If a riverside farmer was quarreling with his neighbor, it was not unknown for him to take revenge during flood time by cutting the neighbor's levee, creating an artificial crevasse, and thus flooding him out. Such behavior ranked on a par with arson and horse thievery, and armed guards customarily patrolled the levee when the river was high. Paradoxically, though, the formation of a crevasse might eventually redound to the benefit of a landowner. A thick deposit of river mud could easily convert a useless backswamp into highly valuable farmland.

*Nowadays, many Cajuns fear that their ancient culture will soon disappear, overwhelmed by the wealth and glitter of twentieth century English-speaking America. One can drive through St. Martinsville, symbolic center of Cajun tradition, and see bumper stickers urging residents to speak French, not English. Meantime, however, English-speaking tourists are invited to bring their money to Cajun country and visit crawfish festivals at Breaux Bridge, the Tabasco factory on Avery Island, and—of course—the Evangeline Oak at St. Martinsville, where Longfellow's heroine pined for her lost amour. It seems doubtful whether the Cajuns can have their tourists, however, and speak French at the same time.

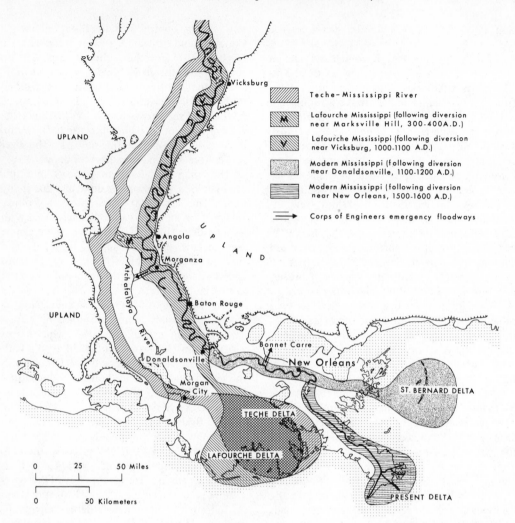

Figure 10. The ancient deltas of the Mississippi. Until recently, all signs pointed to the probability that the Mississippi was on the verge of jumping out of its present course, either into Lake Pontchartrain at Bonnet Carre, or, more probably, into the Atchafalaya at Morganza. Either course would have proved disastrous to New Orleans, and the Army Corps of Engineers has built controlled spillways at both locations to permit overflow in time of flood, meanwhile keeping the Mississippi from leaving its contemporary course. (H.N. Fisk, *Geological Investigation of the Atchafalaya Basin and the Problem of Mississippi River Diversion* [Vicksburg: Mississippi River Commission, 1952]. Modified by William D. Thornbury in *Regional Geomorphology of the United States* [New York: John Wiley, 1965], p. 61. Used with permission of author and publisher.)

have damaged the St. Bernard Delta less than the others, and its tattered birdsfoot outlines forms the coast of Louisiana in the eastern part of the New Orleans metropolitan area. As for the present river course, the Mississippi has occupied this location for several hundred years, with only minor changes.

It is easy to think of this chronicle as mere geologic antiquarianism, with nothing to do with the present condition of New Orleans. That idea would be wrong for two vital reasons. First, as we have seen, there is almost no human habitation in southeast Louisiana except on old natural levees of the Mississippi or its distributaries. And since old river courses run parallel to each other, separated by swampy troughs, the roads do too—a fact which helps explain why travel in and through the Cajun country is so impossibly difficult and why for most of history the Cajun area has been so ill-connected with New Orleans (Figure 2). Second, and of more immediate importance to New Orleans, the Mississippi was on the verge of jumping its traces again, just as Americans arrived on the scene. If the river were to change course *below* New Orleans, it would be awkward, to put it mildly, requiring an entirely new navigation system from the Gulf of Mexico. That problem could be handled, however, even through it would be expensive. A diversion *above* New Orleans would spell nothing less than catastrophe, since the port of New Orleans would no longer be located on the Mississippi River, but instead on a stagnant bayou.

Two diversions were imminent, and both were prevented in the nick of time (Figure 10). One diversion was threatening the east bank of the river about thirty miles above New Orleans at a place called Bonnet Carré (Figures 3 and 10). Indeed, floodwaters had more than once broken through and formed a crevasse which took great volumes of river water and mud from the Mississippi directly into Lake Pontchartrain. Happily, the crevasse had been stopped up, but the situation remained dangerous; at that location the river floods at about twenty feet, and Lake Pontchartrain is essentially at sea level. If the river had gotten loose, it would have gone directly to the Gulf by way of the lake, instead of taking 130 miles by way of its conventional route. Meanwhile, the shallow lake would rapidly have begun to fill up with mud.

A second potential diversion was even more serious, since it was located not only above New Orleans, but above Baton Rouge as well. The weak spot was near the small town of Morganza on the west bank just south of the Mississippi state line (Figure 2). Had the river broken through the levee there, it would have poured into the slot between the present natural levees and the Mississippi and the ancient levees of Bayou Teche (Figure 10). This slot, a swampy wasteland about twenty miles wide, is occupied by a sullen slough called the Atchafalaya River, which leads grudgingly but more or less directly to the Gulf. The Atchafalya route would have saved the Mississippi about half its distance to the sea, and if the

main river had jumped into the Atchafalaya, it might well have stayed there.

The Army Corps of Engineers has repaired both danger points, and, in a stroke of genius, has guaranteed New Orleans an indefinite future, free from flood. Both at Morganza and at Bonnet Carré, great concrete floodgates have been built, which prevent breaching of the levee, but which can be opened intentionally if a flood crest approaches New Orleans. Thus, if the city is threatened, the Bonnet Carré Floodway can be opened to allow surplus water to pour into Lake Pontchartrain. Since the Bonnet Carré Floodway was finished, it has been opened several times, each time bringing the flood crest to safe levels at the city. Only once —in the recordbreaking flood of 1973—has the Morganza Floodway been opened, and although New Orleans was again spared, the diversion severely damaged a number of settlements, including the rather substantial town of Morgan City (Figures 2 and 10).

THE CATALOGUE OF DIFFICULTIES

A summary of what is wrong with New Orleans' site makes an awesome list:

1. The main and oldest part of New Orleans is built on natural levees of the Mississippi, rarely over fifteen feet above sea level. The solidest material on the levee is silt.

2. Most of the contemporary city lies at or below sea level. The Mississippi River normally flows at ten to fifteen feet above sea level and floods at about twenty.

3. Behind the city, at sea level and below, was a half-flooded swamp, with no foundation material worth mentioning and, until about 1900, a breeding ground for malaria. After heavy rains or river floods, there is no way for the water to get out except by evaporation or by pumping it out.

4. Bedrock for foundation material consists at best of compacted clays, but one must dig a minimum of seventy feet below the surface muck to find them.

5. The only avenues into the city until recently were by way of the natural levees. In flood time, the levee could be cut almost anywhere by the sudden and unpredictable formation of a crevasse. At best, the city had poor highway access to the outside. During floods, it might have none at all.

6. Until recently, there was serious risk of the Mississippi changing course upstream, thus leaving New Orleans isolated on a dead-end bayou.

7. Most of the adjacent areas of southern Louisiana are unpopulated, thus depriving the city of a nearby hinterland. Nearly all the scanty population lives on natural levees of old river courses, which are separated by belts of backswamp which slice the delta into north-south strips. The backswamps are barriers to east-west land transportation, and the natural levees are barriers to east-west water transportation.

8. The entrances to the Mississippi are 120 miles downstream from the city. Until artificially removed, mud and sandbars made navigation hazardous at best and sometimes threatened to block it completely.

9. Hurricanes periodically strike the Gulf coast from the south and drive very high tides ahead of them. Areas high above sea level are safe, but most of contemporary New Orleans is substantially below the safety level.

10. The entire city is built on land which is gradually sinking, and some of the city is built on land which is rapidly sinking.

The geologists Kolb and Van Lopik epitomized the area by calling it "a land between earth and sea—belonging to neither and alternately claimed by both." Mrs. Trollope, typically, was less kind: "I never beheld a scene so utterly desolate as this entrance to the Mississippi."

THE SUCCESSFUL SITE

But a million people inhabit a city in this desolate and dangerous place and, judging from what they say about it, a large literate proportion of the citizenry are delighted with their fate. Inevitably one must ask what impelled the building of a city at this particular spot and what permitted it to succeed amidst a sea of environmental troubles.

It is not enough to say that the city's founders were ignorant of local site conditions. That simply is untrue, for they understood the Mississippi Delta a good deal better than many contemporary New Orleans real estate dealers. Rather, one must scan a map of the lower Mississippi much as the early explorers must have scanned it. (Many early maps were surprisingly good, and they had to be, for lives depended on

them.) They were looking for high ground, of course, but that meant going to the site of Baton Rouge, the last and southernmost point along the river where the banks are free of flooding (Figure 1). It was a tempting target, and for a while early explorers had convinced themselves that the site could be reached by entering Lake Borgne from Mississippi Sound, continuing through either Chef Menteur Pass or the Rigolets into Lake Pontchartrain, thence via Pass Manchac into Lake Maurepas and up the Amite River to the back side of the natural levee near Baton Rouge. Thence a short portage led across the levee to the Mississippi (cf. Figure 2).

This route was used sporadically for a long time, but it was mainly important as a political boundary. The Amite defined the northern limit of the "Isle of Orleans" (the Mississippi was its southern boundary), the area that Jefferson wanted to buy from Napoleon in his original 1803 negotiations. It also served as the boundary between British and Spanish-French possessions. Since most settlers circumspectly kept to their own sides of the Amite, it became one of the sharpest cultural boundary lines in the United States—and remains so today: to the south are French Catholic Cajuns; to the north Scots-Irish Protestant Upland Southerners (cf. Figure 6).

But Baton Rouge was an inconvenient distance upstream for ocean-going ships.* And the sluggish Amite was an awkwardly out-of-the-way route for coastal vessels to gain a Mississippi portage. If there were an easier route, it would obviously be better.

That route was found early in the game, shown to Bienville and Iberville in 1699 by the Choctaws, who had been using it for a long time. From the Gulf coast the route began the same as the way to Baton Rouge—from Mississippi Sound and Lake Borgne through the

---

*The Army Corps of Engineers now maintains a dredged forty foot channel to Baton Rouge, which is thus the head of ocean-going navigation on the Mississippi. Despite this high-sounding title, the port of Baton Rouge is no challenge to New Orleans. The main effect of the deep channel is to make the riverbank accessible to oil and chemical tankers and ocean-going barges, which draw up alongside the levee to load and unload cargo. As a result the picturesque old Cajun farmsteads on the river are being replaced by refineries and chemical plants. The day is not far off when the seventy miles of river between New Orleans and Baton Rouge will be an unbroken line of heavy industry.

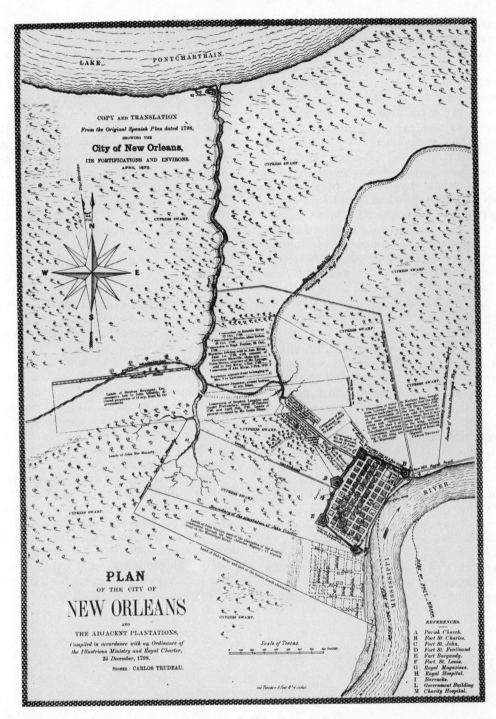

Figure 11. Carlos Trudeau's Map of New Orleans, recopied in 1875, shows how New Orleans commands the portage from the Mississippi to the headwaters of Bayou St. John and thence by water to Lake Pontchartrain. The portage is now Bayou Road. Canal Carondolet was later deepened and used for navigation. The turning basin can be seen below one of the towers of the wall. Peter de Marigny's estate was still not subdivided. "Alluvial Gravel" along the riverbank is the *batture*. (Courtesy of the Louisiana Collection, Special Collections Division, Tulane University Library)

passes into Lake Pontchartrain (Figure 2). Instead of continuing west to Lake Maurepas, however, the little shallow draft vessels turned south into Bayou St. John, which as we have seen flows into Lake Pontchartrain directly off the backslope of Bayou Metairie's natural levee (Figure 11). Bayou St. John is only about four miles long, but from its "headwaters" it is only a two mile portage to the Mississippi itself, mainly across the well-drained land of the natural levee. In sum, it was by far the easiest way to get into the great river from either the Gulf of Mexico or the sheltered waters of the Gulf coast. It was at the place where the portage met the river that the French decreed that their city would be founded—the capital of New France on the Mississippi, and the fortress that would command the wealth of North America's interior. Le Blonde de la Tour's city plan today delineates the French Quarter of New Orleans. It was, to put it mildly, a successful choice.

One can protest, of course, that this explanation is too facile, that it is one thing to found a city, but quite another to make it survive, much less flourish. Early settlement does not guarantee long run success. Tadoussac, for example, predated Québec, just as Mackinac predated Detroit, and Plymouth predated Boston. Clearly, too, the Bayou St. John portage is utterly unimportant in New Orleans twentieth century life—marked only by a ruined fort, a few historical markers, and two streets with picturesque names—Bayou Road and Grand Route St. John. Bayou St. John itself is channelized along the edge of City Park and serves largely decorative purposes (Figure 3). What made the difference was that, below Baton Rouge, the banks of the lower Mississippi were almost uniformly obnoxious, although a purist might argue that they grew slightly more repulsive as one moved downstream. What Bienville did, with the faltering support of the French government, was to create an oasis. When slight "improvements" were made —in the form of a church and a three foot artificial levee to keep out the worst floods— early New Orleans was light years better than the horrid swamps that surrounded it and travelers on the Mississippi headed for it like a haven of the refuge, which indeed it was. Thus, while the term "Isle of Orleans" technically refers to all land between the Amite, the Mississippi, and the Gulf, the real isle was the city itself—an island of civilization in an ocean of wilderness.

One should not then feel too sorry for New Orleans, either in its early days or now, despite its appalling site. The very awfulness of that site gave the inhabitants a certain cheerful esprit de corps. They had conquered the swamp and were clearly pleased with themselves. This special feeling was not limited to the city, either, and New Orleans gained a reputation not merely as a city in the wilderness, but as a beacon which shone with special brilliance, and a prize most eagerly to be sought. Once that happened —only shortly after the founding of the city— no other place had any hope of competing with New Orleans for command of the Mississippi and what it represented.

Thus it was that New Orleans began its career, a cultural island in large part because it was first a physical island. Paradoxically too, it was a place which was miserably connected with its immediate surroundings, but superbly connected with the rest of the world. An outpost of high civilization on a savage shore, it is no wonder New Orleans felt itself a special kind of place.

The Stages of Metropolitan Growth

CONCERNING GEOGRAPHY, HISTORY, AND CITIES

An old aphorism says that "geography doesn't change." That is plainly untrue, as the changing geography of the Mississippi Delta proves. Still, many geographic patterns are conservative and slow to change, often because they represent a considerable investment of energy, and comparable expenditures are required to change them. To state the proposition differently: more than a few important geographic patterns—human as well as physical—are inherited from past time, and we must look into the past to understand them. Thus, if we are to make sense of the contemporary geography of New Orleans, or any other place for that matter, an efficient way is to turn the clock back and try to reconstruct the geography of the past, blood ancestor of the present. More accurately, we must examine the geograph*ies* of the past, for we live with a host of inherited geographies.

For purposes of understanding New Orleans, it is helpful to return to 1718, and the spectacle of Bienville confronting the primordial wilderness. First of all, as Freud has taught us, the beginnings of an organism when it is weak and malleable are often more important than its later, lustier days. It is the old story of the bent twig; early episodes often establish patterns and set habits for a lifetime to come. Second, Bienville symbolizes in a rather pure form the *kinds* of elements that were to make New Orleans (or any other place) the way she is today. On the

one hand, Bienville had certain motivations, and these were determined and conditioned not only by his personal quirks and ambitions but in a larger sense by the temporal and spatial milieu from which he came—a postfeudal French empire, torn by internal dissensions, but grasping for wealth and glory. On the other hand, Bienville was sharply limited in what he *could* do. The limitations were several, but at a general level are exactly the same that all of us labor under today—the exigencies of physical environment; a technology which enables us to manipulate that environment; a certain level of wealth that lets us put that technology to work; and not the least, the social institutions, political philosophy, and psychological habits which ultimately guide what we would *think* about doing—or refrain from doing.

THE FOUR AGES OF NEW ORLEANS

In New Orleans it is helpful to think of several major historic-geographic episodes—each fairly stable, but each begun and ended by brief outbursts of activity which left the city much changed. Each period differed from the ones before and after because each was dominated by different kinds of people, with different attitudes, and with different tools at their disposal. When each period was done, New Orleans required a new map—actually an old one with erasures, and new sections glued on—the new sections different in location and in pattern from the old ones, often because basic modes of transportation were changing and new land was available to new kinds of technology. The city's population changed, both in numbers and in ethnic composition, partly because new kinds of jobs were becoming available and partly because old ones were disappearing. Most noticeable, if not most important, the city's appearance changed, with different street patterns, different styles of building, and changing uses of land. Above all, each period marks a time when the city was related to the outside world by new kinds of communication that changed the areas with which the city was connected. When the episode was over and the city was ready for a breathing spell, New Orleans had changed in fundamental ways—those who made decisions for the city were different, its economic and social connections with the outside were different, and its internal geography had changed. And, after each upheaval, the city stood in quite a different position in the ranking of American cities, and it faced in new directions.

Four such periods mark the evolution of New Orleans' present-day geography. Although the beginning and ending dates are obviously arbitrary, each period marks a time when the rather fickle city linked its fortunes with different parts of the nation or world.

During the first period, from 1718 to about 1810, New Orleans was a European city, both in physical form and human orientation. The period spans the time of Spanish and French rule, and ended when a flood of American immigrants overwhelmed the city in unprecedented numbers with unprecedented ideas.

During the second period, New Orleans was America's western capital. Instantly wealthy from its economic lordship over the continental interior, the city spread far outside its European walls, meantime taking on new patterns which form the city's geographic skeleton today. The period ended about 1865, less the result of the Civil War than the seizure of New Orleans' old hinterland by Northern railroads and upstart Northern railroad cities.

During the third period, hardship matured the city, which consciously set about to avert economic disaster by remaking itself physically. Although it fell drastically in national rankings, it emerged by the midtwentieth century with a new stability, extensive new territory, and a quite different geographic form—a composite of old and new attitudes and technologies.

The last period, which began about 1945 and continues today, sees New Orleans undergoing some of the most sweeping changes in its history, grappling with new competitors, new technologies, and unprecedented social problems. As before, her geography is once more changing—as usual, the combination of her own efforts and of outside forces largely beyond her control. And inevitably, her contemporary geography is a pastiche of present forms, laid atop and beside the patterns of the past.

The European City (1718–c. 1810)

New Orleans did not grow to become a city; it was decreed a city from the moment of its founding—rather as Venus sprang full-born from the sea. And if in her early years she was somewhat muddier than Venus, the city's founders laid the plans for a capital of a scale and magnificence to suit the territory which she was to rule.

The city's plan was laid out by French engineers in a gridiron pattern—symmetrical, with a central square facing the river (Figure 12). To contemporary Americans, there is nothing strange about this pattern, for it seems much less "European-looking" than, say, the winding streets of old Boston or lower Manhattan. But the gridiron was not merely a convenient way to lay out the land; it represented the New Europe, planted with classical perfection on the barbarian shore. As in Philadelphia, whose streets were laid out in a gridiron from its very beginning in 1682, New Orleans' street plan was a declaration of intention. There might not be enough people to fill the grid right away. (New Orleans' grid was not filled until after 1800, and Philadelphia's not until the midnineteenth century, but in both places the plan was there before the people and the settlement was obviously meant to be permanent.) It did not matter particularly if the city's great masonry fortifications turned out in reality to be a rather higgledy-piggledy wooden palisade. The walls were there in the mind. After all, great cities needed great walls, built to the latest standards of military architecture (Figure 11). Indeed, it did not even matter what the land was like, and it was a considerable time before Frenchmen grasped the notion that New Orleans was not built on hills (Figure 13). The plan represented a perfected, purified Europe, ready to be stamped into the soil of the New World wherever Europeans willed it.

From the beginning, image was more im-

Figure 12. Jacques Nicholas Bellin's handsome Map of New Orleans, 1764, shows New Orleans' gridiron pattern without pretentious walls, and only about half-occupied with buildings. However, this area, now the French Quarter, was a statement of classic intention. (From Bellin's "Le Petit Atlas Maritime recueil des cartes et plans des quartres parties du monde," Paris, 1764. Courtesy of the Louisiana Collection, Special Collections Division, Tulane University Library.)

portant than reality. The Place d'Armes (now Jackson Square) with its new church gained a reputation as the finest thing for hundreds of miles. Never mind that the place was a weedy lot and the church a primitive wooden building. New Orleans had already begun to gain a reputation as a terribly important place, but, to Americans, one that was foreign, papist, and therefore dangerous to national aspirations in the Mississippi valley.

As in Canada, France's erred by failing to populate the place adequately. Part of it stemmed from absent-mindedness (France had other things to think about in the eighteenth century), and part of it resulted from deliberate policy. Growing fear of heretics and Englishmen had pushed France into the disastrous policy of screening overseas emigrants to ensure their political reliability. The result of the policy—especially harmful in Canada—meant that only safety conservative persons were considered suitable as landowners, and most conservative Frenchmen preferred living in France to living in the Mississippi Delta, even with its mythical hills. The populating of New Orleans was extremely slow, therefore, and its governing class was suspicious and xenophobic even by Bourbon standards. As for the rural Acadi-

ans who came to people the countryside after the 1750s, they were even more extreme in their views. Hounded from their homes in maritime Canada, they did not look kindly on anyone who was vaguely Protestant or English. Nor did things change much when the Spanish took over in 1767. Spain had even worse domestic troubles than France, and her glittering but rickety Latin American empire gave her even better reason than France to regard New Orleans as a sideshow. Slow migration, moreover, produced a chronic labor shortage, and slaves were imported from the beginning. By the end of the eighteenth century more than half the city's population was black, and the figure has remained high ever since.

Despite neglect, New Orleans continued to grow, largely the result of American settlement in the Ohio valley which sought trade outlets through the city. Even within the limits of the Vieux Carré,* the main direction of growth

*The Vieux Carré (literally, the "old square," or "old district"), was delineated by the palisades on three sides, and the Mississippi River on the fourth. Today, the Vieux Carré is officially recognized as an historic district under the Louisiana Constitution, and its official boundaries are Esplanade Avenue, Rampart Street, Canal Street, and the river. These same boun-

Figure 13. New Orleans: a symbol as well as a city. This highly stylized print shows a well-scrubbed classical city, with some highly imaginary hills in the distance. (Ambroise-Louis Garneray, *Vue de la Nouvelle Orleans*, c. 1830. Aquatint. Courtesy of the Louisiana Collection, Special Collections Division, Tulane University Library.)

was upriver, a trend which would never be reversed. Simultaneously, with boats pulled up at the levee—already raised artificially by several feet—the riverfront and the Rue de la levée (now Decatur Street) began to exhibit a line of docks and commercial buildings which would eventually, under American rule, grow so wide and high that one would find it difficult to walk along—or even see—the river.

Clearly the city was reaching out, but it was still relying on water routes. Building roads was just too difficult, the river too accessible. To be sure, a road had been run along Gentilly Ridge (later to be dubbed the "old Spanish Trail" and later U.S. 90), which theoretically led to the Gulf coast, but it was very troublesome to maintain; the Rigolets and Chef Menteur Pass

daries are well known and recognized by nearly every adult Orleanian.

posed formidable barriers, and it was much easier to go east by boat. And along the river, atop the natural levee, was a River Road about fifty miles long (only eighteen miles of the total lay below the city), but it was of trivial importance compared to the Mississippi itself. New Orleans was literally an island.

The best way to get in or out of the city was still by way of Bayou St. John, and that route had been much improved after Governor Carondolet ordered a canal built to connect the bayou with the backside of the natural levee. Originally laid out as a drainage canal, it was converted so that boats could come up to the rear of the city and unload (Figures 7 and 11). (No locks were built to raise canal boats to the level of the Mississippi for fear the levee would be breached and the city flooded.) At the end of the canal, a few blocks behind the cathedral in the never-never-land between backswamp and natural levee a turning basin was built, giving its name eventually to Basin Street and ultimately determining the location of a thriving commercial waterfront area and of accompanying bawdy houses.

Both canal and basin remain as a part of the city's present landscape, although both are considerably transformed. After canal boats were replaced by railroads, the canal was filled and became a branch line of the Southern Railway (Figure 14). The basin, no longer used, was taken over by the city and, after remaining vacant for a long time, became the site for the public auditorium where New Orleans society gathers for the most exclusive

of Mardi Gras balls. The red light district became a public embarrassment and was eventually removed to make room for a suitably sanitary public housing project. The bawdy houses survived next to the railroad station long enough to give New Orleans a lively reputation for night life. Along Basin Street in the fancy houses black and white musicians joined to entertain the bordello patrons with the blues and ragtime that contributed to the ancestry of jazz. The combination was fortuitous and intriguing—except for natural levees, Spanish governors, railroad barons, and ladies of the night, we might have had no jazz.

Architecture in the old French city is naturally assumed by tourists to be French,

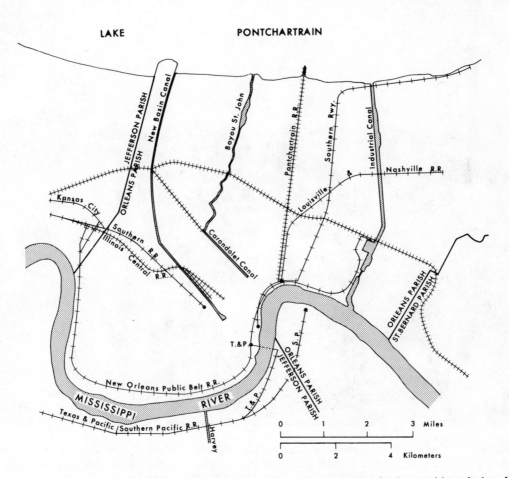

Figure 14. Main rail and canal lines, about 1926. Line names are modernized to avoid confusion. Note absence of central railroad station. Also close correspondence between modern expressway system and earlier rail system (cf. Figure 3). (After a map prepared by the City Planning and Zoning Commission, Harland Bartholomew & Associates. Courtesy of the Louisiana Collection, Special Collections Division, Tulane University Library.)

but most of it is not. New Orleans was Spanish for the last thirty years of the eighteenth century, and during that time two great fires burned up most of the city, so the rebuilding was naturally in the Spanish mode (Figure 12). Thus the "French" Quarter looks a good deal more like Castille than like the Ile de France. A good share of that old Spanish city still stands, a monument to neglect, New Orleans conservatism, and the benevolent ministrations of the Works Progress Administration. Latin

American visitors, according to legend, feel more comfortable in New Orleans than in any other big American city. It is not surprising, for the Vieux Carré, with its stucco buildings standing directly next to narrow sidewalks, occasional ornaments of ebullient cast iron, and flashes of tropical gardens in interior courtyards, is decidedly reminiscent of colonial Spain (Figure 15).

The European period came to an end abruptly with the Louisiana Purchase and the sale of

Figure 15. The middle of the French Quarter, looking down Orleans Street from Bourbon Street toward St. Louis Cathedral. The Mississippi is beyond the cathedral, out of sight. Most buildings here postdate the fire of 1794 and predate the Civil War. The street pattern is the ideal late eighteenth century European gridiron. Buildings directly on the street with private spaces within hearken back to medieval times. The absence of modern high buildings results from the Vieux Carré Commission's architectural controls. (Courtesy of the Greater New Orleans Tourist and Convention Commission)

New Orleans to the United States. Too much is made of the exact date, since official transfer failed to oust Creoles from the seats of power. But neither France nor Spain could have held the city much longer as part of their overseas empires. Americans were flooding into the Mississippi valley at exactly the same time that France was finishing a revolution and sporadically at war with half of Europe. Spain was in worse shape, unable to hold her Latin American colonies even against Indian guerillas. It was manifestly the destiny of the United States to have New Orleans; there were too few Europeans to hold it against the tide of frontiersmen sweeping into the valley. In all, New Orleans enjoyed too important a location and too flamboyant a reputation to be ignored much longer. The city's geographical chickens had come home to roost.

America's Western Capital
(c. 1810–c. 1865)

The United States Census first counted New Orleans in 1810 and, to nobody's surprise, she emerged as the largest city west of the Appalachians. In the whole country she was outranked only by the four East Coast giants—New York, Philadelphia, Boston, and Baltimore (Figure 5). From an underpopulated French colonial capital, she had suddenly become a big city—and she was shortly to become much bigger.

American migration had mainly done the job (population tripled in the first seven years after the purchase), but the process was circular. New Orleans was primate city of the new West, and that very fact stimulated migration to the city.

The Commercial City. Business was booming—then as now a largely commercial business with very little manufacturing. And prospects were excellent, as more and more Americans poured over the Appalachians into the Ohio valley and into the new lands of the Deep South. Europe was building new industry, and so was New England, and both places possessed an insatiable appetite for Midwestern foodstuffs and Southern cotton. Furthermore, these goods were bulky, and, until some kind of dependable land transportation became available, they had to be shipped out by river, no matter where they were eventually headed. That meant steamboats, and a lot of them. Morse's *Gazeteer* of 1823 remarks with a tone

of astonishment about New Orleans that "there were 50 steam-boats on the eastern waters connected with the commerce of this city". That was a driblet compared with what was coming. Captain Glazier, the urban chronicler, described the levee in 1883, long after steamboats were obsolete, and even then the scene was remarkable. "Along the riverfront are congregated hundreds of steamers, and thousands of nondescript boats, among them numerous barges and flat-boats, thickly interspersed with ships of the largest size, from whose masts fly the colors of every nation in the civilized world.... The throng which comes and goes upon the levee, merchants, clerks, hotel runners, hackmen, stevedores, and river men of all grades, keep up a general motion and excitement, while piled upon the platforms which serve as a connecting link between the watercraft and the shore, are packages of merchandise in every conceivable shape ..." Altogether, New Orleans had entered a golden age. Between 1810 and 1840, the city's growth rate exceeded any other large American city, and if the same rate had continued during the 1840s, New Orleans would shortly have become the country's second largest city.*

Internal Divisions. Within New Orleans, conditions were somewhat less golden. As Captain Glazier observed later, "to the French Creoles as a class, who during their long alienation had still at heart been thoroughly French, to become a part of a republic, and that republic English in its origin, was intensely distasteful. This was the deluge indeed, which Providence had not kindly stayed until after their time. They withdraw into a little community of their own, and refused companionship with such as sacrificed their caste by accepting the situation and adapting to it ..."

Part of it had nothing to do with caste, of course. The old "Quarter" (the Vieux Carré, the Creoles called it) was getting crowded and obviously would not hold the increasing number of newcomers even if they had been made welcome, which emphatically they were not. As population spilled outward, it established pat-

---

*Indeed, according to the 1840 census, she almost was. Baltimore and New Orleans had almost exactly the same number of people—102,313 and 102,193 respectively. Only New York, with more than 300,000 people, was larger.

terns which would be permanently etched into the urban geography of New Orleans.

First of all, it was established in which direction the city would grow, and what the internal character of the new city would be. The natural levee, of course, was the only place to settle, and the city pressed into sugar plantations which had lined the river's banks both upstream and downstream from New Orleans. (These additions to the city were called faubourgs, or, roughly translated, "suburbs.") Most of the Americans chose to settle upstream ("Uptown") from the French Quarter, and immediately next to it—rather like a medieval marketplace clustered outside the walls of a fortified European town. The boundary line between established Creoles and newly arrived Americans was what John Chase calls a "name-less no-man's-land," sharply drawn between the two cities. Later on, a navigation canal was planned along the boundary, and a huge right of way was reserved. The canal was never built, but Canal Street was named for it—in the best New Orleans' tradition, in honor of a myth. Canal Street presently became an enormously wide boulevard (Figures 16A and 16B), and the median was called "the neutral ground," a geographical recognition of the armed truce between Creoles and Americans. The phrase is now part of standard Orleanian patois, and means the median strip of *any* boulevard.

Downstream, in the Faubourg of Joseph Marigny, settlement was slower and considerably less affluent. There, population was dominated by Creoles who had spilled out

Figure 16(A). *City of New Orleans and Suburbs.* Classic example of an urban "bird's-eye view," all the rage in the late nineteenth century. Typically, the city layout is accurate, but the surroundings are much romanticized; here, the backswamp is transformed from a cut over cypress swamp into a manicured English park. This chromolithograph was evidently made for the Cotton Exposition of 1883, whose grounds are shown as a darkened rectangle uptown. (See Figure 16B for location key. Print by Theo. Pohlmann. Gustave Koeckert, publisher, 1883. Courtesy of the Louisiana Collection, Special Collections Division, Tulane University Library.)

from the overcrowded Vieux Carré and by new immigrants, mainly Irish and German, who formed the city's white lower classes. But to the proper Creole this was foreign territory too, and the effect was to confine the French Quarter on both its Uptown and Downtown sides. Since the river formed a third side, the only Creole options were to pack more people into the Quarter, which they did; or to mix with the despised foreigners, which they ultimately and gradually did; or to spread beyond the walls toward the backswamp, which they also did (Figure 9). Another option—to settle across the river—was not taken up until late in the century, and even then not very enthusiastically.)

Happily for the Creoles, their allotment of backswamp was less ghastly than the Amercans'. The sharp bend in the Mississippi where the Vieux Carré is located is accompanied by a lakeward salient of the natural levees. This salient extends far enough northwest to merge with the lower natural levees of Bayou Gentilly and thus form a low saddle between the Vieux Carré and the head of Bayou St. John. This saddle came to be known by geologists as Esplanade Ridge, named for the great boulevard which follows its crest. It was Esplanade Ridge

which formed the old Bienville portage of 1699, and now, 150 years later, provided the hard-pressed Creoles with a way of expanding their territory inland. The main axis of the ridge is barely above sea level, but it was enough. The Esplanade in time became the great nineteenth century artery of suburban Creole New Orleans and it is still a fine street.

Meantime, antagonisms between the several parts of the city ripened to the point where in 1836 the city was formally divided into three self-governing "municipalities," the First Municipality being the French Quarter, the Second being the new American city in Faubourg St. Mary, and the Third the Downtown Creolecum-immigrant city (Figure 7). The Third was of little importance to the city's decisionmakers and has remained so since. In modern times, its heart is the Ninth Ward, a blue collar white and Negro area which is terra incognita to the city's elite, and noticed mainly as the butt of bad jokes.

Although the formal political division proved unworkable and was abandoned, the antagonisms left tangible marks on the growing city. For example, streets change names as they cross Canal Street (Royal becomes St. Charles, Chartres becomes Camp, and so on; Figure 4).

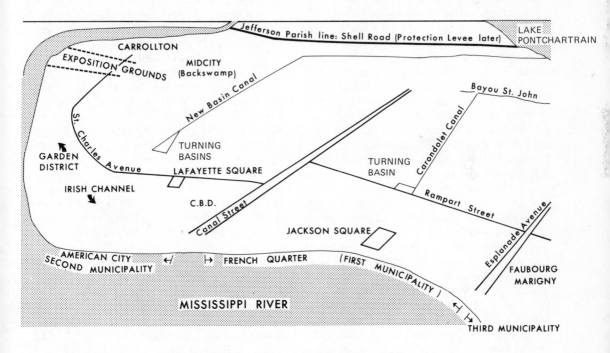

Figure 16(B). Location key for Figure 16A.

Each city had its own great hotel, although the St. Charles in the commercial American city was naturally larger and more ostentatious than the St. Louis on the French side. (Both hotels went through several architectural reincarnations, but both were eventually demolished.) The American city had its own Lafayette Square, hoping to match the grandeur of Place d'Armes on the French side, though never quite succeeding. Important things like churches and burial grounds were sharply segregated and usually duplicated. New Orleans, with its two self-sustaining centers, was rather like a double-yolked egg.

Even navigation canals were duplicated, although more for economic than for ethnic reasons. As the American city grew upstream, the Carondelet Canal behind the French Quarter was farther and farther away from the focus of commercial activity, which continued to move Uptown. In 1832, therefore, construction began on a "New Basin Canal" which by 1838 had connected Lake Pontchartrain directly with the back of the American city. It was an exact American counterpart to the Carondelet Canal of the Creoles (Figures 7, 9, and 16).

The new canal left its imprint on New Orleans in two important and permanent ways. First, it established another major route into the city from behind—a route which ultimately became the main umbilical cord from the central and western United States. Alongside it were built several railroad lines, the most important of which eventually became the main line of the Illinois Central to Chicago. Still later, when the canal was abandoned, part of its right of way was used as the route for Pontchartrain Boulevard, the main approach for the Greater New Orleans–Mississippi River bridge, and Interstate 10, the main route from Baton Rouge, Houston, and the West (Figures 3 and 14). Alongside this long-standing routeway there developed a belt of low intensity commercial and warehousing facilities which occupies a wide swath across the "Mid-city" area of New Orleans. Today, as a result, one enters New Orleans from the north or west on an expressway flanked by auto junk yards, lumber yards, warehouses, breweries, and the like. For a city that supposedly breathes romance, it is a strikingly unromantic entrance.

Second, the New Basin Canal profoundly altered the population geography of New Orleans. It was an expensive thing to build, for it had to be hacked by hand through a pudding of muck and buried cypress stumps. To do the job, Irishmen were hired in great numbers, just as they were hired in the North and West to build railroads. New Orleans became the only Southern city with any substantial number of new European immigrants. As in so many ways, New Orleans seemed a Southern city with Northern habits.

Most of the immigrants were settled between the levee and the end of the new canal's turning basin—long since filled and now partly occupied by the New Orleans Transportation Center and the Superdome. This strip happened to coincide with the rather seedy outer fringes of the booming business district and seemed a proper place to put the obviously inferior immigrants. The area where the immigrant district abutted the riverfront quickly came to be known as "Irish Channel," a rather tough low class area where nice people did not live (Figure 16B).

The American elite, meantime, were moving farther uptown, into what is now called the "Garden District," so named because large mansions were set back from the street (Figure 17)—in contrast with the old Spanish practice of building one's house *on* the street and turning inward toward an enclosed court. The use of the word "garden" simply reflects English word usage—the gardens are what most Americans call "front yards." The Garden District is now one of New Orleans' most picturesque and desirable residential neighborhoods, perhaps the largest and best-preserved antebellum residential area in America. Except for the French Quarter, it attracts more tourists than any other part of the city. (Like the French Quarter, the Garden District has acquired status as an "historic district" and thus legal means are available to prevent architectural instrusions.) The Tourist and Convention Commission says little about the Irish Channel, which has retained its rough, rather seedy character—now half ghetto, half skid row.

The Street Pattern. The pattern of streets in the new steamboat city was at once curious and portentous, for it was both cause and effect of important things in the city's life. The basic layout goes back to the time before the sugar plantations were gobbled up by the city, when property lines and often field lines extended back from the river, perpendicular to the levee

Figure 17. Antebellum Garden District mansion, corner of Prytania and Fourth Streets. Setting houses back from the street was an American custom. The cornstalk iron fence allegedly was uprooted from Vieux Carré, and is one of the few "approved tourist attractions" outside the downtown area (cf. Figure 15). (Courtesy of the Greater New Orleans Tourist and Convention Commission)

(cf. Figures 7, 9, and 3). The pattern was familiar to those experienced with land patterns in certain parts of Europe, where long narrow landholdings extended back from roads and rivers alike. The purpose was the same in Louisiana: landowners needed access to the road, and there was only one road—the Mississippi. Since the only good land was on the natural levee, with land values dropping to near zero in the backswamp, and since the owners needed access to the river, there was only one solution—to slice the two mile band of natural levee into narrow strips, "long lots" perpendicular to the river.* But, since the river was not straight, the strips were not parallel. Behind convex curves of the river, the boundaries fanned out; on concave curves, they were pinched. Where New Orleans was expanding most rapidly in the American city, the meander was convex, so that plantation lot lines formed a fan-shaped pattern—today the most conspicuous feature on any street map of Uptown New Orleans (Figures 9 and 3; see also Frontispiece).

These lot lines were reinforced in two ways. First, they were obvious places to dig canals—not for navigation, but to drain excess rainwater from the natural levee into the backswamp. (See Figure 3, upriver from New Orleans, where similar canals drain contemporary natural levees; cf. Figure 8). Second, when it came time to build main streets, they were often put along property lines, and thus ran along the canals. In such instances, rights of way were often extremely wide. In the early days, these drainage canals were noisome sloughs, the object of bitter complaint, and the canalside streets were unpleasant places—where traffic was heavy, churned to a muddy gruel. (Stories are told of animals mired so deeply that they died in place and were abandoned to decompose.) Later on, the canals were lined with concrete, and eventually covered, to form great wide boulevards. The neutral ground was a fine place to put horse car tracks, and it was not long before these useful boulevards were bedecked with flowers and lined with great trees. During the nineteenth century, as the city spread Uptown, property line after property line became boule-

*Similar long lots occur wherever seventeenth and eighteenth century Frenchmen settled and subdivided rural land in North America—throughout Quebec; along the lower Great Lakes (the Detroit River is lined with them); and in spots along the upper Mississippi, the Wabash, the Maumee, and elsewhere.

vard after boulevard—Melpomene, Jackson, Louisiana, Napoleon, Jefferson, Broadway, and eventually South Carrollton avenues, to name but the main ones. To glance at the maps, one might suppose that these boulevards diverge from a central focus in Mid-City, and it is easy to conclude that Mid-City is therefore a humming beehive of activity. Quite the contrary. The boulevards naturally converge in one place because they are radii of a half-circle whose circumference was already drawn by the Mississippi River. Much of Mid-City is today a derelict wasteland, its character set decades ago when it was an uninhabited swamp.

Cross streets simply followed the river—approximately in concentric curves; more exactly in a series of straight tangents to the curve, each tangent jogging slightly when it crosses one of the radial boulevards. (With straight streets, it was possible to lay out bits and pieces of a grid pattern, but the converging radial streets force constant adjustments which can be seen everywhere throughout the pre-1900 city [Figure 18]).

None of these tangential streets possessed important drainage canals, since they ran parallel to the river and only served as feeders to the arterial canals. There was no natural need for wide rights of way, and in the early days none were provided. Close to the levee in particular, the tangential streets are narrow, utilitarian, and occasionally colorful—like the unpronounceable Tchoupitoulas (see Appendix B) which serves the docks; and Magazine Street, once the main commercial artery of Uptown and today spotted with antique shops and neighborhood stores. But Orleanians had been forced into building wide streets at periodic intervals, and eventually it became a pleasant habit, providing an otherwise crowded city with occasional great shady boulevards, which today must be put very high on the list of New Orleans' urban amenities.

Thus, despite the high cost of land, it was quite natural to run a great boulevard Uptown, parallel to the river. That boulevard, Nyades Avenue, later to be renamed St. Charles Avenue, was placed along the rear boundary line of the long narrow riverfront land grants—the front, of course, being the river itself. Under French law these grants ran back forty *arpents* from the Mississippi. (One *arpent* = 180 feet; hence, forty *arpents* = 7,200 feet, or nearly a mile and a half). The effect was to locate St.

Figure 18. Wedge-shaped blocks result when radial streets fan out from a convex curve of the river, and/or when grid patterns do not exactly accord with old property lines. St. Roch Street to the left is part of Fauberg Marigny grid; Franklin Avenue to right is part of the Ninth Ward grid. As of 1973, this was a bluecollar, heavily Italian neighborhood. Architecture is typically varied—early twentieth century to the right, midnineteenth century Southern commercial arcade to the left. House behind Sal's Pumbing and Heating is a very common two family Creole cottage, probably well over 100 years old. Cross street is Chartres Street; Mississippi is about two blocks behind the photographer.

Charles Avenue about halfway between the clatter of the docks and the stench of the backswamp, insulated from both by a decent distance (Figure 3). In effect, the boulevard bisected the habitable part of the natural levee and became the main residential artery of the American city—the counterpart of Esplanade Avenue Downtown. (It also was the route of the New Orleans and Carrollton Railroad, which was deliberately built to open the Uptown area to suburban development.) Much later on, Claiborne Avenue and Fontainbleau-Broad Avenue, were built roughly concentric with St. Charles. Neither of these later streets holds the Orleanian's very special affection as does St. Charles Avenue, the first and grandest of the great unnecessary boulevards. Visitors to New Orleans may dislike certain aspects of the city, but most agree on the charm of St. Charles Avenue. Today, even the most aggressive new-look politicians have been unable to persuade Orleanians to abandon the last of the city's streetcars, which wobble quaintly along the neutral ground of St. Charles Avenue, past wonderful antebellum and Victorian houses, brushing against oleanders and Spanish moss as they make their runs from Canal Street along the whole length of the old American city. Officials of New Orleans Public Service, Inc. (NOPSI), which operates the city's excellent transit system, force a tight-lipped smile when the streetcar is mentioned, for maintenance costs are outrageous and the nominal fare hardly begins to pay for operation. But tourists and Orleanians alike are delighted, and the St. Charles streetcar is now as firmly entrenched in New Orleans as the cable cars on Nob Hill in San Francisco. It is difficult to prove, but no less obvious, that St. Charles Avenue maintains much of its charm and therefore its environmental health partly because of the beloved streetcar. (In the early 1970s, the federal government joined the growing list of the streetcar's admirers and declared the whole line a National Historic Property—the oldest operating streetcar line in the United States, or so it is said.)

Curiously, the street pattern of New Orleans profoundly influenced the pattern of white and black population, as both spread out across the growing city. And the racial patterns, like the patterns of streets, are still with us.

Racial Geography in an Old Place: Superblocks and Backswamp Ghettos. In early New Orleans, as in most Southern towns, social segregation between races did not necessarily imply geographical segregation—except at the most microscopic scale. Negro slaves, for example, were commonly housed on the quarters of slave owners, and a racial map of the Vieux Carré would have produced an intricate salt and pepper pattern. Even free blacks usually did not live very far from their work—and since many worked as domestics, they necessarily lived in or close to white neighborhoods.

As the city grew beyond the Quarter, however, and spread upriver along the natural levee, geographic segregation began to appear in two quite different forms. First of all, the indispensable domestics (especially after emancipation) commonly were housed in the back streets behind affluent whites, but within walking distance. Similar practices in other Southern towns, and even in the North, led to blacks being put in small houses in back alleys with whites in bigger houses on the streets (Figure 19). Whites did not associate socially with the blacks, but they lived close by and often they played together as children. (Booth Tarkington's *Penrod* describes the pattern in a fictional midwestern town of the beginning of this century.)

In New Orleans, the pattern took a characteristically peculiar turn. In the new American city, many of the biggest houses where the richest whites lived were located along the great boulevards, and the boulevards, in turn, were commonly separated by five or ten or fifteen smaller streets. The boulevards, in consequence, circumscribed "superblocks" half a mile or so square, and subdivided into several scores of ordinary city blocks. Inasmuch as blacks lived behind the big house, often several blocks away, each superblock tended to develop affluent white perimeters with Negro cores (see idealized map, Figure 20). Thus, St. Charles Avenue was solidly lined with wealthy whites, as were Napoleon and Jefferson Avenues, which crossed St. Charles about eight blocks apart (Figure 21). Back from all three streets, however, blacks lived in a small nuclear cluster, and this cluster has survived to this day. Then as now, however, there were poorer whites who could not afford mansions on the great boulevards, and the cores of the superblocks were seldom entirely black.

Such patches of black population by no stretch of the imagination can be called "ghettos" in the contemporary Northern sense. Unlike the Northern ghetto, these Negro neighborhoods of New Orleans were quite small and multinucleated, with fuzzy boundaries. Internally, they contained a fair amount of open space, and the architecture was not conspicuously different from that in white areas of comparable income. If America had to have racial segregation, the New Orleans pattern was less malevolent than that of most Northern cities. Neither whites nor blacks were very far from persons of the other race, and, since each group knew their respective neighborhood to be geographically stable, neither felt particularly threatened by the other.

Unfortunately, there was another less benevolent form of racial segregation, and it is the ancestor of some of New Orleans' worst contemporary ghettos. It resulted from the fact that the poorest blacks simply lived where they could. In other cities in later times, such areas were found "down by the tracks." In antebellum New Orleans, it was either along the *battures* or the backswamps. The *batture* is the area on the riverside of the artificial levee, without flood protection and without private ownership. At the foot of Canal Street, the *batture* was used during low water periods for mooring boats and stacking cargo; ultimately it grew so valuable that warehouses and wharves were built there, its possession was

Figure 19. Little shotgun houses for black domestics were commonly located behind big houses of white slave owners or post-bellum employers (cf. Figure 20).

fiercely contested, and new levees were built to protect it against flooding. (Thus, the city moved into the river, at the same time building a commercial barrier between the residential city and the Mississippi.) Away from the docks, however, the poorest blacks would squat on the *batture* in makeshift shacks, abandoned when the river periodically rose and carried them away. The *batture* ghettos were obviously temporary and of little long run importance in fixing racial patterns.

Not so the backswamp. With whites occupying the highest and best part of the natural levee in all three municipalities, blacks were pushed into the demiland on the inland margin of the natural levee, where drainage was bad, foundation material precarious, streets atrociously unmaintained, mosquitos endemic, and flooding a recurrent hazard. Along this wretched margin there developed a discontinuous belt of black population, interrupted by the commercial zones along the Carondolet and New Basin canals and by the later building of boulevards which attracted affluent whites. By the midtwentieth century, however, the backswamp black belt had grown so crowded that the nonblack interstices were filling up, and the old backswamp ghettos were beginning to merge into something that looked like that evil Northern phenomenon, the superghetto (Figure 21). Thus, while New Orleans has always had one of the highest proportions of black population of all big American cities, she has—until recently—been one of the least segregated geographically. Recent changes in that condition must be listed as one of the least heartening aspects of New Orleans' contemporary social geography.

Regularities in an Irregular City. It is easy to conclude from this catalogue of municipal peculiarities that New Orleans' urban growth

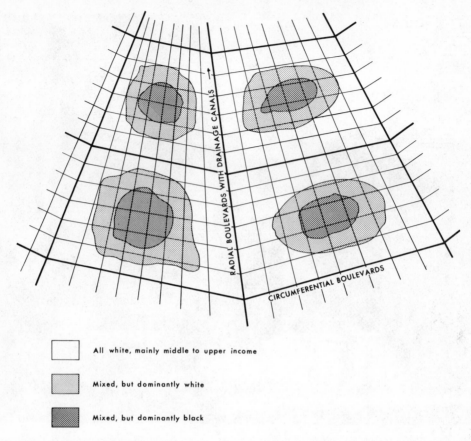

RADIAL BOULEVARDS, WITH DRAINAGE CANALS

CIRCUMFERENTIAL BOULEVARDS

☐ All white, mainly middle to upper income

▦ Mixed, but dominantly white

▨ Mixed, but dominantly black

Figure 20. In this idealized Uptown neighborhood, affluent whites live along boulevards, or near them. To the rear, black population increases in proportion and density, so that each "superblock" is a separate nucleus of black population. Cores of superblocks are rarely all black, although boulevards are usually all white (cf. Figure 21).

before the Civil War obeyed special rules which applied only to it—and nowhere else. It is a tempting conclusion, but untrue. Sociologists and geographers long ago noticed that growing cities in a free economy tend to develop patterns of land use in concentric rings—a central business district, which gradually merges into a ring of warehousing, thence into a wider ring of low income housing, with a ring of higher income residences on the outermost fringes. Such concentric rings have been described in city after city throughout the Western world. Other scholars observed that cities also tend to be sectoral—that is, when a certain kind of land use or a certain kind of people begin to congregate and expand on one side of a city, the expansion will fan outward from the city along major roadways, eventually to form patterns like the wedges of a pie. Both sec-

tors and concentric rings can be found in New Orleans, too, although the peculiar topography so distorted the regularities that one must hunt hard to find them. Nevertheless, the general principles were struggling to emerge, and if one looks in the right place, they are easy to see.

The sectors are most obvious—the large American sector projecting upstream, the low income Third Municipality downstream, the French sector blunted by the backswamp but thrusting a narrow wedge lakeward along Esplanade Ridge. And the concentric rings are there too, if only in segments, as a slice of a rainbow will appear only in one quarter of the sky where sun and rain occur simultaneously. In New Orleans the concentric rings are clearly formed only where the city was developing without obstacles—and that meant mainly Uptown in the American sector along the natural

Figure 21. Negro population, New Orleans, 1970. Source: Block statistics, U.S. Census of Housing. See text for interpretation.

levee. By the midnineteenth century, rings had formed which can still be seen—the civic core along Canal Street, fading into the commercial and warehousing zone upriver, thence into the slumlike Irish Channel, and finally grading into the genteel "suburbs" of the Garden District and ultimately out St. Charles Avenue. A similar, but even more compressed series of rings appeared along the Rampart Street fringe of the French Quarter, past the turning basin of the Carondelet Canal, and extending along the stylish Esplanade into the suburbs at the head of Bayou St. John, with a nearby race track and jockey club to mark the affluence. All of this emerged in full bloom by the turn of the twentieth century, but the seeds were sown long before. What distorts the general patterns in New Orleans are the peculiar bicultural core of the city, the curious racial geography, but above all the stern constraints of local landforms and soil. Modern technology has weakened those constraints, but they were very powerful when the city was forming. Thus, the regularities are there, but one must know how to look for them.

End of the Golden Age. New Orleans' decline from glory also followed a predictable pattern, but even there, the observer can be so distracted by local particulars that long term trends are hard to see. This essay is not the place to review Farragut's daring seizure of New Orleans in 1862, the closing of the river, and General Butler's rude behavior to New Orleans' ladies. But the Civil War was a lurid episode in New Orleans' history, and according to local legend, it was the war that put a sudden and cruel end to the city's lordly dominance over the Mississippi valley. Whole Mississippis of tears have been wept over the event, but the tear-dimmed eyes failed to see that the city's decline resulted from nothing more romantic than an upheaval in the technology of transportation. On the horizon to the north was a cloud no larger than a man's hand, issuing from the smokestacks of the new steam locomotives that were hauling goods directly from the Midwest across the mountains to the Atlantic coast or, more cheaply, to the lake ports, whence goods were taken East by the Erie and other canals.

The numbers tell the story. When railroads got to Chicago and Saint Louis, New Orleans no longer enjoyed a monopoly over the Mississippi valley's trade, and both cities presently overtook New Orleans in population—St. Louis about 1860, Chicago five years later. The Union Pacific was finished in 1869, and by 1875 the combined population of the Bay Area cities exceeded New Orleans. Before the end of the century, six more railroad-industrial cities of the midcontinent had surpassed New Orleans in size—Pittsburgh, Detroit, Cleveland, Cincinnati, Buffalo, and Minneapolis. By the 1890s, New Orleans had dropped to thirteenth place in the nation's metropolitan hierarchy.

But it was no sudden catastrophe that caused New Orleans to be eclipsed. Nor, in fact, did the city suffer except in relative terms, for population continued to grow in a stately sort of way. It was simply that New Orleans had reached maturity at about the same time that the Northern cities were brawling adolescents. The youthful debutante found herself a middle-aged dowager, and her feelings were wounded. Small wonder that the Civil War was used to explain the injury, for the war served New Orleans —as Robert Penn Warren remarks about the South as a whole—as the "great Alibi," excusing all sorts of ills and evils. The war *did* play a role, but it was not in the usual sense of having destroyed New Orleans; rather, it speeded the industrialization of the North, and most particularly it stimulated the building of Northern railroads.

The Mature City (c. 1865–c. 1945)

If the Civil War shocked New Orleans, it did not numb her as it did so much of the South. The main reason, perhaps, was that New Orleans retained very considerable economic advantages from before the war, and that, while things were very bad afterwards, the city discovered that things were not quite so bad as they seemed. First of all, river traffic had begun to revive in a new form, while simultaneously the city found that she had rather willy-nilly become a railroad center. Second, New Orleans' location at the junction of the Mississippi valley and the Gulf of Mexico turned out to be marvellously advantageous for plucking the wealth of new commercial agriculture that had begun to flower both in the American South and in Latin America. Finally, it turned out that the city's decisionmakers were not the

lotus-eating dilettantes of song and story, but realistic tough-minded men who were willing to make some long range bets on New Orleans' future and to hedge those bets by rebuilding a substantial part of the city. By the end of the century, New Orleans was rather like a patient who has just finished recuperating from major surgery—slimmer and healthier than before the operation, but with a certain caution that dampened the flamboyance and insouciance that preceded the illness.

The River and the Railroads. The railroad, it turned out, did not replace the river as a transportation route. What it did was reduce the romance considerably by driving the gorgeous but inefficient general cargo steamboats out of business. (Mark Twain describes that sad process in several brilliant chapters of *Life on the Mississippi.*) Still, the railroads could not compete with water transportation for hauling bulk cargo in no special rush to reach a destination. Thus, the Northern railways carried off the Midwest's general cargo and hurried it eastward, but much of the heavy bulk goods continued to come leisurely through New Orleans— especially grain from the upper Midwest, and coal from the newly opened fields of Illinois and western Kentucky. The key to this traffic was the barge—first of shallow draft and hauled individually (originally they were little more than rafts), then, as the river's channel was deepened, of deeper draft and hauled around in great tows that looked like huge moving islands. By the end of the century the city had established a near monopoly over bulk cargo from the central and upper Midwest. At the same time, more sophisticated river craft, combined with roads and railroads, had reached out for general cargo as well, and by midtwentieth century the city had spun a web of trade that extended over a midcontinental region that was larger even than that of antebellum days.

And, contrary to legend, the South did rise again, for Europe and New England wanted more cotton after the war—not less. In the best prewar year, 1859, the South had produced a little over five million bales, but by the late 1890s, ten million bales a year was routine. The boom began to deflate after World War I— what with the boll weevil, exhausted soils, and competition from Indian and Egyptian cotton fields—but New Orleans had a good share of the American cotton-marketing facilities at the time when it was most lucrative, and the profits carried the city through what otherwise might have been some very bad times. The cotton boom also helped give New Orleans a more Southern flavor than she had ever had before—or was to have again in the future. Correspondingly, the slow decline and eventual disappearance of the Deep South "Cotton Belt" in the twentieth century did more to dilute that flavor than any other single thing.

Resurrection of commerce with the interior did not depend entirely on the river, for while railroads were somewhat delayed in coming to New Orleans (just as they were delayed throughout the South), the 1870s saw the beginning of an integrated Deep Southern rail system with New Orleans at its hub. The city's advantage was simple: she remained the only genuine big city in the South, and, with her long experience in handling cargo, she became a natural magnet for any railway in the region. New Orleans was fortunate, for there were several Gulf ports with better harbors—and better land approaches. All of New Orleans' railroads had to be built on piles and had to cross miles of uninhabited swamps before reaching the city. Any number of other coastal towns—Mobile, for example—would have seemed more reasonable choices, but New Orleans had the head start and shortly became the nation's main rail outlet to the Gulf of Mexico.

This is no place to recount the assemblage of short lines that eventually became New Orleans' railroad system. It took a long time to put it together; indeed, it was the 1950s before the city was able even to condense its five individual railroad stations into a single terminal.* When the system was finished, however. New Orleans had extended six major tentacles into the interior of the continent (Figure 22). The backbone of the system was the Illinois Central's north-south line to Chicago, the self-styled "Mainline of Mid-America." The IC reinforced New Orleans' river connections with the Midwest and strengthened the city's already strong trade associations with Illinois—a relationship which it retains to this day. To the west and northwest, the Southern

*The timing was ironic. No sooner had New Orleans gotten its first genuine union passenger terminal than the American passenger train sickened and fell into a coma. The terminal now serves mainly as a bus station.

Pacific, the Kansas City Southern, and the Texas and Pacific Railways threw New Orleans' trade net over an extremely large area which included upstate Louisiana, most of eastern Texas, Arkansas, and eventually Oklahoma. Northeastward the Southern Railway and the Louisville and Nashville reached through Alabama and on through central Tennessee to the Ohio valley, although farther east New Orleans' thrust was blunted by the expanding hinterland of Atlanta, which was rapidly turning itself into the rail capital for the whole eastern South. It was not the last time New Orleans would have trouble with Atlanta.

Despite these successes, railroads were not the city's forte. New Orleans had gotten into the game too late to contest the dominance of Chicago and St. Louis over the midcontinental region, and the coastal South was, until the discovery of oil and gas, one of the poorest parts of the nation's poorest region. Fortunately for New Orleans, she did not need to rely on the sandy coastal plain for her revenue. Appropriately, this half-foreign city found new wealth in overseas trade. New markets were opening in Latin America, and New Orleans was waiting to exploit them.

The Latin Connection. New Orleans had special affinity for Latin America from the very beginning, when the city was merely an outpost of Spain's Caribbean and Gulf empire. With the decline of Spanish fortunes and the extension of American hegemony westward and southward, New Orleans saw Latin American independence as an obvious virtue. New nations would surely seek new markets, and after all, who could foresee the eventual extent of the United States' political domain? Looking still farther ahead, what more logical place was there for a new focus of Latin American trade than the great Gulf port at the mouth of the Mississippi?

Disappointingly, the Latin American wars of liberation produced more immediate chaos than trade, and New Orleans became a compulsive dabbler in the Byzantine world of Central and South American politics. (Perhaps her experience with Louisiana politics had made that inevitable.) As early as 1822 an expedition had been fitted out in New Orleans to support Bolívar, and during the 1830s and 1840s the city served as a base for Texans in their wars with Mexico. Innumerable filibustering ex-

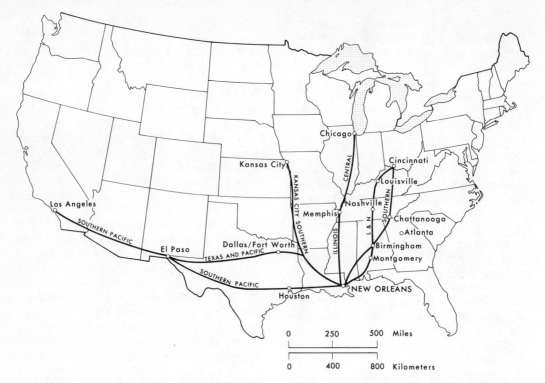

Figure 22. Railroads into New Orleans. Main lines are shown where New Orleans is a major terminus (all routes are generalized). Note excellent connections with the Midwest, especially via the main line Illinois Central. Note also the absence of main lines to the eastern South, where Atlanta dominates.

peditions were launched from New Orleans against hapless Central American states, and when the Caribbean countries were one by one turned into "banana republics" toward the end of the century, it was partly a result of collusion between Latin politicians and Orleanian entrepreneurs.

The Latin American linkage proved very profitable. Americans had been drinking prodigious quantities of coffee for a long time, but after the turn of the century their passion for bananas became equally awesome. New Orleans was a prime port of entry for both products, and if the Guatemalan lower classes did not become rich from cutting bananas and picking coffee beans, a good many Orleanians got rich selling them, while in the meantime the city spun another economic web across midcontinent America (Figure 23).

The result of these political and economic connections was to make New Orleans a kind of Latin foothold on the American shore, and the city in turn spread its tentacles far beyond the

banana coast. Latin commercial offices lined the wharf-front streets, and the city eventually became the home for a consul from every one of the Spanish-speaking Latin republics. Some of the ties were informal, as rich *Latinos* would come to New Orleans on holiday, or send their sons and daughters to learn English at Miss So-and-So's Finishing School or Colonel Somebody's Academy for Young Gentlemen, or to study the Napoleonic Code at Tulane University's famed law school. (A New Orleans education could be counted on to be genteel and safety conservative.) Less formal still was the spattering of political refugees who had fled their native land after some abortive coup and, while plotting the next one, enjoyed the convenient hospitality of New Orleans' growing Latin American community.

In time the Latin American population grew fairly large, although how large depends on who was doing the counting—about 25,000 if one believes the 1970 U.S. Census; 65,000 if one takes the total of Latin American consulate

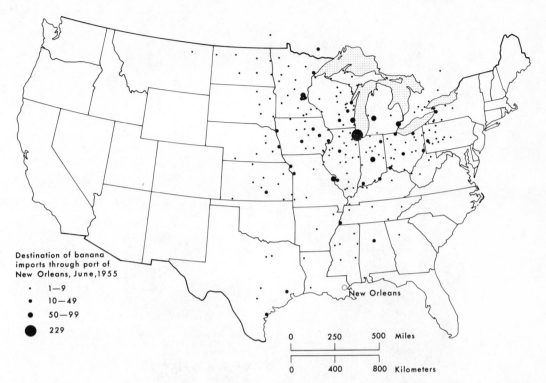

Figure 23. New Orleans, banana imports, June 1955. This apparently exotic map is an indirect geographic measure of New Orleans' critical role as link between Latin America and the United States' interior. Source: Donald J. Patton, *Port Hinterlands: The Case of New Orleans* (College Park: The University of Maryland, February 1960).

estimates and adds Puerto Rican and Cuban figures from a local Spanish language radio station; or 80,000 according to the local office of the Social Security Administration. But absolute numbers are less important than the fact that New Orleans never developed a big conspicuous Spanish-speaking district but instead a number of small *Latino* neighborhoods scattered about the city. One important reason for the absence of a ghetto is that *Latinos* came into New Orleans over a long time and had time to become assimilated. (There was never any deluge, as of Puerto Ricans in New York or Cubans into Miami.) For another, many of them were affluent and bilingual, so they found no need to huddle together for mutual protection. Above all, there were and are no big homogeneous groups from a single country. (The largest national group is Honduran, with substantial numbers from Guatemala and Nicaragua. For a brief time, the Cuban population was fairly large, but by 1973 and the embargo on Cuban refugees, the most noticeable Cuban

neighborhoods had seemingly evaporated—evidently gone to other cities or assimilated into the New Orleans population at large.)

In sum, New Orleans found its Latin connection an agreeable one, both profitable and colorful. And in their turn, it is said, Latin Americans enjoy New Orleans, if for no other reason than the Spanish appearance of the Vieux Carré, which they find familiar and comfortable. At least the Tourist and Convention Commission thinks so and has mounted a substantial advertising campaign to lure Latin Americans to the Orleanian vacationland (Figure 24).

The Cotton Exposition and its Long Run Consequences. In retrospect, New Orleans might possibly have regained its health after the Civil War without artificial stimulation. Perhaps the railroads and barges would have come without enticement, and quite possibly Latin America would have sent her bananas and coffee and people too. As matters turned out,

NUEVA ORLEANS
Aquí navegan todavía para usted Los Viejos Vapores.

Venga a pasear por el Mississippi en los antiguos vapores como aquellos que conoció Huckleberry Finn. (Claro, ahora tienen aire acondicionado.)
Visite las bellas plantaciones de antaño. Conozca la Bahía de Nueva Orleans.
Aquí tenemos toda una variedad de tours para que usted y su familia se diviertan. Desde un recorrido por el Barrio Francés hasta estos paseos en vapor por el Mississippi... Y todo esto está a sólo dos horas de México. Consulte a su Agente de Viajes.

Venga a oir el jazz - el verdadero jazz que nació aquí en Nueva Orleans. Los mejores músicos tocan para usted dondequiera que vaya.

Venga a saborear los platillos de nuestra Cocina Criolla. Son únicos en el mundo !

En Nueva Orleans lo estamos esperando.

Figure 24. The U.S. Travel Service's advertising appeal to Latin American tourists is essentially the same as to others—jazz, food, and air-conditioned Huckleberry Finn, all only two hours from home. (Courtesy of the Greater New Orleans Tourist and Convention Commission)

however, the city fathers decided to take a hand. They did two things, both of which profoundly affected the city's long run growth and changed its internal appearance. The first was to stage an exposition. The second was to rebuild the city's port facilities from top to bottom.

The exposition of 1884–1885 was in the best late nineteenth century tradition—a glittering extravaganza that would last a year, and attract tourists and businessmen from far away. The great 1851 exhibition in London,

with Prince Albert and the Crystal Palace, had set the standard for such affairs, and Philadelphia's Centennial Exposition of 1876 had shown what they could do for American cities. In 1884 New Orleans opened hers—"The World's Fair and Cotton Centennial Exposition," naturally—which announced to the world that the Civil War was over and New Orleans was open for business again.

It is doubtful whether New Orleans sold any more cotton as a result, and the exposition itself did not even break even. But there is no doubt that the city's appearance was considerably changed thereby. On the one hand, the wonders of institutional late Victorian architecture bloomed as they had never bloomed before, with all the fanciwork and Carpenter Gothic gew-gaws that so glorified the Picturesque-Eclectic mode. (Two of the most admired buildings housed respectively the Grand Rapids Furniture Pavilion and that of the Republic of Mexico. Despite differences in financial provenience, the two buildings looked wonderfully similar from a distance.) New Orleans had always enjoyed her domestic architecture on the flamboyant side, but the Cotton Exposition pulled out all stops. The results were admired and imitated throughout the city, but especially in wealthy areas, which to-

day contain some of the most exuberant Victorian architecture in America (Figure 25).

But to New Orleans in the long run, the important thing about the Cotton Exposition was its site and what happened to that site after the exposition was over. As matters stood in 1884, the location was almost predetermined, for it had to be in the American part of the city, in a place that was big, well-drained, and accessible by public transportation. Only one place met the description, a small rural tract which remained between the advancing edge of Uptown and the recently annexed suburb of Carrollton. The boundaries of the fairgrounds followed old French property lines in a quarter-mile swath completely across the natural levee—a distance of about two miles between the river

Figure 25. Late Victorian styles were flamboyant and widespread in New Orleans. Note elevation of the main floor, originally a precaution against flooding. The big shady verandah has disappeared with rising building costs and air conditioning after World War II. Cement pots and lawn furniture are endemic throughout middle-aged parts of New Orleans.

and the backswamp. St. Charles Avenue and the Carrollton Railway to downtown New Orleans cut squarely across its midriff (Figure 26).

When the exposition was over, New Orleans followed Philadelphia's example and turned its fairgrounds into a great park. On the river side of St. Charles it remained as Audubon Park, a pleasant bosky ground with great oaks and little lakes, much beloved of Sunday strollers, golfers, and bicycle riders of unstrenuous persuasion.* Lakeward from St. Charles the land was secured for the city's two biggest universities—Tulane, the self-styled "Harvard of the South," and Loyola, New Orleans' most prestigious Catholic institution. Thus, the Cotton Exposition passed into memory, but the grounds did not. Adjacent areas were changed also, and the margins of Audubon Park and the university campuses became one of New Orleans' most favored locations for the scholarly and the affluent. Today, the whole university area remains as one of the city's wealthiest (and whitest) neighborhoods (see Figures 27 and 21).

The New Port. The immediate purpose of the Cotton Exposition was to improve New Orleans' public relations, but no amount of publicity would change the fact that the city's economic foundation—the port of New Orleans—was in rickety shape. Just as railroad technology was putting steamboats out of business, bigger and faster ships were making old port facilities obsolete. Nor was it merely a matter of building better wharves—although that was involved. The big new ships required deeper navigation channels, efficient means of getting cargo to and from the wharves, and above all an integrated administration of the port to ensure that things were to run smoothly and that facilities were kept in competitive shape. In New Orleans, however, these conditions plainly had not been met. By 1870, according to Leonard Huber, the state of the port had slipped badly. The fall resulted partly from the Civil War, but not entirely.

Part of the trouble stemmed from silting at the mouth of the river's main distributaries. In the lower river, a fifty foot draft is commonly maintained by natural processes, but

across the bars the depths ranged between twelve and twenty feet—and sometimes much less. These depths were awkward but adequate for shallow draft sailing ships in antebellum days; they were no good at all for new deep draft steamships, which sometimes had to anchor outside the bars for days, waiting for safe passage. It was a wasteful way to do things, and shipping companies had begun to mutter about going to Mobile or Gulfport to land their cargo. After lengthy and expensive dredging by the corps of engineers proved futile, New Orleans applied such pressure that Captain Eads was permitted to build his famous South Pass jetties, which, after they were finished in 1879, forced the river into a narrow channel and literally flushed the bars away.

Meantime, physical facilities inside the port had been deteriorating badly. Even so, the prospect was less grim than it might have been, for New Orleans had two intangible assets—which she retains today. First of all she had plenty of time to think about reforms—more time, indeed, than she had any right to. As Donald Patton and other careful students of American ports have noted, a port's customers tend to be extremely conservative. New Orleans had accumulated a large body of customers over the decades, and they would drop away most reluctantly.

The city's second asset was and is institutional—a long tradition of intelligent city supervision of the port. Under French and Spanish rule all wharfage had been government property and private use was at public pleasure. This arrangement continued under American rule, although somewhat less formally. Thus, the nineteenth century had seen a rather erratic alternation between state and city administration and between public and private supervision of port facilities. After the Civil War, the public had surrendered considerable authority to private lessees, who had proved increasingly sloppy as the years went by. When it became clear that something had to be done, therefore, there was ample precedent for public interference.

There is no need to plow through the complex sequence of events whereby New Orleans reorganized its port authority. James P. Baughman has carefully described the labyrinthine process, which extended over many years and involved innumerable political bodies. Suffice it that when New Orleans perceived the port

---

*Audubon Park also contains a small artificial hill, built (so the story goes) so that the children of New Orleans could see what a real hill looked like.

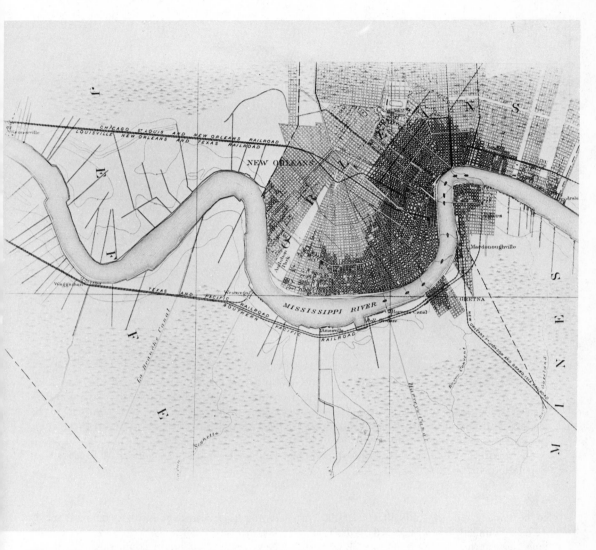

Figure 26. New Orleans urbanized area in 1890. City is still compact, and largely confined to the natural levee. (Compare 1863 map, Figure 9). Most streets back of the city are imaginary. Uptown street pattern abruptly ends with Orleans Parish flood protection levee. Note convergence of streets following old French lot lines in uninhabited Mid-City swamp. Old course of Bayou Metairie is shown by contour lines just east of Kennerville, west margin of map. (Cf. Figure 7.) Source: New Orleans Quadrangle, U.S. Geological Survey, 1890.

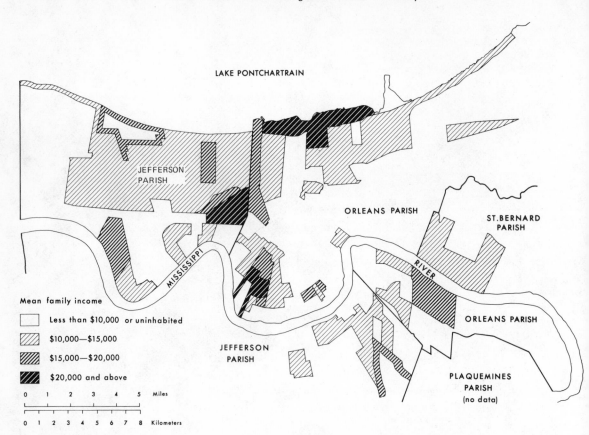

Figure 27. Affluence in New Orleans. Extreme wealth occurs mainly in middle-aged suburbs—Lakefront dating from the late 1930s; Old Metairie, from the late 1920s; the University-Audubon Park district along upper St. Charles Avenue. Affluence in the older part of the city is confined to the Garden District and French Quarter, although figures appear low because census tracts also include poor areas. Large swath of upper middle income on the north side of the city is post–World War II white suburbia. Essentially all affluent areas are white (cf. Figure 40). Source: U.S. Census of Population, 1970.

to be endangered, she took drastic action. In 1896, a landmark law was passed by the Louisiana legislature, establishing the Board of Commissioners for the Port of New Orleans, popularly known as the "Dock Board." This law, together with later amendments, gave the board authority over all water frontage in Orleans Parish and considerable portions of river and canal frontage in adjacent parishes. Within this area, the board had authority to expropriate private property, to demolish and rebuild structures at will, to operate any facility that it chose, and at its pleasure to lease portions of any facility to private operators.

In most other American cities, such behavior would have been denounced as rampant socialism—which it certainly was. For a city with New Orleans' supposed conservatism, it would appear unorthodox, to put it mildly. But Orleanians took it calmly. The port was simply too important to be left in the hands of inept or slothful operators.

The Dock Board went to work in 1901, zestfully tearing down decrepit facilities and rebuilding according to the latest standards of design. Within the next ten years, a good share of the port had been totally rebuilt and facilities greatly expanded. In the public's name, the board built cotton warehouses, coal and bulk storage facilities, one of the biggest grain elevators in the world, and a host of other things, big and small. To complement the massive building program, the government also took control of waterfront railroad facilities, heretofore fragmented among various competing private companies. Under the aegis of the Public Belt Railroad Commission, the lines were consolidated, rebuilt, and subsequently operated as a unit under city management (Figures 14 and 38). Altogether it was a great improvement, eliminating duplication, speeding the movement of goods by more efficient switching, and considerably reducing port costs.

Ignoring details, one should note three things. First of all, the city was willing to use any means necessary to preserve the health of the port. If the means were arbitrary or even socialistic, so be it. Second, there would be no nice regard for political boundaries. If the port spilled over into adjacent parishes and towns, well then, the old boundaries would be ignored. (The Port of New York Authority would presently discover the same thing independly, as would the metropolitan governments of Toronto, Miami, and elsewhere much later.) Third, the new facilities had all been built at about the same time, and, as the city would find to its dismay later on, they would all become obsolete at about the same time. But that was a long time in the future, and meantime the port was booming.

The Crowding City. The city was booming, too, and for the first time in New Orleans' history, space was running out. By Southern standards New Orleans had always been a crowded city—partly from European architectural tradition; partly because the city had to be packed onto the finite area of the natural levee. Some of the pressure had been relieved as the city began spilling across the river, the result of excellent ferry service and new jobs in large West Bank* railyards where transcontinental trains were marshaled before or after crossing the Mississippi River ferries. But the West Bank towns of Algiers and Gretna were still country villages (even though Algiers had been annexed to New Orleans), and most Orleanians preferred the East Bank, especially as streetcar lines got better and better and people could live considerable distances from their work. (The streetcars had begun going electric

*See Appendix A for explanation of the term "West Bank."

in 1893, and by 1902 all lines were consolidated under one management.)

New foreign immigrants increased the pressures still more. Irish and German immigration had subsided after the Civil War, but presently a new wave surged forward—this time Italians who took up the menial jobs that their predecessors were abandoning as they moved up the social and economic ladder. Eventually these Italians were to constitute the city's largest white ethnic minority and they continued to set New Orleans apart as the only Southern city with a substantial number of unassimilated European migrants. Meantime, they added more people to an already crowded city.

Only three options were open to accommodate more people—to expand the city lakeward from the natural levee, to let settlement crawl father and farther along the levee, or to crowd more people onto the same land. The first option, lakeward expansion, was out of the question for the moment. Although several short railways and "shell roads" had been run out to new resorts and amusement parks on the shore of Lake Pontchartrain, the intervening backswamp was still uninhabitable, and the lakeshore was a dangerous place to live (see Figure 26). The lake was shallow, and if a storm from the southeast combined with high tides on the Gulf, Pontchartrain had a nasty habit of backing up and flooding everything in sight. A few shoreline residents, mainly fishermen, had solved the problem in Malay fashion, by building wooden shacks on stilts and hoping for the best. Generally, it worked, but not always.

Expansion along the natural levee was limited too. On the Uptown side, settlement abruptly stopped at the Orleans-Jefferson parish boundary, which happened to be the boundary of the Orleans Parish Levee District (Figure 26; Figure 16B). There, a so-called "protection levee" ran back from the river toward Lake Pontchartrain, and while it kept Orleans Parish dry, the neighboring Jefferson Parish Levee District had to fend for itself— which it did badly. On the Downtown side, in the working class descendent of the old Third Municipality, growth was even more precarious. There, officers of the Orleans Levee District had been less than energetic in providing flood protection in an area whose income and political influence were small. Periodically, parts of the Downtown area found themselves under water, and new settlers were not eager to share the experience. Expansion downstream was very slow (Figure 26).

The remaining option was to pack more and more people into the same space. That feat was accomplished as land costs rose and the owners of large suburban lots were persuaded to subdivide their holdings into increasingly narrow slices. It did not have to be that way, of course, for there are other obvious ways of increasing urban densities. Philadelphia, Baltimore, and Boston, for example, had built three story row houses for decades, and New York had begun erecting walk up tenements that were even higher. But New Orleans was suspicious of multistory residential quarters—perhaps because she feared that foundation material was inadequate to support big buildings; perhaps because she was just Southern enough to insist on keeping houses separated from each other by some kind of yard, no matter how small. Furthermore, the city never took to apartment living, and even row houses were not much favored— this despite the shortage of land. (The famous Pontalba buildings on Jackson Square, sixteen individual row houses under a single roof, are much admired by Orleanians, but their form was rarely imitated) (Figure 28). Given the physical constraints and cultural prejudices, however, there was little option but to build long narrow houses to fit the long narrow lots.

The architectural results were striking in

Figure 28. Decatur Street, the riverward margin of the French Quarter, looking Uptown. The magnolia tree at right is in Jackson Park. Behind it is the Upper Pontalba building. To the left, the Jax Brewery is part of a commercial rind that cuts most of old New Orleans off from the Mississippi, just left of the picture. In the distance along Decatur are old warehouses and seedy seamen's bars. The large high building on the right is One Shell Square, finished in the early 1970s and the visible symbol of Texification, naturally the highest building in New Orleans. To the left of Shell is the Marriott Motor Hotel, 1,000 rooms and symbol of new efficient tourist industry, seen by many old-timers as a threat to the French Quarter.

the extreme. The most popular low cost house was known as a "shotgun," allegedly because one could fire a shotgun in the front door and have all the pellets emerge from the rear (Figure 29). The shotgun house simply consisted of a string of rooms lined up one behind the other, usually without benefit of hallway. The gable of the house ran perpendicular to the street, and the house was rarely more than a story and a half high. In its most elementary form, the shotgun could be very crude, serving as what was euphemistically called "rental housing"—more plainly, the cheapest house on the market. Very often, however, the Orleanian penchant for decoration produced at least a modest efflorescence of finials, brackets, and spindles, which latter-day Orleanians have embraced with unrestrained delight. Commoner

even than the shotgun was a so-called "bungalow," or "double tenament," which resulted from putting two houses under one roof—each long and low like the shotgun, but with a common inner wall and central gable (Figure 30). (For some reason, Orleanians would accept two houses under one roof, but no more than two.) Bungalows cost more than shotguns usually, and embellishments were commoner. Then, too, to avoid possible flood danger, many of them were elevated on pilings five to ten feet high. (Although New Orleans' houses seldom have cellars, these understories were often scooped out, walled in, and turned into an informal ground floor, which Orleanians call "basements.") The result was a very substantial two story double house, with the first main floor well above ground level. Even a

Figure 29. Prototypical shotgun house, one story high, single room wide. Louvred front doors and floor length windows are typically Caribbean, affording ventilation before air conditioning. Next door is a two family bungalow—a double-barreled shotgun, split down the middle. Such houses were built in New Orleans all during the last half of the nineteenth century for low income people; many Negroes still live in them.

Figure 30. Double bungalows, very common in New Orleans. It has lately become fashionable for whites to buy and refurbish shotguns, bungalows, and other such houses—recently unfashionable and left for Negroes. This is Algiers, West Bank New Orleans. Such renovations have forced major shifts in the geography of black population in New Orleans.

simple shotgun could be raised in the same way; such a house is called a "raised bungalow," with a higher roofline than an ordinary shotgun, and a much higher social status.

Scholars have wondered for a long time where the idea of the shotgun and bungalow came from, but nobody really knows. It seems likely that they were found in the countryside around New Orleans and may have come originally from some modification of an Indian "long house"—although that is only conjecture. In any event, they were apparently not invented in New Orleans to meet specifications of the city's peculiar lots, although that story is in wide currency. Rather, the houses were found to meet New Orleans' peculiar needs, and they were built by the thousands. Furthermore, when Orleanians were finished adding their own favorite embellishments—Carpenter Gothic gim-

cracks, tiled gables, and louvered French doors in front—they looked like nothing else in the United States. Around World War I New Orleans builders gradually began adopting other architectural fads, but by then square miles of the city were covered with shotguns, bungalows, and an astonishing variant known as the "camelback," which begins as a one or two family bungalow in front, but rises to two stories in the rear (Figure 31).

The result, as of about 1910, was a city that was aggressively *sui generis* in appearance, a place of great charm to natives and visitors alike. Today, unfortunately, the average short term tourist in New Orleans is unaware of this highly picturesque half of the city—perhaps because unimaginative tourist agencies see nothing extraordinary about this amazing collection of domestic buildings, but more

Figure 31. A camelback house, evidently dating from that late nineteenth century. Origin of this unusual house form is uncertain, but may have resulted from tax laws which assessed the value of a house according to its height along the streetfront, but paid no attention ot how high it rose at the rear. Whatever its origin, the camelback form can be found in river towns to the Ohio and Mississippi valleys as far away as Louisville—mute testimony to New Orleans' cultural connections along the highways of the continental interior. Domestic architectural eccentricities like this occupy huge areas of pre–World War II New Orleans and contribute heavily to the city's picturesque un-American look.

probably because tour directors are ignorant of workaday New Orleans, since they seldom venture beyond their own "approved" Tours-of-the-French-Quarter, Tours-of-the-Garden District, and Special-Two-Hour-Tours-of-the-Harbor-by-Boat. Meantime, however, increasing numbers of Orleanians have begun to "restore" middle-aged shotguns and bungalows (Figure 30), sometimes embellishing them strangely with muted Williamsburg hues and Colonial eagles. While the avant-garde may snigger, the results are often charming—as was much of New Orleans itself at the end of the nineteenth century.

Pumps, Canals, and the Spreading City. Then, abruptly, everything changed. New Orleans discovered that she had the capacity to drain the backswamp. For better or for worse, New Orleans would never be the same again. A. Baldwin Wood, a gifted engineer and later the director of the city's Sewerage and Water Board, designed a heavy duty pump that made it possible to raise huge volumes of debris-laden water a short vertical distance, and to do it fast. It was one of those potent inventions that people in later years would take for granted, but just as high speed elevators changed the geography of New York City by making skyscrapers possible, the Wood pump revolutionized the urban geography of New Orleans by suddenly opening to settlement areas which were thought forever closed.*

One might have expected that New Orleans would have exploded geographically, just as dozens of Northern cities exploded once electric streetcars had made rural areas available for the building of detached suburbs. (To be sure, a few suburbs were planned at the end of car lines on the north shore of Lake Pontchartrain, but the distance was too great to encourage New Orleans to learn new habits of commuting.) Growth did occur, of course, mostly northward toward Lake Pontchartrain, but it was remarkably slow, considering the pressures of population in the old parts of the city (compare Figures 26 and 32). There were several reasons for delay.

First of all, draining the swamp was a major undertaking, requiring money and time. In addition to the pumps (which were huge and very expensive), an ambitious system of new drainage canals had to be built to carry the swamp water to locations where it could be lifted either to Bayou Bienvenue and thence into Lake Borgne (the usual dumping place), or, in case of serious flooding, via standby canals to Lake Pontchartrain. New levees also had to be built to protect newly drained land. Furthermore, people were learning that swamp "soils" were not soil at all, but a thin gruel of water and organic material that shrank and settled when the water was removed, and then settled some more. Thus, although the backswamp surface had originally stood at about sea level, pumping caused it to drop considerably below sea level. Flood protection had always been important in New Orleans, but in this new city below sea level it was now literally a matter of life or death. Clearly, the Mississippi River levees had to be raised, a whole new network of dikes built along Lake Pontchartrain to keep out tidal surges, and then a line of inner protection levees raised to connect the levee systems of lake and river. Even inside wealthy Orleans Parish, the work turned out to be very costly, and in the thinly populated Jefferson and St. Bernard levee dis-

tricts, large scale drainage of backswamps was financially out of the question. Thus, while Orleans Parish passed its original legislation to install its pumping system in 1899, and although much of the middle city had been pumped out within another decade, the neighboring parishes would wait another fifty years —until after World War II—before they could install large scale pumping and drainage facilities.

But even in Orleans Parish, conventional buildings could not be erected in the backswamp simply because surface water was removed. Houses, sidewalks, and streets had a disconcerting habit of sinking—unless sand or other permeable material was brought in to form a foundation pad. For bigger structures, piling had to be driven, often to considerable depths. It was costly business.

Expansion into the backswamp did not occur overnight, therefore, nor did it occur in random locations. Subdivisions of the early 1900s were largely concentrated on the natural levees of the old distributary channels—Bayous Metairie and Gentilly—where elevations were five to ten feet above sea level and silty soils helped prevent subsidence of foundations. On the margins of the old distributary levees, real estate dealers contrived ingenious ways to make land and thereby money. In Gentilly Terrace, for example, a middle income development begun around 1910 on the lake side of Bayou Gentilly, the developer built lots like polders, by the simple expedient of scooping dirt from the streets and piling it up in pads on either side.

Such building was expensive, however, and it had the effect of restricting the northern part of New Orleans to fairly affluent people with white skins. Part of the reason for this racial segregation had legal roots. The early 1900s, after all, saw an outburst of anti-Negro propaganda and Jim Crow legislation throughout the South, and it was exactly at that time that the city's population began rolling northward toward the lake. Most real estate dealers in the newly drained northern parts of New Orleans simply would not sell to Negroes, but even if they had, few blacks could have afforded to live there. North of Metairie Road and Gentilly Boulevard, therefore, the new areas were almost lily white, and even today there are few blacks north of that line. Established black

*It also revolutionized the geography of the Netherlands. Dutch engineers came to New Orleans to learn how Wood pumps worked, and fifty years later the Zuyder Zee had been drained.

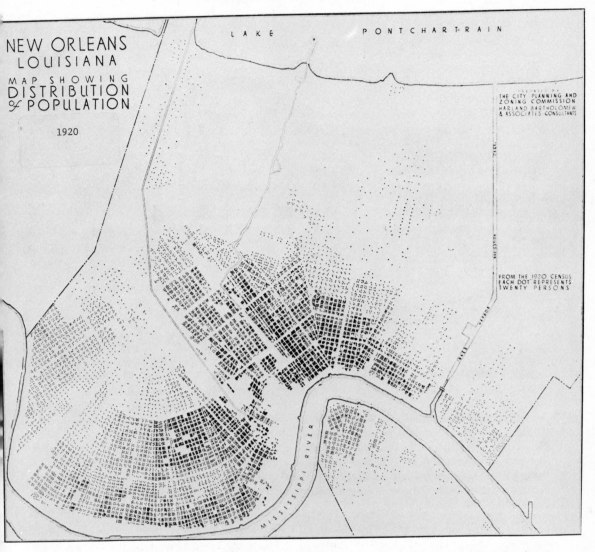

Figure 32. Population distribution, 1920. The pumping system had just begun to allow people to live in the backswamp. Note high densities in the old Creole part of the city between the Vieux Carré and Bayou St. John, and in the emerging backswamp ghetto, just west of the central business district. Ill-tempered Lake Pontchartrain still kept the lakeside part of New Orleans uninhabitable. (Courtesy of the Louisiana Division, New Orleans Public Library)

neighborhoods continued to expand, however, mainly toward the newly drained margins of the old nineteenth century "backswamp ghetto." The Wood pump, as it turned out, was a powerful agent to accelerate residential segregation in New Orleans.

Despite the high cost of land, the city continued to creep northward toward Lake Pontchartrain, and the pace increased with the economic boom of the 1920s. With pros-perity came new architectural fashions, now for the first time out of the Golden West. It was the day of the California bungalow (Figure 33), but, as with earlier architectural fads, New Orleans added its own touch—white stucco, red tiled roofs, and an astonishing efflorescence of concrete sculpture, leaning heavily toward man-sized neoclassic urns and sinister cement wolfhounds arranged symmetrically on either side of the front steps. "Mission style"

Figure 33. The "California Bungalow," hugely represented on the right, was the Golden West's first major contribution to American domestic architecture. With big porches and overhanging shade-giving eaves, it was enthusiastically adopted throughout the South, an architectural signal perhaps that the South was again ready to join the Union. 1920s New Orleans is full of them.

houses also enjoyed great vogue, as real estate developers loudly invoked the city's Spanish ancestry. Today, large areas of north central New Orleans have the look of a middle class Hollywood under the reign of Louis B. Mayer. It is not at all unpleasant.

The New Lakefront. By the mid-1920s, with population moving inexorably in the direction of Lake Pontchartrain, it was obvious that something had to be done about the lakefront. At the most primitive level, the old lakefront levee was inadequate to protect the growing city against floods from the bad-tempered lake. The lakeshore itself was seedy and disagreeable, lined with fishermen's shanties on stilts, and occasionally spotted by amusement parks which were connected with the city by street-car lines. Thus, it was almost inevitable when,

in 1924, the state legislature commissioned the Board of Commissioners of the Orleans Levee District to design and execute a plan that would modernize the levee, make the lakefront more attractive, and simultaneously concoct a scheme whereby the lakefront improvements would pay for themselves. It was a large order, but the Orleans "Levee Board" (as it was more commonly known) was equal to the challenge.

Louisiana levee boards are considerable creatures, mandated by the state constitution not merely to keep their districts dry, but given all kinds of money and power to accomplish that purpose. Boards can levy taxes, expropriate land inside or outside of their districts, run rights of way through lands belonging to other public bodies, and even maintain their own police forces. They are rich and powerful institutions (especially in wealthy Orleans

Parish) and, since board members are appointed by the governor for terms which run concurrently with his, they are intensely political. They may choose to cooperate with municipal governments but are under no obligation to do so. In effect, the levee boards are worlds unto themselves.

Thus, everybody expected the board's plans to be ambitious, but when they were unveiled, even blasé Orleanians were astonished. For five and a half miles, a stepped concrete seawall would be built on the floor of Lake Pontchartrain, 3,000-odd feet out from the existing shore. The area enclosed by the seawall would then be filled, using material pumped in from the lakebottom outside. Behind the seawall, the filled area was raised five to ten feet above the lake level—which meant that it would be one of the highest parts of the city. When the job was done, New Orleans would gain not merely a better levee, but an entirely new lakeshore, with about 2,000 acres of prime and pristine land which the Levee Board could do with as it wished (Figure 34).

The public development alone was breathtaking. New Orleans, which had spent 200 years cutting itself off from the Mississippi River with an insulating rind of docks and warehouses and railroad yards, suddenly discovered that it had a clean public waterfront lined with beaches, boulevards, and parks, not to mention a new municipal yacht harbor. It is some measure of the project's scale that a municipal airport was added to the Lakefront scheme almost as an afterthought. When the airfield was finished in 1934 (with the enthusiastic encouragement of Huey Long), it was one of the biggest and best in the country.

The Depression came, leaving the Levee Board in sore financial straits, but it merely stimulated the Lakefront development, for much of the construction was taken over by the Works Progress Administration, which simply picked up where the Levee Board had left off. (A public work of this magnitude was meat and drink for the WPA.)

To an outsider, however, perhaps the most astonishing thing about the Lakefront development was the way in which expensive public land was summarily and casually converted to private ownership. To be sure, the Levee Board had to pay off its bonds. Thus, the rental of

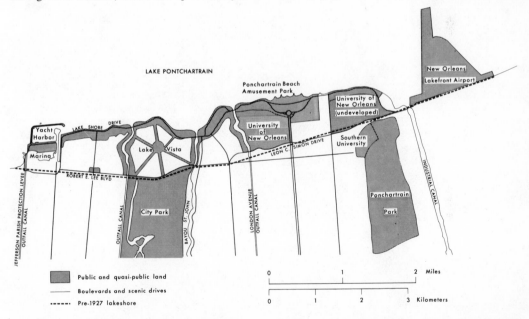

Figure 34. Lakefront New Orleans, 1926 and after. The natural shoreline of Lake Pontchartrain was a smooth curve; see dashed line. All land north of the line is fill, nearly all since 1927. Bayou St. John, once the main entrance to French New Orleans, now serves decorative purposes. Unshaded areas are mainly private residential, including some of the most affluent parts of the city, sold by the Levee Board to help pay for the project (cf. Figure 27). Area around Pontchartrain Park is isolated black upper middle class neighborhood.

land to an amusement park or an airport authority could be explained as prudent acts which provided New Orleans with better public facilities and earned a profit at the same time. Nor could anyone object when considerable land was turned over to Louisiana State University for its New Orleans campus* after World War II. But about half of the Lakefront project became private real estate, sold by the Levee Board to help pay off bonds. The new developments were elaborately planned, conspicuously the Lake Vista project, designed in the "city beautiful" tradition of Radburn, New Jersey, with a central common, pedestrian avenues, and dead-end streets to provide "sanctuaries" for children. Altogether, it was very

*Louisiana State University in New Orleans (LSU/ NO) was renamed the University of New Orleans (UNO) in 1975.

handsome, and because it was laid out with public funds, officials were careful to insist that lots would be equally available to rich and poor alike—what Mayor Maestri happily described as the "poor man's project." It seems doubtful if anyone really believed it, considering the premium location and abundant amenities, and nobody was really surprised when the Lakefront area became the wealthiest area in the New Orleans metropolitan area (Figure 27)—amid public outcries that the law had been persistently violated during the auctioning of land. Nevertheless, Lakefront was and is an ornament to the city—one of the very few places where twentieth century city planning has truly improved a large area of an American city. Lakefront is a handsome place, no matter what one thinks of the political means by which it was achieved.

The New and Uncertain City (1945 and After)

As in most other cities, the Depression paralyzed New Orleans' booming growth, and while it lasted there was no significant building except for public works projects. World War II brought a return of prosperity, but the shortage of labor and materials continued the moratorium on building, which lasted for several years after Japan's defeat. By the late 1940s things were moving again, but New Orleans found herself in a new kind of world that operated under different rules than she had known before. The new rules, furthermore, were being made in irritating sorts of places—not the Clevelands and Detroits that had overtaken New Orleans in the late nineteenth century by sheer exercise of industrial muscle, but in shiny new air-conditioned cities of the West and South (!), whose nouveau riche economies rested on aircraft, electronics, and sunbathing. It was bad enough to be overtaken by Houston and Dallas-Fort Worth, but quite insufferable when the 1960 census showed Miami and the vexatious Atlanta to be larger than New Orleans. Worse still, there were unsettling changes afoot in New Orleans itself. It was no consolation at all to know that cities all over the country were sharing a similar trauma.

Changes took various forms, but at least four were so serious that in combination they bid fair to convert the city into a fundamentally different kind of place than she had ever been before. At this writing, New Orleans is grappling with all of them and will doubtless continue to do so with varying degrees of success.

The first was a change in the technology of

shipping, which in turn threatened the city's economic foundation, the port of New Orleans. The second change—an irreversible one—was the sudden suburban explosion of New Orleans out of its old confines, menacing the economic and physical integrity of the old city, and confronting adjacent regions with environmental challenges that they were ill-equipped to meet. Third, with suburban sprawl and the growth of black population came a rapid change in the function of the central business district and the adjacent French Quarter. Finally—and closely associated with the suburban explosion—was an ominous growth of segregation in New Orleans, the alienation of black and white populations, and the decay of inner city neighborhoods and public services. The combination of problems all arriving simultaneously was profoundly disquieting, especially so to Orleanians who were coming to understand that while their city was unique in many ways, it was not immune to the various ills that America's urban flesh is heir to.

REVOLUTION IN THE PORT

Of the four problems, the most tractable originated in the port of New Orleans. The port's difficulties were rooted in technology and were therefore subject to technological remedies. But while the problems were curable, they were no less important or expensive. As Professor James Kenyon has demonstrated, New Orleans depends much more heavily on income from overseas maritime commerce than any other large port in the eastern United States. (In 1967,

New Orleans received $3,839 per capita in waterborne foreign trade; her closest rivals were Baltimore with $849 and New York with $842.) Furthermore, her industrial base is relatively small—14 percent of its work force in manufacturing, compared with a national average for cities over 200,000 of about 28 percent. Thus, if the port is sick, New Orleans has very little to fall back on save tourism—an enterprise that is notoriously undependable from season to season. Then, too, the scarcity of manufacturing industry means that the port of New Orleans derives most of its revenue from *transshipment* of goods, rather than shipment of goods that originate locally. In consequence, New Orleans has a relatively small captive market of shippers who must use the port's facilities. Most of the customers are at least theoretically free to take their business elsewhere.

Competition between ports has always been lively in the United States, but postwar times brought several changes which inflamed that competition and which endangered New Orleans' second rank position among American ports. On the one hand, land transportation was changing. Trucks (and even airplanes) had begun to challenge the railroads' traditional domination of long distance freight haulage, and by the 1960s the interstate highway system was making all kinds of unlikely places suddenly accessible to cheap, flexible transportation. Simultaneously, railroad mergers meant that companies which had previously funneled all their custom through one preferred port now had several ports to choose from. (Thus, the Illinois Central, which had sent Midwestern produce routinely through New Orleans, merged with the Gulf, Mobile, and Ohio with its own preferred port of Mobile.) And, with completion of the St. Lawrence Seaway in the late 1950s, Chicago suddenly became a deepwater seaport, threatening New Orleans' long standing domination over Midwestern trade areas.

But the most disruptive change came from new shipping technology—container vessels to begin with, and then, about 1970, barge-carrying ships. It is easy to understand why containers upset old ways, for they represent the genius of simplicity. They are standard-sized steel boxes that can be transferred quickly from the hold or deck of a ship and put on a truck dolly or special flatcar to be hauled away. Although containers can be carried on conventional freighters, special "container ships" are much more efficient. The 1970 Bechtel Centroport Study notes that a conventional freighter needs two or three days in port to transfer 1,000 to 2,000 tons of cargo. A modern container ship can transfer 5,000 to 10,000 tons in the same time and with small danger of pilferage or damage by weather. The advantage over conventional modes is so great that by 1970 planners were freely forecasting that more than half of all general cargo would soon be diverted from old-fashioned freighters to the new container ships (cf. Figures 35 and 36).

Barge-carriers are even more unconventional—even mind-boggling. Variously known by the trade names "LASH" (the Central Gulf Steamship Company's "lighter aboard ship" vessel) or Sea-Bee (the Lykes Company's comparable vessel), these cavernous ships are equipped to lift sealed barges of special dimensions into a specially designed hold, where several dozen barges are stacked in long tiers, rather like trays of pizza in a gigantic oven. In some ways, the barges are even more versatile than containers, since they can carry either bulk cargo or general cargo. (On the other hand, containers can be handled by conventional freighters, whereas barges cannot.) The barge-carriers, according to the Bechtel study, can unload their tonnage about twice as fast as a container ship, and about ten times as fast as a conventional general cargo ship.

Barge-carrying vessels are so new that it is still unclear exactly what kind of alongshore facilities will be required to handle their cargo. At the moment, port authorities in New Orleans are inclined to favor barge-carriers over container ships, since containers can be off-loaded onto planes, trucks, barges, or trains, whereas barges are obviously confined to waterways. Thus New Orleans, at the intersection of the Intracoastal Waterway and the Mississippi, is clearly better off with barge-carriers than is, say, Mobile or Beaumont or Houston. Longshoremen too prefer barges to containers: the need to load and unload containers quickly makes for intensive but erratic employment, whereas barges can be handled in a more leisurely way, thus providing steadier and more reliable jobs. It will be several years, however, before the technology of handling barges is completely worked out. One can only suppose that it will require major changes in the geography and design of the port.

Figure 35. Traditional method of handling general cargo, here cotton and barreled products, probably oil. Congested docks are colorful but highly inefficient (cf. Figure 36). (Courtesy of the Greater New Orleans Tourist and Convention Commission)

That has already happened with container ships. The vessels are large and make profits only if they are kept moving constantly. It is particularly important that container ships be loaded and unloaded quickly and that port stops be kept to a minimum. To shippers, the new vessels offer unprecedented economies of scale; to port directors they hold out an ominous future, for if one port is equipped to handle containers quickly and efficiently, other competing ports will be bypassed to wither and slowly die. Furthermore, the situation will grow worse for the second runners, since the big East Coast ports are expecting a majority of their general cargo to be handled in containers within a few years—and the most valuable cargo at that.

For New Orleans, then, the message was clear: if the port was to retain its dominance of a midcontinent hinterland and justify its self-styled title of "Centroport, U.S.A.," it would have to build container facilities, and do it before some other enterprising Gulf port had seized the lead. Nor was it merely other Gulf Coast ports that New Orleans had to worry about. New Orleans' far-flung hinterland has brought the city enormous wealth, but the region's very size makes it vulnerable to raiding by competing ports, especially along its margins. Thus, distant ports like New York or

Figure 36. Loading cargo by container. Standardized large scale transfer of goods is cheaper and more efficient than traditional methods, but requires costly special equipment and huge dockside areas. Most of the New Orleans waterfront is obsolete as a result. (Courtesy of the Board of Commissioners for the Port of New Orleans)

Chicago (or even Oakland-San Francisco) could damage New Orleans badly, providing they had direct connections to parts of New Orleans' hinterland (which they do), and providing they could handle containers faster and therefore more cheaply than New Orleans.

Professor Kenyon notes that New Orleans' port directors are—along with their New York counterparts—among the canniest and most enterprising in the nation, but the New Orleans Dock Board was curiously unenthusiastic about the container business. Kenyon suggests two possible reasons. First of all, sea-going con-

tainers are heavier and costlier than land containers, and shippers are reluctant to send them very far inland, especially if they must return to port empty. Because New Orleans' trade area covers an abnormally large territory, containers seemed less attractive than they would to New York or Baltimore, with their smaller, more compact hinterlands. Second, New Orleans trades heavily with "underdeveloped" areas in Latin America, where modern container facilities are unavailable or poorly understood. Whatever the reason, New Orleans delayed so long that she suddenly found most of her port facilities obsolete. Emergency measures were needed. If nothing else, the sudden discovery that Japan, with her supermodern merchant fleet, had become New Orleans' best customer may have prodded the Dock Board into action.

With the same energy with which she had rebuilt her port at the turn of the century, New Orleans began again in the 1960s—a long term project that is slated to require three decades for completion. This time, however, it was more than a mere overhaul of existing facilities: most of the existing port facilities would be torn down, and the main functions picked up and moved to the east end of the city (Figure 37). It would be the most drastic change in New Orleans economic geography since the city's founding. To justify such efforts, of course, the deficiencies of the old port had to be legion.

They were. About the only things the Mississippi River wharves of the early 1900s had to recommend them were their access to the Public Belt Railroad and the fact that they did not stick out into the river—as did New York's. But for efficient operation, container docks needed large alongside assembly areas, big open "stuffing sheds," large rear yards for assembly of trucks or railroad cars, and huge expensive cranes for moving containers quickly between ships and marshaling areas. The riverfront was simply impossible (cf. Figures 35 and 38). Trucks were forced to use crowded city streets, and the expropriation of enough land to make proper facilities available would have been prohibitively costly. No sensible Dock Board would invest in large scale refurbishing in an area where payoff would be so small.

The Dock Board's decision was to wipe the slate clean and start afresh (Figure 38). By 2000 AD, twenty-nine existing wharves will be retired, leaving only the Henry Clay, Nashville, and Napoleon Avenue wharves open on the river. The rest will be torn down, and, if all goes as planned, New Orleans will have a riverfront uncluttered by wharves for the first time since Bienville landed. Indeed, if the city's excellent Parks and Recreation Department (NORD) has its way, the city may end up with a waterfront park system the equal of any in the country.

In place of the old facilities, an entirely new port is under construction in the marshes east of the city. The scale is very large, and there are signs already that the new development is pulling the whole metropolitan area in an eastward direction.

The reasons for locating here go back to the 1920s, when the Dock Board and the city collaborated to build a deep-water canal between the Mississippi River and Lake Pontchartrain (cf. Figure 39). This Inner Harbor Navigation Canal (more commonly called the "Industrial Canal") was only incidentally for lake-to-river shipping, for it was presently attached to the Intracoastal Waterway which led off eastward to Lake Borgne and the Mississippi Gulf Coast, thus leaving Lake Pontchartrain more or less free for recreation. But mainly, the Industrial Canal was designed to provide more dock space, and, equally important, more room for industrial development that the Dock Board hoped to attract to New Orleans. The canal was finished in 1921 and connected to the river by locks in 1923. By 1934 a long-standing project to improve the West Bank Harvey Lock and Canal was finished, linking the Mississippi with Bayou Barataria, western Louisiana, and the Texas coast (Figure 39). Both the Harvey Canal and the Industrial Canal became central links in the newly finished Intracoastal Waterway, which, by federal legislation, eventually led from the Rio Grande to the Florida Coast (Figure 1). (Traffic grew so heavy by 1945 that the Harvey Lock had to be supplemented with another at Algiers; cf. Figure 39).

The whole system worked beautifully, but not exactly as planned. Instead of heavy industry, the Industrial Canal became lined with facilities to serve the bulk cargo barges that plied the Intracoastal Waterway—storage yards for sand and gravel being fairly typical. The salubrity of New Orleans' atmosphere was thereby preserved, but industrial jobs were not created. Indeed, the city's main success in attracting big industry was through the federal government's acquisition of the Michoud Industrial Facility, some dozen miles east of the city, where NASA eventually began building Saturn rockets (Figures 3 and 37). (The Michoud facility probably results less from New Orleans' advantageous location on the Intracoastal Waterway than from the power of Louisiana's congressional delegation.) The arrangement has been something less than satisfactory, for the Michoud payroll fluctuates wildly, reflecting the fickle congressional enthusiasm for funding space programs.

Figure 37(A). Oblique aerial photo from Uptown New Orleans, looking downriver across Downtown toward New Orleans East and the Gulf Coast (see Figure 37B for key to locations). (Photo by Sam R. Sutton; courtesy of the Board of Commissioners for the Port of New Orleans)

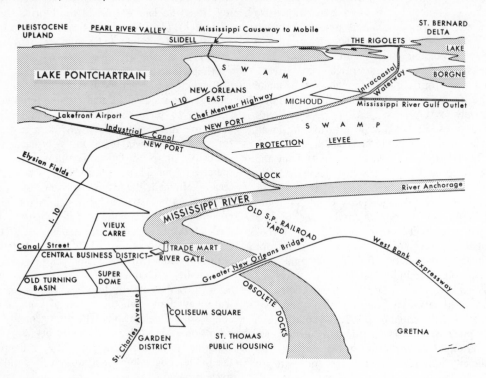

Figure 37(B). Key to locations in Figure 37A.

Figure 38. Looking upriver toward the Greater New Orleans Bridge from Trade Mart Tower, foot of Canal Street. Wharves and Public Belt Railroad separate Uptown New Orleans from the Mississippi. These wharves are obsolete, however, because of inadequate marshaling space for modern containers. Long term plans call for the dock facilities to be cleared and converted to public use—perhaps recreation. Note thunderheads in distance, typical of New Orleans' summer. Dredge in river is removing sediment deposited on inside curve of river meander.

When the Dock Board decided to build a new port of New Orleans, however, the obvious location was the junction of the Industrial Canal with the Intracoastal Waterway (Figure 39). Not only was there plenty of open space available (one hesitates to call it "land"), transportation facilities were excellent—two mainline railways, Interstate-10, and "MR-GO," the Mississippi River–Gulf Outlet Canal, nearby. The MR-GO headed straight for the Gulf, and thus cut off forty miles from the winding river passage (Figure 2). Although it was promoted as a route for deep sea shipping, it turned out to be no such thing—since to get from MR-GO (near sea level) to the river, some ten feet above, ships had to pass through the Inner Harbor Lock, a passage which often was so backed up with ships and barges that delays of several days were not uncommon (Figure 39). Most ocean ships still come to New Orleans by river, not willing to risk the cost of delays at the lock.

Thus, while the new site seems attractive, it requires very considerable improvement—not the least of which is turning swamp into something approaching dry land. Meantime, the first step is under way with the completion of large new container terminals along France Road and plans to excavate a gigantic new harbor and turning basin in the swamps behind the Ninth Ward.

Such a habor will not work, however, unless deep draft ships can get from the harbor to the Mississippi quickly—and, since the Mississippi

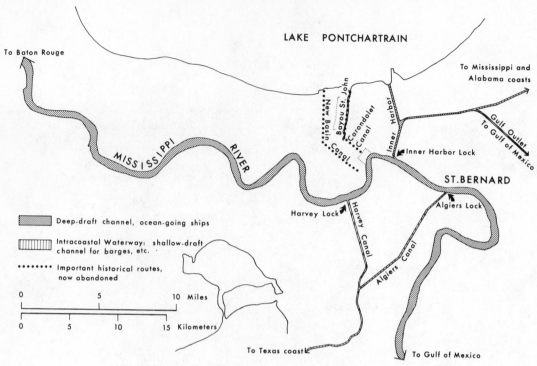

Figure 39. Waterways through New Orleans

continues to flow ten to fifteen feet above the new facilities in the backswamp, large scale locking is necessary. The old Industrial Canal Lock simply will not do, for while it is deep enough for most ocean vessels, the big fast container ships simply will not tolerate the delays. Thus, New Orleans' shiny new port will grow cobwebs unless the lock is either enlarged or relocated. According to the Corps of Engineers, it would cost over $358 million to expand the existing locks, since they are located in expensive built-up land. By contrast, the Corps estimates less than $200 million to build a brand new lock and connecting canal, which would run from the MR-GO to the river at Violet, a village in St. Bernard Parish about ten miles downstream from the present lock. At the present writing the Violet project is stalled, opposed by downriver residents who fear that a new canal would cut off their escape routes during hurricanes and might act as a funnel for floodwaters into their neighborhoods. The issue remains unresolved, while the Corps of Engineers looks nervously around for alternative locations. Nobody, it seems, wants a lock in his back yard.

Meantime, the Dock Board is hedging its bets by rebuilding a small number of Mississippi River wharves for container vessels—chiefly at the Nashville and Napoleon Avenue facilities. Simultaneously, the state of Louisiana says it intends to build a so-called "Superport"—a deep draft habor and terminal that would be built offshore in Gulf coastal waters. The Superport is conceived to service vessels of 100 foot draft and more, and while its promoters suggest that it would handle all sorts of cargo, it is obviously designed for bulk carriers—mainly supertankers, which are growing more and more super by the year. There is considerable economic logic to this location, since the Mississippi Delta is figuratively floating on oil and gas, and since the river below Baton Rouge is rapidly being lined on either bank with refineries, chemical plants, and the like. Although the state of Louisiana stands to collect considerable revenue if such a venture is successful, it is hard to see how New Orleans will gain much from the bargain. After all, the movement and processing of bulk cargo is increasingly automated and there is considerable advantage to moving big bulk facilities to cheap land far away from the city—not closer in. Plainly, however, southern Louisiana is booming, although it may turn out that Houston oil men gain more from the boom than the average resident of southern Louisiana, much less New Orleans. Furthermore, Orleanians do not take lightly the fact that crude oil does not mix well with oysters, crabs, and shrimp, which are caught in large delectable numbers off the south coast of the delta. An oil spill could be an economic disaster for the fishermen, and a culinary disaster for Orleanian trenchermen. Orleanians take shellfish seriously. It is one of their greatest virtues.

THE SUBURBAN EXPLOSION

It is easy to be hopeful about the future of the port, largely because it is firmly controlled by intelligent responsible men, who understand how the port works and want to make sure it continues working. It is harder to be optimisic about New Orleans' physical growth, especially since the end of wartime building controls in the late 1940s. From that time to the present, the metropolitan area has simply exploded into the swamps—first toward the East Bank section of Jefferson Parish; more recently into the eastern reaches of Orleans Parish and beyond; and, although the main surge is yet to come, now southward from the West Bank in the direction of Bayou Barataria. Between 1950 and 1975, the built-up area of metropolitan New Orleans about doubled in size, and there is little sign that the expansion is subsiding. Because the new additions have been so sudden—and because they are different in population and appearance from the old city—New Orleans has become two cities in the last twenty-five years or so. Within is the compact old prewar city. Around it in all directions is the new exploded tissue of suburbia.

The results have not been fortunate. As in dozens of other North American cities, New Orleans' suburban landscape is compounded of new cars, new roads, an insatiable appetite for inexpensive houses with open space, deficient land use controls, unrestrained greed by land sellers and house builders, a studied reluctance of municipalities to cooperate with one another, and an almost pathological desire of local governmental officials to see their particular bailiwicks grow.

In addition, however, New Orleans' subur-

ban sprawl is peculiar in several ways. Most of the newly developed land is built on muck and is sinking at various rates. Much of the land is subject to extremely dangerous flooding. And because New Orleans began spreading out later than most American cities, most suburban growth has been compressed into a very short span of time—mostly from 1960 onward. As a result, the new areas lack the architectural variety of places that grew at different times and in different styles. The contrast between homogeneous new suburbs and the extravagantly varied old prewar city is, to put it mildly, invidious.

Until World War II, New Orleans' patterns of urban growth had differed sharply from those of other big American cities. Outside the protection levees, roads were expensive to build and the swampland atrociously intractable for buildings. The Wood pumps had changed all that by the 1920s, but no sooner had the suburban expansion begun than depression and war combined to smother it.

East Bank Jefferson

But new roads were abuilding, and they would determine the direction in which metropolitan New Orleans would grow (see Frontispiece). Before World War II, there were two main highway routes out of the city—Chef Menteur Highway to the east, and the braided path of River Road and Jefferson Highway westward to Baton Rouge (Figure 3). These roads, and a few other inconsequential roads, were all tied to natural levees, either of the Mississippi or, like the dead-end roads to Lafitte and Yscoloskey, of distributaries of the river (Figure 2). The great break came in the early 1930s, when Governor Huey Long, with customary disregard for tradition and the laws of nature, had his new "Airline Highway" built from Baton Rouge to New Orleans—slashed in great expensive swaths across the quivering swamp (Figure 3).

For twenty years, very little happened along Airline Highway—during the 1930s because nobody had money to speculate in real estate, and after the war because nobody wanted to plunge into the swamps while alternative land could be had inside the city. To be sure, a few roadside commercial buildings sprang up, but nobody saw them as a portent of the time when Airline Highway would become the longest ugliest scar of strip commercial development in Louisiana.

Thus, during the 1930s and 1940s, and even into the 1950s, the city's main growth was internal—filling up undeveloped interstices, or building immediately adjacent to built-up areas. Even today, behind the Lakefront area, one can find patch after patch of houses that might be described as "Cape Cod Veteran," interspersed with the older more substantial neo-Spanish villas of the 1920s.

Then suddenly, in the late 1950s, New Orleans acted like a pail that had slowly been filling—and spilled over. It was a different sort of expansion than the city had experienced before. No longer did building advance like a wave from established neighborhoods on the edge of the city, but instead began to be spattered in apparently random distribution beyond the Orleans Parish line, generally following the axis of Airline Highway. Jefferson officials, who suddenly found taxes deliciously rising, promptly dubbed the parish "Progressive Jefferson" and began to build new levees and streets as fast as revenues accumulated. That was very fast indeed, for Jefferson was soon to boast the highest per capita income of any parish in Louisiana.

To attract more people (as if they needed attracting) East Bank officials achieved two great coups—the new multilaned Veterans Memorial Highway, which cut straight across the parish to the St. Charles Protection Levee; and the new Moisant Airfield, shortly to become New Orleans International Airport (Figure 3). Meantime, promoters had succeeded in funding the most ambitious project of all, the Lake Pontchartrain Causeway, a twenty-four mile span to the "Ozone Belt" of St. Tammany Parish—a bucolic area which had long served as retreat for wealthy Orleanians (Figure 2). The causeway was touted as "the World's Longest Bridge," and indeed it proved too long and too costly for easy commuting. The approach to the causeway, however, obviously dubbed Causeway Boulevard, became the main street of East Bank Jefferson, and sprouted strip commercial development which outdid the most egregious developments along Airline or Veterans highways. (By 1973, Veterans Highway had accumulated such extraordinary strip commercial blight that the New Orleans *States-Item* ran a series of features about how ugly it was.)

The core of East Bank Jefferson—quintessentially suburban—the huge Lakeside Shopping Center, set in a great desert of asphalt parking lots. Along Causeway Boulevard a crop of boxlike buildings emerged, and the Jefferson promoters promptly dubbed the whole area "Fat City," an elegant phrase which describes what presumably happens to the pocketbooks of those who are clever enough to buy or rent land there.

Just as the neo–Los Angeles landscape of East Bank Jefferson differed from old New Orleans by some light years, the population also differed. The area's high average income did not result from any large influx of the very rich (Figure 27). Rather it was a combination of middle and upper middle income migration of whites, together with the fact that poor people and black people were discouraged from moving to Jefferson by economic and other constraints. A comparison of contemporary racial and income maps of New Orleans shows the results of the process by 1970: the most extensive areas of poverty in East Bank Jefferson (Figure 40) correspond to a few patches of black population near Airline Highway and the Illinois Central Gulf Railroad tracks (Figure 21). At the other end of the scale, there is only one area of very rich people, the plush neighborhoods of old Metairie, focused on the Metairie Country Club, cheek by jowl with the Orleans Parish line (Figure 27). In sum, the only important departures from middle and upper income were inherited from prewar times.

(It is not much comfort to know that the same kind of intraurban migration has occurred within dozens of other American cities since World War II. In nearly all of them, the migration has caused suburbs to be more and more homogeneous, the central cities increasingly alienated from the middle class.)

By the early 1970s most of the land in East Bank Jefferson had been used up. The completion of I-10 across the parish to center city New Orleans—the road replete with four gigantic cloverleaf interchanges—simply brought coals to Newcastle, and by 1973 the whole area from Orleans Parish to the St. Charles protection levee resembled one gigantic ill-planned subdivision. (Beyond, in St. Charles Parish, I-10 is built on concrete piles, and for ten miles it cuts through an almost pristine wilderness of marshgrass and cypress. To drive from St. Charles' wild beauty and cross the protection levee into Jefferson's endless suburbia is surely one of the most jarring cultural shocks

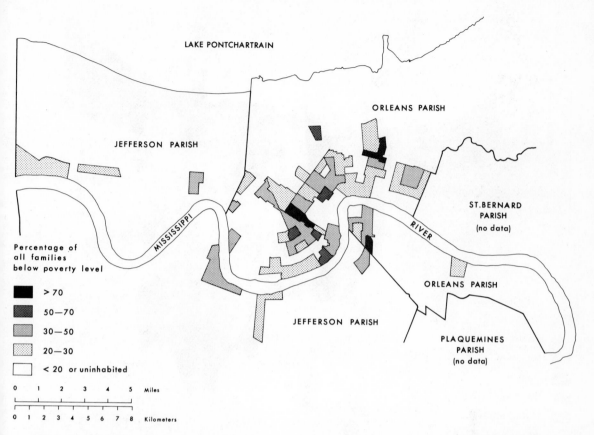

Figure 40. Poverty in metropolitan New Orleans, 1970. The map shows the percentage of households in each census tract whose income falls below the poverty level, as defined by a federal interagency committee. The poverty threshold was set in 1969 as $3,743 for a family of four and is adjusted to take into account family size, sex and age of family head, number of children, etc. Given the definitions, this map obviously shows the city's big areas of serious hard-core poverty. Note the close correlation between poverty and black population, especially in public housing (cf. Figure 20). Note also the low incidence of poverty in suburban areas which developed after 1950 and in fashionable areas of the old city—Vieux Carré, Garden District, and the university district.

awaiting a motorist anywhere in America.) And, as typically happens in the last stage of building a subdivision, the last areas are filled up with multifamily buildings, heavily populated by young couples with young children who are using the "garden" apartments of new *new* Jefferson as a camping ground until they acquire enough money to move elsewhere. By 1973, however, over 40 percent of the New Orleans metropolitan population lived in Jefferson Parish—a population increasingly distinguished by medium-high income, medium-high educational levels (Figure 41), and a lack of domestic roots. It is easy to find people who are fond of old New Orleans. It is almost impossible to find people who are in love with

Jefferson Parish, and it shows in the look of the place.

Eastern New Orleans

I-10 was merely the last in a series of highways which "opened up" East Bank Jefferson, but the process was almost finished anyway. In eastern Orleans Parish between the Industrial Canal and the Rigolets, however, I-10 was the open-sesame which by the early 1970s was converting swamps into a vast new sea of suburbia (Figure 42). And beyond in the piney hills of St. Tammany Parish, of Hancock and Pearl River counties, Mississippi, real estate speculators were beginning to multiply like rabbits.

As of the early 1960s eastern New Orleans

Median School Years Completed, 1970

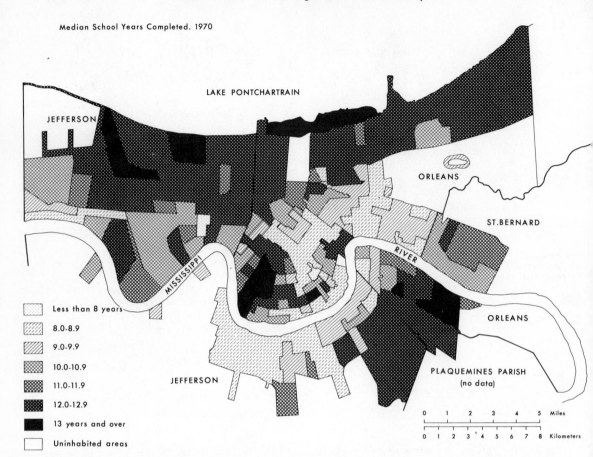

Less than 8 years

8.0-8.9

9.0-9.9

10.0-10.9

11.0-11.9

12.0-12.9

13 years and over

Uninhabited areas

Figure 41. Education in metropolitan New Orleans, 1970. High educational levels obviously occur near Tulane-Loyala and the University of New Orleans, but high levels elsewhere reflect wealth and high prestige—new affluent suburbs, the Garden District, and Vieux Carré. Low education is associated with blacks (cf. Figure 21) and blue collar workers—e.g., Ninth Ward, downriver from the Vieux Carré; West Bank Jefferson's shipbuilders; and dockworkers who live near the river in Uptown New Orleans. (Courtesy of Hugh G. Lewis)

(Figures 37A and 37B) showed signs of duplicating the experience of East Bank Jefferson—only ten years later. Already, helter-skelter strip commercial and residential building had begun to spring up along the relocated Chef Menteur Highway, which struck out across the wetlands in a manner reminiscent of Airline Highway. So far, there was no interstate highway, and the delay had given land speculators a chance to learn the astronomical profits that could be turned by securing large chunks of land along an interstate corridor and holding it. Thus it was that huge new land developments were neatly arranged along the whole right of way of the new I-10 East—with the warm cooperation of the Louisiana Highway

Department, which built large interchanges in advance of subdivision building.

When I-10 was connected to the mainland by a gigantic causeway-cum-bridge across the east end of Lake Pontchartrain (Figure 43), there remained little doubt about the direction of New Orleans' main growth for the next few years.

By the 1970s construction was already under way and on a grand scale, with several enormous projects contemplated for the future. The largest is called "New Orleans East," fifty square *miles* (32,000 acres) owned by a single corporation (Figure 44). According to promotional literature, it will be a "totally planned community where 250,000 people will eventu-

Figure 42. I-10, Heading east through the swamps toward the Lake Pontchartrain Bridge and the Mississippi coast. Ostensibly, the road was built to allow people to get into the city quickly; the actual effect was to promote a suburban exodus out of the city. The swampland to the right and left is shown on drawing boards as becoming one of the largest planned residential areas in the United States. Previously, the area was thought unfit for human habitation. The water in the ditch at the right marks the surface of the water table under "normal" conditions. Recent hurricanes have put this and nearby areas under several feet of water.

ally live, work, and play." The advertisement goes on to observe that "it is the largest singly owned parcel of land to lie within the corporate limits of any major city . . . and is equal to one-fourth the total area of New Orleans itself." As of 1973, pieces of New Orleans East had begun to appear, with billboards at big new freeway interchanges, and bits and pieces of actual development here and there. Much of it seems to portend another East Bank Jefferson, but one must be comforted in the knowledge that it had all been planned in advance (Figure 44).

Still farther out, beyond the Rigolets, other big developments are under construction. One of them, called "Eden Isles," a large area of marsh on the edge of St. Tammany Parish, ad-

vertises itself as a "total community," offering "a refuge for Orleanians fleeing the noise and congestion of the city," and promoting its virtues vigorously over local television. Frontage on water is guaranteed for nearly all residential lots by the simple expedient of making land by digging canals, thus making the whole area look like a large marina. According to the promotional literature, "sites are raised to a minimum of 6½ feet above mean sea level," and Everyman has access to Lake Pontchartrain, the Rigolets, and Mississippi Sound, merely by getting into his boat and sailing out from the dock in his front yard.

Such developments are raising serious questions about the wisdom, much less the safety, of

Figure 43. Looking toward New Orleans from the I-10 causeway across the east end of Lake Pontchartrain. All major arterial highways into the city cross great watery wastelands like this and remind one forcibly that New Orleans is an island. Such bridges have made the city newly accessible, but have simultaneously made possible explosive growth into heretofore inaccessible areas. Behind us from this viewing point, suburbanization is rapidly taking over the Pleistocene upland on the north side of Lake Pontchartrain.

the new New Orleans. Subsidence is a nagging and expensive problem everywhere. New houses are commonly built on concrete pads, laid on sand, and undergirded by thirty foot piles sunk into the mush on four foot centers and held firm by a process delicately known as "skin friction." Such heroic tactics add considerably to the cost of building and they prod developers into selling property as quickly as possible, even though it might be wiser to let it settle for a few years. As a result, a new owner often has the enriching prospect of watching yard, driveways, and sidewalks sink, while his house stands firm, supported by skin friction. (If the water mains or sewers are sheared away, it becomes even more exciting.) By the time the area is ditched and sprayed against mosquitos,

there may be nothing more than a broken driveway to remind the owner that he is living in a wetland environment. Memories are short.

Some reminders would be helpful, however, if only for public safety. The main danger in eastern New Orleans is from hurricanes, which frequently and randomly strike the Gulf coast of the United States with varying degrees of ferocity. Two recent hurricanes—"Betsy" in September 1965, and "Camille" in August 1969—have been extensively documented by the U.S. Army Corps of Engineers, and, although the corps is too politic to say so in plain language, the reports make it clear that extensive building in the marshes of eastern Orleans Parish is inviting serious trouble.

The worst threat from hurricanes does not

Figure 44. Planned development east of New Orleans. Interstate 10, to the left, and conspicuously shown on the billboard, has triggered this growth. Footings of the billboard are about five feet below sea level. Much of the area was heavily inundated during Hurricanes Betsy and Camille, 1965 and 1969.

come from high winds, even though wind velocities, which in Camille exceeded 200 miles per hour (Figure 45), can (and did) shred wooden houses to toothpicks. Rather, the main dangers are "tidal surges," fearful events which occur when high tides are pushed by high winds into constricted channels. On August 17, 1969, in the cold language of the engineers' report on Camille, "at Pass Christian (on the Mississippi coast, Figure 45) a reliable high-water mark of 22.6 feet was found; less reliable debris marks of 24.6 and 24.2 were also found in the vicincity." Shortly before, the storm had "sideswiped the mouth of the Mississippi River" with "estimated wind velocities of 140 to 160 mph ... while tide levels up to elevation 16 feet above mean sea level overwhelmed the protective levee system and flowed into the developed areas."

Camille is supposed to have been the worst storm to hit the North American coast in recorded history, and it is easy to believe. Where the storm struck the Mississippi coast, it wiped out large parts of Pass Christian and neighboring towns, killed 137 people, and did over a half a billion dollars worth of damage in Mississippi and Alabama alone.

It is worth remembering that Camille missed New Orleans by some fifty miles, but even so, much of southeastern Louisiana was flooded (Figure 46). It is worth remembering too that Betsy, although a milder storm than Camille, approached the city on a disturbingly unpredictable course (Figure 47), caused "massive breaks" in the levee system below the city, and flooded huge areas of eastern Orleans Parish—then uninhabited, but now slated for "planned residential development" (Figures 44 and 46).

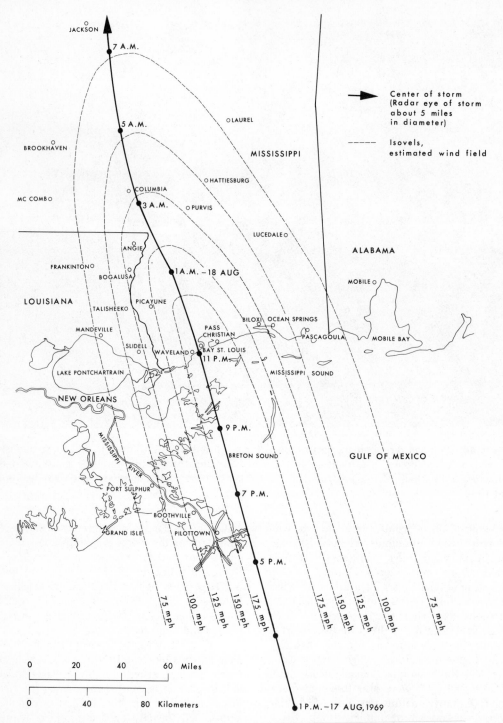

Figure 45. The path and windfield of Hurricane Camille, August 1969, perhaps the most destructive storm to hit the Gulf Coast in historic time. New Orleans was fifty miles away from the center of the storm—a critically important distance, it turned out. Several Mississippi coastal towns were practically obliterated. (U.S. Army Corps of Engineers)

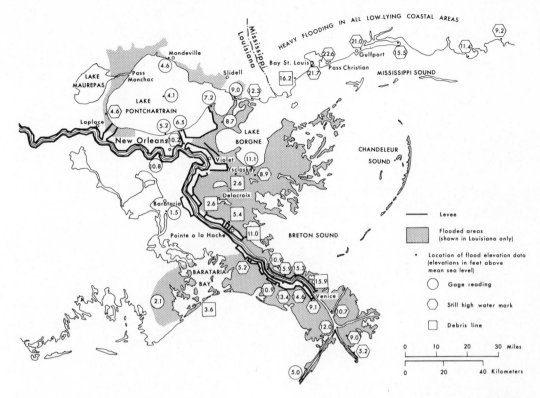

Figure 46. Flooding by Hurricane Camille in southeastern Louisiana, August 1969. Shaded areas were inundated. Numbers denote depth (in feet) to which surface was flooded. (Note: depths of high water are shown in Mississippi, but not extent of flooded areas. U.S. Army Corps of Engineers, New Orleans Engineer District.)

Real estate developers are reassuring, however. In the Eden Isles subdivision with its sea level canals and residential lots six and a half feet above sea level, the advertisements read: "Eden Isles . . . for the rest of your life!" To ensure long life, the state of Louisiana has helpfully erected signs along highways, directing people how to get out (Figure 48). During Camille, some 69,400 people were evacuated from flooded areas in south Louisiana, but, as the Corps of Engineers' report chillingly comments, "in the heavily developed areas of metropolitan New Orleans with a population of over 1 million, prestorm evacuation in most cases is not feasible." It is therefore a relief to know that the New Orleans East developers anticipate a population of a mere quarter million, most of whom have not read the engineers' report, which explains why damage estimates may not be very reliable: "Surveyors must use judgment based on available evidence to decide whether waters floated the structure and the winds sub-

sequently demolished it, or whether floating debris driven by wave action in an area of high surges pounded the structure, or if a combination of two or more of these factors constituted the force of major destruction."

Meantime, construction goes on, and Greater New Orleans grows greater by the day. And real estate advertisements wax eloquent about marinas, golf courses, and fun-in-the-sun, but remain strangly quiet about hurricanes.

The West Bank

Growth on the West Bank, both in Orleans and Jefferson parishes, has been a trifle less hair raising, having lagged behind the East Bank because it is awkward to get back and forth across the Mississippi. There are two automobile bridges in the metropolitan area—the Huey P. Long Bridge, inconveniently located upstream in Jefferson Parish, and built to accommodate the narrow vehicles of the 1930s; and the Greater New Orleans Bridge, which

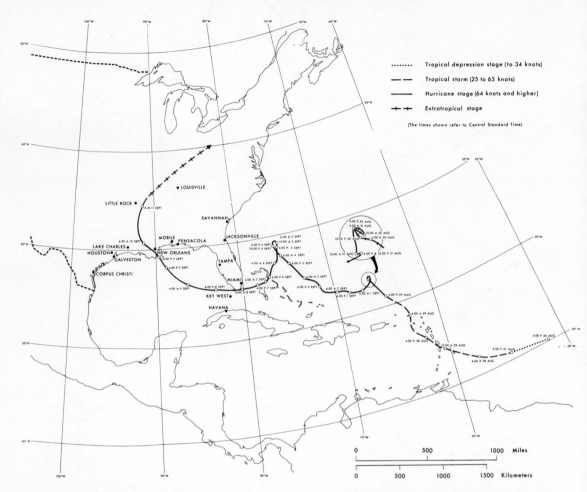

Figure 47. The path and windfield of Hurricane Betsy, 1965. Hurricanes do not always oblige forecasters by following predictable courses. Until three days before Hurricane Betsy hit the Louisiana coast in 1965, the storm was of only academic importance. Compare Figure 45 and note that Betsy passed New Orleans to the west by about the same distance that Camille passed the city to the east, four years later. (U.S. Army Corps of Engineers)

offers a splendid view of the river and business district for drivers waiting in the middle of the bridge for traffic to become unjammed. Frustration has mounted, and new bridges have been proposed at several Uptown locations, midpoint between the older two. Napoleon Avenue was the site of one such proposal, but it was greeted with cries of outrage from Uptown residents, who exhibited selfish prejudices against ripping out oak-lined boulevards to build four lane divided elevated bridge ramps (see Figure 56). Meantime, other promoters had evidently learned the lessons of I-10 and began urging a southerly "bypass" around New Or-

leans, variously proposed as I-29, or I-410, or the "Dixie Freeway."

Few responsible people really believe that such a road is needed for purposes of bypassing New Orleans. Transcontinental traffic stays north of Lake Pontchartrain and has no reason to come near New Orleans. Intracity traffic that wishes to avoid traffic jams in the downtown area can use I-610, which cuts straight across the city's midriff and misses the central business district by two miles (Figure 3). The proposed project *does* have two purposes, but neither have anything to do with "bypassing." First, the West Bank would get one and pos-

Figure 48. Hurricane evacuation route, Paris Road, near New Orleans East. The signs are ominous, but the fine print in the engineers' report is even more so: "in the heavily developed areas of metropolitan New Orleans . . . prestorm evacuation in most cases is not feasible."

sibly two new bridges that would be part of the federal interstate system and thus, under federal law, transfer 90 percent of the cost from the Baton Rouge highway budget and pass it on to Washington. Second, if the road cut far enough southward, it would "open" all kinds of new territory for suburban development.

Critics of the proposal point out that much of the territory is not merely swampland, but is actually under many feet of water (Figure 3). They also note that the project impinges on a proposed national park south of New Orleans. They charge that the real estate promoters are not looking for a bypass at all, but that they got advance inside information on where the "bypass" would be located, bought up the land, and are simply waiting for the road to be built—thus making enormous profits at public expense. The promoters naturally deny

any wrongdoing, and counter by arguing that the road is "needed" because the West Bank's main artery—the West Bank Expressway—is no expressway at all, and is dangerous. While that happens to be true, it is less than persuasive, since the expressway could easily be improved by building an elevated highway down its wide neutral ground. This suggestion is generally ignored, since it is plain that many West Bankers (and speculators with West Bank real estate holdings) simply want new roads and bridges—and without more argument. Possibly it escapes West Bankers that completion of the project would quickly turn the area into a 1980 version of East Bank Jefferson. The promoters obviously know that, and if the public does not, it is merely because they do not keep their eyes open. Perhaps, in view of what has already happened to so much of New Orleans suburbia, the public feels the issue is lost, and no longer cares.

CHANGES IN THE CORE

When a city suddenly develops a suburban ring like New Orleans', the new growth represents more than mere territorial addition. It is a jarring change that sends shock waves through the entire metropolitan area, but nowhere more intensely felt than in the central city. At the root of things are demographic shifts, and a selective migration of people. It has happened over and over again in American cities. Just as the new suburbanites are overwhelmingly white and generally affluent, the central city is left with a disproportionate number of nonwhites, many of whom are poor and badly educated. Furthermore, the suburbanites take their wealth with them, not only eroding the tax base of the central city, but eventually causing jobs themselves to move out. In 1970 in the New Orleans metropolitan area, for example, only 39 percent of Jefferson Parish's work force commuted to Orleans Parish. Of the Orleanians themselves, some 23 percent worked outside the parish. Farther out the figures were even lower, and in St. Tammany—which advertises itself as "close to downtown New Orleans"—only 17 percent actually worked in New Orleans.

Retail stores move to the suburbs even faster than jobs. Thus a suburban worker may commute into the city, but his wife does all her shopping in a neighborhood shopping center. The New Orleans City Planning Commission in 1970 reported that the central business district's share of total metropolitan area retail sales dropped steadily—from 42 percent in 1948, to 34 percent in 1954, to 27 percent in 1958, to 24 percent in 1963.

New Orleans, however, is better off than the numbers suggest. The city's 24 percent in 1963 compares marvellously with such places as Dallas or Phoenix, whose central business districts retained less than 9 percent of metropolitan retail sales. Furthermore, in absolute volume of retail sales, downtown New Orleans is palpably alive—especially at night, when most American cities have barred their windows and abandoned the streets. When Orleanians go out for a night on the town, they still customarily head for the central part of the city.

Most Americans quite properly view decaying downtowns as symptoms of general urban rot—or, even more broadly, of a rotting society. When a city like New Orleans turns out to be partly immune to a nationwide disease, it is worthwhile inquiring into the cause of immunity. Fortunately, the causes of downtown health are fairly obvious in New Orleans, but less fortunately, many American cities are incapable of profiting from New Orleans experience. For them, it is simply too late.

First of all, the processes of downtown decay started fairly recently in New Orleans—compared with other cities. The delay was largely a function of delayed suburbanization, which in turn resulted from the high cost of draining surrounding swamplands. (Most cities have not had the advantages of location in a morass.) Second, despite suburban sprawl, New Orleans remains a fairly compact place, and from most parts of the metropolitan area downtown is not very far away. Third, as all Orleanians know, and as Professors Chai and Juhn of UNO have shown, the city has for a long time been informally governed by a very conservative elite who feel fiercely possessive about their city and who are very slow to make major changes. This conservative group has often been damned by "progressive" elements in the city, but despite the conservatives' alleged sins and wickednesses, they deserve much credit for preventing the orgy of downtown destruction that eviscerated so many American cities in the name of "urban renewal," and has so obviously speeded the exodus to the suburbs elsewhere. St. Louis, to name but one, discovered its mistake after the destruction was over, and by then the city was beyond salvation. In New Orleans, they made the discovery by accident, but possibly just in time.

Salvation of and by the French Quarter

For no explanation of New Orleans' downtown vitality would make any sense unless there had been a solid physical core of architectural interest and permanent population on which to build. That core is the Vieux Carré—the old "French Quarter"—without which New Orleans' downtown area would probably not be very different from any other old American seaport. The "Quarter," as Orleanians call it, performs several vital functions simultaneously.

Most important, the Quarter serves as the city's chief symbolic totem, and most city residents love it dearly. To be sure, some Orleanians profess to loathe it—because it is "dirty" or "dangerous" or "full of hippies and tourists" or simply because "it isn't the way it used to be." While there is much truth in these complaints, it is also true that most Orleanians feel strongly about the Quarter because it is the real core of the city and everybody knows it.

Second, the Vieux Carré attracts large numbers of tourists, who stay out until all hours of the night and spend large sums of money. The best estimates come from a 1965 survey by Hammer, Green, Siler Associates, who found that 1,800,000 people came to New Orleans during the year, and spent about $170 million —which makes tourism the second largest moneymaker in the city. The survey found that most tourists, furthermore, were "influenced" by existence of the Quarter in their decision to visit New Orleans—and that tourists who stayed in the Quarter spent more than their counterparts who lived outside. Since the time the survey was made, a good many more hotels have been built downtown, and these figures probably need to be multiplied by a factor of two or three.

A sizable proportion of tourists, it turns out, come from the Midwest—more even than from Louisiana, Texas, and Mississippi combined. And despite the popular image of Midwestern tourists as clean-cut Disneyland-visiting families with 2.3 children, New Orleans' tourist population includes a considerable number of people who have heard that the Quarter is eccentric and hope for a chance to exhibit a bit of their own eccentricity. It is hard to know exactly how many Bohemians and small town Southern runaways come to the Quarter for that reason, nor is it easy to estimate how many Dr. Jekylls check into French Quarter hotels and emerge half an hour later as Mr. Hydes. There is, of course, a sizable admixture of "ordinary tourists," some of whom come to see the sights, to buy antiques on Royal Street at inflated prices, or merely to watch the year-round carnival that the Uptown end of Bourbon Street has recently become. Whoever the clientele may be, the New Orleans police understand them very well, and all sorts of aberrant behavior is tolerated in the Quarter (especially on Bourbon Street) that would subject perpetrators to instant arrest in other cities, not to mention other parts of New Orleans.

To a good many Orleanians, however, the Quarter's eccentric image is a mixed blessing. A 1969 Gallup Poll caused much anguish when it announced a general public appraisal of American cities. New Orleans, it turned out, stood highest in public esteem for its fine restaurants (only New York and San Francisco were ranked higher)—no surprise after the Hammer, Green, Siler survey that found a good many people visited New Orleans primarily to eat or be seen eating at elegant places. In addition, New Orleans ranked high (fifth in the nation) for being "interesting and different," and even received "honorable mention" for its "gay night life" and its "beautiful setting" (!). But to the dismay of the Chanber of Commerce, the list of twenty cities perceived as "good places to live" omitted New Orleans entirely. Shortly thereafter, the city raised the budget of the Tourist and Convetnion Commission considerably, and that body began energetically to advertise the city's virtues for homebodies as well as sinners. It has not proved easy. New Orleans has apparently been associated with Bourbon Street too long to acquire a reputation for domestic tranquility overnight.

Irrespective of publicity and hoopla, however, the Vieux Carré's ancient and not-so-ancient buildings provide desirable homes for a growing population of permanent residents. Some of these residents are drifters with marginal incomes; there are still plenty of dilapidated houses in the Quarter. But increasing numbers are affluent folk who pay dearly for the privilege of living in the Quarter and parking their Mercedes-Benz in a Spanish courtyard. In the two Vieux Carré census tracts, for example, the median 1970 value of an "owner-occupied housing unit" came to $44,100 and $37,000 respectively—this against a metropolitan area median figure of $20,000. Most dwellings in the Quarter, however, are not single houses, nor are they owner-occupied. Rather, most are in multiunit buildings—apartments with smaller and fewer rooms than one ordinarily finds in other parts of the city. The population that inhabits such places includes many single people and childless couples—well-educated people (Figure 41) whose relatively high incomes give them considerable surplus to buy creature comforts. In population, then, the Quarter's permanent population seemingly resembles that of Greenwich Village, but there is a major difference. Manhattan would survive quite nicely without the Village, but without the Vieux Carré, center-city New Orleans might very well be an empty shell.

Obviously, the preservation of the Vieux Carré has served New Orleans very well, but unhappily for other cities that might learn from New Orleans' example, preservation until recently was largely accidental. For most of the nineteenth century, the Quarter was ignored by Americans who were too busy pushing their brash new city upriver to pay attention to the crowded old European town. Meantime, many old Creole families stayed in their familiar homes, sheltered against the world outside, but the years were taking their toll. New generations moved out to cleaner and airier quarters, while old buildings crumbled. (Fortunately, the crumbling was slow since many of the old Spanish buildings were very stoutly built.) By the beginning of the twentieth century, much of the Quarter had suffered severely—not so much from rot, as from attrition by the city along the edges (Figure 49). On the Uptown side, Iberville Street had become a kind of alley to service the rear of Canal Street stores. Rampart Street, of proud name, faced on the abandoned Carondolet turning basin and the Storyville red light district and had gone to ruin. Along the waterfront, a thick growth of docks and warehouses had cut once-lovely Jackson Square completely off from the river (Figures 28, 37, and 49), and Decatur Street was spotted with seamen's bars and flophouses. Toward Esplanade Avenue, skid row was alive and well. In sum, the Vieux Carré was being affected by adjacent areas, but it was doing precious little affecting itself.

It is not clear exactly why New Orleans began to pay attention to the Quarter and to regard it once more as the core of the city. To be sure, the city had always felt sentimental about it, even as it fell apart, and slim volumes of pencil sketches periodically appeared to remind Orleanians that they did not need to visit Tintern Abbey to see genuine ruins. The official pamphlet of the Vieux Carré Commission is typically vague: "With the coming of the 1920's and '30's there was a rebirth of feeling for the Vieux Carré—and New Orleans began at long last to realize that unless something was done to preserve what was left, that soon the whole Quarter would disappear." The remark implies some spontaneous generation of interest, but as John Chase has observed (in *Frenchmen, Desire, Good Children . . .*) it was the WPA that was chiefly responsible for

showing Orleanians what they had and how to preserve it.

Perhaps there is a lesson: outsiders sometimes are useful for showing natives the virtues of their home places. However it happened, a state constitutional amendment in 1936 authorized creation of a "Vieux Carré Commission," with power to regulate architecture through control of building permits. Meantime, with WPA money and talent, substantial parts of the Quarter were reconditioned, with primary attention to the area around the French Market and Jackson Square, where five crucial buildings were restored—St. Louis Cathedral, the Cabildo and Presbytère next door, and the two superb Pontalba buildings that flank the square.

As tourists flocked in, it quickly became obvious that rehabilitation was not merely an exercise for aesthetes, but would pay handsomely. It also became clear that the processes of slum making had been reversed. Land values began to rise, and rehabilitations were increasingly financed by private capital.

It was not done without a fight, of course, and again New Orleans' experience may be applicable elsewhere. The Vieux Carré Commission exercised its authority with vigor, insisting that the Quarter's Mediterranean character be retained. It was, in consequence, routinely denounced as "standing in the way of progress." That it was, if one accepts the usual definition of "progress" as meaning the demolition of distinguished old buildings to make room for new ones of any sort. But the commission's goals were both comprehensive and subtle, and its successes can be credited in large part to its steering a careful and credible path between two insupportable extremes. At the one extreme, the commission did not attempt to freeze the Vieux Carré in the manner of a Colonial Williamsburg; instead, it recognized that for the Quarter to survive, it had to perform a contemporary function, and that meant change was inevitable. At the other extreme, the commission did not pin its hopes on preserving a handful of "historic" buildings and letting the rest go hang—in the manner of preservationists in too many other American cities and towns where "historic sites" are surrounded by white picket fences and used car lots. Rather, it argued that the Quarter's value stemmed from a quality of total environment—the *"tout ensemble,"* they

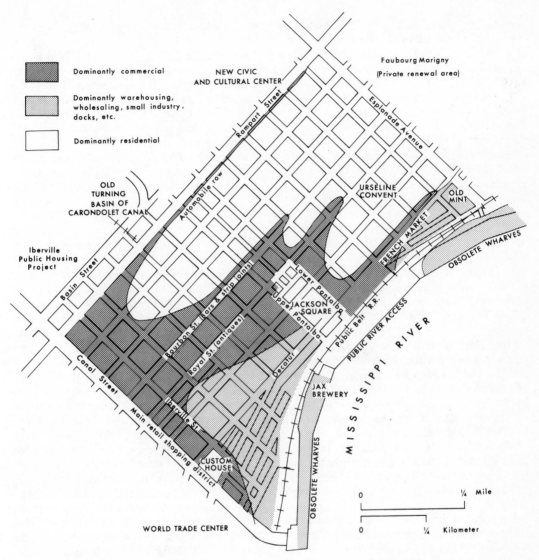

Figure 49. Land use in the French Quarter, 1968. Contrary to common belief, the Quarter is neither homogeneous in use nor uniformly picturesque in appearance. Note rind of commercial and warehousing on three sides, and infusion of more commerce from Canal Street. (Generalized from map in *Plan and Program for the Preservation of the Vieux Carré* [New Orleans: Bureau of Government Research, 1968].)

called it—which required that any change, even to modern buildings, had to be in keeping with that environment. Enforcing this viewpoint, of course, put the commission into conflict with innumerable developers and speculators to whom the *"tout ensemble"* was merely an unpronounceable impediment to quick profit. But the Supreme Court of Louisiana endorsed the commission's authority in a land-

mark 1941 decision that kept the commission in business and saved the integrity of the Quarter.

But the Vieux Carré's defenders won their greatest success in the early 1960s when they beat back federal plans to build an elevated interstate highway along the Mississippi. This "Riverfront Expressway" (I-310) was promoted as an essential part of an "integrated" transportation network for the city, but opponents retorted that the highway would form a Chinese Wall between the Quarter and the river and would ruin Jackson Square and the French Market—the very vitals of the Quarter. The arguments were butressed by a multivolume study of the Vieux Carré—organized by the Bureau of Government Research, but to which all manner of Orleanians and outsiders contributed time and money, and which still remains the definitive study of the Quarter. The expressway fight will be remembered for a long time, for it turned old friends into bitter enemies and shook the city to its roots. But the result was total victory for the preservationists, and humiliating defeat for the highwaymen, who took their plans elsewhere. Outside New Orleans, it will be remembered as one of the first times that the federal highway establishment was forced to cancel a major urban highway project for environmental reasons.

The New Orleans victory gave heart to others in San Francisco, Nashville, Washington, D.C., and elsewhere who subsequently fought and defeated the powerful federal highway lobby on similar grounds. There is no monument on the riverfront at Jackson Square to mark this victory, but there should be.

There is no danger any more that interstate highways will be put through the French Quarter. If anything, the Quarter is endangered by too much success, as more and more people compete for the same space. In a free market, there would be little doubt how the issue would be resolved. Hotels, restaurants, and night clubs would spread rapidly into the Vieux Carré, and a substantial part of the Quarter has already taken on such functions (Figure 49). But without the stern hand of the Vieux Carré Commission, it would be only a matter of time before the whole Quarter would be overrun by tourist facilities, and indeed many Orleanians complain that has already happened. While that is not quite true as yet, the pressure from tourism has already changed the Quarter substantially, and in consequence the Quarter itself is profoundly affecting adjacent areas (Figure 50).

The main pressure is from Canal Street, the traditional commercial center of New Orleans, where new high-rise hotels have been built just outside the jurisdiction of the Vieux Carré Commission. The largest is the forty-two story Marriott Hotel, with nearly a thousand guest rooms and a drive-in "motor lobby," but the Marriott merely portends bigger things to come (Figure 51; cf. Figure 28). It is also a measure of what would have gone inside the Quarter, had not the commission imposed a ban on high buildings and on new hotels inside the Vieux Carré. Meantime, as commercial tourist facilities press downriver into the Quarter, rents are rising ahead like the swell that precedes a breaking wave. These increased rents have already caused speedy renovation of old houses on the Downtown side of the Quarter, and areas that were only recently slums have suddenly become fashionable. Most of the black population, unable to afford the new high rents, decamped several years ago, and it grows increasingly hard for white people of medium income to keep even modest apartments (Figure 50). Meantime, the city has renovated the old French Market and opened Jackson Square to the river—a decision partly prompted by the Dock Board's abandonment of obsolete docks along the Mississippi.

As these two waves of higher rent roll downstream and lakeward, genuine residential neighborhoods are being squeezed into the northeast corner of the Quarter. Middle income white people are fleeing across the Esplanade downstream into old Faubourg Marigny, where early Victorian shotgun houses are emerging with newly painted brackets and the "For Sale" signs of fashionable realtors. As might be expected, the ghetto is recoiling under the pressure of higher rents, and Faubourg Marigny is being transformed as the Quarter had been transformed years before. (Exactly the same process, in Washington, D.C., transformed Old Georgetown in the 1930s and is now working along the edges of Capitol Hill.) One can applaud the architectural results, but the continued displacement of blacks and compression of already overcrowded ghettos is disquieting, to say the very least.

Texas in Downtown New Orleans: Superdome and Rivergate

But the profoundest effect of the refurbished Quarter was felt on its Uptown side toward Canal Street, New Orleans' traditional business district (Figure 51). Had New Orleans been an ordinary city, lower Canal Street might have gone the way of lower Woodward Avenue in Detroit, the way of old main streets in innumerable American cities. Indeed, the

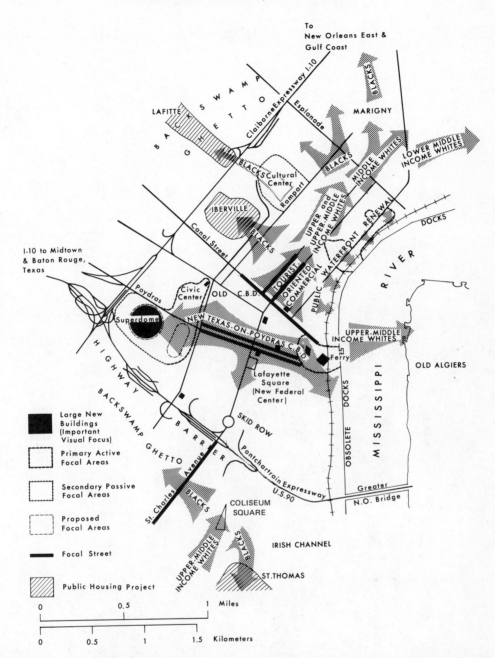

Figure 50. Center city New Orleans in transition. Arrows suggest the direction of changes in downtown New Orleans, largely prompted by revival of the Vieux Carré and the symbiotic revival of lower Canal Street. Note in the Quarter: blacks ejected by middle income whites, in turn ejected by upper and upper middle income whites, in turn under pressure from tourist-oriented commercial uses—an index of who is able to pay rents at various levels. Upstream from Canal Street, the new Texan CBD is pushing into skid row, while upper income whites move into the lower Garden District from other directions. Again, blacks are pushed into less desirable areas with lower rents.

lower two blocks of Canal had been lined with seedy bars and what were euphemistically called "hotels," and blight was slowly spreading up the street toward Maison Blanche, the city's biggest department store. Several things reversed the process, however, so that today lower Canal Street is taking on a newly scrubbed countenance of shiny prosperity (Figure 52).

The Quarter was the main cause. Lower Canal had served as a kind of osmotic membrane between the Vieux Carré and the central business district, so that when the Quarter began to revive, nourishment seeped across into the business district itself (Figures 49 and 50). Then, with the Dock Board's decision to abandon its riverfront wharves, there came a chance to open up Canal Street to the Mississippi, and revive the ancient liason between the city and its river. It all began with the huge new Rivergate project, whose central figure is the thirty-three story International Trade Mart and the Rivergate Exhibition Center just behind it (Figure 52). Unlike so many other big convention centers, which appear to have been dropped into an urban wasteland as if in desperation, the Rivergate Center achieved instant success, though its success is more a result than a cause of what lies nearby. The Trade Mart houses many of the city's port-related activities—consulates, shipping lines, and the Dock Board—while conventioneers across the street at the Rivergate find themselves in one of the happiest urban environments in America. To one side is the Mississippi, with its ferry boats and excursion ships; to the other are a dozen excellent hotels, history and doughnuts seven blocks away at Jackson Square, antiques on Royal Street, strip joints on Bourbon Street, and a good many of America's best restaurants scattered between (Figure 4). The Rivergate's promoters advertise persuasively that the facility is within easy walking distance of everything, which is true if "everything" in New Orleans is confined to a few blocks in the southwestern one-fourth of the Vieux Carré. If the tourist pays attention to the advertising, that is very nearly all he will see; routinely, many tourists come away from New Orleans having walked up Bourbon Street for four blocks, and returned on Royal. It is a pity, for there is more to New Orleans than one corner of the French Quarter, charming as that corner may be.

The Rivergate was finished in 1968, the Marriott Hotel in 1972. Neither could have succeeded without the Vieux Carré next door. Farther away, however, the business district was in sore straits, and uptown beyond Common Street things went downhill rapidly. The trouble went back to the nineteenth century, when the Uptown area was flanked on riverside by docks and railroads, on lakeside by the old canal turning basin, railroads, and warehouses. Between these two poles, St. Charles Avenue made its way uptown past Lafayette Square and Lee Circle, once a lovely part of the city, now becoming skid row. Things were bad enough when the railroads and riverside docks were healthy, but after World War II both went into decline, and so did the business district between. The coup de grace fell with completion of the Greater New Orleans Bridge, whose elevated ramps cut straight across the area to finish the job of neighborhood ruin (Figure 4).

It is something near a miracle that downtown decay was gradually reversed, but the technique turned out to be more expensive and even more controversial than renewal of the Vieux Carré. As the Uptown side of the business district visibly came to pieces, it was plain that the blight would spread unless a barrier were erected against it. That barrier had to

Figure 51. Lower Canal Street, seen from the top of the International Trade Mart, looking toward Lake Pontchartrain and the towers of Jefferson Parish's "Fat City" in the far distance. Canal Street was the dividing line between the old Creole French Quarter to the right and the commercial American city on the left. With its wide "neutral ground" (now used for busses), Canal was long New Orleans' main street; Maison Blanche, the city's traditional "big" department store, is the large light-colored building, partly hidden by the high-rise hotel. The whole area is in transition: main businesses are moving uptown (to the left), while tourism, symbolized by the slick new 1,000 room Marriott Hotel, puts heavy pressure on the Quarter. Lower right is old Custom House, 1849, the point from which distances in New Orleans are measured and the scene of many events of symbolic importance in the city's history.

Figure 52. Downtown New Orleans; Canal Street at St. Charles, looking toward the River, and the International Trade Mart Tower. (The big Rivergate convention center projects a half-arch colonnade just in front of the Trade Mart.) Note the flamboyant nineteenth century commercial buildings on the left, increasingly in unprestigious uses, alternating with shiny high-rise buildings, like the Marriott Hotel at the left.

stand somewhere between the bridge ramps and the still healthy fringes of the Common Street financial district. The logical line was a compromise along Poydras Street, which runs diagonally between the foot of Canal and City Hall (Figures 4 and 50).

The city was obviously incapable of rebuilding Poydras Street, but it could and did build anchors at either end of Poydras, and then actively encourage new construction along the intervening distance. The Rivergate would furnish one anchor, its strength guaranteed by proximity to the Quarter. The northern end of Poydras posed the real problem, and although activity buzzed around the new civic center with its boxlike city hall, state and city fathers decided that more heroic measures were needed.

New Orleans would build a "domed stadium" to house athletic events and large conventions and to be a magnet of activity which would complement the Rivergate complex at the other end of Poydras.

There is nothing unusual about civic stadiums, of course. Indeed, New Orleans was overdue for one. The annual Sugar Bowl football extravaganza had outgrown the old Tulane Stadium, and the arrival of the New Orleans Saints had created mild hysteria for the home football team. What was extraordinary about the stadium was the Babylonian scale of the whole thing—although more properly it was Texan, both in size and inspiration (Figure 53).

Physically, it would be big enough "to put the Houston Astrodome in the end zone," as

Figure 53. Like the building it represents, this futuristic rendering of the New Orleans' Superdome has a Texan inspiration. Superdome is also symbolic of the new New Orleans—outdoing Texas in bigness, shininess, and the size of its color TV screens. Although its cost is Texan, the scale of purported corruption in building it is strictly Louisianian. (Courtesy of the Greater New Orleans Tourist and Convention Commission)

one enthusiast prophesied. It would be named the "Louisiana Superdome," with 72,000 permanent seats and room for more on the floor. The dome would rise twenty-seven stories above the old railroad yards and be altogether the most visible thing in New Orleans—perhaps in the whole South. (It is advertised, without conscious comparison to St. Peter's Cathedral, as the "world's largest room unobstructed by posts.") Never mind that it was originally estimated to cost $35 million but turned out to cost almost five times that much. (Herman Kohlmeyer, one of its original bond brokers, was quoted by Burck in *Fortune* as calling it "the most extravagant thing I've seen in my life," and in Louisiana that is quite a statement.) Never mind if skeptics sneered that the Superdome would be filled only half a dozen times a year, and then its departing crowds would create Texas-sized traffic jams. Never mind that its legislative foundation was slippery, and the cost of retiring bonds might hang like an incubus on New Orleans' financial back for generations to come. (The weekly

Courier headlined its August 31, 1973 issue "The Damned Stadium: Blueprint of a Scandal" and devoted a double page spread to a chart which purported to explain "how the Scandal works," naming in the process many of the city's leading personalities.) If Houston had its Astrodome, New Orleans would have its Superdome, bigger and perhaps better. Superdome politics have a familiar Louisiana ring about them—and while the financing is quintessential Huey Long, the whole scale of the thing is ostentatiously un-Orleanian.

For the Superdome is more than just a very large building. It is a symbol of fundamental change in New Orleans psychology from the old days when the city was run by a handful of old-timers, whose status was confirmed by membership in one of the elite "krewes"—the secret societies that ostensibly organized Mardi Gras parades and balls, but additionally organized New Orleans' formal and informal government. The old, closed, conservative city was open for business, and open with a vengeance, all with a very strong flavor of Texas and Hollywood. Blue bloods watched in horror, as a new Mardi Gras krewe called "Bacchus" was organized—its membership publicly bourgeois. Bacchus' fourth king, for example, was not an old-time Bourbon, but comedian Bob Hope, specially imported from Hollywood to play the role. In olden days, Hope might have been challenged to a duel under the oaks at dawn. In the early 1970s, a million Orleanians and tourists cheered him down Canal Street, as the hoi polloi flaunted its new power in the face of the elite.

More than a few old-timers view the changes with dismay, at some variance with Mr. Kohlmeyer, who observed that the Superdome has been "a real shot in the arm for the community." Whether that is so or not, it has certainly proved a shot in the arm for Poydras Street, which is rapidly replacing Canal Street as the main business artery of New Orleans. As of 1973, the catalogue of new buildings is impressive—a twenty-two story headquarters finished for the Lykes Bros. Steamship Company, a new federal complex under construction at Lafayette Square, and numerous other buildings rising nearby or on the drawing board. Perhaps the most portentous project is "One Shell Square," a gleaming white sixty story advertisement that Texas oil had settled on Poydras Street to stay. Significantly, it was the highest building in New Orleans and fundamentally changed the city's skyline with its huge neo-Seagrams profile. But there will surely be more and higher.

In sum, New Orleans central business district looks to be in healthy shape—marvellously healthier than most American cities of a million or more people. If the health has a new and radical look, its roots are old and conservative—physically embedded in the eighteenth century French Quarter and in a municipal elite whose new blood still has a rather blue Bourbon color to it, at least in political philosophy. As broker Kohlmeyer is supposed to have remarked, "The man who built the Taj Mahal didn't ask the permission of the people. Ditto here."

Racial Geography and the Future of New Orleans

It is easy to be optimistic about New Orleans' economic future, but its social future is another matter. As in most other big American cities, New Orleans' main malady is racial.

The facts are devastatingly simple, and in combination they portend no good for the city. In New Orleans, as elsewhere, blacks are relatively poor and ill-housed, and their neighborhoods poorly attended by municipal services. Educational levels are low (Figure 41; cf. Figure 21), crime rates high. Meanwhile whites flee and the proportion of blacks continues to increase, as do the isolation and alienation of a population that sees itself abandoned and abused. It is a sorry tale, and no less sorry for being typical of city after city across the United States.

New Orleans' racial experience is especially poignant, for its racial history was less flawed than in many other American cities. In some ways, to be sure, New Orleans was and is a very Southern city for blacks. Thus, as Chai has shown, blacks constituted 45 percent of the city's population, but only 3.6 percent of its "Level I leadership." (In 1973, not one of the city councilmen was black.) Furthermore, to the city's white majority, it was unthinkable that blacks would share equal facilities, and most blacks perhaps did not expect it.

Nevertheless, New Orleans' racial attitudes were consistently less embittered than, say in Montgomery or even Baton Rouge—and certainly less than in Chicago or Newark. Thus, New Orleans sweated through the hateful summer of 1967 quietly if nervously. Part of the credit for tranquility goes to intelligent mayors, but deeper roots stem from the city's Creole heritage and the rather easy-going attitude of the French toward racial mixing. Part of it stems from nothing more complicated than interracial musicmaking, for white Orleanians are intensely proud of the ragtime tradition and are not unconscious that blacks were largely responsible for its invention and preservation. Part of it, perhaps, is economic: blacks have worked beside whites for a long time in New Orleans, especially on the docks, and there were no periodic economic catastrophes to provoke the recurring large scale unemployment of blacks that so poisoned race relations in Detroit auto factories or in the boll weevil belt of the rural South. But a major reason for New Orleans' history of good race relations—or at least the absence of overt violence—was the traditional geographical fragmentation of black neighborhoods in the city.

Professor John Adams of the University of Minnesota has observed that two conditions commonly presage racial violence—the expectation of a better life that is routinely frustrated, and ghettos so big that blacks see only blacks, where resentment feeds incessantly upon itself. New Orleans satisfied neither of these conditions. The New Orleans Bourbon elite never dreamed of holding out to blacks the expectation of better living conditions, and if the streets fell into disrepair in black areas, that was the way things had always been (Figure 54). Then too, if a black felt especially aggrieved, he could do what millions of other Southern Negroes had done—get on a train and go North, more often than not to Chicago at the other end of the Illinois Central Railroad. (It is unprovable but quite likely that New Orleans' bitterest racial dissatisfactions were shipped off with unhappy migrants to Chicago,

relieving pressures in New Orleans, but with explosive results in Chicago—a kind of differential migration of hatred. And later on, California apparently received some of New Orleans' exported racial troubles. Huey Newton, the Black Panther, first gained a violent reputation in Oakland, but his home town was New Orleans.) And as long as New Orleans' ghettos remained small and fragmented, there was little chance for resentment to reach critical mass, particularly if the ghetto was not too crowded. Quite accidentally, New Orleans' distaste for high-rise buildings and its Southern predilection for open space probably helped to relieve tensions that incited violence in the crowded streets of Harlem and South Chicago.

It is disquieting to note that nearly all of these things are changing—mainly in the direc-

Figure 54. Backswamp ghetto, just inland from Faubourg Marigny. Low profile semidetached houses are common in New Orleans; straight-pitched overhanging roofs are nineteenth century Creole design. Although the city has obviously done little to encourage streetside amenity (poor pavement and lack of trees is typical), population densities here are much lower than in comparable parts of big Northern ghettos.

tion of probable future trouble. At the base of it, the city has grown more segregated in recent years. Most obviously, New Orleans' multi-nuclear ghettos has been growing together, especially in the old backswamp areas where the poorest Negroes always lived. Significantly, the location of ghettos had not changed much. Back in 1940, for example (the earliest census date for which we have detailed racial data at a large scale), the black neighborhood cores were located in the same places they had been for more than a century, but individual Negro neighborhoods were smaller and were separated from one another (cf. Figure 55). Since 1940 black population had grown and spread, but there has been very little leapfrogging into new parts of the city, especially not into affluent neighborhoods. One major exception is the Pontchartrain Park development where blacks were allegedly given their own golf course to avoid pressure to integrate white golf links during the 1950s. Not surprisingly, Pontchartrain Park was 99 percent black by count of the 1970 census, and the subdivision is cut off from the outside by canals and railroad tracks so securely that it takes an expert to find the

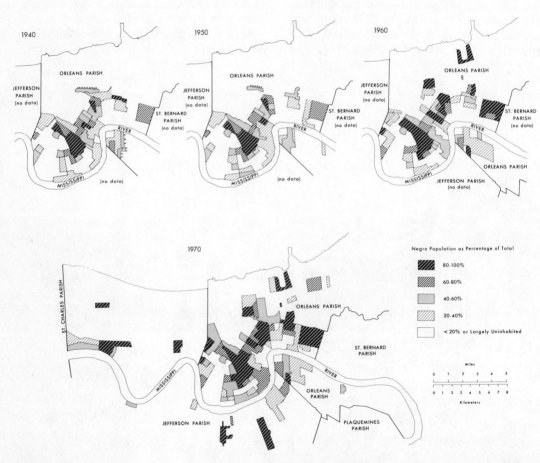

Figure 55. Negro population, New Orleans, 1940, 1950, 1960, 1970, mapped by census tract. Note that growth of Negro population has not resulted in substantial changes in *location* of Negro neighborhoods; instead, areas of Negro population have grown steadily blacker and have spread somewhat from their earlier boundaries. Meantime, newer areas of the city toward Lake Pontchartrain are almost lily white, with a few conspicuous exceptions—like Pontchartrain Park, horseshoe-shaped area in northeastern part of 1960 and 1970 maps. The result is increased segregation. Note, however, that mapping by coarse units of census tracts does not reveal the real intensity of neighborhood segregation; compare Figure 21, 1970 Negro population mapped by block.

entrances. In no sense is Pontchartrain Park an integral or integrated part of the city.

The same is true of New Orleans' ten big public housing projects, which are now almost 100 percent black and mostly isolated from the mainstream of city life. By standards in other cities, New Orleans' public housing is reasonably good—fairly well built, with moderate population densities and considerable open space. The first projects were completed in 1938, when segregation was still legal, and four were reserved for whites—Iberville, Florida, St. Thomas, and Fischer. Desegregation did not bring integration to any of these projects, however, since each served mainly as places of refuge for blacks displaced from housing in nearby neighborhoods. Iberville, considered one of the best because it was especially well built and located close to the French Quarter, took in black refugees from the Vieux Carré who could not afford to pay skyrocketing rents. St. Thomas has served exactly the same function for the lower Garden District, where private renewal is displacing blacks from old elegant houses, and Florida apparently took in people from the enormous infamous "Desire" Project, generally regarded as the worst in the city, (Three out of four Desire families have incomes which fall below the census' definition of poverty; see Figure 40).Thus, while the projects sometimes provided better housing from a physical standpoint, the rapid switchover from white to black population has merely replaced one kind of segregation with another.

To make things worse, black neighborhoods have endured increasing pressure from whites bent on "improving" the city. One form of pressure has come from freeway building, and while there is no direct evidence that highways were deliberately located in black neighborhoods, a comparison of racial maps with highway maps makes the conclusions inevitable (cf. Figures 3 and 21). Experience in other American cities suggests that urban highways are often located where political opposition is weakest—presumably the reason why the Highway Department abandoned its Vieux Carré schemes, but found no difficulty running Interstate-10 along North Claiborne Avenue, thus converting the main street of New Orleans biggest Negro neighborhood from a broad landscaped boulevard into a dingy concrete cavern (Figure 56). While the short run costs of road building doubtless were relatively low

on North Claiborne, one must wonder what it will cost in the long run to repair the social damage wrought by the expressway, or if it can be repaired at all.

The other form of pressure is equally strong, and emerges when whites "discover" the architectural virtues of an old black neighborhood. As of the early 1970s, three such areas were being "reclaimed"—Faubourg Marigny, already mentioned; the lower Garden District around Coliseum Square; and "old Algiers," just a five minute free ferry ride from the foot of Canal Street (Figures 50 and 30). All three are areas of fine flamboyant Victorian houses which had been abandoned by upwardly mobile whites, and it was quite natural when poor Negroes moved into them. All three are well worth preserving, and if something is not done, their wooden buildings will surely disintegrate from neglect, moisture, heat, and termites. Thus, on architectural grounds, one must applaud the restoration. But the blacks have fled, unable to pay the new high rents (Figure 50). Some whites may be comforted that the blacks are out of sight and out of mind, but such processes cannot help but make New Orleans more and more segregated, alienated, and prone to violence.

By contrast with other big cities, New Orleans has a good record for housing its black population—if one counts units and does not look too closely at individual structures. According to the Taeubers, between 1940 and 1960 the city built about as many housing units for blacks as it did for whites—half again better than either Memphis or Birmingham, a fact which may help explain the difference in the three cities' histories of racial violence. But at the same time, the "index of residential segregation" crept up and up. New Orleans' 81.0 was already high for a Southern city in 1940, but it was up to 84.9 in 1950 and 86.3 in 1960. Since the Taeuber's define the index as meaning "the minimum percentage of non-whites who would have to change the block on which they live in order to produce an unsegregated distribution," it would require that 86.3 percent of New Orleans' nonwhites move for integration to be achieved. It is small consolation to know that most other American cities are neither much better nor much worse than New Orleans in this respect, but it is even less comforting to review the record of racial violence in cities with similar indexes.

Typically, racial tensions have seriously

Figure 56. Elevated expressway now occupies a boulevard through a black neighborhood. Comparable projects have been effectively fought off by residents of more affluent white areas of the city. (The occasion for the crowd is a "jazz funeral." Courtesy of the Greater New Orleans Tourist and Convention Commission.)

damaged the public school system. Southern states were never noted for extravagant support of public schools, and when money had to be split between two separate racial systems, the results were truly miserable—especially on the Negro side. Public schools in Southern Louisiana were particularly rickety since many Catholics sent their children to parochial schools and disliked paying school taxes from which they derived no immediate benefit. Affluent Protestants often emulated the Catholics, and New Orleans gradually developed a system of private schools—some fair, some excellent—which served not merely to educate, but functioned as gatekeepers for admission into the city's ruling elite.

Brown v. *Topeka*'s order to integrate schools, therefore, was a severe blow to an already sickly public system. Affluent whites in Orleans Parish avoided sending children to integrated schools by enrolling them in private and parochial schools or by moving to whiter parishes outside. Many white families who could not afford to take those steps did so anyway. (St. Bernard and Plaquemines parishes, under the semifeudal rule of Leander Perez, never bothered to conceal their hostility to black immigrants, and the black population is consequently small. Jefferson Parish, with only one black school child out of five, has developed a large scale busing system that keeps the white-black ratio as homogeneously high as possible.)

As a result, the last decade has seen whites abandoning public schools in Orleans Parish at precisely the same time as the black school population has been increasing rapidly (Figure 57A and 57B). As this essay is written, the departure of middle income white families with school age children from Orleans Parish resembles a stampede, and school administrators grow more apprehensive by the day. The fear that integration would ruin New Orleans' public schools apparently is turning into a self-fulfilling prophesy. Meantime, the hope that the school system can serve to ease racial tensions is doomed in Orleans Parish unless present circumstances literally reverse themselves. The prospect is bleak.

It is always hazardous to predict the future course of human affairs. In matters of race, however—which have too often decided whether American central cities live or die—too many signs in New Orleans point in ominous directions. Although several recent mayors have tried with some success to increase the number of black city employees, the progress is painfully slow, and while segregation increases, blacks grow increasingly restive. So far there has been no outbreak of major violence, but there is no guarantee against it. White Orleanians know it, and within the city they huddle together in white enclaves—or flee to the suburbs, where one can go for miles without seeing a black face. Neither tactic bodes much good for the city's future.

YET STILL A FINE CITY?

Unlike New Yorkers and Bostonians, most old-time Orleanians courteously refrain from giving unsolicited advice about how other people should run their cities. Quite naturally, Orlean-

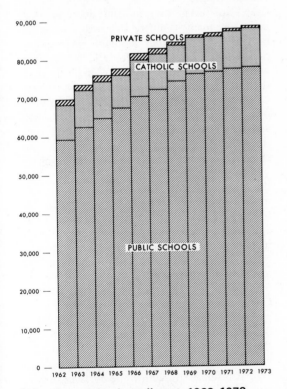

(A). Negro School enrollment, 1962-1973.

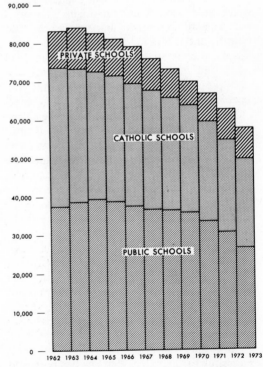

(B). White School enrollment, 1962-1973.

Figure 57. Graphs show precipitous decline in white school enrollment in Orleans Parish, reflecting white outmigration. Compare simultaneous increase in Negro enrollment; change is especially drastic in public schools, which most Negroes attend. Note also relative increase but absolute decline in white enrollment in private and Catholic schools. Source: Stanley Fitzpatrick. *Facts and Finances 1972-1973* (New Orleans: New Orleans Public Schools, Orleans Parish School Board, 1973)

ians do not take kindly to advice from outsiders on how to run their own. New Orleans is different, we seem to have agreed—so different that she has little to learn from other places, and so different that she has little to teach them.

Perhaps we need to reform such habits of thought and consider that the rest of America may have a good deal to learn from New Orleans and vice versa. The lessons may not be immediately obvious, and they may be easier for an outsider to recognize than the ordinary Orleanian—many of whom rarely move very far beyond the precincts of their beloved city. (A very unofficial unscientific survey of several freshman classes at the University of New Orleans in the summer and autumn of 1973 revealed a surprising number of young Orleanians who seldom traveled outside New Orleans and showed little desire to do so.)

One ventures to suggest that the great failures of urban America have been general failures which stem from common origins—the overcrowding of workers' quarters in the last century, the failure to keep air and water clean, the destruction of neighborhoods by railroad tracks and auto expressways and airports, the cruel pressure on blacks to live within the confines of an "inner city," the decay of central business districts, and so on through the dismal familiar litany. To the degree that these failures are epidemic, it is because most American cities are tied to a national model of behavior. One city does something, and presently all are doing it. Our impatience is our undoing, for by the time we discover Los Angeles' mistakes, every other city has made the same mistake itself. American cities are like lemmings.

By contrast, the great successes of urban America have been highly particular ... cities that have danced to a different drum. San Francisco's successes are San Franciscan—not somebody else's. Boston is successful to the degree she is Bostonian—not because she has conformed to some standard national model.

And the same is true of New Orleans—successful to the extent that she has preserved her individual identity. It is significant, perhaps, that San Francisco and Boston and New Orleans have all failed most miserably in precisely those areas they share with the rest of the country—sprawling suburbs, faceless and interchangable downtown buildings, expressways that murder neighborhoods, slum clear-

ance programs that wreck whole sections of the city and expel the people who lived there. In the United States, at least, urban success requires aberrant behavior.

One can push the argument too far, to be sure. Cities should not encourage freakiness—that way lies Disneyland. Nor should cities resist innovations just because they are innovative; no sensible person denounces chlorination of New Orleans' water simply because God put no chlorine in the Mississippi River. But we should not be afraid to talk—as Albert Bush-Brown talks—of our "right to a fine city," and to recognize that fine cities are made from the delicate interweaving of tangibles and intangibles which take time to weave, and which are not easily mended once they are torn.

Thus New Orleans. Bourbon Street does not make the city a wonderful place, nor the French Quarter, nor superb food, nor Mardi Gras, nor even the humane urbanity that makes so many ordinary Orleanians so extraordinary—but the *tout ensemble* that speaks of special people, rooted for a long time in a special place. If this is true, or even partly true, then other American cities should look to New Orleans for guidance, and should look to their own special qualities for their own special salvation. (New Orleans, meantime, might consider declaring such things as nationally franchised restaurants to be crimes against the city.)

Conversely, the two most potent forces that threaten to destroy the special qualities that make New Orleans a fine city are not particular to New Orleans, but are parts of a national epidemic. One is suburban sprawl. The other is increasing racial segregation. Both are obviously related, both produce alienation and hostility, and both may have gone so far that they may be irreversible. But it is plain to a reader of New Orleans' history that the city began to lose its special qualities at about the time that Mr. Wood's swamp pumps made it possible for affluent whites to flee the city in their automobiles, leaving behind the fine old city to become a great black ghetto with white enclaves. As the city becomes blacker, poorer, and more segregated, as the suburbs become whiter and more sprawling, it becomes harder and harder to put the urban Humpty Dumpty back together again. New Orleans becomes more and more like the rest of the country.

There are no obvious antidotes to suburban

Figure 58. Definition of place by civic act: Mardi Gras Parade on St. Charles Avenue. (Courtesy of the Greater New Orleans Tourist and Convention Commission)

sprawl and racial segregation in New Orleans. Indeed, in the context of urban America in this last third of the twentieth century, there may be no solution except to abandon our cities and start afresh. Some Northerners seem quite ready to do that, but the new urban models usually look better on the drawing board than they do outdoors in the cold light of day. Levittown is Levittown everywhere, and it is still doubtful whether Reston really works. But New Orleans clearly did work—and it may yet, if Orleanians resist the temptation to act like everybody else. And if they abandon efforts to keep their fine city, their sin will not be easy to pardon.

Yet New Orleans retains two special advantages which may still hold out some hope. First of all, she does remain a fine city, despite recent depredations. Second, she has always been a laggard, and laggards have a special advantage over those at the forefront of progress. They can—to paraphrase Lincoln Steffens —look over into the future to see if it works. From New Orleans' vantage, her racial future is writ large in Detroit—her suburban future projected in the deserts around Phoenix—the future of Poydras Street on display in Houston's anonymous parody of a downtown.

New Orleans, of course, may choose to go that way—and failure to act will guarantee it. But if the city is to choose another course, time is running out. For most of her history, she was an island, protected against national fads by the insulating swamps, by Creole aloofness, by poverty, by a host of natural and artificial devices which kept the world at arm's length. Over that long time, New Orleans has had the leisure to plant and nurture the special qualities that made her a fine city. But the barriers are down, and the world is crowding in.

The city fathers have recently been saying rather stridently that "Pride Builds New Orleans." And so it has. But pride alone is not enough. New Orleans will remain a fine city only so long as she remains a special place, and contemporary America is not tolerant of special places. New Orleans will remain a special place only if she takes special measures to define the qualities that made her that way (Figure 58) and to defend them with all the power at her disposal. Failing that, she will go the way of Houston and Phoenix. After that, pride will scarcely make any difference.

EPILOGUE

Again and again we read that the nucleated city is a lost institution in the Western world—an antique relic whose time is past. It may be so, especially in the United States, which started city building late in mankind's urban career, and whose automotive technology has already destroyed more cities than Atilla ever dreamed of. But the Great City, for all its warts and flaws and corruptions, is surely one of the great accomplishments of human kind. It is too soon, perhaps, to know whether we can build suburbs to rival the center of Paris or shopping centers to rank with the markets of Florence or Peking, but one may be pardoned for doubting it. What we do know is that genuine cities already exist —urbane, cosmopolitan, self-conscious centers of civil affairs.

There are not many places like that left in the United States, but pre-1950 New Orleans is surely one of them. Just as surely, it is threatened by the same forces which have already destroyed less lusty cities all across the New World and are even now assaulting the gates of the Old World's finest cities. If Americans really mean it when they say that the creation and preservation of humane environments are worthy national goals, then the protection of New Orleans' civic integrity is clearly a matter of high national priority. Clearly too, the matter cannot be left to the tender mercies of the free market, much less the obsolete medications prescribed by schools of urban planning.

Plainly, there is no simple way to turn back the host of enemies which already besiege New Orleans—be they racial hostility, suburban sprawl, or nothing more sinister than the rising tide of mediocrity that threatens to flood the city with tourist gimmicks and Houston plastic. Indeed, there may be no solution at all: perhaps democratic automotive society is simply incapable of creating and preserving delicate physical environments—those treasured spots like New Orleans which can never be re-created, but which are so easily and readily plundered. But if this nation cannot find methods to protect a New Orleans from despoilation, and if it cannot find ways to employ those methods, the failure will cast serious doubt on our ability to protect any valued part of our national environment.

Appendix A

Concerning Directions in New Orleans

Americans, accustomed to grid pattern towns with streets that run north-south and east-west, are often lost in New Orleans. They will remain lost until they relax and remember that conventional compass directions mean nothing and the Mississippi River means everything.

The river divides the metropolitan area into two equal parts, called "East Bank" and "West Bank." This locution causes confusion immediately, since the Mississippi has perversely turned eastward through New Orleans, so that "East Bank" is really north of the river and "West Bank" is south. Never mind. Remember that "East Bank" is where travelers from the Atlantic coast would first arrive, and that is where most of the city is located. "West Bank" is where visitors from California come from, with a lot of swamps and new suburbs. Keep in mind, too, that Orleanian directions ignore convolutions of the river and for a short distance opposite the central business district it is flowing due north; thus, East Bank is really west, and vice versa. It is a helpful concept to remember when one is driving across the Greater New Orleans Bridge, heading west with the sunset behind. It is a mere detail; Orleanians look at the big picture.

On the East Bank, where most people live, there are four cardinal directions: "Riverside," which means toward the river (no matter where the river is), and "Lakeside," which is the direction toward Lake Pontchartrain, and generally north. The other two directions are "Uptown" and "Downtown." Uptown is upriver from Canal Street and is roughly equivalent to the old American city. Downtown is downstream from Canal Street, including the French Quarter and so on. Visitors beware: "Downtown" does not necessarily mean the central business district to an Orleanian.

Finally, some streets are labeled with compass directions. In the Lakeside areas with a conventional grid pattern, there is no problem. Riverside, however, such directions cause mass confusion until one notes that streets receive their directional labels where they cross Canal Street. Thus, *"South* Claiborne" heads northwest in the Uptown area, but is so designated because it *started* from Canal Street heading southwest.

Appendix B

A Pronouncing Gazeteer of South Louisiana Names

NOTE: This abbreviated list of Louisiana pronounciations reflects the fact that, in southern Louisiana, things are *sui generis*—often more American than French, but not recognizably either. There are no general rules of pronounciation, therefore, and the visitor simply must memorize the commonest aberrations. The closest thing to a rule, perhaps, is that southern Louisiana pronounciations of French words sound like a Deep Southerner who has had a bad course in French a long time ago. Indian words are pronounced like a Deep Southerner who has never had a course in Indian at any time.

AMITE: AY-meet (sometimes AH-meet)
ATCHAFALAYA: 'chah-fah-LAH-yah
BIENVILLE: BYEN-vill (no trace of French pronunciation)
BONNET CARRÉ: Bonny Carry
BURGUNDY: bur-GUN-dee
CAJUN: KAY-jun
CONTI: KON-tie
IBERVILLE: IH-bur-vill (not EE-bur-vill)
LAFOURCHE: La-FOOSH
MANCHAC: MAN-shack
MELPOMENE: MEL-po-mean
METAIRIE: MET-urry (or MET-ry)
MICHOUD: MEE-shoe

MOISANT: MOY-zant
NEW ORLEANS: A complicated business. Note to begin with, that no Southerner pronounced "New" as the Yankee "NOO." It is always "NYU," as the British commonly do it. As for the "Orleans," "AW-lens" is the way well-spoken natives do it. "OR-luns" or "OR-lee-uns" will pass for Yankees and radio announcers. But "or-LEENS" is forbidden when talking about the city. "Orleans Street," however, is pronounced just that way: "or-LEENS."

Incidentally, the exclusive uptown "Orleans Club" makes a stab at French locution, where it comes out, "or-lee-AHN"

In summary, try it as "nyu AW-lens." If your tongue is Yankee and can't cope, try "nyu OR-luns."

(Incidentally, "NO-luns" or "NAW-luns" are often heard but considered hicky.)
PLAQUEMINES: PLACK-a-minn
TCHOUPITOULAS: chop-a-TOO-lus
THIBODAUX: TIB-ah-doe
VIEUX CARRÉ: vee-YOU ka-RAY (This pronunciation approximates French more closely than most other Orleanian words or phrases, but a Parisian still recoils to hear it spoken.)

Appendix C

New Orleans Periodicals

A few local periodicals containing important information on New Orleans and vicinity.

The Courier (weekly tabloid). Similar to *Figaro*.

Dixie Roto (see *New Orleans Times-Picayune*). Frothy in general, but contains at least one —sometimes more—solid item on the city and region, often available nowhere else. Sunday supplement to *Times-Picayune*.

Figaro (weekly tabloid). A trifle brassy, but the main source of information about unofficial and underground New Orleans.

Louisiana Business Survey (quarterly publication of the Division of Business and Economic Research, University of New Orleans.) A scholarly periodical for economic and social matters concerning New Orleans. Short papers, rarely over half a dozen pages. Heavy on reports of current business statistics.

New Orleans (official monthly publication of the Chamber of Commerce of the New Orleans area). Slick but solid; one of the best "city magazines" in the country.

New Orleans Times-Picayune (daily and Sunday mornings; includes Sunday supplement, *Dixie Roto*). The city's prestige paper; journal of record for the New Orleans area.

New Orleans States-Item (daily except Sunday; afternoons). Same ownership as *Times-Picayune*, but more local news. Often contains fine serial features on city and regional problems.

Bibliography

Adams, John S. "The Geography of Riots and Civil Disorders in the 1960's." *Economic Geography* 48 (January 1972): 24–42.

Arellano, Richard G., and Manuel M. Alarcon. "New Orleans and Visitors from Latin America." *Louisiana Business Survey* 2, 1 (January 1971): 14–15.

Ayers, H. Brandt, and Thomas H. Naylor, eds. *You Can't Eat Magnolias.* New York: McGraw-Hill, 1972. (A publication of the L.Q.C. Lamar Society.)

Baughman, James P. "Gateway to the Americas." In Hodding Carter, ed., *The New Orleans 1718-1968,* pp. 258–87. New Orleans: Pelican Publishing House, 1968.

Bechtel Corporation. *New Orleans Centroport, U.S.A., Master Plan for Long Range Development.* A report prepared for the Board of Commissioners of the Port of New Orleans, an Agency of the State of Louisiana. New Orleans: March 1970.

Blassingame, John W. *Black New Orleans, 1860-1880.* Chicago: University of Chicago Press, 1973.

Burck, Charles G. "It's Promoters vs. Taxpayers in the Superstadium Game." *Fortune* 87, 3 (March 1973): 104–13, 178–82.

Bush-Brown, Albert. "Your Right to a Fine City." *House and Garden,* March 1968, pp. 118ff.

Calhoun, James, ed. *Louisiana Almanac, 1973-74.* Gretna, La.: Pelican Publishing Co., 1973.

Carter, Hodding, ed. *The Past as Prelude: New Orleans 1718-1968.* New Orleans: Pelican Publishing House, 1968. (A Tulane University Publication.)

Chai, Charles Y.W. "Who Rules New Orleans? A Study of Community Power Structure. Some Preliminary Findings on Social Characteristics and Attitudes of New Orleans Leaders." *Louisiana Business Survey* 2 (October 1971): 12–16.

Chamber of Commerce of the New Orleans Area. *The New Orleans Area Story.* New Orleans: Flambeaux Publishing Company, n.d. [but probably 1972].

Chase, John. *Frenchmen, Desire, Good Children . . . and Other Streets of New Orleans.* 2nd ed. New Orleans: Robert L. Crager & Co., 1960.

——. *Louisiana Purchase.* New Orleans: The Hauser Press, 1954, 1960.

Christovich, Mary L.; Roulhac Toledano; Betsy Swanson; and Pat Holden. *New Orleans Architecture.* Vol. 2; *The American Sector.* Gretna, La.: Pelican Publishing Company, 1972.

Chubbuck, James; Edward Renwick; and Joe Walker. "An Analysis of the 1970 New Orleans Mayoral Election." *Louisiana Business Survey* 1, 3 (July 1970): 6–12.

Collin, Richard H. *The New Orleans Underground Gourmet.* 2d ed., rev. New York: Simon and Schuster, 1973.

Davis, Jack. "Can Anybody Save the Business District?" *Figaro* (New Orleans) 2, 19 (May 12, 1973: 1, 6–9.

Dufour, Charles L. *Ten Flags in the Wind: the Story of Louisiana.* New York: Harper and Row, 1967.

Farrier, Dean Grimes. "Impact of Environmental Legislation on the Transportation Decision-Making Process in New Orleans: The Derailment of the I-310 Riverfront Expressway." *Journal of Urban Law* 51 (1974): 687–722.

Federal Writers' Project of the Works Progress Administration for the City of New Orleans. *New Orleans City Guide.* American Guide Series. Boston: Houghton Mifflin Company, 1938.

Feibleman, Peter S. *American Cooking: Creole and Acadian.* New York: Time-Life Books, 1971. (Time-Life Foods of the World Series.)

Filipich, Judy A., and Lee Taylor. *Lakefront New Orleans: Planning and Development, 1926–1971.* New Orleans: Urban Studies Institute, Louisiana State University in New Orleans, 1971.

Fisk, H.N. *Geological Investigations of the Alluvial Valley of the Lower Mississippi River.* Vicksburg: Mississippi River Commission, 1944.

———. *Geological Investigation of the Atchafalaya Basin and the Problem of Mississippi River Diversion.* Vicksburg: Mississippi River Commission, 1952.

Fitzpatrick, Stanley. *Facts and Finances 1972–1973.* New Orleans: New Orleans Public Schools, Orleans Parish School Board, 1973.

Fleishman, Joel L. "The Southern City: Northern Mistakes in Southern Settings." In H. Brandt Ayers and Thomas H. Naylor, eds., *You Can't Eat Magnolias,* pp. 169–94. New York: McGraw-Hill, 1972.

Gagliano, Sherwood M., and Johannes L. van Beek. *Geologic and Geomorphic Aspects of Deltaic Processes, Mississippi Delta System.* Report no. 1, Hydrologic and Geologic Studies of Coastal Louisiana. Baton Rouge: Coastal Resources Unit, Center for Wetland Resources, Louisiana State University, February 1970.

Gallup, George, and the American Institute of Public Opinion. Reports of a poll on American attitudes toward particular cities. *The New York Times,* September 7, 1969, p. 59; and September 8, 1969, p. 25.

Gilmore, H.W. "The Old New Orleans and the New: A Case for Ecology." *American Sociological Review* 9 (1944): 385–94.

Glaab, Charles N., and A. Theodore Brown. *A History of Urban America.* New York: Macmillan, 1967.

Glazier, Captain Willard. *Peculiarities of American Cities.* Philadelphia: Hubbard Brothers, 1883. Esp. ch. XX, "New Orleans," pp. 264–80.

Greater New Orleans Tourist and Convention Commission. Annual reports.

Hammer, Greene, Siler Associates. "An Economic and Social Study of the Vieux Carré, New Orleans, Louisiana." Technical Supplement to *Plan and Program for the Preservation of the Vieux Carré.* New Orleans: Bureau of Governmental Research, December 1968.

Hansen, Harry, ed. *Louisiana: A Guide to the State.* (American Guide Series, originally compiled by the Federal Writer's Program of the Works Progress Administration of the State of Louisiana.) Rev. ed. New York: Hastings House, 1971.

Hayward, John. *A Gazetteer of the United States of America. . . .* Hartford, Conn.: Case, Tiffany, and Company, 1853.

Hilliard, Sam Bowers. *Hog Meat and Hoecake: Food Supply in the Old South, 1840–1860.* Carbondale: Southern Illinois University Press, 1972.

Housing Authority of New Orleans. Monthly memoranda from deputy executive officer to executive director concerning occupancy of St. Thomas, Iberville, and Florida Avenue projects, January 2, 1968–September 4, 1973.

Huber, Leonard V. *New Orleans: A Pictorial History.* New York: Crown Publishers, 1971.

Jefferson Parish Planning Department. "Residential Construction Trend in Jefferson Parish, Louisiana, excluding Kenner, Gretna, Westwego and Grand Isle, 1960–1971." Metairie, La., March 21, 1973. Mimeographed.

Juhn, Daniel S. "Managerial Thinking in the New Orleans Area." *Louisiana Business Survey* 2 (October 1971): 12–16.

Kenyon, James B. "Elements in Inter-Port Competition in the United States." *Economic Geography* 46, 1 (January 1970): 1–24.

Key, V.O., Jr. "Louisiana: The Seamy Side of Democracy." In *Southern Politics in State and Nation,* ch. 8. New York: Alfred A. Knopf, 1949.

King, Grace E. *New Orleans, the Place and the People.* New York: The Macmillan Company, 1895.

Kniffen, Fred B. *Louisiana, Its Land and People.* Baton Rouge: The Louisiana State University Press, 1968.

Kolb, Carolyn. *New Orleans: An Invitation*

to Discover One of America's Most Fascinating Cities. Garden City, N.Y.: Doubleday and Co., 1972.

Kolb, Charles R. *Distribution of Soils Bordering in the Mississippi River From Donaldsonville to Head-of-Passes.* Vicksburg, Miss.: U.S. Army Waterways Experiment Station, Technical Report no. 3-601, April 1962.

Kolb, Charles R., and J.R. Van Lopik. *Geology of the Mississippi River Deltaic Plain, Southeastern Louisiana.* 2 vols. Vicksburg, Miss.: U.S. Army Engineer Waterways Experiment Station, Technical Report no. 3-483, July 1958.

Morse, Jedidiah, and Richard C. Morse. *A New Universal Gazetteer* ... 4th ed. New Haven: S. Converse, 1823.

New Orleans, City of. City Planning and Zoning Commission. *Major Street Report,* 1927.

———. *Community Renewal Program.* New Orleans: City Planning Commission, n.d. [but apparently 1970].

Newsom, Robert T. "Worker Mobility in New Orleans, 1960 to 1965." *Louisiana Business Survey* 1, 1 (January 1970): 1-4.

Newton, Milton B., Jr. *Atlas of Louisiana: A Guide for Students.* Baton Rouge: Louisiana State University, School of Geoscience, 1972. (Miscellaneous Publication 72-1).

Official Guide of the Railways and Steam Navigation Lines of the United States. ... New York: National Railway Publication Company, published monthly.

Patton, Donald J. "General Cargo Hinterlands of New York, Philadelphia, Baltimore, and New Orleans." *Annals of the Association of American Geographers* 48, 4 (December 1958): 436-55.

Patton, Donald J. *Port Hinterlands: the Case of New Orleans.* College Park: University of Maryland, February 1960. (Office of Naval Research, Contract 595[05] NR 388-033.)

Peirce, Neal R. "Louisiana: An evocation." In *The Deep South States of America: People, Politics, and Power in the Seven Deep South States,* pp. 13-122. New York: W.W. Norton, 1974.

Price, Reynolds. "Dodo, Phoenix, or Tough Old Cock?" In H. Brandt Ayers and Thomas H. Naylor, eds., *You Can't Eat Magnolias.* New York: McGraw-Hill, 1972.

Plan and Program for the Preservation of the Vieux Carré: Historic District Demonstration Study. New Orleans: Bureau of Governmental Research, December 1968. See also Technical Supplements:
1— Environmental Survey (Marcou, O'Leary and Associates)
2— Legal and Administrative Report
3— Economic and Social Study (Hammer, Greene, Siler Associates)
4— The Vieux Carré, New Orleans, Its Plan, Its Growth, Its Architecture (Samuel Wilson, Jr.)
5— New Orleans Central Business District Traffic Study (Louisiana Department of Highways)
6— Summary Report: Evaluation of the Effects of the Proposed Riverfront Expressway (Marcou, O'Leary and Associates)
7— Technical Report on the Effects of the Proposed Riverfront Expressway on the Vieux Carré, New Orleans, Louisiana (Marcou, O'Leary and Associates)

Regional Planning Commission. *History of Regional Growth of Jefferson, Orleans, and St. Bernard Parishes, Louisiana.* New Orleans, November 1969.

Reissman, Leonard, et al. "Housing Discrimination in New Orleans: Summary and Recommendations." Based on a series of reports prepared for the New Orleans City Planning Commission. New Orleans: Tulane University Urban Studies Center, April 1970. (Mimeographed.

———. "Sociological Components of Community Renewal in New Orleans." A report prepared for the City Planning Commission of New Orleans. New Orleans: Department of Sociology, Tulane University, c. 1965.

Rushton, Bill. "The Damned Stadium: Blueprint of a Scandal." *The Courier: The Weekly Newspaper of New Orleans* 10, 17 (August 31-September 6, 1973): 1, 12-18.

Sanford, Terry. "The End of the Myths: The South Can Lead the Nation." In H. Brandt Ayers and Thomas H. Naylor, eds., *You Can't Eat Magnolias,* pp. 317-29. New York: McGraw-Hill, 1972.

Saucier, Roger T. *Recent Geomorphic History of the Pontchartrain Basin, Louisiana.* Technical Report no. 16. Baton Rouge: Louisiana State University Coastal Studies Institute, June 1963.

Saussy, Gordon A. *The Dynamics of Manufacturing Employment Location in the New Orleans Metropolitan Area.* Research Study no. 16.

New Orleans: Division of Business and Economic Research, College of Business Administration, Louisiana State University in New Orleans, 1972.

Slusher, David F.; W.L. Cockerham; and S.D. Matthews. "Mapping and Interpretation of Histosols and Hydraquents for Urban Development." Alexandria, Louisiana: U.S. Department of Agriculture, Soil Conservation Service. Paper presented before Soil Science Society of America, Miami, Florida, October 30, 1972. Mimeographed.

Smith, Robert J., ed. *1973 Annual Directory, Port of New Orleans.* New Orleans: Board of Commissioners of the Port of New Orleans, 1973.

Smith, T. Lynn, and Homer L. Hitt. *The People of Louisiana.* Baton Rouge: The Louisiana State University Press, 1952.

Somers, Dale A. "Black and White in New Orleans: A Study in Urban Race Relations, 1865–1900." *The Journal of Southern History* 40 (1974): 19–42.

Taeuber, Karl E., and Alma F. Taeuber. *Negroes in Cities: Residential Segregation and Neighborhood Change.* A Population Research and Training Center Monograph. Chicago: Aldine, 1965.

Thornbury, William D. *Regional Geomorphology of the United States.* Esp. chs. 2 and 3, "The Continental Margins" and "The Coastal Plain Province." New York: John Wiley & Sons, 1965.

Trollope, Frances. *Domestic Manners of the Americans.* London: Whittaker, Treacher & Co., 1832. Numerous reprintings and revisions. Among the best is Donald Smalley, ed., for Vintage Books. New York: Alfred A. Knopf, 1949.

U.S. Army Corps of Engineers. *Report on Hurricane Betsy, 8-11 September 1965 in the U.S. Army Engineer District, New Orleans.* New Orleans: U.S. Army Engineer District, November 1965.

———. *Report on Hurricane Camille. 14-22 August 1969.* New Orleans: U.S. Army Engineering District, May 1970.

U.S. Bureau of the Census. *Census of Housing: 1970. Block Statistics, New Orleans, La., Urbanized Area.* Final Report HC[3]–101. Washington, D.C.: U.S. Government Printing Office, September 1971.

———. *Census of Population and Housing: 1970. Census Tracts, New Orleans, La., Standard Metropolitan Statistical Area.* Final Report PHC[1]–144. Washington, D.C.: U.S. Government Printing Office, February 1972.

———. *Statistical Abstract of the United States: 1972.* 93d ed. Sect. 33, "Metropolitan Area Statistics," pp. 837 ff. Washington, D.C.: U.S. Government Printing Office, 1972.

U.S. Census Office, Department of the Interior. "New Orleans, Louisiana." In *Report on the Social Statistics of Cities,* compiled by George E. Waring, Jr. Part II, "The Southern and Western States." Washington, D.C.: U.S. Government Printing Office, 1887.

U.S. Department of Commerce. Environmental Science Services Administration, Environmental Data Service. *Climatic Atlas of the United States.* Washington, D.C.: U.S. Government Printing Office, June 1968.

Vance, Rupert B. *Human Geography of the South.* Chapel Hill: The University of North Carolina Press, 1935. See esp. ch. XI, "The Delta, Plantation Heritage," pp. 261–74.

"Vieux Carré Commission, Its Purpose and Function." New Orleans, n.d.

Williams, T. Harry, *Huey Long.* New York: Alfred A. Knopf, 1969.

Wilson, Samuel, Jr., and Bernard Lemann. *New Orleans Architecture.* Vol. 1: *The Lower Garden District,* Mary L. Christovich and Roulhac Toledano, eds. Gretna, La.: Pelican Publishing Company, 1971.

Wilson, Samuel, Jr. "The Vieux Carré, New Orleans, Its Plan, Its Growth, Its Architecture." Technical Supplement to *Plan and Program for the Preservation of the Vieux Carré.* New Orleans: Bureau of Governmental Research, December 1968.

Woodward, C. Vann. *Origins of the New South 1877-1913.* Baton Rouge: The Louisiana State University Press, 1951. Paperback reprint, 1970.

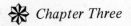 *Chapter Three*

The Cities by
San Francisco Bay

Frontispiece. The new San Francisco, seen from Treasure Island east of the Embarcadero. Photo courtesy of San Francisco Convention and Visitors Bureau.

The Parts that Make a Whole

To the traveler who comes to San Francisco by water under the Golden Gate Bridge, the contrast between the bare hills to the north and the mass of sparkling buildings to the south is striking indeed. To the airborne visitor who swings around the south end of San Francisco Bay, the checkerboard of lights and snaking freeways is strange in that it is broken into so many separate segments. To the Amtrak passenger who rides by Carquinez Strait on the way from Sacramento to San Francisco, the little towns along the southern shore seem oddly isolated. But it is soon clear that the grassy hills of Marin County and the terraced houses of Daly City, the continuous suburbs and the isolated towns, the steady glow of Oakland and the shimmering lights of San Francisco are all part of a single urban system, one that runs some hundred miles north-south and thirty-five miles east-west.

THE COUNTIES ROUND THE BAY

The city and county of San Francisco may steal center stage from Alameda, Contra Costa, Marin, and San Mateo counties, to which it is statistically joined in the San Francisco-Oakland SMSA with a population of 3.1 million (Figure 1). But there are other components to this extensive region. To the south is the San Jose SMSA and to the north an infant urban system is tabulated in 1970 as two units—the Santa Rosa SMSA and the Vallejo-Napa SMSA. These four contiguous statistical units around the San Francisco Bay together encompass an

intricate mesh of cities and suburbs that has functional unity and a total population of 4.6 million. Locally the term nine county region is used by governmental agencies to denote a level of economic and political integration that is also recognizable as the Daily Urban System (Table 1).

The DUS consists of two core counties— San Francisco and Alameda—plus seven suburban counties divided into two groups, the inner three and the other four. Contra Costa, Marin, and San Mateo counties are closely linked to the core counties in a functional articulation that shows up clearly in commuting patterns, although some residents of San

Table 1. San Francisco-Oakland Daily Urban System

County	Percentage of County Labor Force Commuting to Core Counties in 1970	Percentage of Labor Force Commuting to San Francisco-Oakland SMSA in 1970
Almeda	82.9	88.3
San Francisco	83.0	88.8
Contra Costa	31.8	90.0
Marin	38.4	90.6
San Mateo	28.6	83.4
Napa	4.5	8.4
Santa Clara	4.3	11.1
Solano	4.1	10.1
Sonoma	5.7	12.4

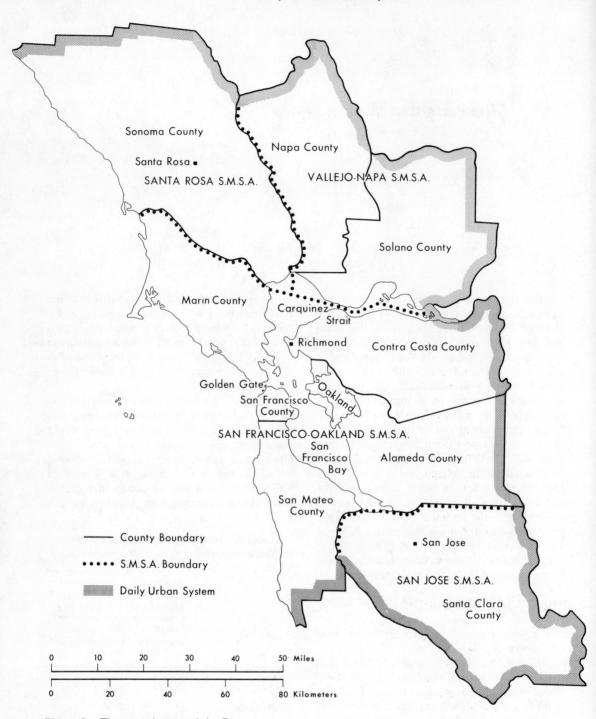

Figure 1. The counties round the Bay.

Mateo County head south to work around San Jose. The four outer counties may send similar numbers of workers to San Francisco or Alameda counties, but they do differ strongly one from another. Sonoma County is gradually being drawn into a "suburb to place of work" relationship to San Francisco. This pattern is directly comparable to that earlier—and far more pronounced—relationship of Marin County. The disadvantage of the extra traveling distance from Sonoma County is countered by lower housing costs. Napa and Solano are still predominantly rural counties that are becoming urbanized. Santa Clara County to the south contains the major city of San Jose and is an economic focus itself, of a magnitude akin to that of Alameda County. It shows a somewhat similar pattern of very high internal employment, as well as peripheral commuting. The San Francisco-Oakland DUS is not a region where a morning inflow is matched by an evening outflow. Instead it is a rather complex network of reciprocity, in which intracounty movement is very important, and within which rush hour traffic flow on the interconnecting freeways is in two directions so that the radio traffic alert may report congestion both ways. People live in the core counties and work in the core. People live in suburban counties and work in core counties. But people also live in one suburb and work in another. That is what builds the network.

A SENSE OF UNITY

In the region, governmental organization has been catalytic in creating a sense of regional unity and geographical identity. Through the public discussion of areawide issues has come support for regional agencies to deal with universal problems such as air pollution; but perhaps more significant than that is an awareness of sets of local issues that form recurrent patterns within the region. For some communities the preservation of their physical amenities is the major issue; for others the excessive speed of growth is causing problems; for yet others social conflict is the prime concern. Although these conditions recur within the region, there is no simple overall design that confines one set of problems to one locality. This emergent metropolitan system is noteworthy for its persistent physical discontinuity, its sheer area, and its diversity. The main theme of this study is the diversity of environment and evolution that has created a complex totality; this account may also convey the sense of fortunate people living in a fortunate place, for that is what it has been.

In less than one hundred years three major cities—San Francisco, Oakland, and San Jose—have played starring, but dissimilar, roles in an extensive—essentially tripolar—urban region. During this time San Francisco has normally taken the lead, though at intervals it has been regionally subservient, yielding pride of place to another part of the region. San Francisco could not compete with Oakland or Richmond as the proposed terminus for a transcontinental railroad. Most commonly the loss of leadership could be ascribed to San Francisco's eccentric location on a rugged peninsula. Nevertheless, today, in spite of its geographical shortcomings, San Francisco is sprouting a cluster of high-rise office buildings set to rival Manhattan in their brash seizure of opportunity. By means of a rapid transit system that will link Contra Costa and Alameda counties to San Francisco county, San Francisco is attempting again to tap a wide economic realm from its spatially constricted base. Regional white collar employment is being concentrated in a small financial district on the site of the original harbor. San Francisco is thereby reenacting a role it has played in the past. Once it was a minor village on a major bay whose fame rested on external trade links round Cape Horn, but within a span of twenty years the settlement took center stage. Recently the Bay Area has become a favored region in the American concept of regional virtue and again the city of San Francisco seeks to become the favored in that region. The tale of how San Francisco became the most famed of many places around the Bay in the days of sail can still symbolize the city's relationship to the entire Bay Area in the days of rapid transit.

An Anchorage Becomes an Entrepot

When the Boston men sailed to the coast in search of hides, their destination was the Bay. San Francisco to them designated a region not a site, just as it did to the Russian fur traders and the whaling ships. But these transients recognized the significance of the location.

> If California ever becomes a prosperous country, this bay will be the centre of its prosperity. The abundance of wood and water; the extreme fertility of its shores; the excellence of its climate, which is as near to being perfect as any in the world; and its facilities for navigation, affording the best anchoring-grounds in the whole western coast of America—all fit it for a place of great importance.

Such were Richard Henry Dana's observations as he sailed out of San Francisco Bay in December 1835. Since he had endured three weeks of incessant rain, his climatic panegyric was remarkable, as was his anticipation of future prosperity, for the *Alert* had "floated into the vast solitude that was the Bay of San Francisco. All around was the stillness of nature." The ship had anchored between a little island called Yerba Buena and a gravel beach on a small bight, also called Yerba Buena. The *Alert* had come to collect hides, not from the Mission Dolores "that has no trade at all," but from the missions and settlements on creeks and rivers tributary to the bay. In those days an agent organized voyages of three or four days by launch to gather a cargo. The supreme virtue of San Francisco Bay was

that it offered access to the interior on an otherwise inhospitable coast where the parallelism of ridge, valley, and coast produced few harbors, and even fewer easy ways to the Central Valley. The glories of the Bay with its wooded islands stood in sharp contrast to the gullied sandhills bare of grass, with few surviving trees, that surrounded Yerba Buena cove. But the importance of a convenient anchorage was recognized, even though the townsite was readily accessible to colonists only by water—because of its peninsular location—and was more convenient for those coming, than for those already there.

In 1859 Dana returned to find the islands shorn of trees and his cove built over to accommodate the city of nearly 100,000 persons that had become San Francisco. The hide trade had ended. "The hides . . . they brought us here, they kept us here, and it was only by getting them that we could escape from the coast and return to home and civilized life." When he came back twenty-four years later he found French cooking to equal that of Paris, as well as a church congregation so congenial in music and sermon that it recalled to him a Parisian chapel. The transformation came by virtue of commerce—not trade *to* the port but trade *through* the port.

SAN FRANCISCO TAKES TITLE TO THE REGION

In 1835, William Antonio Richardson, who had been appointed harbormaster when the Bay was

declared a port of entry for the newly sanction-
ed trade to the Mexican Republic, built a tent
of redwood and hide on the sandy slope above
the cove, there dealing with incoming vessels
as well as trading with the ranchos. As a primordial wholesaler, he also ran a transportation
service on the Bay using two salvaged schooners
for transferring goods. In 1836 Jacob Leese
sailed into the cove, built a large house next to
Richardson's tent, and proceeded to trade his
cargo on the plaza in competition. Land and
building lots in the settlement were located on
the basis of a rectangular survey of Yerba
Buena that was commissioned of a Swiss sea
captain Vioget in 1839. By 1841 thirty families
were settled, and a Hudson's Bay Company
post flourished.

After 1841 a renewal of trade restrictions
against foreigners sent the whalers off to the
Sandwich Islands, and ended other trade. The
existence of the Mexican Customs House on
Portsmouth Square ceased to give the village
much advantage over the pueblo at Sonoma,
or the agricultural center at Napa on the Napa
River since external trading was now forbidden.
There were other embarcaderos around the Bay
from which internal exchange could be effected, and this kind of trade between one settlement and another required no single assembly
point where all goods would be collected prior
to transhipment. To be predominant in external
trade was a gift of locational advantage held by
Yerba Buena, but the gift was dross in a territory not organized for colonial trading—that
is to say, for the export of a large volume of
goods. When the situation of Yerba Buena
offered little profit, the disadvantages of its
site became more apparent. Every description
mentions sand and dust, wind and fog, as well
as fleas, but more striking are the accounts of
the difficulty of getting around.

Bartlett, the first alcalde (mayor) under
the American flag in 1846, paid attention both
to the problems of site and to the potential
asset of location. He ordered a revision of the
Yerba Buena survey and appointed Jasper
O'Farrell town surveyor. O'Farrell extended the
grid of small rectangular blocks westward, and
to the south he added a new grid oriented to
the trail that had led to Mission Dolores. There
he utilized blocks some four times as large as
those in the original grid (Figure 2). The two
grids met at an uneasy junction along Market

Street. In *The Making of Urban America* by
John Reps, the clear reproduction of *View of
San Francisco, Formerly Yerba Buena, 1846-7*
shows the gap between the surveyor's dream
and what existed on the ground. The O'Farrell
map conveys the impression of a large, well-
ordered settlement: the engraving reveals how
modest were those streets and how sparse the
buildings.

Bartlett also managed to reap the potential
benefit of the town's location at the entrance
to the famous Bay. In the face of a plan to in-
corporate the name Francisca in the title of a
new town being platted on Carquinez Strait
at the head of San Pablo Bay, Bartlett issued
his declaration "that the name San Francisco
shall hereafter be used in all official communications and public documents, or records,
appertaining to the town, . . . so that the town
may have the advantage of the name given on
published maps."

BUILDING A HARBOR

In 1848 Sam Brannan reputedly led 893 of
the town's 900 inhabitants on the first rush
to the American River diggings for gold. By
the end of the year San Francisco housed some
2,000 men on their way to the diggings. The
world traveler and correspondent Bayard Taylor arrived on the Pacific Mail Steamship Company's *Panama* on August 18, 1849, to report
on doings in California for the *New York
Tribune,* and he recounts his first view in
Eldorado.

> Yerba Buena Island is in front; southward
> and westward opens the renowned harbor,
> crowded with the shipping of the world,
> mast behind mast and vessel behind vessel,
> the flags of all nations fluttering in the
> breeze! Around the curving shore of the bay
> and upon the sides of three hills which rise
> steeply from the water, the middle one
> receding so as to form a bold amphitheatre,
> the town is planted and seems scarcely yet
> to have taken root, for tents, canvas, plank,
> mud, and adobe houses are mingled to-
> gether with the least apparent attempt at
> order and durability.

The renown of the harbor rested on events
rather than on natural configuration. Because
the waters of Yerba Buena Cove were so shal-

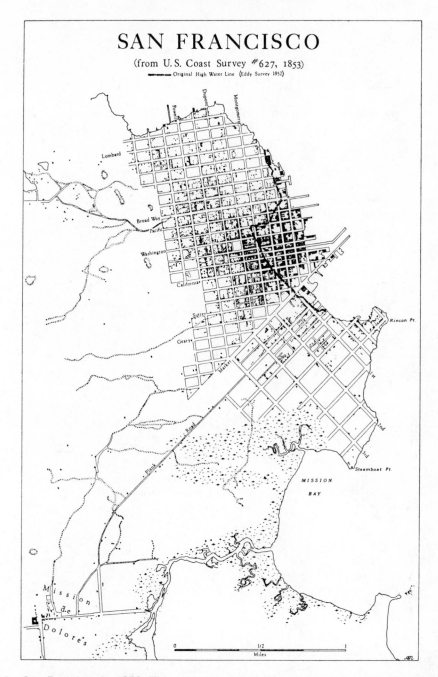

Figure 2. San Francisco in 1853. This map shows the encroachment of the city on the mudflats of Yerba Buena Cove below the original high water line, and the virtual isolation of the trading town from land. Except for the "Plank Road" across the marsh at the head of Mission Bay, the city was framed by marsh, steep hills, or sand dunes. It was along the wharves extending the streets to deep water that San Francisco made its contact with "the world" and "the diggings." Source: James E. Vance, Jr., *Geography and Urban Evolution in the San Francisco Bay Area* (Berkeley: Institute of Governmental Studies, University of California, 1964), p. 19.

Figure 3. Filling the cove.

Table 2. Vessels in San Francisco Harbor, October 31, 1851

Type	Number
Ships	59
Barks	97
Brigs	81
Schooners	55
Ocean Steamers	9
Miscellaneous	2
Store Ships[a]	148
Total	451

[a]Many of the vessels in the harbor had been abandoned when their crews rushed off to the goldfields. They were subsequently used as stores or lodging places to augment the scanty premises available.

Source: Frank Soulé et al, *The Annals of San Francisco* (New York: D. Appleton and Co., 1855), quoted in *Subsidence and the Foundation Problem in San Francisco,* a report of the Subsoil Committee of the San Francisco Section, American Society of Civil Engineers, September 1932.

low, piers had to be built out from the beach for more convenient unloading of cargo. By 1850 nine wharves stretched into the cove, the longest of them extended 975 feet, and in all the wharves had a total length of 6,000 feet. The spaces between the wharves were soon cluttered with abandoned vessels (Table 2) and sand and garbage were also dumped there. Soon cross links were built between these piers. A network of streets extending the landward grid was created and commercial activities advanced into the cove (Figure 3).

Goods, Money, and People: The Mercantile Base

San Francisco was a port with a highly specialized entrepôt function, and it presents in exaggerated form the character of a mercantile settlement. The hinterland of the port was far removed, at least a riverboat ride away, and there was virtually no trade area in the immediate vicinity of the town. It fitted no neat settlement hierarchy. Business activities hinged on goods, on money, and on people, and these three elements gave rise to a segmented urban base. This commercial life was at first spatially intermingled, but functional segregation soon emerged amid intense economic speculation and a three part business district emerged.

CONSTRUCTION AND RECONSTRUCTION

Rapid construction and a fluid pattern of building use within the town were prompted in part by the need to build and rebuild after the six fires that leveled the settlement between December 24, 1849, and June 22, 1851. The fires that destroyed so many merchants' stocks forced them to replace wooden buildings by brick as soon as possible, specifically along Montgomery Street, and this meant importing building supplies. Granite for the Parrott building came precut and numbered from "the most accessible granite quarry"— in China. Bricks, window frames, and glass for the Montgomery Block constructed in 1853 to restore confidence after the 1852 depression came from France. One hotel, the Graham

House, was "imported bodily" from Baltimore. In 1849 ready-made houses had been imported from Canton.

The building frenzy was accompanied by enormous speculation in land. According to Bayard Taylor, land bought for $20,000 was sold a year later for $300,000. The instability in land prices matched the ups and downs on the gaming tables that were such an element in city life, and these in turn reflected a famine and feast pattern in trading goods. A barrel of alum bought for $6 soon sold for $150, since it was the only one in town. Demand for goods was so unpredictable to the remote suppliers on the East Coast that an item in short supply and grossly inflated one week would be hard to give away the next. This business instability was compounded by a shortage of actual money as neither available gold dust nor coins matched the scale of monetary transactions, so a complex credit structure with short term interest payments flourished.

FUNCTIONAL LOGIC IN A MERCANTILE CITY

That order emerged in this volatile economic condition is due to the different space demands of business dealing with goods, with money, and with people. But a fine-grained sorting of land use within the settlement was favored by the initial street layout, too. The blocks north of Market Street were small, some 275 feet by 412 feet, and many were divided by an interior alley or street. The clustering of even a few business establishments of one kind in a short distance would create a focus.

According to Bowden, in a definitive study of the San Francisco Central District, of the 1,273 establishments in San Francisco in 1850, the wholesaler with stocks was predominant, and 29 percent of the city's establishments could be so classified. The merchant had to cling to the wharf. As piers extended out into the cove the wholesalers with stocks who were dealing with incoming ships and outgoing riverboats moved out onto the piers, for the warehouses needed to be on the water. The wholesalers who dealt in produce, liquor, and wine turned north toward Clark's Point, for that was the pier for the diggings in the Sacramento and San Joaquin valleys. The wholesaling of bulky items such as lumber and building supplies was soon forced away from the central piers. Shipping activities and wholesale functions became more and more locationally specific, passenger embarking and disembarking tended to stay north and the handling of goods went south. The waterfront itself became characterized by a clustering according to the type of trade and goods handled.

A large part of the entrepôt function was financial. San Francisco served as the conduit for bills of trade, for bank drafts, and for credit, which in turn involved express agents like Wells Fargo, shipping agents, and the ancillary services of insurance and underwriting. A shift of financial establishments to the wharf heads presaged the rapid growth of a singularly complex financial district on the filled land of Yerba Buena Cove. An informal stock exchange was set up in a saloon in the Montgomery Block. The face-to-face nexus of dealers flourished and their economic activities were given enormous stimulus by the Comstock Lode discoveries of 1859. Mining stocks boomed, and in 1862 the San Francisco Stock and Exchange Board was organized. San Francisco's primary role as a banking center was assured by involvement in the silver boom in Nevada, the Central Pacific Railroad, and the Central Valley land development that had

started with wheat in the 1850s. At first many financial operations had been conducted upstairs over retail shops, but soon banks sought the ground floor.

Buildings tended to be very low, for the successively extended and enlarged business district lay on unconsolidated fill that was to be subject to extreme earthquake hazard until either the fill consolidated or superior building techniques could take foundations to bedrock. From the start, the filled land of the cove had been subject to tidal washing and scour, but stone and earth embankments were built to prevent this erosion. However, the impact of the 1868 earthquake showed that much of the business district was built on poor ground. In low buildings, usually two or three stories high, businesses clustered on streets according to their primary concern, whether with insurance, stock trading, or shipping.

The third functional component of early San Francisco stemmed from the demands of a tremendous inflow of people. Hotels and lodging houses for all classes of persons were prominent. Entertainment and gambling loomed large. Restless people shopped—men for work clothes, women for fancy goods, and everyone for groceries and household hardware. In the early years, when Portsmouth Square was the center of social life, retailing clustered there, but the gradients of Nob Hill and the slight extension of the Chinese quarter on Grant Avenue made inland expansion impossible. Therefore stores turned south toward Market Street, but not across that 110 foot wide street. The 825 feet by 550 feet blocks south of Market Street were simply not conducive to retail uses. The center of retail trade was ultimately established at Union Square, some seven blocks south and a little west of Richardson's tent site.

Although the configuration of the early business district related most directly to the waterfront, a threefold segregation of activities was in progress in the first flush of mercantile prosperity. This division into separate parts not only took place quickly, it also persisted for a long time, in spite of changes in external relationships of the port.

San Francisco and the Rest of the United States

San Francisco was not a conventional port. It was a place to which people and goods came on their way elsewhere. It was the first convenient point for transshipment and the constant comings and goings created an aura of excitement and of surging vitality. The importance of the settlement to trade for a wider region stemmed from the advantage of the port for communication with the outside world—a condition of situation rather than of site. So long as connections with the eastern United States were by water, San Francisco had no peer; it was the only link with civilization for an expanding economy. This held true in the technology of clipper ships and steamers, but as soon as landward connections were improved then the advantage of being the closest harbor to ocean waters paled, and the deficiencies of an eccentric site on the tip of a peninsula became more apparent. What really took place was a complete reversal of vantage point. The links by sea became less vital than the links by land. When Frémont had named the straits "Golden Gate" because they were reminiscent of the Golden Horn of Byzantium, he little knew how appropriate the name would prove. When Hittell wrote of Carquinez Strait as the "Silver Gate" he remarked a shift in economic importance from the gold of the Mother Lode to the silver of the Comstock Lode. His naming of the second gate, the one that led inland, also pointed up a new orientation that would be important in the exchange of information before it was significant in the exchange of goods.

BRIDGING THE INFORMATION GAP

On March 3, 1847, an act of Congress authorized the secretary of the navy to call for bids to carry mail to California and Oregon. By the end of 1848 the United States Mail Steamship Company was feeding passengers to Chagres, Panama, whence they traveled overland to Panama City to wait for passage to "the Coast." The Pacific Mail Steamship Company vessel *California* reached Panama on January 17, 1849, and was able to load 365 of the 1,500 persons waiting there. Thereafter, a regular complement of over 300 moved northward every month, whereas a slowly accelerating return passenger load reached similar proportions by September of that year. Concurrently, gold dust shipments that had started at around $300,000 per sailing rose to around a million dollars. By the spring of 1850 news of returning passengers was published on the East Coast and letters began to flow. Wiltsee describes communication in the following passage:

> From the inauguration of the "gold rush" steamers, they had been the sole conveyors of the news to and from California. The columns of the entire local press of the state and the Pacific slope were dependent for their news of the outer world upon the newspapers from abroad, received on the arrival of each steamer. In the intervening two weeks until the next arrival, the columns of the Pacific press would contain only local items. . . . It was a bi-monthly blossoming in-

to a bewildering abundance of world news to relapse into complete obsolescence until the next steamer arrived.

In San Francisco the first and fifteenth of the month became "steamer days" when business accounts were rendered. Service was now reliable, though this had come about only under pressure of competition from the Law's Line sailings that had been advertised to give better service.

In fourteen months an enormously lucrative trade had developed, one that served three functions: first, the carrying of persons to and from the West Coast; second, the carrying of goods and gold dust; and third, the exchange of news. Soon three companies vied for the trade; cutthroat competition resulted in lowering fares which cut into profits; and more space became available than there were persons wanting to sail. The Comstock Lode dicovery in 1859 was the last bonanza that triggered an upsurge of passenger travel and that did something to compensate for the dropoff in bullion shipments which had once run as high as $2.5 million but by 1859 had fallen back to half a million.

Although change in volume characterized the first two functions of a maritime link, it was in the third component—namely, the carrying of news from coast to coast—that radical change came first. There was a transformation not in scale of operation but in the means and direction of transmittal. The old order is recorded by Bayard Taylor, who describes the arrival of mail on October 31, 1849, after a three month void: "Thirty-seven mail-bags were hauled up to the little Post Office that night, and the eight clerks were astounded by the receipt of forty-five thousand letters, besides uncounted bushels of newspapers." A forty-four hour seige ended with delivery to the private boxes, but a week later it could take six hours of standing in line to get to the post office window. For inland delivery there were private agents willing to serve the mines, and they did a lucrative business, for official arrangements to carry mail to an inland destination were erratic in the extreme.

A decade later, the inauguration of the Pony Express service in April 1860 was followed, in July 1861, by a Post Office directive requiring that mail be sent by overland stage unless specifically marked "by steamer."

This was an absolute reversal of previous practice and marked the turnabout in connectivity. In October 1861, the completion of a telegraph link at Salt Lake in Utah meant that California newspapers carried national crises daily, instead of bimonthly. California had truly come into the Union.

For the movement of goods, the geographical situation of San Francisco was still important in the 1860s, for it would take the completion of railroad ties to trigger a real dispersion of manufacturing and trade from the central city. Although the existence of potential rivals round the Bay had long been recognized, the long-standing reputation of San Francisco as *the* port would leave no rival in the national perception of where commercial power rested. The other settlements would develop their own specialized port activities, but those would not steal the general trade from San Francisco. Benicia was a clear potential rival for San Francisco in that it had a far superior anchorage with immediate access to deep water and ample space for a town site at the Silver Gate, the Strait of Carquinez. Indeed, on the advice of letters received in New York in early 1849 vessels had been cleared from New York to Benicia with large cargoes. Bayard Taylor comments, "Now anchorage is one thing, and a good market another; a ship may lie in greater safety in Albany, but the sensible merchant charters his vessel for New York." The disadvantage of an inland location was even more marked for "New York of the West"—more an ambitious real estate promotion than indicative of the settlement's effectiveness as a rival. Taylor allotted agricultural produce and a fair share of the inland trade to Benicia; and he left the supplying of mines to Stockton and Sacramento City; but "San Francisco takes the commerce." Although San Francisco did indeed take the commerce—and kept it— a dispersion of waterborne commodities round the Bay spawned the growth of specialized factory ports. Later, completion of the railroad link further shifted trade to the landward shore.

THE DISPERSION OF SPECIALIZED TRADE INITIATES THE FACTORY PORTS

Up to 1868, wheat destined for Europe from the increasing acreage in the Central Valley came from within 120 miles of San Francisco. It was taken in sacks to San Francisco and there transshipped from the riverboats to the sailing ships that would go round the Horn. The completion of the Central Pacific Railroad to Oakland in 1869 initiated a new alignment for the trade. Some wheat had moved from the Santa Clara valley to San Francisco by rail, but as soon as there was access to Oakland, the route for that crop changed, and Santa Clara wheat was added to the volume moving from Modesto to Oakland. Saunders attributes the shift to three main causes: one, the rail line to Oakland had an easier grade than the San Jose to San Francisco route; two, the cargo could move straight from the railroad to the loading point; and, three, the high port charges for which San Francisco was notorious could be avoided. Since 1863 the improvement of San Francisco's harbor had been financed by state-authorized levies that were placed on freight hauled to and fro and on freight stored, and on a daily wharfage charge while a ship was berthed. These made San Francisco an expensive destination or shipping point. Because Oakland suffered from shallow water, wharves were built far out into the Bay for the ferry boats in 1863, and this set a precedent for the Southern Pacific Company's Long Wharf. Completed in 1871, it extended two miles into the Bay and supported large grain warehouses. In a reversal, San Francisco lost preeminence in the grain trade to Oakland and Vallejo. The trade did not stay long in these two ports, however, but moved—when the Southern Pacific skirted the shore after 1879—to a line of even smaller loading places along the south side of Carquinez Strait where natural deep water offered a great time saving in efficient transhipment as well as a 50 cents per ton saving on rail-shipping fees. Some of those small ports were the most logical places to build factories for the processing of raw materials—for milling flour for example—and Crockett today has a major sugar refinery, which began life as a wheat warehouse.

Explosives at Hercules, cement at Redwood City, petroleum at Richmond and Oleum, steel at Pittsburg—all examples of specialized manufacturing towns that depended for their origin on a dispersion of trade from San Francisco and on the possibility of developing numerous small industrial ports. But even more fundamental was the completion of the rail link between the Bay region and the rest of the country.

BY LAND AND BY TRAIN

In rather the same fashion that one narrow entrance had concealed access to the Bay from sailors for so long, so did the coastal ranges limit freedom of entry to the region for the railroads building from the East. There were only three practicable routes to the Bay Area, and none of these provided a direct link with the city of San Francisco. To the north of Carquinez Strait, Jameson Canyon offered good access to Vallejo. The route through Carquinez Strait on the south shore led to Richmond or to Oakland. The third gap, Suñol Canyon, which was the original route of the first transcontinental line, also ended in Oakland. Not until 1910, when the Dumbarton Bridge was completed, would this first route tie directly to San Francisco (Figure 4).

True, the first railroad built in the Bay Area had linked San Francisco to San Jose in 1864, but this early start could never compensate for the indirectness of any transcontinental link for that route. And the other railroad connections for San Francisco required ferry trips. Consequently, the poverty of the San Francisco site relative to railroad access was a shortcoming that enabled the East Bay—most especially in Oakland, but also Richmond—to capture the transshipment function. It was more logical to ship goods to and from the last landward point on a transcontinental journey. Further, the East Bay had the immeasurable advantage of large expanses of flat open ground. A division of shipping functions that started with the completion of the railroad has—in the intervening century—switched much wholesaling to the East Bay. In the same manner that in the 1860s a diversion of specialized commodities initiated manufacturing at points around the Bay, so in the 1960s a geographically logical distribution of function has developed with the growth of the port of Oakland.

THE EASTWARD SHIFT OF TRADE IS COMPLETED

The prophecy that San Francisco would take the commerce has been fulfilled—even today there is no challenge to its financial role—but recently Oakland has taken the trade expressed as a port function. In 1962 the port of San Francisco was still ahead in tonnage, but in the

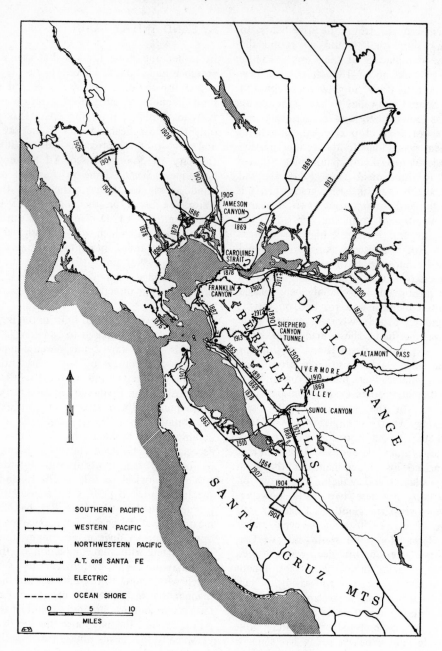

Figure 4. By train to the Bay. Only steam railroads and the heavier and more long distance traction lines are shown. The Petaluma and Santa Rosa Railway in Sonoma County ultimately came into the Northwestern Pacific system, the Sacramento Northern from Oakland eastward through Shepherd Canyon tunnel to Sacramento came into the Western Pacific system, and the Peninsular Railway around San Jose was controlled by the Southern Pacific from its inception. Source: James E. Vance, Jr., *Geography and Urban Evolution in the San Francisco Bay Area,* (Berkeley: Institute of Governmental Studies, University of California, 1964), p. 37.

next two years the two came closer together, and since 1965 Oakland has assumed the lead. Both ports are predominantly general cargo handlers. Oakland receives sheet steel and shaped iron and steel, fruit and vegetable juices, and molasses, as well as exporting frozen vegetables, animal fats, grain mill products, and scrap metal. In these items Oakland shares some of the character of the factory ports that dot the remainder of the Bay shore. Round the Bay the main commodity measured by tonnage received and shipped is that of most American ports—petroleum and petroleum products; Redwood City, Carquinez Strait and, above all, Richmond, are the sites of refineries and tank farms. But items such as sugar and molasses (the California and Hawaiian plant at Carquinez Strait); coke and petroleum asphalts (San Pablo Bay); and sand, gravel, and cement (Redwood City) are reminders of the factory processing that shows up at diverse waterbound locations.

Both Oakland and San Francisco handle a remarkable variety of products; 135 and 125 separately listed Standard Industrial Classification (SIC) categories of commodities as reported in *Waterborne Commerce, 1971.* San Francisco's trade is predominantly foreign, with imports at 847,346 tons as compared to exports at 538,542, and only the receipt of fuel oil, jet fuel, and sand shows up significantly in domestic trade. Oakland's exports at 1,070,411 tons exceed imports of 846,452, largely because of the scrap metal outflow. But Oakland, in addition, has as much coastwise trade and internal trade as foreign. It is perhaps the large component of domestic trade that

most emphatically points up the contrast between the present-day roles of these ports, as compared to the 1850s, when San Francisco's water links to interior California were so vital to its entrepôt function.

The port of Oakland is the third largest container port in the world, measured in tonnage, in acreage for container storage, and in berths and in cranes. In the U.S. it is exceeded only by the Port of New York. Figures published by the Port of Oakland (Table 3) show the impact of the introduction of containers in 1962. Prior to containerization of cargoes, Oakland handled some 2.5 million tons per year, primarily fruit juice and canned foods for Europe. During the ten years of growth in container shipping, container cargo alone has increased to 4.5 million tons. Oakland has four terminals with twenty-five berths in all, and has a seventy acre Sea-Land facility as well as the forty-eight acre Seatrain facility and the Matson container terminal at the 140 acre Seventh Street docks located on the transformed Southern Pacific mole. The port has 1,000 acres of industrial and commercial land with a further 11,500 of undeveloped land, part of which is underwater. Expansion of the port has entailed Bay filling, and some organizations have opposed it, though without creation of new land no comparable harbor facility could have emerged.

Four main advantages have been cited to explain this successful growth. First, Oakland has large open storage areas near the berths permitting container, truck, and railroad car parking. Second, Oakland has good railroad access; it is served by the Southern Pacific,

Table 3. Container Cargo and the Port of Oakland (1,000s of tons)

Year	Container Cargo	Break Bulk General Cargo	Total Container and Break Bulk General Cargo	Bulk Liquid	Bulk Dry	Total Port Tonnage
1962	55	733	788	1,386	380	2,554
1964	321	638	959	1,131	420	2,510
1966	708	1,079	1,787	831	402	3,019
1968	1,531	1,000	2,530	469	391	3,391
1970	3,651	762	4,413	373	813	5,598
1972	4,577	998	5,576	320	640	6,535

Source: Port of Oakland.

the Western Pacific, and the Atchison, Topeka and Santa Fe, all of which have tracks, or spur trackage, leading from the port. Third, within three miles of the port there are some forty truck terminals, and access to east-west and north-south freeways is as convenient as the rail connection. Finally, Oakland has a large hinterland that is growing in population and in industrial significance—even though the city itself experienced a slight drop in population in the last decade. To the city of Oakland, it is of no little importance that the port provides 23,000 jobs and that 32 percent of those are held by minority employees. Using a multiplier effect of three, it is estimated that one in five Oakland residents depends on the port, because to the 23,000 persons directly employed by the port must be added another 46,000 persons in indirectly dependent jobs.

The port of San Francisco boasts that it is the fourth largest coffee port in the world, a status that the breeze confirms since some of the beans are roasted close to the Ferry Building. Until recently it also boasted of some 250 passenger vessel sailings or calls annually, though this number is dropping. San Francisco has the maritime union hiring halls for the Bay Area and a long list of shipping services —twenty-four chandlers, three maritime carpenter firms, and no less than ninety-one ship brokers. A hundred years of history still shows.

The port of San Francisco divides into two sections at the Ferry Building. The northern section has twenty-seven piers of which seven currently are withdrawn from maritime use. The piers persist to Hyde Street (which is well known to tourists who have ridden the cable car to the Buena Vista Café and the Maritime State Park) and are predominantly general cargo piers, although two specialize in newsprint and four in fish, while one is a passenger pier. Plans for the waterfront call for the abandonment of ship handling north of the Ferry Building and the building of recreational facilities, commercial premises, and apartments. To the south of the Ferry Building nine of the thirty-seven piers are closed, but in contrast to the northern section there has been major construction to the south since 1950. A high speed grain terminal has been built, as well as container facilities and roll-on roll-off capacity. The most publicized development is the LASH

terminal—the Lighter Aboard Ship system. Utilizing this method port time is cut to a minimum and a vessel can serve several piers at one stop. The "mother" ship carries forty-nine lighters and can be loaded to capacity in twenty-four hours using a crane with a gantry for loading containers. The Pacific Far East Line plans to have six such vessels in service. The forty-eight acre LASH terminal is at the southern extremity of the waterfront and San Francisco is expecting further expansion in the area in the next five years.

Despite this activity it is likely that Oakland will maintain its newfound leadership. San Francisco will retain what passenger trade there may be, but the handling of bulk cargo is likely to shift to Oakland. San Francisco is anticipating an increase in container cargoes but, as the port for a regional market, San Francisco suffers from the insuperable problems inherent to a peninsula location. In contrast to Oakland, where excellent rail connections make it possible for as much as 65 percent of its cargoes to move by rail, about 75 percent of San Francisco port traffic moves by road. This puts a severe burden on freeways and above all on the Bay Bridge. Any port construction on the San Francisco waterfront will entail more transbay traffic. Gradually the eastward shift of industry and wholesaling that started with the completion of the transcontinental railroad links (the first in 1869 and the third and last in 1910) has gathered force, and it makes good geographical sense. The economic well-being of the region demands that there be some sharing of functions that can be allocated to their most appropriate location. When it was possible to anchor quickly off Yerba Buena Cove, the immediacy of that anchorage was convincing proof of its superiority. But now that growth within San Francisco has shifted the focus of its port far south of the Bay Bridge, it requires navigation very similar to that needed to reach Oakland's wharves, and the landward advantages of the port of Oakland come into play. As economic activities have shifted over the years there has been a gradual dispersion of shipping to foci around the Bay. Specialized cargoes had fostered factory ports, and modern technology has contracted trade to fewer points.

The contribution of ocean, bay, and river

traffic to the many embarcaderos round the shore had been easy to see, but once water-borne trade is concentrated to highly specialized craft, the number of essential waterland contacts is sharply reduced—for instance, to a container port in Oakland, oil terminals on the Contra Costa shore, a few specialized factory ports, and to the trade to which San Francisco clings. In the meantime a host of new functions has appeared. The Bay could no longer be just a shipping artery but would assume other functions too.

The Physical Stamp on an Urban Design

In no other American metropolitan area does the physical environment play a greater role in shaping a modern urban region than in the Bay Area. The sheer physical diversity of conditions within a small geographical area has permitted the deliberate selection of alternative options for development. It is demonstrable that the distribution of land and water has been a major influence in shaping urban function in this region. It is also demonstrable that the San Francisco Bay itself is a component of the regional economic system. Although other elements of the physical environment have been obtrusively influential too, their impact is not as immediatley obvious as is the role of the drowned valley that comprises the center of the region.

THE "VAST SOLITUDE" HAS GONE

Every loaded city dump truck that heads toward the Bay is reducing a scarce resource, for San Francisco Bay is a literally diminishing asset. Nichols and Wright calculate that since the mid-1800s the Bay has lost 11 percent or fifty-three square miles of its water area. In addition, marshland and tidal sloughs had lost 60 percent of their original 313 square miles by 1968, though half of that loss was to salt evaporation ponds. The attrition of this resource has taken many forms. There has been a clear reduction in the area of the Bay. There has also been deterioration in the quality of water within the Bay which in turn has had a deleterious impact on potential functions of the water body.

Concern over water quality has been manifest on two issues—the impaired volume and condition of water flowing into the Bay from the Sacramento and San Joaquin drainage basins, and the threat of salt water intrusion upriver from the ocean. A reduction in speed and volume of freshwater outflow started in the days of hydraulic mining, but the completion of Shasta Dam in 1944 was the start of massive impoundment that was followed by massive water transfer—most recently to Southern California—accomplished by an interlocking system of rivers and canals that reduced river flow to the Bay. The diversion of water to agriculture creates polluted discharge as well as making a shortcut in the hydrologic cycle. As a consequence, fertilizers joined the industrial and municipal wastes that had been discharged into the Bay for a long time. It is clear that the deterioration of water quality has been a complex sequence, one that has impaired water supplies as well as affecting such processes as fish spawning.

The reduction in the area of the Bay has also had drastic impact. A shallow water body can activate water purification by oxygenation; a diminution in surface area reduces this ability. Marginal marshes and ponds support wildfowl and it is these borderlands that are lost first. Some authorities argue that the sheer size of the Bay means that it acts as a weather modifier and that changes in temperature and air circulation would be consequent to a change in surface area. The complexity of uses served by the Bay were publicly recognized only when serious questions about its future were raised. Everyone had always taken for granted the recreational and aesthetic qualities of the San Francisco Bay and the shrinkage of the resources was not widely recognized, nor was the contradictory nature of many of the demands placed on the water body properly realized.

The publication in 1959 of the so-called "2020 Report" by the Army Corps of Engineers—who were responsible for reconciling some of these conflicts—brought a rude awakening. The report showed that if all parts of the Bay less than twelve feet deep were filled—and such filling would be economically feasible—then little more than a river would remain in some sections (Figure 5). Active citizen concern prodded the state legislature into establishing the Bay Conservation and Development Commission (BCDC) in 1965. The commission, after initiating a series of exhaustive studies during a four year moratorium on fill, produced a Bay Plan in 1969 that called for reserving half of the 276 mile shoreline for five priority uses—ports, water-related industry, water recreation, airports, and wildlife preserves. After legislative acceptance the commission was charged with requiring adherence to its plan, and was given some jurisdiction over a one hundred foot shoreline strip.

Control over dumping and dredging may well reduce problems associated with development on made land. The present shoreline has been created out of natural and manmade deposition of unconsolidated fill, much of which is in urban land uses. Relative to earthquake hazard, serious geologic questions remain unanswered, but few zoning codes or building codes recognize the complexity of subsurface conditions. Of prime concern are the water content of sediments (usually more than 50 percent by weight), the load-bearing strength, potential for compression, and a sharp differentiation between dry and saturated volume. Such complexities produce locally unique settling rates that may be compounded by the subsidence of adajcent land. In the Santa Clara valley, for instance, up to thirteen feet of subsidence was recorded between 1912 and 1967.

That building on Bay fill poses future problems has long been known. In 1932 a comprehensive report from the San Francisco section of the American Society of Engineers documented the foundation problem that existed, especially for buildings on filled-in Yerba Buena Cove and Mission Bay. Maintenance of street grade had plagued the city engineer's office since 1850; indeed south of Mission Street you can still see houses with garage entrances so far below street level as to be inaccessible. Yet in defiance of visible warnings of cracking stucco and warped roof lines large scale urban development has taken place on land fill. In San Mateo county in the 1960s Foster City—designed as an economically integrated town to house 35,000 on 2,600 acres—was built on reclaimed sea level salt marsh islands. Municipalities are by no means consistent in their attitude toward their shoreline properties. Berkeley has more ardent advocates of Bay conservation than most cities; it also has motels and new restaurants marching out across a marina built on the city dump. Further invasion is inhibited by the knowledge that continued attrition of the San Francisco Bay could eventually condemn the complex metropolis to an anonymous future—just one more endless suburban carpet uninterrupted by that stretch of water which now gives both internal contrast and the great visual peace that so distinguishes this double metropolitan area.

THE QUESTION OF EARTHQUAKES

The San Francisco Bay region is subject to frequent, widely distributed earthquakes; from 1850 to 1927, about 1,000 were recorded. Perhaps two or three in 150 years are internationally known (1906—8.3 on the Richter scale); though more that have caused physical damage are locally recognized (San Francisco, 1957—5.3, or Santa Rosa, 1969—5.7).

Around the Bay there are four historically active fault zones—the San Andreas, the Sargent, the Calaveras, and the Hayward (Figure 6). A detailed map of epicenters of earthquakes greater than 0.5 occurring in 1969–1970 shows three nonparallel belts not more than four miles wide and generally about two miles wide, trending northwest-southeast. This earthquake activity was localized in narrow surface zones that descend almost ver-

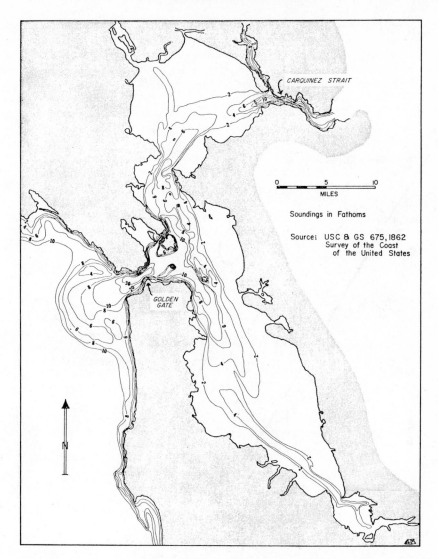

Figure 5. The Shallow Bay. The contours show the configuration that existed prior to the deposition of the main load of silt and mud that came from hydraulic gold mining. The general shallowness of the bays should be noted, as well as the absence of deep water inshore, except off Yerba Buena Cove (already filled in 1862), Point San Pedro in Richmond, and Sausalito and Tiburon. Source: James E. Vance, Jr., *Geography and Urban Evolution in the San Francisco Bay Area*, (Berkeley: Institute of Governmental Studies, University of California, 1964), p. 11.

tically some ten miles. Movements producing earthquakes on the San Andreas, Hayward, and Calaveras faults shift rock masses seaward of those traces—i.e., toward the northwest, in a horizontal plane. Each of these faults has generated large earthquakes resulting in surface displacement and major damage to buildings. On the surface the major faults are evidenced by local relief features such as offset streams, scarps, and one of the most persistent features, sag ponds. After land fill and subsequent housing developments have completely obscured fault-created ponds, reports of flooded basements or local subsidence reveal their location.

The best known of the four active faults is

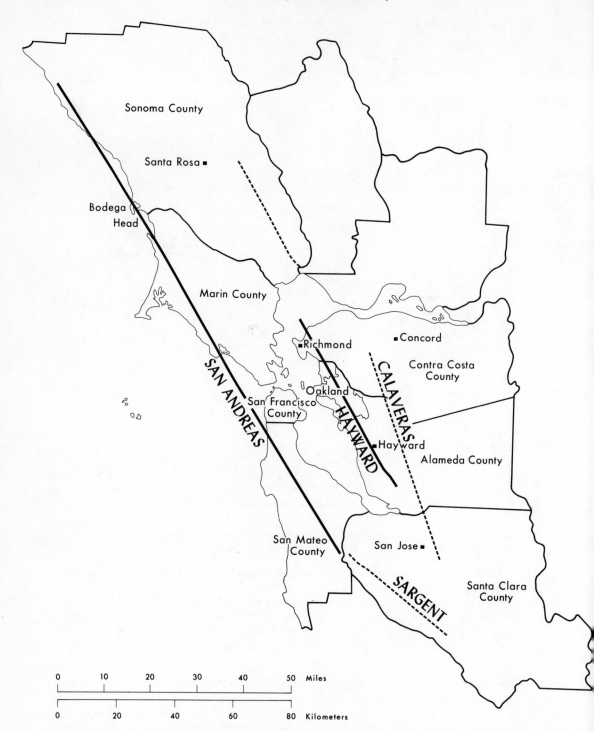

Figure 6. (a) Active faults in the San Francisco Bay region. Based on San Francisco Bay Region Environment and Resources Planning Study, U.S. Department of Interior and U.S. Department of Housing and Urban Development. Miscellaneous Field Studies Map MF-331.

the San Andreas; movement along this fault in 1906 caused horizontal displacement of up to twenty-one feet in Marin County. South of the junction with the Sargent fault in Western Santa Clara County, as much as half an inch per year of continuous creep is being recorded, as well as many small quakes. To the north of that junction, earthquake activity is intermittent, and it centers around four distinct foci; there is very little tectonic creep. A similar contrast between northern and southern segments is true for the Hayward and Calaveras faults.

The abundance of small earthquake activity and creep of the southern portions suggests that strain is being relieved along those active faults. It also appears that, along the San Andreas fault as a whole, portions that are seismically quiet are those that have been subject to abrupt faulting in the past, generating major earthquakes. Certainly, being on a quiet portion of the fault does not diminish risk, but may instead presage large earthquake hazard. On the more active portions of the faults, tectonic creep is a real problem; tunnels, dams, pipelines, and aqueducts must be monitored constantly. An example of this is the tunnel carrying the new rapid transit system from Oakland to Concord under the Berkeley hills.

The consequences of this physical instability are not limited to any single land formation. Certain potentially hazardous situations can be envisaged where public or private precaution would be appropriate. The area within a thousand foot trace of a fault is considered the most vulnerable territory, but there is little evidence of any differential development within these zones. Large public buildings, including schools, have been built on plotted fault traces. (Figure 6b). Multiple dwelling units have been permitted within fault zones, as well as the public parks and single family dwellings that might have seemed more appropriate uses. A noteworthy exception is the series of lakes and watershed land along the San Andreas Fault valley on the San Francisco peninsula. The concept of geologic hazard was invoked in a suit to prevent construction of a nuclear power plant on Bodega Head in Sonoma County, but it has seldom prevailed as a specific constraint on public or private development.

After the 1906 earthquake and fire very de-tailed recommendations were published by numerous authorities. For example Humphrey, in the U.S. Geological Survey Report of 1907, noted: "In earthquake countries, water-supply pipes, at least, should be laid so as to avoid the action of slips, settling, and ground movements of all kinds." Other parts of that publication deal with fire insurance practices as well as building structures. It was obvious in 1906 that physical damage occurred substantially on so-called poor ground—either on Bay fill or on alluvial soils. San Jose and Santa Rosa were cities critically affected by the 'quake, whereas Berkeley and Oakland were thought to have suffered far less since they were on solid ground. (Subsequent reports on Santa Rosa have confirmed a local island of poor ground that is subject to severe damage.) Within the city of San Francisco there was great variation in damage between districts built on solid rock and those on filled water courses or onetime mud flats (Figure 7). And it need not be the earthquake shock itself that causes damage. In a century, nineteen tsunamis have been measured at the Golden Gate with a recorded maximum reach of 7.4 feet. A marine wave following the Alaska earthquake in 1964 caused extensive damage in Crescent City, California; around the shores of the Bay even a modest tectonic shock wave could be hazardous now that building has encroached farther into the Bay. It is not physical conditions per se that merit consideration: rather it is combinations of conditions.

PEOPLE EVEN TALK ABOUT THE WEATHER HERE

The San Francisco Bay region offers an extraordinary range of climatic options, not just in the thirty miles from the coast to Walnut Creek or the one hundred mile north-south axis, but also from one district to another in a single city. The Sunset District on the ocean side of San Francisco is ironically named when stratus clouds the view so often, whereas the Mission District on the east side might have merited the sobriquet "Sunrise District." Felton remarks a 6 percent differential in hours of possible sunshine received from one part of the city to another, and residents are aware of far higher variations from one neighborhood to another. An intricate meshing of land and

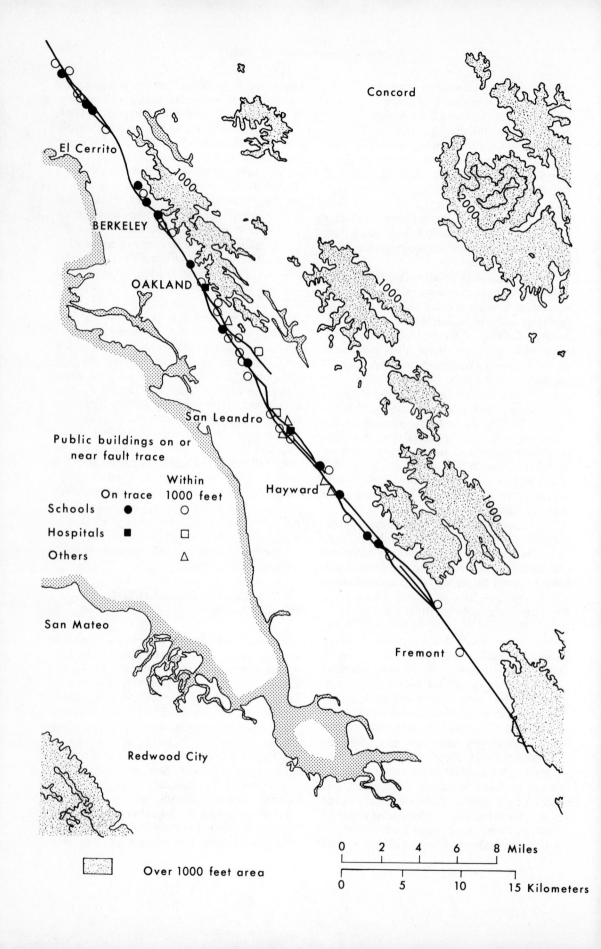

Concord

El Cerrito

BERKELEY

1000

OAKLAND

San Leandro

Public buildings on or near fault trace

	On trace	Within 1000 feet
Schools	●	○
Hospitals	■	□
Others		△

Hayward

1000

1000

2000

1000

San Mateo

Fremont

Redwood City

▨ Over 1000 feet area

| 0 | 2 | 4 | 6 | 8 Miles |

| 0 | 5 | 10 | 15 Kilometers |

water, varying exposure to breezes that have passed over the offshore cold upwelling, an extreme variety of relative relief—all these conditions exist and have been cited to explain the high degree of microclimatic variation. This variation can be seen most readily in temperature regimes, in the incidence of fog, and in amounts of precipitation.

These conditions have influenced the speed and location of suburban development. More significant than a determination of early or late residential accretion has been the perception of choice in climatic environment. Those who enjoy sun can have it, those who abhor rain can avoid it; an Orcadian would feel at home on Point Reyes, while a Sicilian might be reassured by the crackling sunshine of the Livermore valley. Lifestyle, housing design, residential layout—all reflect differing leisure options whose diversity is stimulated by the range of climatic options.

In 1853 the successful orchards of Alameda were evidence of its pleasant climate, and gift lots to those who would erect a $50 building attested the force of early residential promoters. In the 1890s the well-to-do San Franciscan could head to the Russian River resorts for a summer vacation. To the city resident there was no need to flee from oppressive heat but rather a desire to enjoy summer warmth as found there. Across the coastal ranges in the East Bay, the estate of Phoebe Apperson Hearst near Pleasanton was, in 1890, a forerunner of the "country club estates" of the 1970s, replete with poolside splendors. For over a hundred

Figure 6. (b) On the Hayward Fault. Schools, hospitals, and other public buildings on or close to the Hayward fault have been shown by A.E. Alquist. Legislation requiring superior construction for such buildings has caused the demolition and rebuilding or repair of schools in 1974. Declaration of proximity to fault traces in real estate transactions is seen as desirable by some. But the real issue still concerns the identification and plotting of active fault traces. Source: U.S. Geological Survey. *Seismic Hazards and Land Use Planning. Geological Survey Circular 690.*

years persons of upper income have selected a suburban environment attuned to their physical preference, and alternative choices were available even before the mobility granted by the automobile made this more commonly the case.

Temperature and Amenity

Around the Bay there are striking variations in temperature régimes according to location relative to the coast. There is a steady increase in average annual range of temperature from the coast to the interior, and even more pronounced is the variation in July daily mean maxima (Figure 8). An additional factor influencing diurnal temperature ranges is proximity to the only sea level exit to the Pacific Ocean. Newark, which sits twenty miles south of Oakland and far removed from the Golden Gate, has summer afternoon temperatures five degrees (F) higher and nights two degrees colder than Oakland, situated immediately south across from the Golden Gate. Today the importance of temperature conditions is still of significance in the context of housing. In the nine counties, reliance on air conditioning is not just a factor of income, it is a highly variable index modified by strikingly varied microclimates as well as by varied economic capacities.

Although it is possible in the Bay Area to choose a housing location attuned to personal climatic desiderata, this is seldom done today. In the past, the relative inability to control temperature conditions within the house meant that the physical design of the house in a sunny location ensured shade, just as the location of the house might well reflect the occupant's climatic preference. Today the house whose two story glass window wall faces the unrelenting western sun will have the view shrouded out by huge screens or permanently closed curtains. To cool the interior exposed to that exaggerated insolation, the switch is flipped to bring rescue via the air conditioner. The societal cost of our neglect of available climatic options and our insistence on aritificially modified conditions is now being recognized as a massive lien on diminishing energy reserves.

Fog and Pollution

Low stratus clouds create a strange July in San Francisco. Warm season air circulation in

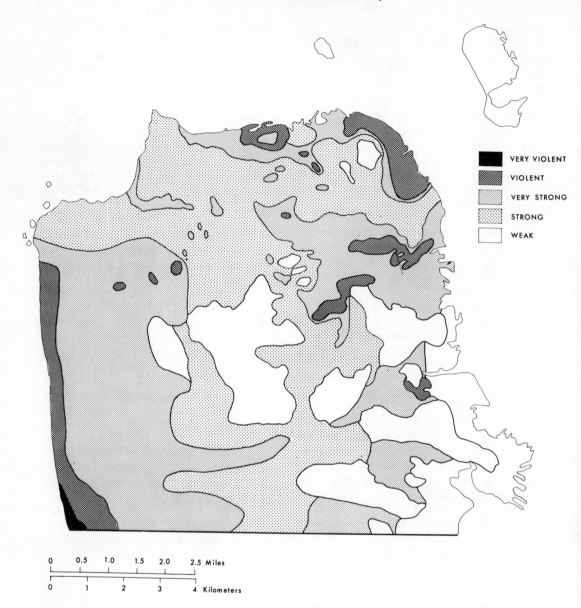

VERY VIOLENT

VIOLENT

VERY STRONG

STRONG

WEAK

0   0.5   1.0   1.5   2.0   2.5 Miles

0   1   2   3   4 Kilometers

Figure 7. Earthquake shock intensity, 1906. The then commonly used Rossi-Forel intensity scale did not distinguish between degrees of intensive damage in a modern city. The Omori scale which was highly regarded since it was an absolute scale and gave degrees of acceleration of shock had the disadvantage of citing evidence of damage to Japanese structures. Therefore a *"San Francisco Scale"* was devised. It was not an absolute scale but rather was a classification of observed phenomena. In the absence of recording devices such evidence is the best available approximation of the degree of shock. The San Francisco Scale (selected observational criteria): A—Very violent; some structures totally destroyed; consistent fissuring in natural earth. B—Violent; general collapse of brick and frame buildings where not unusually strong; breaking of sewers; compression or displacement of well-ballasted streetcar tracks. C—Very strong; brick and masonry badly cracked; frame buildings lurched, occasional falling. D—Strong; general but not universal fall of chimneys. E—Weak, occasional fall of chimneys and damage to plaster, partitions, and plumbing.

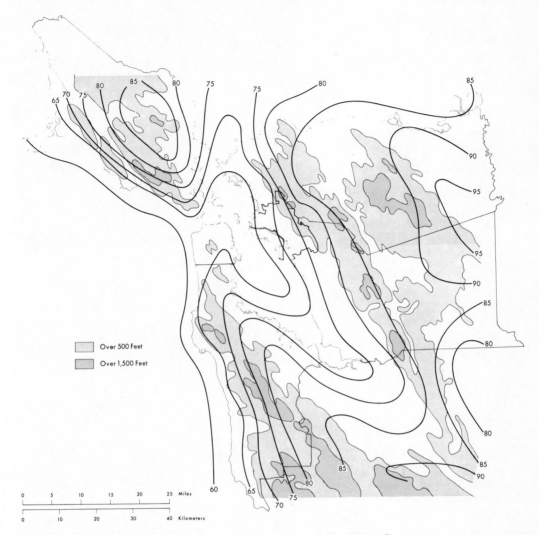

Figure 8. Daily mean maximum temperature for July, 1951–1960 (F°). Source: A. Miller. Land-Sea Boundary Effects on Small Scale Circulations, Progress Report no. 2., Meterology Department. San Jose State College. 1966.

the Bay Area is controlled by the persistence of relatively high pressure and low temperatures over the Pacific Ocean, and high temperatures and low pressures over the Central Valley. An intensified landward breeze is particularly marked from May to August. The incoming maritime air is restricted to a shallow layer, capped by a warm stable air mass; this phenomenon—the familiar summer inversion—is particularly pronounced in September, when a casual drive to the top of the Oakland hills will reveal significantly higher temperatures at a 1,000 feet elevation than farther down the

slope. The trapped cool air is modified in passage over the cold ocean upwelling off shore. If the resulting surface cooling is pronounced enough then surface condensation occurs, visible as great combers of fog rolling through the Golden Gate and around Mount Tamalpais —often held back by Twin Peaks and Mount Davidson in San Francisco, but otherwise cresting like a great surfing wave driven by differential pressure. The incidence and persistence of fog is a function of proximity to the ocean and relative relief. In July, San Francisco records 68 percent of possible sunshine hours as compared

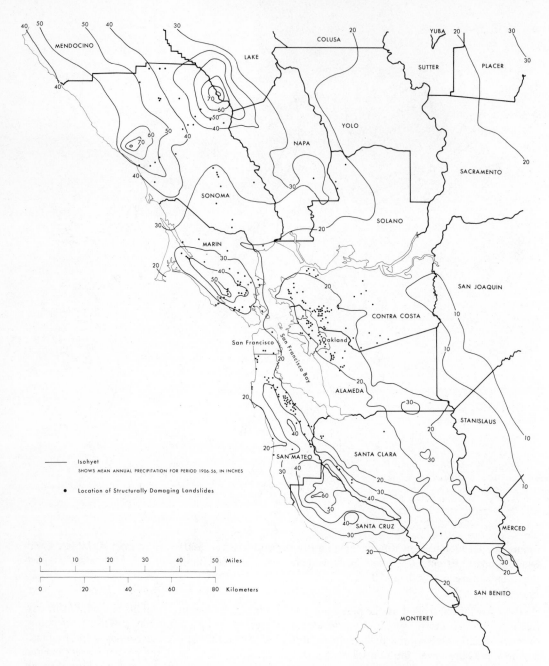

Figure 9. Average annual rainfall, San Francisco Bay region, 1906–1956, and landslide locations, Winter 1968–1969. Source: Department of Interior, U.S. Geological Survey.

with 87 percent at San Jose, or 95 percent 2,375 feet above sea level at Mount Tamalpais.

Because the fog is so limited in vertical extent it is channeled to an extraordinary degree by surface relief, and on a midsummer afternoon a literal river of fog may run swiftly through the Golden Gate and San Pablo Bay to Carquinez Strait. In late summer, when the pressure gradient inland declines, a very low inversion can develop over the Bay. Miller estimates that over Oakland the average height of trapped maritime air is 1,400 feet in summer and, when it exists, about 300 feet in winter. The height of the inversion is a critical meteorological determinant of the severity of air pollution conditions when pollutants are trapped near the ground in a persistent smog layer. Comparable conditions can develop with rapid cooling on clear nights. Smog in general and particulate matter *in sensu stricto* can be observed very easily around the Bay because of the many vantage points that normally offer an unimpeded view of fifty miles or more. Any reduction of visibility can easily be checked by reference to familiar landmarks, and a perception of air quality can be measured visually as well as by smell or by discomfort.

This awareness of a deterioration in air quality gave ready support to those who urged that a regional agency would be the only way to tackle the problem. In 1955 the state authorized nine Bay Area counties to form an air pollution control district; consequently six did so join together. Controls over domestic burning, industrial waste disposal, and automotive emissions have been observably effective in halting the deterioration of air quality. The recognition of the smog problem first created a willingness to support and finance a regional special district, and as such it fostered regional unity. But the perception of air quality has also created an awareness of regional differentiation. According to the Stanford workshop, in 1970 the per capita emissions for industrialized Contra Costa County were twice those for the Bay Area as a whole and four times those for Marin County. The rate of increase in smog in the newly urbanized Livermore valley is unusually high, for it is prone to develop a Los Angeles-like basin inversion. There is a growing recognition of local conditions of air quality that could be reflected in differences in the demand for housing.

Rainfall and Landslides

Amounts of rainfall received show as much variation from one place to another around the Bay as do other weather elements. A simple relationship between aspect and relief has traditionally been called on to explain the range of rainfall from twelve inches near Sunnyvale to the fifty-two inches on the northern flanks of Mount Tamalpais, though a closer study of rainfall records makes the story look more complex. Whatever the causes, there is a considerable variation in amounts of rainfall within short distances. Rantz has established a correlation between the total amounts of precipitation and depth-duration-frequency, suggesting that it is reasonable to look at average rainfall amounts in conjunction with geologic conditions to study land slippage potential (Figure 9).

In an area where state freeways cross abrupt ranges, and housing is creeping up formerly avoided slopes, the potential hazard from landslides is severe indeed. For the winter of 1968-1969 a conservative estimate of loss from slide damage in the nine counties was $35 million, according to Taylor and Brabb. In that winter fifty-eight slides were reported in Alameda County, one affecting twenty-six houses; and seventy were reported in Contra Costa, causing $3.6 million in road maintenance costs. In subsequent years Marin County has been prominent in local winter news broadcasts as houses start moving downslope. The isohyetal map suggests that this skew will continue. As a consequence of increasing slide problems, pressure is mounting in Marin to forbid any building on slopes of 30 percent or more to reduce private losses.

In summary, it is not just that people talk about the weather here. The complex relationships between temperature and energy demand, rainfall and slide potential, and inversions and air quality are all factors in a locally distinctive urban landscape. The kinds of questions that are now raised in environmental impact studies are issues that have been integral to differentiated development around the Bay. In the San Francisco Bay region, the singular diversity of climatic options points to the need for locally specific planning decisions attuned to particular conditions. And an appreciation of the variety of climatic conditions is a not inappropriate background to the study of how this urban landscape has evolved.

The Creation of a Social Fabric by Alternative Modes of Public Transportation

To understand the patterns of residential space that developed in the Bay Area's pre-1940 suburbia, it is useful to make a crude distinction between blue collar workers and white collar workers, between those whose place of factory employment was somewhere within the metropolis and those whose office or store employment was focused downtown. In other words, it is important to note the different destinations of journeys made by similar modes of transportation. Moreover, the public transportation systems that were a major formative constraint in patterning residential distribution in the Bay Area by no means were restricted to a simple radiating design. To bridge the Bay that formed the core of the region there were the ferries, from San Francisco to Alameda Island and Oakland, as well as to Marin County. The railroads served three different destinations in Richmond, Oakland, and San Francisco. And the rich mixture of street railroads and the cable cars supplemented the ubiquitous trolley cars.

Ferries, railroads, and trolley cars all gave distinctive service and charged very different prices for movement over similar distances. Some journeys to work could only appeal to higher income classes, whereas others were relatively cheap, though the trip might cover a greater physical distance. This system of independent pricing within different parts of the region resulted in spatial sorting by income class that distinguished Marin and San Mateo counties from Alameda County as potential residential locations for persons

working in San Francisco. On the two sides of the Bay two radically different daily mobility patterns emerged, as well as two different forms of suburbia. Parts of the Bay Area began to emerge as distinctive complementary segments of the whole.

Even considering only a single mode—the trolley car—alternative workplace-residence patterns can be seen. Some routes focused on a central business district, others on a ferry terminal; and there was also linear development serving both residence and workplace outside the core. The distances that separated the factory from the office were often greater than the distances that separated worker housing from middle class housing. This did not mean that different social classes were integrated within suburbia. The coexistence of housing for markedly differing income groups, all tied to a trolley wire, merely meant that workers might board cars going in opposing directions, or might transfer at different points. This produced a highly detailed residential fabric, particularly in the East Bay.

SAN FRANCISCAN SUBURBS IN THE NINETEENTH CENTURY

The notion of suburban living, the creation of a residential environment at the edge of the city, came early to San Francisco. In 1850, when blocks adjacent to Portsmouth Square were already characterized by ethnic association—Sydneytown, Germantown, or the Chinese quarter—blocks a little farther away were regarded as socially superior, and lots half a mile south of town, in Happy Valley, were selling for $3,500.

A formal suburban experiment was that of South Park. In 1852, George Gordon from Haworth, Yorkshire, who had married a barmaid and therefore had been obliged to emigrate beyond a social *cordon sanitaire,* laid out sixty-four lots around an oval square located between 2nd and 3rd streets and Brannan and Bryant. The oval had an ornamental iron fence and was furnished with English sparrows and roses, to be admired by the prominent citizens to whom lots were sold (Figure 10). For a time this was a good address, but locationally it was doomed. Gordon had chosen his site close to the only practicable area for waterfront extension, and soon South Park was neighbor to industry and bulk shipping. Railroad freight yards followed immediately to the south, on the filled Mission Bay, as well as, in 1889, the S.P. depot (Figures 2 and 3). Indeed, by 1870 South Park was declining rapidly as a neighborhood of social distinction.

In the 1860s a succession of good addresses was recognized in San Francisco, shaped primarily by accessibility. Besides such private toll roads as the Mission Plank Road, the Folsom Plank Road, and the San Bruno Turnpike large houses with pleasant gardens were built. Nordhoff in 1872, writing for the benefit of "Travellers and Settlers," remarked that most of San Francisco was "smoothly laid with wooden pavements. . . . Go where you will, within fifty miles of the city, and you will find smooth hard roads, broad avenues . . . roads which you may drive at the rate of ten or twelve miles per hour and do no harm to your horse nor tire yourself." But the area that could be effectively regarded as suburban could not rely on road access; it was too distant to reach each night by horse-drawn vehicles. Instead, that access had to come via the railroad. The wealthy San Franciscan who looked to suburbia turned south, because it was only from that direction that rails could reach to the city on the peninsula.

In 1863 the rail line to Redwood City was completed, and it reached San Jose the next year. The route from San Francisco southward was circuitous. The easiest course lay west of San Bruno Mountain to avoid the marsh, sand, and rough going on the Bay side of the mountain, and the length of this big loop did not encourage much nearby development. Then, too, the terminus in San Francisco at Eighteenth Street and Valencia was well away from Portsmouth Square, so that to reach it meant another fare for the commuter; it was too far away to encourage a walk from the business district. So in spite of frequent service and good traveling time, the railroad did not stimulate extensive suburban growth southward on the San Francisco Peninsula. In fact it promoted exclusive suburban development. Bion Arnold, discussing the impact of rail networks on residential patterns, stated that the fare structure was the critical element. It cost much more per mile to go by train than ferry. Moreover, fares were higher on the peninsula rail line than on the East Bay rail network. The peninsula was, however, favored by a landscape amenity furnished by huge trees and an intervening park landscape that encouraged the creation of estates and country clubs. Burlingame had fox hunting and polo, Hillsborough became the "city of millionaires" with no stores, and Atherton, as well as Belmont, followed the same kind of pattern. Today these towns maintain their social cachet, though the commuter rail line that fostered them guarantees no survival of train service in the future.

IN SAN FRANCISCO PROPER

Within the city of San Francisco, once the terrain barrier of Twin Peaks was breached in 1918, high density housing followed trolleycar lines west to the beach both north and south of Golden Gate Park. These were urban housing developments rather than suburban, even though they were constructed on sandy fog-shrouded wastes; they consisted either of stucco apartment buildings or that local phenomenon, the house built over a garage on a narrow lot, with the front door approached by stairs beside the garage. Variants on that form would range from single family houses joined in row style to duplex and fourplex buildings. The provision of the garage in no way reflected an inconvenient distance from the trolleycar line; instead it foretold the assumption that Californians, even within an urban environment, would be car owners.

In addition to these extensive tracts, there were what Gertrude Atherton dubbed "those restricted residential quarters called subdivisions . . . with pretty names, St. Francis Wood,

Figure 10. South Park, San Francisco, circa 1855. Daguerreotype, maker unknown, whole plate. Courtesy of the Oakland Museum. After the destruction of the 1906 fire, tenements and a hotel were built in spite of a location totally outmoded for any residential use. Today South Park sits as a tiny, predominantly black, ghetto surrounded by industry, on the same street oval that Gordon platted.

Ingleside Terrace, and Sea Cliff." They were islands of higher income housing, marked off by imposing gateway entrances to a subdivision that might or might not have lots commensurate in size with the pillars at their gates. These "suburbs" relied on the automobile as a supplement to the trollycar. Like others much farther out on the peninsula, their household breadwinners would work in downtown San Francisco.

TRAVELING TO WORK FROM THE EAST BAY

Regular ferry service between Broadway, in Oakland, and the San Francisco ferry slip had started in 1851, to be followed by an integrated ferry and rail connection from San Francisco to Seventh and Broadway in Oakland in 1863, and a ferry to Alameda in 1878. These ferries were cheap; the water crossing took twenty minutes, and weekend tripping was encouraged. Clerks earning a meager wage could emulate suburban living by crossing the Bay by ferry, and all the transbay residential districts could be reached within an hour. By the 1880s the original small holdings on Alameda Island had been covered by modest housing. The East Bay resident who worked in San Francisco would disembark at the wooden ferry terminal at the foot of Market Street, within easy walking distance of all parts of downtown. In 1873, 2.6 million passengers a year rode the ferries, and patronage doubled in the next four years. Largely because of the low ferry fares, the East Bay had become suburbia for the less affluent workers, the clerk as well as the factory worker. It had its own affluent citizens as well, mostly those who chose to live in the city in which they worked—Oakland.

By 1880 six suburban rail services focused on Oakland. The four Southern Pacific steam lines—some of which ran along streets—were electrified in 1911. Where these heavy lines could not be justified, an extensive trolley system was built. By 1910 the Key System and the Southern Pacific electric lines formed a close mesh of routes spread across the flat plain north and south of Oakland (Figure 11). Land speculation and suburban tract development went hand in hand with the building of new streetcar lines that would reach peak mileage in 1924. The increasing passenger travel in Oakland was made up in part by those refugees from the 1906 San Francisco fire who stayed to live in the East Bay, even though they returned to work in San Francisco. For the region as a whole this was a period of great immigration, but Oakland grew faster than San Francisco (Table 4). By 1912, forty million people a year were crossing the Bay by the ferries, and at the peak there were 400 ferry trips a day from Oakland. As many people moved from Oakland to San Francisco daily as from suburban Oakland to downtown. The peak of transbay water travel came in 1924; after then, numbers declined on the ferries until they were rendered obsolete by the completion of the San Francisco-Oakland Bay Bridge in 1936. The railroad continued ferry service for its passengers for whom Oakland was the rail terminus until 1958. Automobile ferries ceased in 1939, although in that year ferries carried a surprising 6,363 vehicles as compared with 22,904 on the bridge.

The reduction in transbay passenger traffic after 1924 suggests that new employment centers were increasing faster outside the city of San Francisco than within. A dispersion of industry and commerce was beginning to have an impact. This was encouraged by the superiority of inland transportation links from the East Bay. For some seventy years, while employment was largely in San Francisco, there had been a divide between workplace and residence; now that phase was ending for part of the employed population. They could rationalize their journey to work by both residing and working in the East Bay.

LIVING—AND WORKING—IN THE EAST BAY

Residential patterns in the East Bay were far from oblivious to terrain controls. Large scale housing speculation—associated with streetcar routes—generally utilized repetitive house design on small regular lots close to the Bay and very irregular lots on the hill slopes. From trolley stops, access upslope was often by paths and steps that would shortcut the circuitous loops needed for road access. The physical character of land went hand in hand with accessibility, to favor an intricate sorting of residential suburbs by income class. The "hills" were expensive, the "flats" were cheap; managers lived in one, clerks in the other.

In the hills a process of dispersed infilling of residential space occurred as automobile ownership became more nearly universal. The areas between the trolley wires were developed to housing that was free from the constraint imposed by a need for public transportation, though residents might later seek bus service. And this became very pleasant suburbia. In-

Table 4. Population in the Commuter District

	1860	1870	1880	1890	1900	1910	1920	1930
San Francisco	56,802	149,473	233,959	298,997	342,782	416,912	506,676	634,394
Oakland	1,543	10,500	34,555	48,682	66,960	150,174	216,261	284,063
Alameda	460	1,557	5,708	11,165	16,464	23,383	28,806	35,033
Berkeley				5,101	13,214	40,434	56,036	82,109

Source: Modified from Bion Arnold.

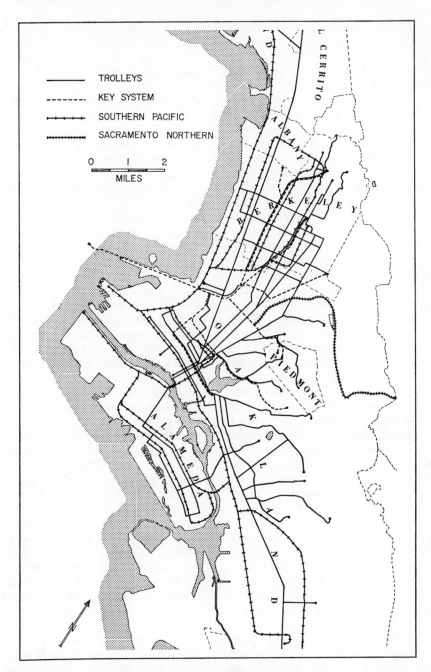

Figure 11. Steam railroad and electric interurban lines. Source: James E. Vance, Jr., *Geography and Urban Evolution in the San Francisco Bay Area,* (Berkeley: Institute of Governmental Studies, University of California, 1964), p. 49. This map does not show street railway and interurban lines at any one time; rather it shows each line at its greatest length. In addition to a number of streetcar lines there were two heavier traction systems, the Key System and the Southern Pacific Electric lines, that were built separately, often competitively, and survived to 1958 and 1940 respectively.

deed, this was a landscape improved by development rather than one despoiled. The first ridge of the East Bay hills is generally steep and grass-covered in its natural state, freshly green in the first winter rains but otherwise dun-colored. When explorers first saw the huge oaks of Atherton they had remarked on the wonderful vegetation of the San Francisco peninsula. No similar words were recorded to describe the glories of the East Bay. A comparison of views sketched prior to settlement with those made after houses and gardens had reached a twenty year maturity suggests forcibly that the wooded aspect of the hills we enjoy today is a pleasing manmade improvement of an originally spartan landscape. And avid gardeners continue to plant shrubs and trees as fast as they trim them.

Generally speaking, increasing elevation provided a better view of the Bay, and a few streets seem consciously designed to give visual access. Only the wealthy Claremont district in Berkeley ignored the amenity of the Bay; there, due to underground utilities, large lots, and big houses, with the whole development approached through a stone-pillared entry gate, residents found social security even though they didn't have a view. But this subdivision is well removed from the Bay. There is a consistent increase in house size from the shore of the Bay inland. This increase, which generally coincides with increasing elevation, is far more marked than any trend toward larger houses in a pattern from city core to periphery.

Relative to blue collar employment in the East Bay, the trolley lines created a new relationship between place of work and residence that is evidenced by the decline in transbay ferry traffic beginning in 1924. In Richmond, Emeryville, and as far south as San Leandro, there are industrial plants associated with trolleycar access for the workers. This pattern was a prototype for the suburbanization of industry that would become more prominent later with the arrival of mass automobile ownership. The dispersion of the 1920s relied on cheap mass travel to plants too large—and too new—to fit close to the city center, though they still needed an ample labor supply. Worker housing was not tied to a particular plant, but had access to a generalized industrial development allied to public transportation. This

was in part because some of these industries used seasonal labor—canning companies, for example—so that there would be a constant shifting about of the labor force. In the East Bay there is a band of industrial plants of the 1920-1930 era located well back from the shore, on what had once been generally dreary mudflats. These plants had no physical tie to the Bay, except perhaps for waste discharge. On the landward side of this band is the worker housing, and the transportation arteries.

Strip and cluster commerce threaded along the streetcar lines; behind them grew the speculators' subdivisions. Vance has termed the resultant metropolis "prairie-form." He notes the pattern of narrow lots and a street frontage module for division, as well as the repetition of the bungalow, which seems to have anticipated the California "ranch house" by two full generations. Some of the most modest of these subdivisions combined exotic gingerbread decorations with very small houses, and these today have a Disneyland charm, as if built to five-eighths scale. The pattern of this early single family house suburbia tied to public transportation still survives, even though that phase of development came to a sad end. A decline in trolleycar patronage was compounded by the necessity to raise fares on rail lines, and this combination accelerated the shift to the automobile for getting to work as well as for leisure. The demise of this era was fundamentally tied to the financial collapse of the overextended trolley line and associated real estate speculations. The rapid growth of Oakland after 1900 had been fostered by the Realty Syndicate, a complex holding company that united street railway systems and land development. Although the company—whose organizer was said at one time to have owned one-sixth of Alameda County—collapsed in 1913, the pattern of housing accretion tied to arterial streets and industrial plants has persisted. Worker housing in the East Bay has continued to be associated with flatlands, and that is where the new plants have been built, now much farther south toward the closed curve at the end of the Bay. Even though industrial workers now commute to work by automobile, the north-south rapid transit line follows the same axis that the trolleycars followed, close to the Bay, and the design of that route was presumably to resurrect an old travel mode.

A LOCALLY DISTINCTIVE SUBURBIA

By the close of the 1930s it was clear that the regional variation in residential landscape around the Bay that had characterized early settlement was not disappearing; indeed it was enjoyed and further refined. Two fundamentally distinct spatial relationships could be discerned; one relied on differentiation in journey to work and type of employment; the other related to housing style and elevation. The latter progressed to the cultivation of peculiar architectural devices. The difference between the blue collar suburb and the white collar suburb was registered more clearly by size of house than by generosity of lot or any locational specificity. The housing of the middle class was not any more dispersed than that of the industrial worker, and they shared the urban frontier. There was physical distinction, however, in style—and in the amenity of immediate surroundings. The most obvious difference would be in the amount of internal space. As to external space, all too frequently a rather large house would be placed on a too small lot so that it would seem to have outgrown itself. Even within exclusive residential enclaves there is a physical massing of houses that fits ill with proclaimed affluence. To the eye of the New Englander, the comfortable suburbs seem crowded and congested.

To further compound the unusual qualities of this suburbia, in the East Bay a strange inversion of amenity can be noted. Although worker housing has meaner streets and narrower lots—as well as a view of sky rather than water—this housing has distinct advantages for some age groups because it sits on a flat lot. That condition gives pleasure to the very young and the very old. It is the children of the well-to-do who have trouble finding a place to ride a tricycle, and it is the well-to-do elderly who have to move out of their old homes to seek a house on one floor that has no cumbersome front entry steps to be negotiated. It is important to note these inherited characteristics from the older suburbs because they play a big part in explaining the small scale diversity that marks the contemporary occupance of this housing. This diversity is in contrast to the more uniform patterns of the suburbia that was created by reliance on the automobile alone. These developments took form east of the Berkeley hills.

EXTENSIVE SUBURBIA IN THE EAST BAY

Behind Oakland, Berkeley, and Richmond a parallelism of ridges and structural valleys hindered housing expansion; only to the south did the shoreland plain broaden. The Berkeley hills, really a series of ridges, trend northwest-southeast for about fifteen miles, reaching 1,000 feet on the average and nearly twice as high in the area behind the university campus; much of the westernmost ridge is in park and watershed land that provides an enormous recreational asset. This barrier was first breached in 1913 by a 3,000 foot tunnel on the interurban line that joined Oakland to Antioch (Oakland, Antioch and Eastern Railway). Despite the improved access, not much suburban growth was triggered by that connection. It was the opening of the twin bore Broadway Low Level (Road) Tunnel in 1937 that effectively brought Walnut Creek into the Oakland orbit. At that time, movement east of the range, which previously had been predominantly north-south along a series of parallel valleys, was supplemented by a direct east-west flow through the range, so that by 1967 almost 30,000 cars traveled westbound in a twenty-four hour period. A third bore that carries a reversing traffic flow, depending upon the heavier direction of movement, now supplements the earlier construction, and the whole is known as the Caldecott Tunnel. In the spring of 1973, 53,000 vehicles traveled westbound; the morning load peaked at 8,000 vehicles per hour, when only 550 were traveling eastbound. The afternoon peak is less directionally biased.

In valleys previously isolated one from another, streams of suburban traffic have accumulated. Walnut groves and small holdings have given way to executive housing (originally the term implied seniority), and the pecking order gives Orinda pride of place. More recently, the term "junior executive" has been utilized to flatter more modest houses. The limitation of space in these valleys has favored a kind of spur track street network and small scale developments. Only much farther out on the Concord plains could the "prairies" of massive housing tracts flourish.

In the valleys and on lower hill slopes the initial development was of relatively large lots—two acres or more—relying on well water and septic tanks or serviced by very small utility districts. The horse, a small paddock, and a sweeping driveway set the image of affluent suburbia. But once a reliable water supply is available through a larger municipal utility district, then small lots become the rule farther out long the same highway. The importance of piped water in initiating suburban development in a seasonally arid area can hardly be exaggerated.

Although the suburban growth of southern Contra Costa County was stimulated by construction of the tunnel through the hills, the development there has been relatively slow as compared with that of Santa Clara County. Moreover, Contra Costa County still does not have as great a suburbanized employment base as do San Jose, Sunnyvale, and Mountain View. For every three who work in Contra Costa County, one works in Oakland; and for every six, one works in San Francisco. The freeway connections through Oakland linking Walnut Creek to the San Francisco-Oakland Bay Bridge were completed in 1973. They essentially parallel the most heavily traveled Bay Area Rapid Transit (BART) line, which opened to San Francisco in 1974. Not just Walnut Creek, but Pleasant Hill and Concord, too, are in the San Francisco orbit, though this applies only to a narrow employment sector of the local population. Presently under study are extensions of BART service to Antioch, or, alternatively, to Livermore and Pleasanton (Figure 21).

It appears that around transit stations, on previously undeveloped land, multiple unit dwellings will take precedence over single family houses. And if linear extension of service continues, then the conversion of agricultural land will be inevitable as soon as utility districts are organized. Many persons touted public transit as a way to concentrate suburban growth into clusters. Though such concentrations do develop around stations, it appears that the ambitious design for expansion will encourage, instead, urban growth at ever more distant points. It seems unlikely that more intensive housing will as yet replace existing housing stock close to stations as most of this housing is less than twenty years old. The pattern of replacement and intensification of housing characteristics around BART stations west of the hills is not likely to appear in Contra Costa County for some time.

INCORPORATION OF AGRICULTURAL LAND INTO SUBURBIA

Although variations in the quality of the physical environment such as degree of slope or elevation or desirable view have played a primary role in shaping Bay Area suburbia, there have been some variations in the pattern of urban growth that need to be related to the prior agricultural use of that land. Most of the early suburbs that spread over cultivated acreage were taking the place of small holdings. These had relied on easy access to market to sell their seasonal produce, but they found in turn that this accessibility became the cause of their own demise as they fell to the developer. With the rapid increase in scale and speed of suburbanization in the 1950s the land that was taken into the urban system was land that had been far removed from the urban frontier and had been in prime agricultural use. In the Bay Area two valleys demonstrate contrast in the rate and inevitability of this kind of conversion process—the Santa Clara valley and the Napa valley.

Post-1946 Development in Santa Clara County

The San Jose SMSA has supported continuous single family house construction for thirty years. It is the epitome of the suburbia that was created by universal car ownership, FHA mortgages, and the GI housing programs. Low density housing tracts replaced the prune orchards, and the valley spawned shopping centers as well as dispersed industrial employment. In 1955 the Ford Motor Company moved from Richmond to a new assembly plant at Milpitas, just outside San Jose, and their white workers moved too. Berger has convincingly demonstrated in a study of those workers who made the move that they were creating a working class suburbia; these were blue collar families who were emulating the middle class move out of the city and Berger suggests that they were specifically different from earlier suburbanites. The mixture of social classes and the existence of large scale dispersed employment, reinforced by the speed of landscape transformation, all combined to create a special image of suburbia here. Indeed, political science texts use successive maps of the built-up area of San Jose as their type examples of postwar growth with its attendant political restructuring. It is not likely that the change processes of the last thirty years will be halted.

Today the Santa Clara valley is the California of the averages; aerospace dominated, it is an extensive suburbia of reasonably priced, single family housing built well apart and only recently becoming more concentrated through an admixture of low rise apartments. Today it is the boom economy where the bust could be catastrophic as seemingly everything depends on industrial growth which offers the quick route to affluence for the one time blue collar worker. The aspiring young population of the new housing areas and shopping centers has, in this social environment, left the old center of San Jose to the Spanish-speakers. The economics of suburban house purchase today makes this new suburbia middle income. These are two car families with domestic mobility for the wife as well as for a journey to work.

Orchards and walnut groves are still giving way to tract housing, and the highways are lined with billboards describing new tracts and citing specific house prices. Because of concern at the loss of prime agricultural land there have been attempts to soften the blow of increasing land assessment and the resultant higher taxes that are most frequently cited as the catalyst forcing landholders to sell their orchards. It is now possible to place land in an "agricultural preserve" status that keeps taxes down so long as the land is kept in agricultural use. But even such favorable tax shelters are not likely to preserve the rural landscape, for suburbia and orchards do not easily coexist. Laden fruit tress are a target for an overnight haul, and a whole years' crop can be lost in the dark of a single night, not to mention the physical damage to trees. Field crops might be profitable under an "agricultural preserve" system, but they would not provide the same kind of landscape amenity that nostalgia demands—one that comes from acres of trees in full blossom.

The Contrasting Case of the Vineyard Lands

That orchards still give way to housing tracts is demonstrated in building permit data for the nine county region. The San Jose SMSA still shows a commanding lead in residential construction, and single family units predominate. To the north of the Bay in Solano and Sonoma counties single family housing also dominates construction (Table 5). It is possible to see in these two new SMSA's at first glance a potential frontier for suburban growth that would mimic the earlier conversion of the San Jose region. Although the flat land

Table 5. First Quarter Building Permits for Housing Units by County, 1972–1973

	Single Family		Multifamily	
	1972	*1973*	*1972*	*1973*
San Francisco-Oakland SMSA				
San Francisco	48	27	1,326	1,952
Alameda	1,613	438	1,606	1,380
Contra Costa	1,191	728	1,084	507
San Mateo	651	511	1,370	1,552
Marin	332	258	310	525
San Jose SMSA				
Santa Clara	2,159	1,441	1,595	1,380
Santa Rosa SMSA				
Sonoma	541	467	298	293
Vallejo-Napa SMSA				
Napa	157	93	43	104
Solano	395	356	337	121

Source: U.S. Department of Commerce, San Francisco Regional Office of Field Operations, "Authorized Construction—San Francisco Bay Area," *Construction Report,* May 1973.

of the Santa Clara valley is much more extensive in terms of acreage still available for development, the orchards and vineyards of the NAPA and Sonoma valleys have potentially the same appeal of water supply, flat land, and accessibility.

But here vineyards have dramatically changed the seemingly inevitable transition from agriculture to suburban housing. Since the mid-1960s major distilleries have entered the winemaking industry of these valleys, taking over small family operations and introducing large amounts of capital. The acreage of wine grapes has increased (Table 6) as the price received for grapes has soared. Since there is a limited amount of land that is suitable for grape growing, the cost of land that can be planted to vines has gone up sharply. Indeed, prices demanded for this kind of land are higher than those paid for land that can be converted to housing. So grapes effectively compete with houses. All through the Napa and Sonoma valleys the construction of recreational suburbs with golf courses and pools is being outpaced by that of overhead sprinkling systems and redwood stakes holding up young vines. Frost used to be thought the major limiting factor, but now the new vineyards run across the hollows and have even caused a Christmas tree farm to sell its stock for household plantings and switch to vines. It seems as if the potential profits in grape pro-duction must seem sufficiently high to make such gambling with nature worthwhile, for there is no great evidence of any introduction of the natural gas heating systems that are advertised in the trade journals. Growers seem to be relying on the spray sprinklers and a few of the large old fans to circulate air out of deeper hollows. Whether increases in wine consumption will keep pace with the increased acreage and the soaring prices of wine is a matter of local concern. In 1974, resistance to high wine prices began to show up for a complexity of reasons—general economic conditions, the impact of the French wine scandals, the high volume of wine stocks following two good production years, and the introduction of some highly advertised medium price varietal wines from former bulk wine producers. Some observers believe that the Napa and Sonoma valley wines will always be in demand so long as they are priced with regard to a reasonable profit, but increasing production costs are compounding the cost increases incurred under the land speculation conditions of the past five years, and the definition of "reasonable profit" is elusive. It does seem inevitable, whether land stays in vines or is sold for development, that the prevailing high land costs will produce a relatively high density residential use. And it is this increase in density that marks a most significant change in suburbia.

Table 6A. Wine Grapes in Napa and Sonoma Counties (Acreage in Wine Grapes)

County	July 1971			July 1975			1975[a]
	Bearing	Nonbearing	Total	Bearing	Nonbearing	Total	Bearing
Napa	12,548	3,000	15,548	13,035	3,244	16,279	16,116
Sonoma	12,424	3,064	15,488	12,682	4,286	16,968	16,724

[a]Bank of America estimate

Table 6B. Wine Grapes in Napa and Sonoma Counties (Annual Planting of Wine Grapes (Acres))

County	1959 and earlier	1960-1964	1965	1966	1967	1968	1969	1970	1971	1972
Napa	6,917	2,602	588	726	651	814	737	935	1,317	992
Sonoma	8,332	1,615	624	355	505	584	667	1,229	1,133	1,924

Source: California Crop and Livestock Reporting Service, California Grape Acreage, 1972.

Table 7. Mobile Homes and Trailers, 1970

County	All Housing Units (1,000)	Percentage Single Family	Mobile Homes and Trailers	Percentage of All Units
Napa	27	78	1,618	6.0
Sonoma	78	80	4,270	5.5
Solano	54	70	2,057	3.8
Santa Clara	336	68	9,833	2.9
Contra Costa	178	76	3,694	2.1
San Mateo	190	68	1,924	1.0
Alameda	380	59	2,918	.8
Marin	71	71	531	.7
San Francisco	310	17	85	.02

Source: U.S. Bureau of the Census, Census of Housing: 1970. Washington, D.C.: U.S. Government Printing Office, 1972.

RECENT TRENDS IN BAY AREA SUBURBIA

If an increase in residential density is to be anticipated, then it is inevitable that mobile home parks and multiple housing will flourish. Where once the single family house tract was a mass housing market now—even though it may be mass appeal—fewer and fewer are able to afford its costs. As a substitute, the mobile home park comes walled with cement block and heavily landscaped; the immovable trailer is really a prefabricated or modular house (Table 7). This is one way of keeping costs down. The other is planned unit development. These units are as often purchased as rented, and offer more profit to the developers and a more intensive use of land. Such a low rise apartment boom is affecting Alameda county now, reproducing a comparable housing that existed long ago in San Mateo County. There it gained a reputation as appropriate for "swinging singles" style; now many such developments in the East Bay and in Marin County are catering instead to families with children.

Just as housing style and economic class categorize some parts of suburbia, so does specific age and income class. As San Jose became the regional model for one form of suburbia, in the valley of Tice Creek just south of Walnut Creek there is another archetype. The warmth and landscape beauty of this ranching valley forms a setting for housing for "mature" citizens where retirement is pictured as a busy round of golf and swimming, sunning and puttering. Had retirement not come earlier and earlier to the affluent, these developments might have become geriatric ghettos. Instead, Rossmoor has become the model for numerous small leisure communities restricted to adult citizens now to be found in the Napa and Sonoma valleys, as well as in the outer reaches of the East Bay. Such tracts provide congenial surroundings, protection, and some assurance that housing outlays will be directed to their owners' particular needs. Medical plans, exterior landscaping shared by all, security guards, and a restricted gate entrance are all features that come with house purchase and maintenance. Neither Oakland nor Berkeley, Richmond nor San Francisco can offer what these residents want, either in physical or social climate.

Ethnicity and Space: Another Patchwork Design

In 1970 in the San Francisco-Oakland SMSA there were six places over 2,500 population whose percentage of black population exceeded twenty-two (Table 8). In sharp contrast, in 1940 blacks made up only 2 percent of the total Bay Area count. The black population of Oakland then numbered 8,462 and that of San Francisco 4,846. In thirty years a new component has been added to the Bay Area—one that is new in proportion and magnitude —and one that is also new in social structure and in distribution.

SOME ASPECTS OF SOCIAL CHANGE

Before World War II, clusters of black population were associated with employment on the railroads—the sleeping car porters and dining car crews who lived not far from the railroad terminals—or with the more dispersed service trade employment that was found in San Francisco. These people were a stable long term group and they were a force in national affairs as well as in the local community. Oakland as a railroad terminus was a center of early labor organization. Although the Oakland membership of the Brotherhood of Sleeping Car Porters was never numerically outstanding on the national scale, nevertheless, this local was strong and active in the struggle to establish the union. C.L. Dellums of Oakland was for most of the union's life fourth vice-president of the brotherhood. In 1968, when A. Phillip Randolph III stepped down, Dellums became president, though by that time the membership

Table 8. Population of Selected Places of 2,500 or More, 1970

Place	Total Population (1,000)	Percentage Negro
East Palo Alto	18	61
Emeryville	3	37
Richmond	79	36
Oakland	362	35
Berkeley	117	24
Pittsburg	21	22

Source: U.S. Bureau of the Census, Census of Housing: 1970, *Block Statistics,* San Francisco-Oakland, California Urbanized Area, Table 1, Final Report HC(3) - 24 (Washington, D.C.: U.S. Government Printing Office, December 1971).

was down to some 2,000 or so. Members of the Oakland black community have been influential in traditional leadership roles and now in new guise others have become conspicuous.

In 1967, when Eldridge Cleaver first met Huey P. Newton at a meeting in San Francisco, Newton countered, "You're wrong, we're not the Oakland Panthers. We happen to live in Oakland. Our name is the Black Panther Party." Since then ideas first expressed in Oakland have had an enduring impact on the national black community.

At the local level black activists have explored alternative means to bring about change. A shift away from overt violence to social

programs has brought some new alliances—
for example, the efforts to work through
black church organizations. And the traditional political structure has been challenged.
On May 3, 1973, Bobby Seale, one time chairman of the Panthers—in a runoff election for
mayor of Oakland—garnered 36 percent of the
vote in a city where the black population comprises 35 percent of the total—but where two
in every five blacks is under eighteen as compared with one in five of whites. And following the election there was a public statement of
intent to take greater cognizance of the needs
of that one-third of the population. The catalytic
qualities of black leadership in Oakland are
evidenced in many realms, and though the sorts
of changes that have taken place in Oakland
are not representative of the degree of transformation occurring in the Bay Area as a whole,
things have changed elsewhere, too. There are
more blacks in leadership positions, particularly in the school districts—which is not illogical,
for it is in the schools that the increasing proportion of black population is most strikingly
evidenced.

A Newly Visible Condition

Prior to 1940, though there was little social
integration between black and white, visitors
to the Bay Area commented on the comparatively easy relationship between members
of the two groups. In former days there were
other minorities who received more attention,
probably because they were more numerous
and because they lived in visible isolation—
for instance, the Chinese. It is debatable whether
the present raised awareness of black-white
differences came because of imported attitudes,
or whether there was a transfer of hostility to
the black from groups previously perceived
as inimical, such as the Japanese. But—by
whatever mechanism—for the black in 1960
"characteristic patterns of racial discrimination and segregation had arrived," according
to Wilson Record.

Two conditions need to be emphasized as
being distinctly different from the national
experience of urban minority populations:
this large black population has arrived over a
very recent time span; and clusters of black
population occur in a widely distributed pattern. These two conditions are integral to
present relationships: first, because neither
blacks nor whites are bound into long established postures, and, second, because there

is no single central city black concentration.
Indeed, there are several distinctive patterns
of black residential space. There is the familiar pattern of a predominantly black central
city that is slowly expanding, as in Richmond;
there is the pattern of several nuclei, as in San
Francisco; there is the scattered diffusion
through middle class suburbia as in parts of the
East Bay; and there is the emergence of new
black suburbs. Just as the changes that have
taken place in social relationships are diverse
and complex, so are the changes that have
taken place in the spatial dimension. It is
especially important to look at some of the
examples of spatial evolution, since there have
been several processes at work simultaneously
within the region. Different things have been
happening in different places and no single
model can synthesize the changes that have
taken place. First, it is useful to examine some
localized conditions that explain the emergence
of spatially distinct black population clusters,
several of which date to the period of most
significant black immigration—the 1940s.

THE NEWCOMERS

From 1942 to 1945 the shipyards at Richmond,
Alameda, Marin County, and San Francisco
needed a large new labor force; one was re-
cruited primarily from the south and south
central states, first white and later black.
Men came and brought their families to Oakland and to San Francisco. There was some
underutilized housing in East and West Oakland, as well as in the Fillmore district of
San Francisco, but the supply was inadequate so the government proceeded to build
new towns of barracklike housing. Temporary suburbs were constructed that were in
part racially integrated at the end of the war,
but most were predominantly black. All of
it tended to become more so, as white workers
moved on to new industrial areas in San Jose
and the outer suburbs, especially to the aircraft industry plants around Sunnyvale.

The second part of the immigration of
the 1940s was made up of returning GIs
who came home from the Pacific through
the ports of Oakland and San Francisco and
found the Bay Area to their liking. They
decided to stay and to bring their families
to the growing region. Black as well as
white servicemen so opted, but the black
housing choice was significantly more limited

in location. For them, moves to suburbs and the new $99 down housing tracts were not possible. Instead, the newcomers settled close to the existing clusters of population that had grown up wherever blacks had been housed during the war. These focal sites persisted even when the employment that had caused them to arise came to an end. In some cases the actual housing units survived, as in Hunter's Point; in other cases the housing was bulldozed away, as in Richmond; but in both cases a black population stayed.

RESIDENTIAL ISLANDS AROUND THE BAY

Since 1950 some new concentrations of black residential space have emerged, and at the same time separate foci have become more clearly differentiated by social class. As employment opportunities have become available to some blacks, an economically stratified black society has developed. To be sure, this society is bottom-heavy; but, as well as the large numbers of poor, there are also the survivors of the railroad employment group and, in addition, there is a significant and growing component of highly educated professionals. The pattern of housing availability that led initially to the growth of several separate black population nuclei has been reinforced by the emergence of a class-stratified population. These young professionals can afford to go into housing areas formerly denied to them by income, and a new dispersion of blacks has begun, this time into suburbia. In a few areas this population is integrated, at least by housing location, but in other cases new clusterings of blacks have appeared (Figure 12). This population is spatially distributed in such a way that the term ghetto must either be redefined from the usage in the Middle West and East or abandoned in favor of another label. No single word can encompass the welfare enclave of South Park in San Francisco and middle class Trestle Glen in Oakland; no one word can characterize the urban isolation of Hunter's Point and the semirural isolation of Marin City. The black population of the Bay Area inhabits many "islands," separated by rough terrain, by nonresidential land use, by income class, and by lifestyle. Much of this isolation derives from nonacceptance by the majority population, but emerging as well are patterns of residential separation through

choice that are a response to black aspiration rather than to white discriminatory practices.

The Case of Richmond

To understand present-day black population patterns in the Bay Area it is well to start with the spatial legacy of war time shipbuilding. In Richmond, for example, Henry Kaiser started building ships in 1941 for the British government at a new shipyard in the Inner Harbor. The initial yard was followed by three others, only one of which (Point Potrero) was intended to be permanent. At the height of activity the yards employed 90,000 people, and it was for this population influx that temporary housing was built on flatland to the south and west of the old city center. Most of that housing was removed after 1946, leaving behind streets complete with utility poles and fire hydrants but otherwise starkly bare. That part of Richmond finally became the site of a major rebuilding program only in the 1960s. Now it is one of the largest areas of moderate income black housing in the East Bay. The shipyard workers divided into the blacks, many of whom stayed in Richmond, and the whites, most of whom moved either toward new housing in the hills to the east of Richmond or on to San Pablo.

Now Richmond is 36 percent black and the major portion of the city west of Interstate Highway 80 is their territory. Richmond is a working class city, with $12,000 the average family income and only 53 percent of the eighteen to twenty-one age group going to college. It is a very American place with hardly any recent immigrants; indeed the largest foreign stock population, which is Mexican, comprises only 1.8 percent of the population. Half the work force of Richmond stays within the county and 20 percent of the labor force is employed in secondary industry. Richmond is still a factory port, one whose trade is overwhelmingly dominated by petroleum products, with scrap metal, sugar, and chemicals trailing behind. Petroleum refining and chemical processing are the main industries, and an entry into the city across the Richmond-San Rafael Bridge brings the smells you might expect. Richmond is a blue collar city where black workers meet white, and this is sometimes a tense frontier. The issue of school integration has caused fiery meetings here. To gauge the separation of population that can develop it is salutary to look at San Pablo, a separate incorporation

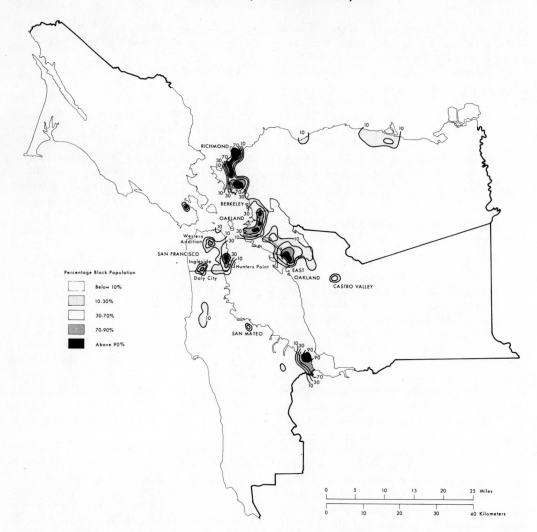

Figure 12. Black population, 1970.

that lies immediately adjacent to the solidly black population tracts of central Richmond. San Pablo is 97 percent white and with an average family income of $10,000 it is less prosperous on the average than Richmond.

The Island that is Marin City

In Marin County the legacy of a war time shipyard has resulted in a very different black population pattern because of a radically different settlement pattern. The Marin Ship Corporation started in 1942 at the northern end of the Sausalito waterfront. Because there was no housing available locally it was necessary to build temporary quarters for shipyard workers. On an open site west of Highway 101 the Marin County Housing Authority erected

housing on behalf of the Federal Housing Administration. This tract, Marin City, was meant to be self-sufficient because of the war time shortage of transportation, though there was some bus service provided. The project itself attracted national notice for its well-designed redwood structures. They stood as an integrated housing development in an otherwise predominantly white county. In 1954 the project was turned over to the Marin County Housing Authority and controversy developed as to its future. Some wished it to remain integrated and suggested the best way to accomplish that end would be to make available a high proportion of owner-occupied rather than rental property, so as to encourage a stable middle class component, both black and white. The proposals for private housing were rejected and, as had been predicted, by 1960 the census tract containing Marin City was over 80 percent black. By 1962, when 300 low rent units had been completed (to replace war time buildings) in the project, it contained 530 families of whom 95 percent were black.

Thus, a once integrated project had become an island of black population, physically separated from Sausalito by a six lane freeway, hemmed in by open space, but sending children to integrated schools in Sausalito. Within Marin City there is provision for only minimum shopping needs as well as taxi service and a feeder bus system. Because the housing project is on unincorporated land, social services are provided by the county government, which is based in the Marin Civic Center located miles away on the other side of San Rafael. Census tract 1290, which includes Marin City, is 90 percent black. There are more women than men living there and two persons in five are under eighteen. Only 13 percent of the eighteen to twenty-one age group are in college and of the sixteen to twenty-one group 28 percent are neither in school nor employed at a job. Finally, 28 percent of all males over sixteen are unemployed.

These figures stand in stark contrast to the rest of the county which is one of the most affluent in the United States. There are small numbers of black families dispersed in many census tracts. In 15 percent of the Marin tracts black family income exceeds white and averages $20,000. Some of these residential areas are close to Hamilton Air Force Base, but others appear to be in areas where predominantly upper income professionals reside. It is ironic that Marin City, which started as an integrated residential project, should now stand out in the way it does as an island of black isolation, in contrast to conditions elsewhere in the county.

And East Palo Alto

The third place where black housing sits across a freeway from a predominantly white area is found in San Mateo County. East Palo Alto—or Nairobi as it would have been called had a referendum promoted by youthful activists not gone down to a three to one defeat in 1968—has been described by Barusch and Nathan as "a blighted suburban community that is a significant step up the economic ladder and out of the ghetto for central city

minorities." Prior to 1946 East Palo Alto was broken into predominantly agricultural small holdings, with a few housing tracts, where the small holdings were mostly owned by Asians. Rapid housing construction raised the population to 8,000, and in the 1950s "blockbusting" techniques caused some white owners to panic. In 1970 the population of 17,837 was 61 percent black with some tracts showing a black proportion of as high as 88 percent.

East Palo Alto has many small lots, but it also has long-established greenery and pleasant surroundings. This is an unincorporated area, but the county supervisors are advised by a municipal council whose members are elected at large from five defined districts. There is a great deal of community influence over police, youth programs, physical planning, and school administration, even though the community is not incorporated. The per capita assessed valuation in 1969-1970 was $1,219—not unique in the county, for white Pacifica has a per capita average assessment of only $1,626. When these figures are compared to the $3,000 to $4,000 levels for other cities in this county —which also includes very wealthy places such as Atherton—the base is demonstrably weak. East Palo Alto is hemmed in by incorporations and cannot hope to gain any more desirable land assets. Given its population structure and physical isolation, a reasonable compromise toward self-determination seems to have been accomplished. The furor over the proposed name change thus did result in some progress; but the underlying problems of inadequate financing remain, and the clearer identification as a black community is only a first step to a more viable suburban status.

The foregoing examples illustrate how three black communities developed outside core cities. The fact that you must look at essentially localized conditions to explain the emergence of such concentrations in the Bay Area generally is not a prerequisite to understanding the distribution of black population in the suburbs alone. What has happened outside San Francisco or Oakland is not so very different from what has happened inside, although the numbers of persons involved are very different, as Table 8 shows. In those cities where the actual number of black residents is high there is a comparable diversity in the distribution and location of predominantly black residential areas that demands local explanation. Of course, some general characteristics of black population in the Bay Area can be attributed to experience shared in common by that group, these are regional variants on the national black urban experience. This black population is markedly youthful, an attribute of the time and manner of immigration. This population frequently clusters close to the Bay or adjacent to railroad terminals, a condition that reflects the original recruitment to work. But in looking for recurring patterns in this population the most striking repetition is that of small scale diversity. Just as the black population outside the major cities is diversely distributed, so it is within those cities. Only Oakland has, in West Oakland, the familiar ghetto image of deteriorated housing stock in a traditional location close to the old city center. And even in Oakland that is by no means the only, nor is it the largest, concentration of black population. Indeed the architecturally distinctive Acorn project that has replaced some of that deteriorated housing stock is racially integrated. The polynuclear pattern of the suburbs is found in San Francisco and Oakland, too.

SAN FRANCISCO AND OAKLAND— AND A BERKELEY POSTSCRIPT

In 1970 the black population of 95,845 made up only 13 percent of San Francisco's total count. This population was primarily located in three islands—the Fillmore district, Hunter's Point, and the Ingleside district. Of these, the first comes closest to the model of the central city ghetto, though it is a comparatively recent cluster of dominance within the longtime cosmopolitan area of the city called the Western Addition. Fillmore is unusual in that it is closely bounded to the north by the high income neighborhood of Pacific Heights, while farther away to the west lies Golden Gate Park, and to the southwest the Haight-Ashbury district has been an area of lively social change. The Western Addition contains some handsome Victorian style housing, much of which is in disrepair but some of which has been taken up and renovated, and in stretching up hill and down dale it offers some sightly views. On the cityward margin the Western Addition has been the site of a major urban renewal project which includes much of Fillmore in its bounds. After local controversy over the first phase of renewal —the WA1 project, which involved clearance—

the second phase—WA2—includes block renovation as well as the construction of new housing that is to serve residents of the area (Figure 13). There are several low rent developments of the San Francisco Housing Authority in the Fillmore district, one dating from the 1940s though others, including developments for the elderly, date from 1972. The core census tract of the Fillmore district, with 7,500 persons in total, is 80 percent black, and the mean black family income is $7,111. In contrast, in the Ingleside district, where the core tract contains only 4,199 persons at a much lower density, the mean black family income is $12,730. This is the black middle income neighborhood within the city, one that first opened up because of an absence of restrictive convenants in the house deeds in the era when such barriers to minority purchase were legal. The third predominantly black residential area, close to the naval shipyard site at Hunter's Point, includes more than 16,000 black residents in three census tracts that are 80 to 90 percent black. Some of the housing dates from wartime emergency construction, other low rent projects date from the 1950s, and demolition for new projects has taken place. This is physically isolated space, within predominantly industrial-zoned territory viewed by nonresidents only if they take a detour on the way to a ballgame at Candlestick Park.

In spite of a black newspaper, the *Sun-Reporter,* and some prominent civic leaders belonging to the black community, in San Francisco black power and influence are lacking. Whether this is due to the comparatively recent growth in the population, to its internal diversity, or to its physical separation into discrete parts is impossible to say, but in citywide debates over the school integration issue, for example, the black viewpoint was far less widely publicized than that of the Chinese.

In Oakland 124,671 black citizens make up over one-third of the city's population. Oakland has been a predominantly working class city throughout its history and the black population finds work in the port of Oakland as well as in local industry. There is a large stock of modest single family housing built in the trolleycar era that has become more dominantly black-occupied in the last ten years, particularly in East Oakland (actually to the south of the city center). Solomon has shown that although maps of Oakland at the census tract level seem to show a steady progressive

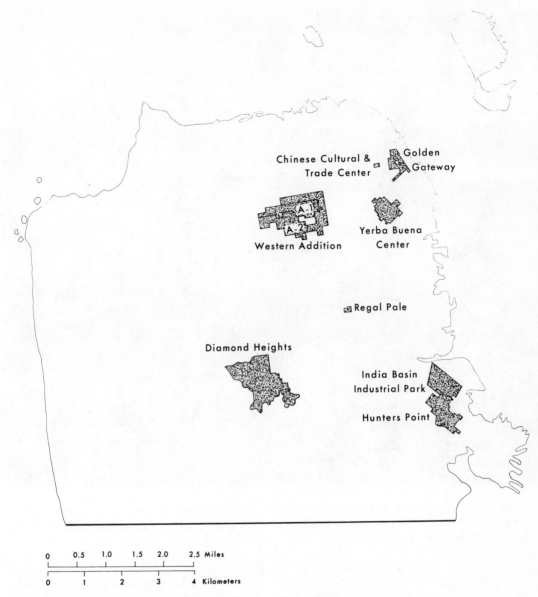

Figure 13. San Francisco redevelopment areas, January 1973.

concentration to two separate masses of black residential space between 1940 and 1970 (Figure 12), when block data are analyzed, a different pattern appears. "It is evident that the patterns of black distribution . . . by no means have smooth transition zones. There are also many isolated areas of black concentration, small areas containing blacks completely surrounded by all white blocks or by blocks containing much lower proportions of black residents." After considering the location of eight conventional public housing projects in

Oakland that conform to the traditional model and were built in predominantly black areas, Solomon examines the potential impact of Oakland's recent implementation of a scatter site policy for low income housing which places projects widely throughout Oakland on the flatlands. An example of a conventional project is the large Acorn development, an integrated low-rise and high-rise housing development that lies next to the Nimitz Freeway close to downtown Oakland and has replaced much of the old black residential core. That would

Figure 14. Lake Merritt and downtown Oakland. Across the Bay is San Francisco beyond the port of Oakland and the San Francisco-Oakland Bay Bridge. Photo courtesy of the Oakland Chamber of Commerce.

presumably tend to reconcentrate low to moderate income population in a single area, whereas the scatter site policy will effect most of Oakland's working class housing areas. Although few if any of the scattered site projects are planned in the hills there are black neighborhoods there too. The middle class Trestle Glen is the home of black professional families. Oakland is struggling to maintain a mix of modest income and moderate income families, both black and white, and to this end the amenity of Lake Merritt with its extensive park and adjacent high-rise apartment buildings—new and old—has been a successful magnet to childless couples and to older persons with grown children (Figure 14). Whether Oakland

will remain a heterogeneous city with Spanish-speaking and Chinese as well as black and white population is a moot point.

Clearly the presence of establishments in the public sector has had a fundamental role in determining the pattern of black population clusters in the Bay Area; public housing projects are obvious enough, but locally the legacy of the war time shipbuilding industry was no less important. Although the consequences of urban renewal programs have not been uniform in their impact, they have tended to redistribute black population. Continuing beyond the influence of demolition or construction, however, is the influence of military establishments in the Bay Area. Certainly the Alameda

Air Station, the Hamilton Air Force Base, and the Mare Island Navy Yard are all neighbor to significant clusters of black population, some of whom are service connected but many of whom have severed their ties with military service and are in civilian employment. And just as some public institutions seem to have stimulated the growth of black population concentrations, so do others show promise of stabilizing a racially integrated condition. It is clear that both Oakland and Richmond are cities where the increase in black population is likely to continue. Housing is available for various income classes and the shift to predominantly black population pattern of housing areas near the Bay is not likely to face any insurmountable obstacle toward the hills, given the employment potential for an upwardly mobile population. In Berkeley a more diverse pattern may develop. The presence of the University of California campus with nearly 30,000 students and numerous allied facilities brings both a constant flux in city population and the introduction of other variables. Some modest West Berkeley areas that have long been traditionally black are now home to young white families. Although there are few of the onetime numerous white blue collar residents left in Berkeley, they have been replaced by modest income persons of new lifestyles. And in the hills the amenity of housing style and design encourages a stable population that clings to its neighborhoods. And those families who leave the city discouraged at change in the school system are matched by others who are attracted by experimental programs. Despite the upheaval generated around the university itself, it is probable that the existence of the campus—plus the unchallenged amenities of the city—make it likely that Berkeley will retain a considerable white population, in contrast to the likelihood that neighboring cities will continue to change their population mix.

THE HOUSING EXPERIENCE FOR OTHER MINORITY GROUPS

Because Californians are newcomers, it is rare to meet a resident whose family has been here for three generations. This is a population that has come by choice; it is not of necessity resigned to conditions that are now perceived as little more than a legacy left by some great-grandparent's choice of home. Instead, these are people who came seeking a direct satisfaction that they themselves preconceived. For some this was to be a one way trip, a journey to seek a new environment where things would be better than in the old. But for others the coming to California was not thought of as a one way trip. Hittell expressed a universal immigrant sentiment when he wrote in 1863:

> For a long time we could not think or speak of this as home. When we first saw the brown mountains and bare plains of California in the fall of 1849, it did not occur to us that we should ever want to live here. There was nothing here to reward ambition save gold.

Few groups felt more strongly that their visit would be temporary than the Chinese. They arrived as laborers, intending originally either to return to China when they had saved some money, or to bring their wives and families to join them later. The Chinese Exclusion Act of 1882 barred further immigration of laborers and also forbade the immigration of any Chinese women except the wives of merchants, and so Chinatown became a predominantly male society. Male Chinese continued to enter either as students or merchants, or by claiming relationship to an earlier immigrant. After 1924 no Chinese women at all were allowed to enter and this embargo continued until 1943. Since that time a series of legislative acts have removed the old taboos and by 1970 there were nearly 60,000 Chinese in San Francisco, many of whom were newcomers, and many of whom were under twenty-one.

Of all the immigrant populations, the Chinese are the one group that has stayed most strongly anchored to their original destination in the city on Grant Avenue. In 1906, after fire had destroyed Chinatown, leading white businessmen set up a Subcommittee on Relocating the Chinese as one of the relief efforts. The Chinese refugees were shuffled all over town and many went off to Oakland. But the Chinese businessmen, through their representative association known as the Six Companies, were well aware of the advantages of their former location next to the central business district and they wanted to get back there. Since they had owned many of the buildings they had occupied, they could stand firm. In any case, the city soon acknowledged that to evict them would involve severe economic loss to San Francisco. So a densely populated city within a city, complete with commercial manufacturing and residential functions as well as a strong internal political structure, was rebuilt.

Since 1960 Chinatown has grown very rapidly beyond the old seven blocks, particularly toward North Beach as the Italians have moved out. Today fortune cookies are as easy to buy on Columbus Avenue as is paneforte. The heart of traditional Chinatown is a familiar place to return to for a meal; it is the home of the elderly; and it is the destination for most new immigrants.

In a perceptive and accurate study the Nees have analyzed the social structure of this core, drawing on the memories of the old-time bachelors as well as the aims of the new working class and the visions of the radicals. They found that in the last few years a sense of community has brought young people, as well as a few prosperous former residents, back to work with youth and the elderly. But however strong is the commitment of these workers, the physical facts of substandard housing cannot be ameliorated. According to city code standards, 77 percent of this housing is inadequate, consisting as it does of tiny rooms with communal facilities occupied by families, not just by single persons. Population densities are comparable to crowded parts of Manhattan, and there are only tiny play areas for the very large numbers of small children. Schoolyards are now kept open during vacations, and roof areas are used as a place to sit or to play, but the alleys are so narrow that it is hard to bounce a ball and the sidewalks so crowded that going along any of the main streets demands concentration to avoid a collision.

There is a new Chinatown made up of young professionals, students, and families who are moving into the apartment buildings several miles across the city from Grant Avenue in a formerly general middle class area to the north of Golden Gate Park that is linked to the old Chinatown by a direct bus route. This is also a densely built-up territory, though the streets are wide, the blocks unusually large and Golden Gate Park is very close. The diffusion through this area—called the Richmond District—has progressed from east to west.

In contrast to this move, which is still with-in easy physical contact of the old core, the move of the assimilated Chinese to San Mateo or to El Cerrito, in the East Bay, means physical separation. Within the Chinese community people are tagged by their home address, and the offspring of the second generation in suburbia are often those who come back to help in the youth programs in the old Chinatown as they struggle to come to grips with their own heritage. In Chinatown itself, once the bitter external hostility of the majority population toward this unassimilated minority lessened, internal dichotomies became more pronounced. This internal dissension was compounded when renewed immigration brought the struggles of China, Taiwan, and Hong Kong to Grant Avenue. But even when these human conflicts are eased, the locational conflict will remain.

Chinatown today is at the edge of a physically expanding central business district. One major motel now flanks Portsmouth Square and the pressure on space is acute. One protection against this encroachment is the small size of individual land parcels in Chinatown. This is perhaps a surer safeguard than ownership by the clan and family associations that control 65 percent of the holdings but that in the final accounting are made up of businessmen first and foremost. If the Six Companies decide to hold firm, then the maze of tenements, shops, and small factories will remain. If they decide to sell what is some of the most valuable land in San Francisco, then change will come. Individual owners of parcels on the edge of Chinatown have already sold, but to accumulate adequate acreage in these tiny blocks to make modern construction worthwhile will necessitate the cooperation of many owners of contiguous parcels. Since the property owners are generally making only a small living from their businesses, the potential profits involved in sale may be irresistable. Only the busiest restaurants and tourist attractions would be immune, and they are the basis of a different kind of community, anyway.

The newest immigrants to press their cause are the Filipinos. Two blocks on the eastern edge of Chinatown have long been called Manilatown. But intense economic competition has driven out many of the old hotels as this area sits between Chinatown and the Golden Gateway renewal project. Parking garages and the new Holiday Inn have found this small area an ideal location, close to stores and the expanding office core. At the same time, immigration from the Philippines has sharply increased and professionals and large family groups have joined the single men who once predominated in the flow. Since there is no room in Manilatown for new arrivals, three or four widely scattered foci for immigrants have developed, and their geographical scatter compounds the difficulty of organizing a community already rent by political differences—as well as by a multiplicity of linguistic and cultural distinctions.

As the Filipinos begin to emerge as a visible ethnic component, the Japanese are becoming less visible. Prior to 1941, the Japanese either lived at the edge of the urban area, engaged with greenhouses and market gardening, or were clustered in a section of San Francisco dubbed Nihonmachi, close to what has become the predominantly black Fillmore. On coming back to the Bay Area from the relocation camps after 1946 few returned to their former core area which in the meantime had become the city's main black area. In the early 1960s, as part of the Western Addition renewal project in San Francisco, a Japanese Trade Center and Hotel were built close to the prewar center of their community. Yet, despite Japanese street signs and imported goods, this is an area more real for tourists than for the onetime resident. Some Japanese do come to shop or to eat at one of the many restaurants, and young activists have started food and recreational programs for the elderly who have clung here. But, by and large, the citizens whose parents or grandparents came from Japan are widely disseminated through the Bay Area.

The American Indian and the Eskimo are most likely to migrate to Oakland; the Mexicans, clustered by village origin, will tend to be drawn to different parts of San Mateo County and San Jose; and the Mission District of San Francisco—once Italian, Irish, and Scandinavian—is now a complex pattern of culturally distinct Latin American groups for whom the label 'Spanish-speaking' conceals rather than reveals identity. The social geography of the Mission District is yet to be written.

The Bay Area as a whole still deserves the description that Bayard Taylor wrote of San Francisco in 1849:

> The streets were full of people, hurrying to and fro, and of as diverse and bizarre a character as the houses: Yankees of every possible variety, native Californians in sarapes and sombreros, Chileans, Sonorians, Kanakas from Hawaii, Chinese with long tails, Malays armed with their everlasting creeses, and others in whose embrowned and bearded visages it was impossible to recognize any especial nationality.

He might have been describing any one of the local college or university campuses, which are themselves our microcosm of the local population mix.

Where Change—or Lack of It—Is the Problem

To isolate three kinds of contemporary change now affecting core cities within the Bay Area is not to argue that these are the only changes taking place; rather, it is to draw attention to different processes in action. To observe change in physical condition is to study obsolescence in actual city fabric; and both in Oakland and in San Francisco efforts to renew or repair that fabric have met with mixed success. To consider change in the retail sector is to observe success made visible, though the self-centered quality of that success can bode ill for interrelated urban functions that are less able to adapt to the rapid shifts in styles of retailing and distribution of retailers that have been symptomatic of the last ten years. To look at change in the office function is literally to see a transformation. In San Francisco the visual impact of a mass of slabs, wedges, and a needle that now blots out landmarks like Coit Tower or the Ferry Building forces the observer to wonder at this massive centripetal growth. It is not just the way it looks, it is the manifold implications of a policy that reconcentrates so much activity, especially employment, in such a small area. Changes in the housing stock, changes in the way in which people shop, and changes in the volume and location of office activities are reshaping the relationship of city to city, and city to suburb, around the Bay.

OBSOLESCENCE AND CHANGE IN THE HOUSING SECTOR

Urban accretion has been relatively recent in the San Francisco-Oakland SMSA, even in the central cities, and the proportions of dilapidated or deteriorated housing stock are low. With few exceptions, the first inner city housing has been replaced by other uses. Older housing is likely to show up either in high middle income districts or in a peculiarly spotty pattern in low income areas. The cult of wooden Victorians came too late to save many in Oakland, but it did save some in San Francisco. Bright paint and renovated redwood shingles come high, and preservation requires either youthful energy or affluence, or both.

In districts of more modest nineteenth century housing there has been a great deal of single lot replacement. In Berkeley, for example, the "San Quentin modern" apartment buildings have been constructed at right angles to the street, with exterior stairs and gallery walks so as to crowd the maximum numbers of units onto a former single family house lot. Under less competitive land conditions, duplexes and fourplexes with parking slots may be the replacement for an old house and garden. There seems to be a fairly constant removal and renewal in these single unit housing areas where lots can accommodate a new multiunit structure. This is in contrast to conditions in more densely built up city districts where whole blocks must fall before regeneration can take place. Some of these physically changing areas may continue to have single family housing interspersed that is very well maintained (as in South Berkeley), and they tend to be racially mixed, or predominantly black. If the suburbs of the 1920s are being transformed slowly, there seems to be no reason why those of the 1930s may not progress in the same way.

The replacement form of the trolleycar tracts of the twenties may involve a gradual shift to somewhat higher population densities.

For the $99 down postwar GI housing tracts the aging process may not be as gradual. The vast amount of this housing introduces a new condition. In some cases the early postwar housing is already changing hands. Black or Spanish-speaking families with steady incomes are moving into such lower middle income suburbs, more often clustering together in ethnic neighborhoods than diffusing. As significant as any shift in racial composition of the population is a tendency for such housing to move from owner occupance to rental. A key to potential deteriorated districts that will concern us is found in this shift in form of tenure, not in the ethnicity of the occupants. Rented property dilapidates faster than that which is owner-occupied; in single family units rental income is barely profitable, and in a seasonally arid climate we see first the collapse of once well-tended gardens. Then a rapid going to seed reveals that the physical construction of much of this speedily built housing will not stand very heavy usage.

Some of the housing built between 1939 and 1960 in the first extensive automobile suburbia will need a new kind of renewal program. Few of these houses will ever merit the preservation accorded to the wooden rural cottage "Californian" or stately "Victorian", now so desired by young professionals.

The 1920s suburban houses with big porches, solid woodwork, and plenty of interior space, using most of their lot for house, are now coming into their own for young families. So long as the style was good, and the supply limited, free market renewal will work. But if the supply outruns demand and the original quality was inferior then that mechanism will not work. This is what may happen to the tracts of early Concord or San Jose.

With respect to residential property, after an early phase of demolition, urban renewal in Oakland and San Francisco until recently has entailed a reshaping of function rather than the replacement of physically obsolescent building stock (Figure 13). This is in part because the 1906 San Francisco fire and the 1923 Berkeley fire effected spontaneous removal (Figure 15). It is true that in Oakland the absence of catastrophe has made necessary the Acorn project, which replaces a deteriorat-

ed residential neighborhood that had become predominantly black and poor. However, renewal projects, particularly in San Francisco, have normally tended to substitute one function for another. In both cities the zone of discard has been viewed as a proper place for offices and stores, with a hotel and convention center, too, scheduled for San Francisco in a six block area south of Mission Street. Between Third and Seventh streets a district of mixed land uses had evolved that included many old hotels housing the single elderly, predominantly male, most of whom were seeking to deal with society on their own terms. These hotels were in many cases in very poor condition and the district had a high mortality rate by fire (Figure 16). In 1964 there were nine times more deaths from fire per thousand population here than for the rest of San Francisco. Pawnshops, bars, liquor stores vending cheap wine, thrift stores, and corner grocery stores with heavy metal grating over their windows together created a functional entity. Initially, in the renewal plan of the 1960s, the resident population was to be moved on to other quarters (presumably to the Tenderloin district north of Market Street and west of the central business district which also included a large number of hotels), but under U.S. District Court action, 1,500 units of low cost housing are now included in the South of Market renewal area. Prior to the completion of that housing, it was estimated, in December 1972, that only 112 people still lived in the twenty-five acres South of Market where the underground convention hall and 1,800 car parking garages are planned. There is some question as to the viability of studio apartments for the elderly in an area where many of their support facilities, especially the small stores, have disappeared. While it is true that a decent place to live is a first priority, some public officials have voiced concern at the plight of single elderly persons stacked up in small rooms who rarely emerge from their isolation. Their immediate physical surroundings are vastly better, and safer, but they do not seem to venture outside the building much.

It may be that the problems of the aging poor, alcoholics, and the socially alienated defy solution. The realization that deteriorating and dilapidated central city areas—for all their obvious shortcomings—might have been pro-

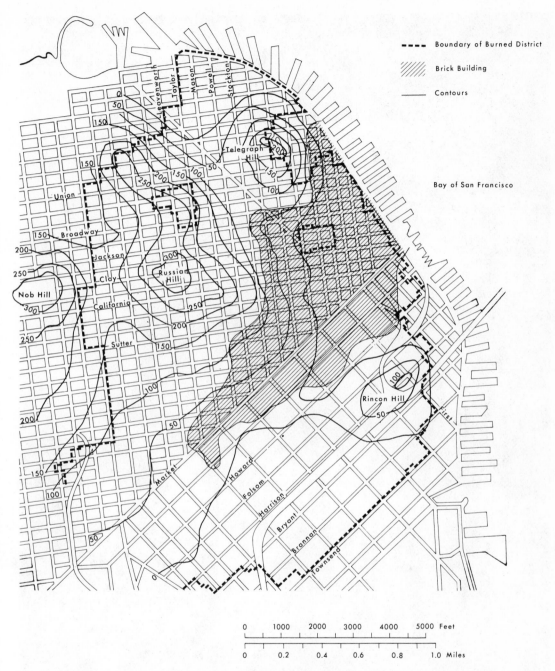

Figure 15. Burned district after the San Francisco fire, 1906. Source: Map accompanying the Report of Richard L. Humphrey, Bulletin 324, U.S. Geological Survey.

viding some other answers to very specific social needs was late in coming, almost too late. That the old hotels served special housing needs has been recognized and efforts have been made to replace what was torn down; but the complex web of supportive circumstances —proximity to a bit of life and action, or the possibility of being left alone to do things that would look odd elsewhere—cannot be re-created. Instead, there will come the surge of

cars to a basketball game or of conventioneers rushing out to see the nightlife.

The complex community that was served by this special social district will have to find a base somewhere else. But in looking around to find the deteriorating housing stock that made a marginal existence possible, the diminution in this stock becomes apparent. The demolition of the old hotels without prior inventory of the needs the district was serving caused a lot of sorrow. And there is little evidence that society is making much provision for the socially alienated for whom the central city is a haven. In San Jose, for example, the pressure of a special population on the fringes of downtown has been further compounded by recent policies imposed on state mental institutions that are having to return former inmates to communities that have no facilities to receive them. The partial closing of the Agnews State Hospital near San Jose has caused patients to congregate in downtown San Jose—posing a new set of problems for police and social workers, as well as for those formerly institutionalized persons.

In all these example the process of change in housing stock is but one step in a sequence of social change that is far more complex than a cursory glance at physical obsolescence would suggest. This is true whether you are looking at the renovated Victorians on the edge of Fillmore that begin to impinge on the ghetto population; whether you are observing the decay of suburban single family housing that opens it up to lower income families for rent; or whether you are seeing decayed hotels replaced by economically viable shining new projects. In every case, the series of changes that are set in motion by the physical crumbling of a building are on a relatively small scale. And that is the great advantage of the Bay Area over other metropolitan systems thus far. What goes wrong does so on a small scale and it has been possible to make some sort of amends, at least up to now.

BAY AREA TRENDS IN RETAILING

In the Bay Area, two counties—Marin and Contra Costa—show up on national tables of unusually high family income, and it

Figure 16. The Mars—A family hotel.

would seem likely that retailing would show a very lively condition in the region. A study by the United California Bank shows that in 1972 Marin County exceeded the statewide average of 8.64 retail outlets per thousand of population with nine outlets per thousand. Contra Costa (6.43), San Mateo (7.46), and Alameda (7.52) counties fall well below the state average. That San Francisco has twelve retail outlets per thousand of population shows the degree to which the traditional pull of the core city has been maintained. The numbers of stores relative to population there has stayed very steady since 1965, with a slight relative increase as the population total has declined. The sales per capita for San Francisco City and County in 1972 stood at $2,926, as compared with an average for the other eight counties in the region of $2,220. This lead in sales was not due to the presence of department stores in San Francisco—for the third year in a row sales in that category declined as the competition of suburban shopping centers showed its effect. And restaurant business did not increase as fast as it did elsewhere, though San Francisco still held on to well over a quarter of the total sales for all eating and drinking places in the nine counties—so that its reputation for good dining is surviving.

Locally, three sorts of retail concentration are worthy of comment—the central business districts of the older core cities, the regional shopping centers, and the neighborhood shopping clusters. The two most striking features in the region are the diversity of trends that have shown up within central business districts, and the emergence of very strong, highly specialized, retailing at the neighborhood level.

The Tale of Four Central Business Districts

The retail trade function that was once viewed as a prime activity at the core of a metropolitan region is less likely now to satisfy the classical image of a central business district. Exceptional to the Bay Area is the demonstration of four distinctively different conditions of contemporary change as revealed by San Francisco, Oakland, San Jose, and Richmond. These represent respectively what we might term old center survival and regeneration; the phoenix rising from the ashes; outlying shopping center victorious; and downtown collapsed.

The first needs to be distinguished from the second in that San Francisco has never faced the downswing that Oakland has experienced. And the third is worth separating from the fourth. San Jose is close to the normal American pattern of the 1960s in the vigor of its outlying shopping opportunities which clearly explain the demise of downtown; whereas for Richmond there is no such surrender to competition, there is just collapse.

Downtown shopping in San Francisco centers on Union Square, but it has changed character in the last decade. Some old retailers like Liebes and the White House have departed, as well as J.C. Penney, but some New York specialty stores have arrived—Tiffany's, Abercrombie and Fitch, and Peck and Peck, for example. In spite of competition from the few suburban shopping centers like Walnut Creek that are located close to high income residential suburbs, downtown San Francisco has kept its grasp on limited appeal goods selling, and has gained added diversity in that category of retail outlets—though losing its dominance in department and dry goods sales. It has also lost some diversity in retail management, apart from the introduction of the Hawaii-based Liberty House (Amfac) that took over the old and floundering City of Paris. Downtown is still the place to go to for women's clothing, jewelry, decorative items, and all sorts of expensive goodies. That the central business district can still exert a pull on the spatially segregated limited appeal goods market is a measure of urban fragmentation in the Bay Area. High income suburbs occur in Marin, Alameda, Contra Costa, and San Mateo counties, so that the most accessible point to most high income shoppers in the Bay region is not in the suburbs, but is still in downtown San Francisco. A suburban location can capture only one portion of that market, as does for instance the Stanford Shopping Center which is a focus for peninsula big spenders who are sufficiently numerous to allow the creation of a suburban limited appeal center. But no other county has enough high income shoppers to support such a center, and so all the suburbs must continue to rely on San Francisco, which is the only easily accessible focus for them all.

San Francisco, unlike many central retail clusters, still carries the three functions assigned to core districts by Vance: "they serve as the area of standardized shopping for people living in and near the core; they serve as a shopping place for this sort of goods for those people who work in the central business district; and they carry on certain highly specialized retail functions for the metropolis." In addition, tourists still include Union Square on their itinerary, though it shares its place with some highly specialized shopping attractions in the vicinity of Fisherman's Wharf.

In contrast to San Francisco's success in responding to change, Oakland's central business district has always suffered from a peculiar bipolarity. Decisions by individual retailers and business leaders have repeatedly produced a pattern of spatial overextension in a linear pattern. In the 1960s the pull was in two diametrically opposed directions—of the lower income group to a refurbished "Washington Street Mall" to the west of the old core (close to City Hall), and of the higher income group toward Lake Merritt to the east. There the new Kaiser office-store complex was built to include a small department store occupied by the White House. The comparative failure of that branch, close to—but not in—downtown, is said to have played a part in the bankruptcy of the chain. It was not big enough to save an ailing company but was big enough to deepen the hue of the red ink. Apart from the shaky retail mix originally present at the Kaiser Center, it was also apparent that the distance between department stores at either end of the shopping district was too great. Only the ones closer to the middle could prosper. They survived, and Oakland has prestigious stores on Broadway that look hopefully to the BART stations at their entrances to lure customers from south, east, and north whence they can come with no change of train.

In 1973 a major renewal development—the City Center Project—attempted to shift the center of retailing back again to the west of city hall, to sites discarded long ago, despite the planners' mall built there in the late 1950s. This is to be a mammoth integrated shopping center, with office space, parking, restaurants, and department stores—specifically Liberty House. The unique condition is that this center will be immediately adjacent to the central business district, within two blocks of a freeway but on the west side of the city where industry, low income housing, and much decaying property remains. This is a classic zone of discard, so the introduction of such a project would be no small gamble. The success of the venture rests on the peculiar vitality shown by Oakland retailing that is mainly due to the lack of hard-hitting competition from outlying shopping centers. In the whole of the East Bay there is barely one outstanding regional center, yet there is a lot of spending money in Alameda County. Whether shopping would be drawn to such an eccentric location as that of the "City Center" is another matter.

In October 1973, when nine blocks had been prepared for rebuilding and the first office block was already completed, the U.S. Environmental Protection Agency announced that all future parking projects to create fifty or more spaces would be subject to review and would require specific permission. The City Center plans have been predicated on the availability of 5,500 parking spaces for workers and shoppers. And late in 1973 it became apparent that urban freeway projects were out of favor, and so the City Center will have to rely on existing street access. Since the project is served by BART—in fact is close to the intersection of the two axes of the system—it might seem that Center would have a great potential advantage over suburban shopping centers. This may well prove to be the case if reliance on the automobile drops significantly; but it will mean some revamping of the project, which is based on the model of Eastridge, San Jose, and was touted as a bold attempt to introduce the design of an outlying shopping center, including automobile convenience, to the central city.

San Jose is the epitome of the old downtown that has decayed and been left deserted by its original patrons. They have gone to suburbia and now favor places like the massive regional shopping center of Valley Fair that was built in 1956 and subsequently so enlarged as to need decked parking. In the old downtown center, store windows show a predominance of lower cost items as well as "Se Habla Español" signs. It has become an ethnically distinctive shopping district, as have so many traditional central business districts—for example, Chicago's Loop and the old downtown of Los Angeles.

The most dramatic, in the tragic sense, of the four city retail centers is Richmond, a retailer's disaster area that has collapsed over a ten year period in spite of the fact that the nearest competing shopping center, four miles away in El Cerrito, has only a modest branch of a department store, and that the major suburban shopping center of Sun Valley is twenty miles away to the east across the mountain range—and even that cannot compare in size or sophistication with the centers around San Jose. Moreover, the universal planning panacea—a mall—was tried to no avail. Downtown Richmond once had one of the two local Macy's outlets outside of San Francisco, as well as a good array of stores, but hardly one retailer remains from the period that ended in the early 1960s. Given the income levels of Richmond, both black and white, the poverty of retail opportunities is remarkable. Black shoppers as well as white have virtually abandoned downtown. Only Montgomery Ward, in a free-standing location close to middle income black housing, survives and, in fact, prospers very nicely. Downtown Richmond has everything but stores—BART, an excellent civic center, an auditorium, a high school, state office employment, and a new federal office building. But no one can imagine that retailers will ever again replace the Tabernacle of God and the numerous missions that now occupy a few of the otherwise vacated stores.

There are, of course, other downtown clusters in the Bay region—Berkeley, for instance —that have considerable vigor. The recent revival in retail activity in Berkeley is concentrated in the restaurant category. Between 1968 and 1972, fifty-eight new eating places opened, offering an enormous variety of cuisine, and by 1972 the city could call itself the restaurant center of the East Bay. This feature of local specialization is not uncommon for the numerous small downtown retail foci within the region; indeed an unusual differentiation of function is far more explicit than would be anticipated from any reference to concepts in a classical central place hierarchy. This differentiation may be a consequence of a highly fractionated residential distribution pattern, which may similarly detract from the ability of free-standing discount houses to prosper. The three White Front stores have been closed, leaving only relatively small discount outlets in the whole region. Bay Area shoppers can buy specialty goods at ware-

house prices, but not much family clothing
or mass appeal goods.

But What About Regional
Shopping Centers?

In a 1959 study of eleven regional shopping centers, Vance reported to the Lund Symposium that all these centers were primarily
of local importance and that each had become
the mass seller to an individual suburb alone.
Since that time centers have brought the total
in the Bay Area to nineteen; more were added
in Santa Clara County than elsewhere, though
each part of the region gained at least one
center. Some of these are "climate-controlled,"
one has decked its parking facilities, and some
are just glorified neighborhood centers. Indeed,
not one can boast to be the biggest, best, or
brightest of its kind, and you must look either
to the vitality of San Francisco or to other
competing opportunities for an explanation of
the patchy quality of suburban shopping.

Shopping in the Neighborhoods

A major cause for the comparative lack of vitality in regional shopping centers may be in
the unusual strength of specialized neighborhood store groupings. Most of these are com-
prised of a series of independently located
stores catering to a locally discrete market
for which they form a functional association.
Some groupings of stores at the community
level are directed at a localized clientele but
were set up as an economic entity. Instead
of catering to the mass market locally they
cater to a locally differentiated market. Thus
Eastmont Mall in Oakland is directed primarily at middle income black shoppers. In
San Francisco, tourists and visitors form a
discrete market and so Ghiradelli Square and
the Cannery offer an appropriate mixture of
stores and restaurants enclosed in prettied-
up nineteenth century factories and warehouses. They are as precisely located close
to well-advertised lures as the stores around
Jack London Square, in Oakland, but the
former have the advantage of the turnaround
of the California Street cable car. Union Street
in San Francisco demonstrates how a series
of independent store owners can get together
to promote their own image—their successful
efforts have led rents to soar on that street.
They offer a rich mixture of specialty stores,
restaurants, and clothing stores directed to regional visitors and white-gloved ladies—the
high middle income trade.

In cities rich in cultural diversity, an array
of ethnically distinctive streets shows not
only the predominant component of nearby
housing, but may also signal changes that are
taking place in that population. In San
Francisco, Clement Street, once Russian in
tone, is now Chinese, marking the migration
of younger and second generation residents
to the avenues north of Golden Gate Park.
The Mission district in San Francisco has a
bewildering proliferation of ethnically distinct stores—central American, Arabic, Mexican, and Indian. Grocery stores are the most
prominent of those to so specialize, but variety
stores, book stores, bakeries, and restaurants
are there too.

The nation knew about Haight Street in
San Francisco and Telegraph Avenue in Berkeley at one point in their trade cycle, but retailing has never stabilized in either since their
days of notoriety. The once magnetic Telegraph Avenue is now more signaled by endless
street hawkers and franchised food offerings
than by the unusual sellers of sandals, custom
furniture, books, and records that once made
it appeal to a wider community than the
putative campus affiliates who now seek
identity there. Elsewhere in the East Bay,
Solano Avenue in Berkeley has blossomed with
oriental rug dealers, natural foods, primitive
interior decor, and restaurants. And College
Avenue, well south of the Berkeley campus,
adds sporting goods to that mixture. The special communities—hip youth, homosexuals,
ecology buffs, and boat aficionados—all have
their own places, not just one store but
visible and viable clusters.

The retailing landscape of the region is a
highly volatile one, with publicized success
stories like Levi Strauss and the blue jean to
set trends that are nationally emulated—
from candles to sandals, from wine tasting
and wine making to natural foods, and now
a plethora of indoor plant sellers is being
succeeded by the quilt makers. The retail
waves advance and recede with the tides
of a mobile population that fluxes in taste
and discretionary spending. It may next decide
to forget about material objects all together
in favor of meditation. But if that happens,
there will be a store to serve that need. The
last fad was the conversation store which

Figure 17. New high-rise construction overwhelming the old buildings, 1972. Photograph: Karl H. Riek.

sold a little talking time—on-tap friendship for the lost and lonely—over a chess board or a cup of coffee. That substitute for the neighborhood bar did not last very long.

THE CHANGE FROM LOW-RISE TO HIGH-RISE

The transformation of the San Francisco skyline over the last decade has destroyed any lingering image of a romantically antiquarian port city wielding wide-ranging financial power, a physical aspect maintained until the early 1960s. The soaring towers of the new financial district may well end up looking more like Manhattan than does the original (Figure 17). The first major building of this era, opened in 1959, was the twenty story Crown Zellerbach building on Market Street, a green glass slab raised above ground on columns that left two-thirds of the site open to landscaping—and general acclaim. Within two blocks the fifteen story John Hancock building—also opened in 1959—used its full site but diminished in mass upward. It innovatively took pedestrians one story above ground around a narrow garden walkway. During the succeeding twelve years twenty more high buildings were erected; at fifty-two stories the Bank of America is the largest mass, though the Transamerica cathedral tower rises to fifty-five. All told, large new office buildings have added over

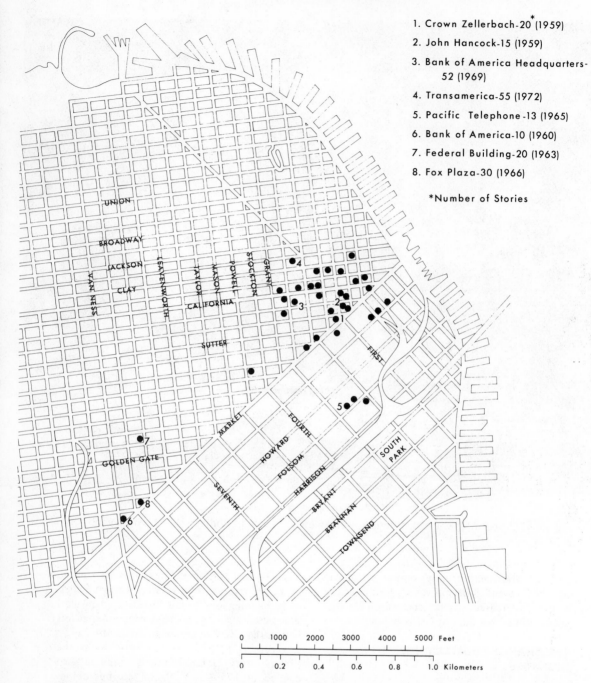

1. Crown Zellerbach-20[*] (1959)
2. John Hancock-15 (1959)
3. Bank of America Headquarters-52 (1969)
4. Transamerica-55 (1972)
5. Pacific Telephone-13 (1965)
6. Bank of America-10 (1960)
7. Federal Building-20 (1963)
8. Fox Plaza-30 (1966)

*Number of Stories

Figure 18. Office buildings constructed Since 1959, with number of stories and year of construction for selected buildings.

one million square feet of floor space per year on the average since 1960, and the annual contribution has been increasing recently (Figure 18).

But not all the construction has taken place

in this contiguous expansion of the original financial district from not much over a dozen blocks to a forty block area. The completion of the thirteen story Pacific Telephone building in 1965 on Folsom Street, three blocks south of Market Street, broke what had come to be a traditional barrier to the expansion of the high-rise core. Since that time, four buildings over thirteen stories have been built along the south side of Market Street itself, though delays over the Yerba Buena renewal project have thus far hindered the start on three buildings set to join the Pacific Telephone building in its present isolation. Although this southward extension from the high-rise district will serve to reduce the pressure of concentrated vertical growth, the location of this "annex" so close to arterial freeways and freeway ramps does pose issues of potential traffic congestion.

Some ten blocks away from downtown in 1960 the Bank of America opened a ten story building close to the Civic Center, where this world's largest bank carries on much of its technical, as opposed to policymaking, functions. The completion of the twenty story Federal Building nearby and the vertically mixed office, retail, and residential block of the Fox Plaza building contribute a second focal point to office development adjacent to two sides of San Francisco's neoclassical Civic Center. This second focus—made up of governmental and administrative offices—is distinctly different from the financial character of the major focus on Montgomery and California streets.

Of the twenty-two SMSAs for which data are given in *Construction Review,* the San Francisco-Oakland area led all others in value of authorized building permits for office buildings for the first three months of 1973 with $30.6 million recorded. The next three in line—Washington, D.C., Los Angeles-Long Beach, and Chicago—recorded $24.2, $23.9, and $22.8 million respectively. The construction activity for San Francisco in, or close to, the foci described above accounts for most of the volume for the SMSA. Informal estimates have suggested that the ratio of new to old office building space now is about one to two. There is some downgrading or abandonment of older buildings as new ones attract prestigious concerns, and in this process the classical Russ building, which was the largest on the Pacific Coast when completed in 1927, has yielded tenants to the Transamerica Tower. In the SMSA in 1972, 101,600 persons were engaged in finance, insurance, and real estate, and 273,500 were in government employment. Of these totals San Francisco was the place of

employment for 67,300 (66 percent) and 91,500 (33 percent) respectively, an increase of approximately 20,000 in each category since 1960. The majority of the first group would be located in the major core and a goodly proportion of the second in the Civic Center cluster. There is strong census evidence to support the visual evidence of a significant increase in the office function of San Francisco relative to the region as a whole.

Such an increase in specialized central function could only occur due to a combination of factors. The concentrated economic growth has been favored by superior accessibility from a disjunctive region, by determined self-enhancement by the San Francisco business community, and by the focusing of public transportation at the old Bay Bridge Terminal. Commuting data for 1970 showed that 139,000 persons gave the San Francisco central business district as their place of work destination. Though many of these people would be employed in retail or service sectors, it is obvious that office employees make up the largest portion of this number.

Within the office core are now to be found high-rise residential towers as well as public parks and a massive new hotel. Therefore, on the weekends this is not an entirely deserted Wall Street of the West. But, with the inrush of the aforementioned commuters it becomes a terribly congested zone from 10:00 A.M. to 6:00 P.M. on weekdays. Many do not like this new vision of gleaming towers and parking garages. It is stunning for the airline passenger who swings in around the Bay, or for the motorist passing by on the freeway, but it is costly in time and effort for those who funnel into this core on weekdays. And there are also those who question the success of this area at ground level. Some parts, such as the Vaillancourt Fountain, are a delight to pedestrians, but along whole blocks the individual is dwarfed by an unbroken wall of a parking structure. In the interior of the Golden Gateway project circulation is taken up one level to create a pedestrian precinct separated from automobile at ground level, but this doesn't altogether work.

However, to carp at the detailed stitching of change is to risk missing the new fabric that is being woven. This new pattern is part of a single design that is derived from the form of the classical single-centered city. In the case of

San Francisco, though, the new high-rise core is a limited purpose focus for an extended urban region within which other functions have become very differently organized. For the office worker this present focusing of transportation modes will not decline. The completion of the Bay Area Rapid Transit system brings four tributary feeders from the region—three from the East Bay, and one from San Francisco and the northern extremity of San Mateo County—to the office core. Now that this concentration of employment is highly visible in glass, steel, and concrete, doubts are being raised within San Francisco (most colorfully by Duskin) as to whether this was, in fact, a desirable strategy for the city as a whole or whether it merely serves special interests.

That the debate about the sorts of changes that are occurrring in core cities is becoming louder can be assigned in part the very speed of the transformation. But behind those initial questions are more fundamental concerns about the very nature of urban change. These concerns revolve around the alternative options to be brought into discussion when mature cities are in need of rejuvenation and restoration. Within cities the debate has been carried by small groups of involved citizens, by business and governmental organizations, and by those whose professional interests give them voice. At the edge of the city, where whole communities are seeing the reefs of immaturity rather than the shoals of maturity, there are as many conflicting points of view about the process of change as there are in core cities. And there, very large groups of citizens become involved.

Whose Limits to Growth?

In 1959 the Army Corps of Engineers published projections of population growth for the Bay Area. Its figure for the year 2000 was 8.84 million. A 1973 Association of Bay Area Governments (ABAG) report calling for "controlled growth" to respond to an estimated increase to 7.5 million could, therefore, be termed "cautiously realistic." Despite the sobering figures, a regional approach to the control of growth is opposed by some East Bay municipalities, which are anxious to set their own goals and feel well able to design their own destinies.

Any discussion of issues relative to future planning in the Bay Area is likely to stress two themes: first, the preservation of open space and, second, the desirability of increased employment opportunities. Thereby a combination of the good life—lived in good surroundings for a limited but diverse population—would tie together economic self-interest and the husbanding of local amenities. An accepted ABAG plan calls for reserving 3.4 million acres for open space—that is, about seventy-five percent of all land in the nine counties. The second theme picks up on the need for three million more jobs. In separated localities the contradictions inherent in conflicting goals focus on issues such as courting new industry and the adequacy of housing supply in a suburban environment, equitable access to open space and the preservation of scenic qualities. The ultimate cynic might argue that if all these desirable goals were to be achieved internally (to produce an urban elysium), then this paradise would surely be beseiged by outsiders crowding to enter the verdant gates. But that, after all, is the eternal Californian paradox.

STRATEGY FOR CONTROLLED GROWTH: MARIN COUNTY

Marin County has been cast as the earliest and most vigorous proponent of the campaign for controlled growth; and the county itself is the focus of seemingly irreconcilable goals. It is a scenically special place, one that has seashore and uplands of unusual beauty that have been preserved—either by private and public foresight, or, by chance, in military reservations. The qualities of the Point Reyes peninsula have been recognized through the creation of the National Seashore; it is likely that a balance between grazing land, with access to beaches, and extensive trails can be maintained, partly because the area is given a little protection from excessive use by the persistence of fog and cool summer temperatures, and partly because of a deliberate policy of not widening the twisting two lane roads.

In October 1972, the federal government established the Golden Gate National Recreation Area which consolidated 34,000 acres and thirty-one miles of shoreline that had been held by private parties, by the federal government, or by the state of California into a single recreational unit (Figure 19). This park is still in the making; municipal and state lands have yet to be turned over to federal jurisdiction,

Figure 19. The Golden Gate National Recreation Area. From Olema in the north the GGNRA stretches twenty-two miles to the Golden Gate Bridge. The northern portion includes 7,500 acres of state parkland; 2,000 acres of federally owned land; 200 acres of county land; and 16,000 of privately owned land. It is largely open land in contrast to the portion south of the Golden Gate Bridge which is heavily used urban land in parks, historic sites, and existing recreational attractions.

for example, but there is already public access to undeveloped portions as well as to existing state parks, and there are developed trails. The bicycle trails and walking paths are well utilized by local residents for whom cycling and hiking are primary recreational activities. Indeed, these residents would see more ambitious facilities as a potential rival for space, or one that might draw persons looking for other kinds of amenities that might detract from the bucolic atmosphere that now prevails. Although some of the GGNRA is within the city of San Francisco, the major acreage is in Marin County, and the creation of this park will exacerbate for Marin the problems that come from having such attractive scenery within the county.

Some idea of the dimensions of this amenity pull can be gauged from a recreational-travel survey taken by the county in the summer of 1972. At that time it appeared that county residents made up less than half the visitors to all but one of the recreational sites surveyed. The exception was a fishing lake where the generally disproportionately heavy use by white residents was also counterweighed by black participation. At Muir Woods, a redwood grove that is under the National Park Service, only 8 percent of the visitors were from Marin County—a local would assert that those people were there showing out-of-state relatives the closest big tree they could find. Certainly the swarm of tour buses and recreational vehicles show massive tourist use. Although it is true that the proportion of local use of facilities increases during the winter season, it is still a fact that people come from all over the Bay Area to use Marin facilities—and that the weekday patterns of commuting congestion are replaced at the weekend by patterns of visitor congestion. When Marin residents refuse to support improvement of an east-west highway system they are reacting against external use; they have been less hostile to improvement of north-south routes which take their 30,000 commuters more rapidly to San Francisco.

Within Marin County, various strategies have been tried in efforts to limit growth—through a moratorium on new water connections in central and southern Marin, in the rejection of a planned water supply pipeline in a county referendum in November 1973, and with proposals for ordinances to halt construction on ridgetops and steep slopes. In Sonoma County, the city of Petaluma attempted to limit building permits to 500 per year. Thus, the tools for "controlled growth" are multiple, and the goals are both overt and covert. Since Marin is a county with few residents drawn from minority groups and with many households of higher than average incomes, the county is dubbed exclusivist or élitist by others in the region, a description hotly denied by those who got there first. In public debates, the overwhelming desire to preserve what they have comes through loud and clear. Minority and lower income groups do not fit easily into the old image of Marin County, any more than jazzy recreational attractions belong on that Point Reyes peninsula recorded in the book "Island in Time." But, whatever their motives, it is clear that people in Marin County have strong views about growth. This is what they talk about and, more significantly, what they vote about.

A CHANGING VIEW OF GROWTH: NORTHERN SAN MATEO COUNTY

In northern San Mateo County three belts of development can be related to north-south transportation axes. For over a hundred years physically discontinuous growth on the Bay side of the peninsula has been tied to the railroad and to El Camino Real—the public highway that first linked the California missions and subsequently was the main axis of development until replaced as an arterial by the Bay-

shore Freeway. Settlement in this zone includes heavy industry on the Bay flatlands as well as residential developments. In sharp contrast, the ridges along the spine of the peninsula and the restricted flat patches facing the ocean were protected from change by rugged terrain and weather. Both areas were reached only by winding roads giving slow access to modest settlement.

Beside the Ocean

The intermittent fog of the coastal stretch made California Route 1 unattractive for commuters. Little road improvement was practicable along the immediate shore because of landslides or marine erosion, and because of the instability that was compounded here by the passage out to sea of the San Andreas rift zone. Both the Ocean Shore Railroad (1907-1920) and Route 1 lost considerable portions of right of way through the years. In spite of the difficulties of commuting to San Francisco, the coast experienced rapid postwar residential growth of low cost G.I. loan housing tracts, and this eventually brought the incorporation of a series of housing clusters into the city of Pacifica in 1957. Massive road construction started edging southward in 1958 and finally carried a four lane divided highway across the spurs and valleys—well inland from the coastal terraces.

Convenient access to San Francisco and the economics of initial development made Pacifica an attractive suburbia in the 1960s, though problems stemming from an inadequate tax base could not be overcome by a high rate of taxation. Inadequate fire protection and the absence of many city services modified the early euphoria. The total lack of industry is crucial. Now that planning controls by the state are exerted over all development 1,000 yards landward from the shore there is no hidden asset to be mined there. The patches of coastal plain backed by very steep slopes have been almost completely built up with single family residences; and only the ridge tops and precipitous slopes remain to be developed. But the city has enacted a hillside preservation ordinance designed to limit growth to the ridge lines. To get up there is expensive and likely to involve either massive road construction or reliance on inadequate access. The political struggles between developers and concerned residents, which bedevil many suburban communities, are here dramatically emphasized by the rugged terrain and locational attributes of this suburb.

What is perhaps more dramatic considering the high percentage of blue collar workers in the city—workers who must necessarily commute outside Pacifica for employment—is the recent rejection of a massive ridgeline development proposal for condominium clusters. A citizen-sponsored referendum turned down the project by a four to one margin in November 1973 despite the heavy spending by the Labor Council of San Mateo in support of the development corporation. Clearly, this workers' suburb did not relish the prospect of more housing units brooding above it on the highlands.

Up on the Peninsula Ridge

Along the spine of the San Fransisco peninsula lies the third axis of development—the one that has been most recent. It was the construction of a freeway in 1968-1972 that triggered the filling of remaining land for suburban growth. Interstate 280 is a scenic highway; it runs beside the lakes of the San Andreas rift zone with their adjacent watershed lands and is furnished as well with some remarkable underpasses and access ramps which are striking in design and aesthetically superb. The visual contribution of the road is not matched by many of the residential units or the new Serramonte shopping center close to the county line. In many places on the newly remodeled slopes there is little tree planting in progress to ameliorate the stark terraces of closely spaced houses that have—since World War II—become as much a San Franciscan feature as the cable car, though some garden apartment complexes shrouded in greenery show that development could be visually pleasing.

It was certainly inevitable that as soon as access improved, this area would be subject to speedy development. The situation was unusual in there being so much empty land within such a short distance of the central city so that it was possible to construct a large volume of readily accessible housing in the late 1960s. It is noteworthy that this recent development does not depart from the classic model that predicates middle income housing lying closer to the city center than upper income residential zones. Usually this social

pattern is attributable to age of housing and progressive outward spread of development of available land. In San Mateo County the land became available late in time but has gone to what the developers must have assumed to be the most profitable use—namely, mass market housing.

In the suburbs of northern San Mateo close to the San Francisco city line, there is an increasing proportion of minority residents. Around Daly City there are initially low cost speculative housing tracts that might well have deteriorated very fast. Many of them were of poor construction or were in locally hazardous places because of proximity to the San Andreas fault. That nothing has changed this fact is evident in cracked stucco, warped roof lines, or basements that flood in any rainstorm. But these areas—once rather inaccessible—have become suddenly very convenient. Not only does new highway construction lead straight to San Francisco but also the BART line starts from Daly City. Since San Mateo county is outside the BART jurisdiction, residents pay no property taxes to the district, nor do they pay the extra sales tax levied within the three included counties. This section of suburbia—once the only practicable destination for the lower middle income family with one car, wishing to purchase rather than to rent—is becoming very attractive to city workers. Since this area is close to a major black middle income housing area in Ingleside, and since the BART line to Daly City runs through the predominantly Spanish-speaking Mission District of San Francisco, this suburbia is potentially familiar ground and it is likely that in the future these areas will come to house a diversified population.

ADVOCATES OF GROWTH IN THE EAST BAY

When Marin County is advocating controlled growth—and communities in San Mateo County are in political conflict of the issue—then the question of future additions to the housing supply in suburbia comes into question. If those already living within the Daily Urban System begin forcibly to exert control over growth—which means some form of limitation at this time, not merely channeling into preferred avenues—then a restricted supply of potential undeveloped acreage will result in even higher prices for land and for houses. It will also mean that development will be accelerated in those localities where it is viewed more favorably. Southern Alameda County is one region in which growth is still viewed favorably. On incorporation in 1956, Fremont, with its ninety-six square miles, was tagged as the city producing the most cabbages in the U.S. Between 1970 and 1972 it grew a staggering 20.4 percent, reaching a population of 121,400, thereby recording the fastest rate of growth in the SMSA. The construction of factories—General Motors employing 13,000, and a large Ford installation across the county line at Milpitas in Santa Clara County—as well as trucking terminals, has been followed by the siting in Fremont of mobile home parks, single family housing tracts, and planned unit developments. Within a hundred feet of the heavily traveled Nimitz Freeway there is a current housing boomlet. This relatively modestly priced suburbia—widely advertised by bill-

boards citing prices just under $25,000—is akin to the one that continues to grow around San Jose.

In Fremont the boom has the added incentive of direct access to rapid transit as well as to local factory employment. The flat fields that only recently produced flowers and vegetables tended largely by Spanish-speaking workers now have a markedly Spanish-surname population living in the houses that permanently occupy the former fields. This conversion to suburban uses has produced a relatively convenient suburbia for many blue collar workers and at the same time has garnered speculative profit for a few. This example appeals to land holders in Antioch and areas even farther east in Contra Costa County. These Contra Costans are actively touting an extension of the Bay Area Rapid Ransit system to their area within the next five years to harvest the same financial windfall that was obtained in the last decade in southern Alameda County.

The Integration of an Urban Region

The movement of goods and people, first by water and then by land, has always been the key to the way the different parts of the Bay Area related one to another. That was true for the Gold Rush steamers, the ferry boats, and the trolleycars; it is no less true when compact automobiles, rapid transit, and revitalized bus systems are the way to go. It is not just a case of changing technology, but also a reflection of new directions in where to go as well as how to get there. And because these choices involve organizing systems, as well as running them, there comes from these designs in physical articulation some evidence of a new fitting together of administrative structures. This is emerging not from theoretically desirable schemes for regional relationships—good as they may be—but from the pragmatic putting together of separately functioning operations like bridges and freeways, or transit stations and bus stops. That is how the parts work together.

BY ROAD AND BY BRIDGE

A map of freeways (Figure 20) shows the eccentric condition of San Francisco relative to the Bay Area network. Whether the grumble of traffic on surface streets unlucky enough to lie between incomplete freeway sections is a preferable substitute to the roar of freeway traffic is a moot point; the antifreeway stance of San Franciscans has been widely publicized. The gap in freeway connections in San Francisco primarily affects (or blesses, your point of view depending largely on where you live) the northern half of the city. Traffic going to and from the Golden Gate Bridge is either forced across Golden Gate Park or toward the center of San Francisco on city streets. The elevated portion of the Embarcadero Freeway that takes traffic to the Bay Bridge from the northern waterfront and the high-rise office core is the subject of a campaign for demolition, although in fact the new tall buildings behind the freeway now obscure any waterview from much of downtown. It is not clear what substitute streets would be utilized should the campaign succeed. On the east side of the Bay it is possible to take alternative peripheral routes. The new Interstate 680 takes traffic to the Benicia-Martinez Bridge from Fremont east of the coastal range, and Interstate 580 offers a partial alternative to the Nimitz Freeway in Oakland, though north of the Bay Bridge there is no alternative to Interstate 80 through Richmond.

In the east-west direction the San Francisco-Oakland Bay Bridge is the strongest integrative link within the region (Table 9) as such it is becoming more and more congested. The increase in traffic averages 4 percent per year, and in 1972 the daily average of 162,000 vehicles (rising to a peak of 200,000 on occasion) meant that the bridge was pushed beyond its capacity of 8,500–9,000 per hour at times. causing waiting lines at the toll booths to get onto the bridge. The institution of a one way westbound fare collection in September 1969 reduced congestion on the bridge itself for

Figure 20. Bridges and main routes.

travelers from San Francisco, but even the extensive East Bay approaches can be taxed at times by the pile-up. An additional bridge—the Southern Crossing—was authorized by the legislature in 1966, to run from Hunter's Point in San Francisco to the Oakland Airport and Alameda Island. The building of such a crossing was indefinitely postponed by local voters through a referendum in 1971, largely, to judge by bumper stickers, on environmental grounds. It was further argued that no further bridges should be built until the impact of the Bay Area Rapid Transit District (BART) on transbay traffic was known.

A LINEAL DESCENDENT TO THE KEY SYSTEM

In 1962 voters in three counties approved a $732 million bond issue, the largest local one ever successfully proposed in the United States. The requisite 60 percent vote was achieved in the sum total with a strong affirmation in San Francisco (66.8 percent) being balanced by less enthusiastic votes in Alameda County (59.7 percent) and Contra Costa County (54.1 percent). By the end of 1973 taxpayers in the three counties had invested $1.4 billion in the Bay Area Rapid Transit system.

Table 9. Traffic on the Bridges in the San Francisco Bay Area, 1972[a]

Crossing	Class I (car)	Truck	Bus	Free	Total
San Francisco-Oakland Bay Bridge	27,442	2,558	433	844	31,279
San Mateo-Hayward Bridge	4,209	810	9	5	5,034
Dumbarton Bridge	1,673	240	1	5	1,921
Carquinez Bridges	7,628	1,158	73	29	8,890
Benicia-Martinez Bridge	4,710	823	6	11	5,551
Richmond-San Rafael Bridge (east- and westbound)	6,874 6,784	915 915	8 8	20 20	7,819 7,819

[a]1000s of vehicles, westbound.
Source: California Division of Bay Toll Crossings.

Enormous sums of money and effusive publicity have been hallmarks of this special district. As of 1974, an eventual cost of $2 billion is being publicly forecast, as well as an annual operating deficit of $30 million. The system itself predicts losing $111 million in four and a half years; in other calculations it has seldom fallen short of its own estimates. BART is a technically complex system performing a spatially simple task of collecting persons from thirty-four widely separated stations and carrying them over axes connected in their central portion (Figure 21). The distance between stations is a consequence of the demand for high speed trains, a provision which also affects the headway between trains and the total passenger capacity of the system. The system is one-third elevated, one-third surface, and one-third subway; the longest underground section is under the Bay. In downtown San Francisco the system is underground, as it was planned to be in a short stretch in downtown Berkeley. Berkeley has placed the entire portion within the city underground at the expense of city taxpayers alone; the larger system is financed by property taxes and a three county sales tax, as well as by the diversion of some San Francisco-Oakland Bay Bridge money and small federal grants.

In September 1972, the first portion of the BART system began operation. This was the Fremont-MacArthur line which runs south from downtown Oakland through predominantly blue collar employment areas to the rapidly growing suburbia of southern Alameda County. After the opening of the line an initial flurry of riders dropped as the novelty wore off but

commuter patronage rose from 2,000 to some 3,500. This pattern of short term decline followed by a steadying off and subsequent slight increment in rush hour riders has held true for other segments of the system (Figure 22). When the line north from Oakland to Richmond opened, in January 1973, that added six stations and a totally new passenger tributary area of low and middle income, black and white, young and old. Average daily patronage over the two lines steadied at 25,000, of whom 5,930 were riding in the two hour morning peak period and could therefore be assumed to be largely commuters. In May 1973, nineteen miles of double track and six more stations were added when the Concord line started operation. That service for the first time brought into the system the predominantly white middle class suburbia beyond the East Bay hills. The six Concord line stations generated over 6,000 trips, and total patronage on the system rose to over 35,000. On the opening of the Daly City line, in November 1973, service to downtown San Francisco from the northern margins of San Mateo County doubled total ridership on the system. During the busy week before Christmas 36,000 persons per day rode that line alone.

In September 1974, the opening of the Transbay Tube linked the East Bay and West Bay portions of the system and average daily patronage rose 65 percent from 69,049 to 113,622 trips daily (Figure 23). By far the greatest increase in passengers occurred on the Concord line, though the Daly City line benefited too, showing destinations for East Bay residents that fall beyond the first Embarcadero

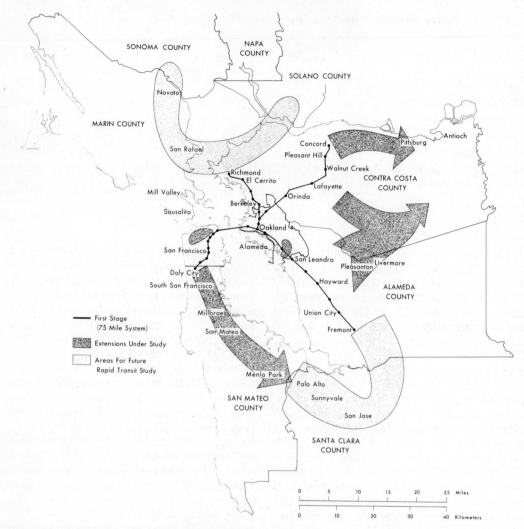

Figure 21.   The Bay Area Rapid Transit System.

station in downtown San Francisco. When ridership is separated into three components, it is apparent that East Bay patronage has been fairly steady at approximately 40,000 per day except for an increase of about 10,000 trips during the gasoline shortage and an increase of half that number during an Alamedia-Contra Costa Transit District strike in late summer. Similarly, fluctuations around a 27,000 daily trip figure for the West Bay reflect transit strikes in San Francisco and gasoline shortages. The October 1974 transbay average daily ridership reached 51,465. Following the opening of the Transbay Tube, bus services on the San Francisco-Oakland Bay Bridge have been reduced. The primary reductions have affected

southern Alameda County, although the Greyhound bus schedules from across the hills have also been curtailed. It is estimated that car traffic on the bridge is down by some 5 percent, which demonstrates the degree of diversion from one public transportation system to another that has occurred to yield the present ridership on BART. The diversion is likely to be further increased when direct service to San Francisco is available from the Richmond line. At present a change of train is necessary on that journey.

It is premature to make a proper evaluation of the accomplishments of BART; a long term impact study is underway and conclusions must await the findings of that group. But certain

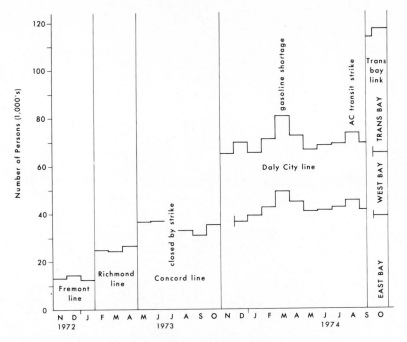

Figure 22. Average daily ridership on BART (excluding holidays).

conditions are becoming apparent. Restrictions by strikes, or inconvenience because of shortage affecting alternative means of transportation, do produce increases in ridership, but these have proven to be temporary. A more sustained impact from the general increase in gasoline prices is yet to be evidenced, and that is true for the effect of increases in metered parking rates imposed by Oakland and Berkeley. There has been a small drop in automobile use—the car pool lanes on the Bay Bridge that were used more heavily during the gasoline shortage have much lighter traffic—and there has been a considerable diversion from buses. In the first three weeks of BART Transbay Tube operation, AC Transit cut seventy-one scheduled journeys, leaving a total of 1632 daily services across the Bay Bridge.

Four hour peak period traffic on BART in the first month of full operation made up 55 percent of total daily trips. In forecasts of ridership the average daily figures are assigned in roughly equal proportions to commuters and other riders, although the peak hour travel figures for the crossing between San Francisco and the East Bay are expected to account for almost twice the load of any other segment. Interruptions of service by labor disputes, inadequate capacity during rush hours, and numerous equipment problems have all played a part in limiting patronage—the day-to-day reliability of train service has yet to be established—but the system can be assessed against its own projections of patronage. For 1975, projections look for 22,000 East Bay peak period travel trips, 25,000 West Bay, and 57,500 Transbay. In general, peak period travel is reaching, or exceeding, projections, whereas total travel trips have generally fallen short—with the exception of special occasions. (In October 1973), the combination of the Veterans' Day holiday and three days of World Series games at the Oakland Coliseum brought average daily ridership for the month to 35,519). Two quite different components of travel need to be remarked—the one coming from regular daily use from fixed locations, residence and workplace, and that originating in intermittent mass movement from a whole series of fixed generators of potential traffic, for example, the downtown shopping cluster or a sports complex.

Data thus far substantiate the view that BART is primarily a commuter service system that will have its major impact for persons living in the East Bay who work in downtown Oakland or San Francisco, or those who live in a small section of San Mateo County and

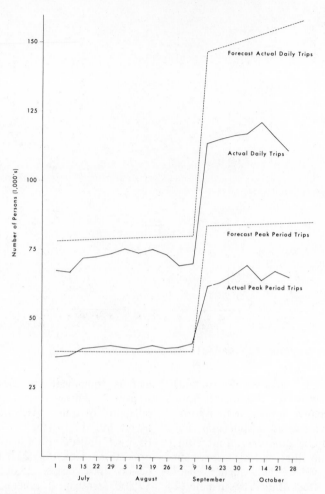

Figure 23. Forecast and actual BART patronage, July through October, 1974. Before the opening of the Transbay Tube actual daily trips fell below forecasts and peak period travel exceeded projected volume. Since the completion of the system this has changed. In October 1974, total four hour peak period travel reached 80 percent of forecast. East Bay trips exceeded forecast by 25 percent (which possibly reflects heavy use by students). West Bay trips reached 80 percent of forecast and transbay attained 56 percent. Presumably, deficiencies of operating equipment accounted in part for that low figure. Of the daily 52,000 transbay riders, 10,000 travel in the two hour morning peak period.

limited portions of San Francisco and work downtown. 1970 commuting data show that one in three persons who record their place of work as the city and county of San Francisco head to the central business district. Of all who give a place of work destination within the San Francisco-Oakland SMSA, 12.5 percent head to the San Francisco central business district and 2 percent to that of Oakland. In the three counties that have

BART service the percentages are 15 and 12.5 respectively. Although BART is of inestimable value for those whose destination is downtown, they are a relatively small proportion of the total work force. For them, the difficulty and cost of parking will guarantee their use of the system. It may well be that rising costs of gasoline will encourage others for whom parking is less difficult—those who work at outlying destinations—to switch to BART. But travel

Table 10. BART Fare Structure[a]

Fares (Example: MacArthur to Fremond costs $1.00)						
Daly City	.35	.35	1.20	1.00	.75	1.25
13	Montgomery	.30	1.20	.85	.60	1.25
14	1	Embarcadero	1.20	.85	.60	1.25
50	37	36	Concord	1.00	.85	1.25
42	29	28	41	Richmond	.45	1.10
27	14	13	23	15	MacArthur	1.00
53	40	39	60	49	34	Fremont

TIME (MacArthur to Fremont takes thirty-four minutes)

[a]The fare pattern for the region is entirely different from the one that prevailed in the days of the ferries and railroads. Of that other fare structure Bion Arnold wrote:

> From a fare standpoint San Francisco, Oakland, Berkeley and Alameda are already unified, while peninsular development is automatically placed under a handicap of considerably over 100% for local service, and 200% for express service, in excess of the basic cost of transportation within the 5-cent zone. While the 5-cent commuter fare reaches to the north of Berkeley, a fare of 13 1/3 cents is charged for the same time distance [on the peninsula].

on BART is not cheap (Table 10) and even at existing fares the system does not come close to meeting operating expenses.

If the merits of alternative travel options are very clear to the consumer then it is easy to anticipate his behavior. When you are talking about easy smooth riding versus freeway congestion, or a simple walk to the office from the station instead of a struggle to park the car, it is clear that BART will be the choice; this is the case for the downtown worker. But when options are couched in more complex terms—high fares as compared with high gasoline prices, or transferring from inadequate or time-consuming feeder service as compared with finding a place to park on the street—then the choice of car versus public transit becomes highly individualized. And that is the situation for the vast majority of workers who live or work close to the lines—let alone for the greater numbers for whom the station is remote at either end of the journey. Critics have always argued that only coercion will drive large numbers of commuters to use BART, citing punitive bridge tolls as a possible method to achieve that end. Constraints on the supply of gasoline, whether by price alone or other means, might seem to be another form of coercion, albeit one brought about by conditions that are national and international rather than local.

BART as a Manipulative Design

Far beyond the individual impact of an alternative means of travel for a few workers is the question of the impact of BART on the overall pattern of movement to work. If a single-centered city with highly concentrated suburban employment foci were to emerge, then the system would be well worth the very large capital costs incurred and would be on the way to avoiding, or at least reducing, recurrent operating deficits. To make the system successful it would not be sufficient to rely on a central city concentration of work force ·alone; additional foci would have to emerge on the lines. And many activities long since gone from core cities would need to return as well to even out the impact of the twice daily commuter bulge and subsequent underutilized equipment.

To accomplish these ends, BART would have to have good articulation with residential areas and it would have to provide satisfactory service to numerous generators of traffic outside downtown. On both criteria BART is deficient. The preexisting dispersed settlement pattern means that feeder services to the fixed rail system must be utilized: for the suburbanite that is a nuisance, and it is easier to go to the garage and get out the car then to contemplate getting on and off bus and train. A two axis linear service stopping at a limited number of points could never adequately serve a scattered residential population, but it could have served more fixed points than it does. BART probably avoids more generators of potential traffic than any other transit system in existence. It does serve Laney College in Oakland, a two year junior college, but it misses San Francisco State University and UC Berkeley. The latter has a well-patronized connecting shuttle bus service that is partially federally funded. In going to Daly City, BART does not go by the Cow Palace. In Oakland the station close to the Oakland-Alameda Coliseum was originally separated from the sports complex by railroad tracks and a divided road. There is now a footbridge connection. But off to the west of the Coliseum you can see the Oakland Airport, although you can't get there by BART.

BART is a regional rapid transit system using a fixed rail technology that is intended to link widely spaced points in the outer region with downtown areas, specifically San Francisco. Accepting Vance's earlier arguments, Zwerling has demonstrated that the preservation of downtown by the maintenance of San Francisco's role as the central city was a prime moving force behind the system, though it was largely publicized and sold to the public as a means of solving automobile dependence and road congestion. That the scheme would benefit no more than a small number of their activities was never given adequate publicity. Now that the system is in operation—and has suffered numerous technological problems—the first blush enchantment is over, and many people are asking the same kinds of questions that only a few raised in 1963 when taxpayers in Contra Costa County tried to question the wisdom and ethic of the proposed system. BART is a limited purpose project that, if successful, would help maintain a high density Manhattanlike core fed by seventy-five miles of rail line. Presumably high density development would be encouraged in the immediate vicinity of the thirty-four stations, but access to undeveloped cheaper land at the edge of suburbia at the end of the lines in the East Bay would be even more effectively promoted. In the 1975 BART patronage projections, Concord and Fremont at the end of East Bay lines are assigned substantially more riders than stations closer in. The assumption of further dispersion of suburban population in those sectors is clear. Indeed AC Transit is experimenting on a contract basis with BART in providing feeder links to suburban communities far beyond the present ends of the BART lines. Whatever develops, this will be a different

settlement pattern from the one created by automobile access, but whether it will be preferable is debatable.

Reservations about the role of BART have not been confined to taxpayers and some geographers alone; competing public agencies have also voiced their concern. According to material prepared by the California Division of Bay Toll Crossings in 1970, estimates of the potential diversion of transbay vehicular traffic to travel by BART range from a low of 7 percetn to a high of 13 percent, but in any case traffic relief from BART is likely to be exhausted essentially by 1976. That narrow debate focuses on the problem of integrating the East Bay with San Francisco, since the question at issue is the desirability of new ways to cross the Bay. In the East Bay, an alternative public transportation system does offer some concrete evidence of existing options in public transit that serve broader needs.

THE ARTICULATION OF PUBLIC TRANSPORTATION

The Alameda-Contra Costa Transit system is a public bus system financed by voter approval in November 1959 of an original bond issue of $16.5 million. Its budget for 1973-1974 was $29.7 million, of which $12.7 million is tax supported and the remainder must come from fares and other revenues. The system has been carrying 180,000 riders daily, though increases since June 1973 have brought this to 200,000 and ridership is running about 6 percent ahead of 1972. In 1973 AC Transit carried 20,000 daily to San Francisco, 10 percent more than in the previous year. AC Transit is an effective local bus system that has rerouted services to connect with BART stations and to avoid route conflict, and the two systems serve somewhat different needs—except for the potential of the lucrative Bay Bridge traffic. The existing express buses do offer advantages—frequent stops close to housing areas and no change of vehicle—though they can fall victim to traffic jams. But then trains have their operating problems, too.

In practical terms, BART and AC Transit will make an effective articulated system eventually, because they must. Whether there could not have been better and cheaper mass public transportation is another point. In

San Francisco, the third BART county, the San Francisco Municipal Railway (the Muni), which runs buses, streetcars, and cable cars, is in recurrent financial straits. It is a cumbersome system that offers service within two blocks to everyone in the city but is therefore a slow way of getting around. With enough of its own problems, the Muni is not showing much interest in offering a feeder service to BART although the two systems physically meet in a complex underground project on Market Street.

Within the region, numerous local transit systems are generally organized under enabling legislation from the state legislature as special districts. Some are authorized specifically to operate a transit system—the Bay Area Rapid Transit District, for example—or a specific part of a transportation system—the California Division of Bay Toll Crossings—but others have the potential for wider activities. The Golden Gate Bridge, Highway, and Transportation District has recently expanded its activities from overseeing the Golden Gate Bridge to running a bus service and starting a ferry service. A more formal mechanism with the goal of coordination of transportation services is the Metropolitan Transportation Commission (MTC). The nine county MTC began functioning in 1971 but expanded its activities greatly when it was designated the agency to oversee federal transportation funding to the Bay Area.

In June 1973, MTC published a proposed *Regional Transportation Plan* which considers everything from the use of bicycles to the need to integrate airport planning into the regional transportation plan. The agency is committed to multimodal transportation systems, to a reduction in dependence on the automobile, and to better utilization of existing facilities. before the construction of new ones. And they show proper environmental concerns, too. The extent to which planning of regional transportation priorities is translatable into public service is yet to be proven. The example of air traffic to the Bay Area is a case in point.

Planning on the Ground and in the Air

MTC clearly states that access to local airports is part and parcel of passenger needs at those airports. Whether by road or rail, there are signs that ground access is going to improve.

What is less clear is the future relationship between the airports in the Bay Area, and since the need to get there is a direct reflection of flights arriving and departing, that has to come into the picture. Forecasts for 1974 projected nineteen million passengers for San Francisco International, six million for Oakland International, and three million for San Jose—a not illogical distribution if you consider the distribution of population within the region. But in 1970, seven times as many people enplaned and deplaned in San Francisco as in Oakland. When the Amtrak passenger is getting off in Oakland, the PanAm passenger is alighting in San Francisco. The congestion in parking garages and at ticket counters in San Francisco Airport is matched only by the ease of access to parking lots and empty ticket counters in Oakland. Oakland is important for nonscheduled carriers, although as regular airlines have become highly competitive with their group fares and special excursion tickets, the number of charter passengers has diminished in relative importance. At the very time that traffic is becoming more and more congested at one airport, another is underutilized. A large proportion (37 percent) of the San Francisco passengers are bound for Los Angeles, mostly on the less costly intrastate airline flights, but others are on their way to a foreign destination via Los Angeles. The concentration of overseas services through the Los Angeles 'gateway' compounds the local limitation of choice in arrival and take-off points. The reduction in numbers of flights because of fuel restrictions is likely further to exacerbate the concentration of flights from San Francisco, a concentration that was first markedly noticeable with the switch to larger aircraft on the introduction of the 747.

In 1974 Oakland is building a second runway on land already filled in preparation. At the same time, San Francisco Airport is to petition to fill more of San Francisco Bay in order to construct another runway. Although local agencies may act rationally and allocate theoretical business to the three airports on the basis of localized demand for services, although they may design access facilities to minimize travel to the airport within the region, and although they may encourage the airports to expand only in response to local-

ized residential growth within the Bay Area—
the actual provision of flight service to a
particular airport is out of their hands. It is
the airlines that determine where planes
land. And the national pattern becomes more
and more concentrated on fewer large airports,
leaving an increasingly reluctant public to find
their way to these fields as best they can. So
the Oakland resident who might like to take
off from the east side of the Bay, from a facility in which he has some tax investment,
and which is less crowded and therefore more
pleasant, is forced to cross the Bay Bridge in
competition with a surge of commuter traffic.
To fly Oakland takes persistance. You may
accept flying by helicopter from there so
long as you do not plan to leave after 9:45 P.M.
and are prepared to pay up to $13.50 one way.

It is not enough, then, for municipalities to
build adequate facilities—or even to articulate
them with other services within the region, as
MTC is effectively suggesting—there are other
limitations on the ability to create a viable
transportation system. There are limitations
over which the metropolis and its areawide
agencies have little influence, however success-
fully they may have struggled to overcome
their own internal rivalries. And in spite of
enthusiastic experiments with alternative
transportation modes, at the present, and
for the foreseeable future, the primary means
of movement from one part of the region to
another is via the freeways, which lack only a
few connective segments. Had there been more
serious consideration of modifications to the
freeway concept within cities—smaller scale
construction; perhaps a significantly different
design for lower speeds that would have been
less land-consumptive—then that connective
tissue might have been completed. Not that a
road system alone would be adequate or desirable, but finally it is the only existing or predictable structure that serves all points within
the established settlement pattern.

THE PARTS THAT MAKE A WHOLE?

The issues and controversies that surround the
creation of a sensible transportation system are
but one thread in the design for the overall
region. Other regional agencies such as the
Bay Conservation and Development Commission (BCDC) or the Bay Area Air Pollution

Control District are responsible for limited
purpose areawide integration of policies in
their own jurisdictions and they face comparable problems. An example of a broader pattern is to be found in the Association of Bay
Area Governments (ABAG).

In 1961, under legislation known as the
Joint Exercise of Powers Act, cities and counties in the Bay Area—responding to pressures
that had come from cities in the region that
were fearful of losing out in power struggles
with the larger cities—formed ABAG. These
concerns had been expressed in the Alameda
County Mayors' Conference where the initial
impetus came from the smaller cities of the
East Bay, but finally Oakland joined the association and was later followed by San Francisco. In 1964 the Department of Housing and
Urban Development (HUD) designated the
association as the agency responsible for the
local review of federal financial grants. Since
the city of Oakland and the city and county
of San Francisco belonged to ABAG, the fact
that Solano County never joined (and that
Sonoma County withdrew following a three
to one citizen advisory referendum in April
1971) was not crucial. More than eighty of the
ninety-two cities in the Bay Area do belong
today, as well as seven of the nine counties.
The major contribution of ABAG has been a
regional plan, commended especially for its
open space recommendations, although any
implementation of recommendations remains
with the local authorities. This is an advisory
body only, and the unwillingness of Solano
County to join, or Sonoma's decision to withdraw, shows the ambivalence of local perception of the regional relationship. Admittedly,
Sonoma County stated that it preferred to be
associated with a group of North Coast counties, but it is to the Bay Area that Sonomans
travel to work.

The great utility of ABAG is that it furnishes
a public forum within which municipalities
can make their views known, and in which they
must struggle to enunciate their local policies.
The difficulties of doing just that were exem-
plified in 1973 when the ABAG general assembly voted on a statement of planning
policy to control growth to the year 2000.
Where San Francisco supported the policy,
Oakland and three Alameda County cities
opposed it. A mature county that has no
room for growth within its own boundaries

may see things differently from areas where further growth might hold the promise of a solution to pressing problems. The ideas that emerge in the formalized setting of ABAG are like those that come up in local political campaigns or in debates over controversial proposals. The kinds of divisions that occur at the regional level can be found down to the level of neighborhoods within cities, and the recognition of these differences may represent a searching for the parochial and human in scale that is the individual's only remaining defense against the increasing anonymity in the scale of the metropolitan existence.

In the Bay Area there have been recent efforts to break down administration within municipalities into smaller units. In Berkeley, in 1972, there was agitation for localized control of police within the city, and current proposals for the revision of the city charter include the concept of the election of some city council members by wards. In San Francisco, a proposal that supervisors should be elected from eleven wards in place of the at large system went down to a two to one margin in November 1973. That such proposals have been defeated by the voters shows that the present systems are deemed adequate, but the very appearance of such ballot measures shows how strong the drive for formal recognition of the small social geographic entity has become.

San Francisco is a city of villages but—unlike Los Angeles—this multinuclear quality is not a result of the way it grew. In Los Angeles there was a subsequent coming together of originally separate nuclei, often separated by considerable physical distance. In San Francisco, a series of distinctive nuclei seem to be emerging through a kind of crystallization process from a heterogeneous mass. The city contains an enormously diverse population within which elements can be characterized by lifestyle, as well as by more traditional associations such as ethnicity. In San Francisco there have always been ethnic neighborhoods, like the old Italian community of North Beach, as well as associations by social class or religious persuasion, and these have been unusual only in their multiplicity, and—with the exception of the Italians and the Chinese—in their small numbers. But in the last twenty years a tolerance of lifestyles that might be regarded less sympathetically elsewhere has attracted newcomers, and this same new permissiveness has encouraged local resi-

dents to define more clearly their own preferred associates. Within a diverse population, segments have developed localized attachments, not only in residential space but in stores and bars, too. The resultant small neighborhoods are internally congenial and coherent, as well as being externally tolerant. This combination of inward concern and outward respect is making it possible for seemingly incompatible populations to live in close physical proximity. Whether the differences between these populations is going to impose a new fragmentation of administration in order to accommodate contrasting priorities of existence is yet to be seen.

THE SURVIVAL OF A MANAGEABLE METROPOLIS

The diversity of population that characterizes San Francisco is mirrored in the different kinds of suburbs that coexist around the Bay. It is clear that many lively neighbors are joint tenants in the urban region. Neither ethnic groups nor social classes are confined to any one sector of the region; there is instead a small scale pattern of local allegiance based on differing perceptions of community needs. Johnson has described this in detail for the working class who live in a mobile home park, and van der Zee has plotted the struggle of the would-be rustic in the metropolis. That the mobile home park and the self-conscious ecological community are unusual is not to obscure the fact that there are many ordinary residential districts within which clearly identifiable social goals set boundaries. The middle class retirement community, the blue collar suburb, or the new immigrant enclave perceive their own priorities very clearly, and this gives rise to conflicting views as to how the different parts of the urban region can interlock, and the extent to which they can—or should—be made part of a single system.

In arguing the merits of a metropolis in which the individual maintains his identity by locally defined allegiance—by touting the merits of his cause as compared with another's—there inevitably comes an awareness of how the preferences of one segment impinge on the choices of another. The suburb that sets a limit on housing growth thereby denies opportunity to the central city minority resident who might otherwise see for the first time the chance to realize the middle class dream.

The conflict between a desire for local autonomy and a reasonable responsiveness to the needs of a wider population has long simmered in the Bay Area. This is not a clear-cut struggle between city and suburb: instead, there are conflicting ideologies that create some unexpected, if not unholy, alliances. The Sierra Club member ends up logically pushing high-rise apartments to save the countryside, and the devoted San Franciscan can find himself opposing a rapid transit system that will undoubtedly enhance central city land values but which will, incidentally, destroy antiquity and amenity in his city and encourage the building of even more tall office blocks.

That contrasting attitudes to urban goals are found from city to city within the urban system shows the persistence of a kind of small scale regional variation that has always been a hallmark of the Bay Area. In the past the region has been blessed by the advantages of diversity. The complex network of communities that grew around the San Francisco Bay allowed independence to its constituent parts. Cities retained some sort of individual flavor that often came from an originally specialized economic function. When these foci were swept up in a tide of metropolitan expansion after World War II they did not disappear into an anonymous and all-encompassing suburbia; instead, they retained their identity and thereby created a metropolis that is a system of parts. A clamor to retain local autonomy may have been originally predicated on political self-interest, but it subsequently proved to have the enormous virtue of retaining a manageable scale in urban affairs. In other American urban systems the symptoms of a populace drowned in a sea of problems seem endemic; in the Bay Area there is still some sense of being in control of an urban destiny, perhaps because the metropolitan area includes so many independent cities and discrete landscapes. And in this may rest the urban future.

Bibliography

Abrew, Carole Joy. "Patterns and Process of Change in Oakland, California." Master's thesis, Department of Geography, California State University, San Francisco, 1973.

Arnold, Bion J. *Report on the Improvement and Development of the Transportation Facilities of San Francisco.* Submitted to the Mayor and the Board of Supervisors, City of San Francisco, 1913. San Francisco: Hicks-Judd Co., 1913.

Atherton, Gertrude. *My San Francisco: A Wayward Biography.* New York: The Bobbs-Merrill Co., 1946.

Bank of America. *California Wine Outlook.* Economics Department, Bank of America NT and SA. San Francisco, September 1973.

BART Office of Research. *BART Patronage Reports.* No. 1, October 1972 through no. 13, October 1973.

Barusch, Phyllis, and Nathan, Harriet. "The East Palo Alto Municipal Advisory Council: A Black Community's Experiment in Local Self-Government." *Public Affairs Report.* Vol. 13, no. 5. Berkeley: Institute of Governmental Studies, University of California, October 1972.

Benét, James. *A Guide to San Francisco and the Bay Region.* New York: Random House, 1963.

Berger, Bennett M. *Working-Class Suburb: A Study of Auto Workers in Suburbia.* Berkeley and Los Angeles: University of California Press, 1960.

Bowden, Martyn J. "The Dynamics of City Growth: An Historical Geography of the San Francisco Central District 1850-1931." Ph.D. dissertation, Department of Geography, University of California, Berkeley, 1967.

Brown, R.D., Jr., and Lee, W.H.K. "Active Faults and Preliminary Earthquake Epicenters (1969-1970) in the Southern Part of the San Francisco Bay Region." San Francisco Bay Region Environment and Resources Planning Study, Basic Data Contribution 30. 1971. Miscellaneous Field Studies Map MF-307.

California Department of Human Resources Development. *Area Manpower Review.* San Francisco-Oakland S.M.S.A. Annual Outlook and Planning Report. Sacramento: 1973.

Cleaver, Eldridge. *Post-Prison Writings and Speeches.* Edited by Robert Scheer. New York: Random House, 1969.

Dana, Richard Henry. *Two Years Before the Mast.* New York: T.Y. Crowell Co., 1907.

Duskin, Alvin. *The Ultimate Highrise.* San Francisco: The San Francisco Bay Guardian, 1971.

Felton, E.L. *California: Many Climates.* Palo Alto: Pacific Books, 1965.

Gebhard, David; Montgomery, Roger; Winter, Robert; Woodbridge, John; and Woodbridge, Sally. *A Guide to Architecture in San Francisco and Northern California.* Santa Barbara and Salt Lake City: Peregrine Smith, Inc. 1973.

Gilbert, Grove Karl; Humphrey, Richard Lewis; Sewell, John Stephen; and Soulé, Frank. *The San Francisco Earthquake and Fire of April 18, 1906 and their effects on structures and structural materials.* Department of the Interior, U.S.G.S. Bulletin no. 324, Series

R, Structural Materials, 1. Washington, D.C.: U.S. Government Printing Office, 1907.

Gilliam, Harold. *Island in Time.* San Francisco: Sierra Club, 1962.

Graves, Clifford W. *Air Transportation and San Francisco Bay.* Report prepared for the San Francisco Bay Conservation and Development Commission. 1966.

Heyman, Therese Thau. *Mirror of California.* Oakland: The Oakland Museum, 1973.

Hittell, John S. *The Resources of California, Comprising the Society, Climate, Salubrity, Scenery, Commerce and Industry of the State.* San Francisco: A.L. Bancroft and Co., 1879.

Huth, Ora. "Regional Organization in the San Francisco Bay Area—1970." Regional Conference—1970, Background Paper no. 1. Institute of Governmental Studies, University of California, Berkeley, 1970.

Johnson, Sheila K. *Idle Haven: Community Building Among the Working-class Retired.* Berkeley and Los Angeles: University of California Press, 1971.

Kennedy, John Castillo. *The Great Earthquake and Fire.* New York: William Morrow and Co., 1963.

Metropolitan Transportation Commission. *Regional Transportation Plan*—Proposed. Berkeley, Calif., 1973.

Miller, Albert. *Smog and Weather: The Effect of San Francisco Bay on the Bay Area Climate.* Report prepared for the San Francisco Bay Conservation and Development Commission. San Francisco: 1967.

Nee, Victor G., and de Bary, Brett. *Longtime Californ'; A Documentary Study of an American Chinatown.* New York: Pantheon Books, A Division of Random House, 1972.

Nichols, Donald R., and Wright, Nancy A. "Preliminary Map of Historic Margins of Marshlands, San Francisco Bay, California." San Francisco Bay Region Environment and Resources Planning Study, Basic Data Contribution 9. 1971.

Nordhoff, Charles. *California for Health, Pleasure and Residence.* New York: Harper and Brothers, 1873.

Radbruch, Dorothy, and Wentworth, Carl. "Estimated Relative Abundance of Landslides in the San Francisco Bay Region, California." San Francisco Bay Region, Environment and Resources Planning Study, Basic Data Contribution 11. 1971.

Rantz, S.E. "Precipitation Depth-Duration-Frequency Relations for the San Francisco Bay Region, California." San Francisco Bay Region Environment and Resources Planning Study, Basic Data Contribution 25. 1971.

Record, Wilson. *Minority Groups and Intergroup Relations in the San Francisco Bay Area.* Berkeley: Institute of Governmental Studies, University of California, 1962.

Reps, John W. *The Making of Urban America: A History of City Planning in the United States.* Princeton, N.J.: Princeton University Press, 1965.

Saunders, Margery Holburne. "California Wheat, 1867–1910: Influence of Transportation on the Export Trade and the Location of Producing Areas." Master's thesis, Department of Geography, University of California, Berkeley, 1960.

Scott, Mel. *The San Francisco Bay Area: A Metropolis in Perspective.* Berkeley and Los Angeles: University of California Press, 1959.

Solomon, Steven Morse. "Turnkey Public Housing in Oakland." Master's thesis, Department of Geography, California State University, San Francisco, 1973.

Soulé, Frank; Gihon, John, M.D.; and Nisbet, James. *The Annals of San Francisco.* New York: D. Appleton and Co., 1855.

Stanford Workshop on Air Pollution. *Air Pollution in the San Francisco Bay Area.* Stanford, 1970.

Taylor, Bayard. *Eldorado or Adventures in the Path of Empire.* New York: Alfred A. Knopf, 1949.

Taylor, Fred A., and Brabb, Earl E. "Map Showing Distribution and Cost by Counties of Structurally Damaging Landslides in the San Francisco Bay Region, California. Winter of 1968–69." San Francisco Bay Region Environment and Resources Planning Study, Basic Data Contribution 37. 1972. Miscellaneous Field Studies Map MF-327.

United California Bank. *Retailing Trends. California and Its Regions.* Research and Planning Division, 1972.

U.S. Department of Commerce. *Construction Review,* May 1973. Vol. 19, no. 5. Washington, D.C.: U.S. Government Printing Office, 1973.

U.S. Army Corps of Engineers. *Future Development of the San Francisco Bay Area, 1960–2020.* Report prepared by Office of

Area Development, U.S. Department of Commerce, Washington, D.C.: U.S. Government Printing Office, 1959.

U.S. Bureau of the Census. Census of Housing: 1970 *Block Statistics, San Francisco-Oakland, California, Urbanized Area.* Final Report HC(3)-24. Washington, D.C.: U.S. Government Printing Office, December 1971.

U.S. Department of Commerce, San Francisco Regional Office of Field Operations, "Authorized Construction–San Francisco Bay Area," *Construction Report,* May 1973.

Vance, James E., Jr. *Geography and Urban Evolution in the San Francisco Bay Area.* Berkeley: Institute of Governmental Studies, University of California, 1964.

Vance, James E., Jr. "Emerging Patterns of Commercial Structure in American Cities." Proceedings of the IGU Symposium on Urban Geography Lund 1960. *Lund Studies in Geography* ser. B, Human Geography. Lund: Gleerup, 1962.

Walton, Sidney F. *ZBC 1994.* San Ramon: San Ramon Valley Counseling, Consultation and Education Services, 1972.

Wiltsee, Ernest A. *Gold Rush Steamers of the Pacific.* San Francisco: The Grabhorn Press, 1938.

Zee, John van der. *Canyon: The Story of the Last Rustic Community in Metropolitan America.* New York: Harcourt Brace Jovanovich, Inc., 1971.

Zwerling, Stephen. "The Politics of Technological Choice: Some Lessons from the Bay Area Rapid Transit District." *Public Affairs Report.* Vol. 14, no. 3. Berkeley: Institute of Governmental Studies, University of California.

Index